Modern German Political Drama 1980–2000

The last two decades of the twentieth century gave rise to a renaissance in the genre of the political drama in Germany. Although political drama has always been a mainstay of German literature, it has been of particular significance during the years surrounding the *Wende,* or reunification, of 1989. This book is the first comprehensive study of politically engaged German drama writing in the 1980s and 1990s, covering the works of key playwrights during the period and providing an analysis of oppositional theater before and after reunification. It treats the range of current political topics and their repercussions in drama writing, including reunification, women's issues, the media, politicized environmentalism and the Greens, and right-wing radicalism. In addition to established playwrights such as Heinar Kipphardt, Franz Xaver Kroetz, and Heiner Müller, the book looks at the younger generation of playwrights not yet fully taken into account by research: writers such as Oliver Bukowski, Dea Loher, Marius von Mayenburg, Albert Ostermaier, and Theresia Walser. It gives an overview of the most important developments in recent German political drama through analysis of more than forty contemporary plays, clearly tracing connections between politics and theater. Each chapter is preceded by a short introduction into the respective political topic, providing the framework for the study of drama as a political tool and making it easy for students to see the multiple ways in which plays respond to political change. This book will be of interest to students and scholars in drama and theater studies and German literature.

Birgit Haas teaches in the German Department at the University of Bristol, and has published widely on drama and theater of the twentieth century.

Studies in German Literature, Linguistics, and Culture

Edited by James Hardin
(*South Carolina*)

MODERN GERMAN POLITICAL DRAMA
1980–2000

Birgit Haas

CAMDEN HOUSE

First published 2003
by Camden House

Camden House is an imprint of Boydell & Brewer Inc.
668 Mt. Hope Avenue, Rochester, NY 14620 USA
and of Boydell & Brewer Limited
PO Box 9, Woodbridge, Suffolk IP12 3DF, UK

ISBN: 1–57113–285–6

Library of Congress Cataloging-in-Publication Data

Haas, Birgit.
  Modern German political drama, 1980–2000 / Birgit Haas.
     p. cm. — (Studies in German Literature, Linguistics, and Culture)
Includes bibliographical references and index.
ISBN 1–57113–285–6 (hardcover: alk. paper)
    1. German drama — 20th century — History and criticism. 2. Political
plays, German — History and criticism. I. Title.

PT668.H33 2003
832'.91409358—dc22

                                                                    2003011241

A catalogue record for this title is available from the British Library.

This publication is printed on acid-free paper.
Printed in the United States of America.

Contents

Preface   vii

Acknowledgments   ix

List of Abbreviations   x

Introduction   1

Part I: The 1980s

1: Outcasts   13

2: Green Issues   31

3: The Memory of the Holocaust   42

4: The Decay of the GDR   60

Part II: The 1990s

5: Reflections on German Reunification   82

6: Women in Society Today   143

7: Terrorism in Germany   167

8: Right-Wing Radicalism in Germany after Reunification   186

9: Media and Politics   207

Conclusion   227

Epilogue   229

Index   235

Preface

IN 2000, WHILE PLANNING A NEW COURSE on contemporary German drama, I discovered to my amazement — and dismay — that the drama of the last two decades had largely escaped people's attention. It was then that I saw the need for an overview of recent developments in German drama. The present study is a result of that realization.

This chronologically structured volume is an examination of the multifaceted political drama in Germany from 1980 to 2000, and not only gives an overview of theatrical developments, but also places the texts in their specific historical context. The years of the "gentle" revolution and reunification, 1989 and 1990, certainly are among the most important dates in German history of the twentieth century. Consequently, the book is divided in two main parts, for the periods before and after reunification, each of which is divided into several subject areas. As the political situation in the eighties was considerably different from that in the nineties, the topics naturally vary. Each chapter begins with an introduction containing a brief summary of political events relevant to the themes of the plays. This anchors the plays in the political developments of the time, and provides a starting point for analysis. The introductory chapters should also help to avoid unnecessary repetition, as several plays refer to one political issue — particularly when it comes to the "Wende," the collapse of the GDR in 1989 and German reunification. Although the political background has formed the primary basis for analysis, intertextual references, biographical issues, and information about theater history are also included. As the analysis of each play is self-contained, the information is also available as a quick reference for any single play. The book presents a broad range of dramatic writing, including examples from East and West Germany, "traditional" postmodernism and innovative realism, and works by different generations.

Acknowledgments

I OWE THANKS TO MANY PEOPLE who contributed in various ways to the writing of this book. First, I must thank the German Department at the University of Bristol for the time and support they have given me in order to complete this work, particularly Anne Simon, who read several of the early drafts. I am also grateful to my German friends Knut Bühler, and Frank and Franziska Reuter, for their support and advice.

I owe an almost unrepayable debt of gratitude to Jim Hardin, not merely for commissioning this volume, but also for his endless supply of patience, his careful reading of the manuscript, and his encouragement, keen insight and perseverance, which brought this book to fruition.

Finally, I must thank Anna Saunders, who patiently read each draft, and whose comments and criticisms helped to shape the current results.

B. H.
January 2003

Abbreviations

BZ	*Berliner Zeitung*
FAZ	*Frankfurter Allgemeine Zeitung*
G	*The Guardian*
Mopo	*Hamburger Morgenpost*
PVjS	*Politische Vierteljahresschrift*
SoZ	*Sonntagszeitung*
Sp	*Der Spiegel*
SZ	*Süddeutsche Zeitung*
taz	*Die Tageszeitung*
TdZ	*Theater der Zeit*
Th	*Theater heute*
ThJ	*Theater heute Jahrbuch*
W	*Die Welt*
Z	*Die Zeit*

Introduction

SINCE LIVING DRAMA cannot exist without performance, this introduction will outline the trends that shaped the broad canvas of the
German stage, and will also explain the repercussions of performance
culture on the writers. Following the postmodern wave of the 1970s,
stage directors gained importance, and a culture of so-called "Regie-
theater" developed, a type of drama that gave directors complete freedom in their productions. Many directors shunned "Werktreue," the
rendering of a dramatic text true to the author's intentions, in favor of
experimental performance. They regarded texts largely as reservoirs,
sources of material that could be cut, rearranged, and turned upside
down completely at the director's discretion. Despite this attempt at
creativity, the theater crisis persisted, for audiences stayed away and
turned to other leisure activities. Postmodern adaptations of classic playwrights also dominated the programs, making it hard for contemporary
playwrights to gain recognition.

An International Theater

Theater programs reveal the plurality and versatility of a theater that is
open to both experimental and traditional forms of drama, as well as
being receptive to international influences. In 1985, the critic Peter von
Becker strongly recommended Alan Ayckbourn's (1939–) realistic and
popular theater as an antidote to the German theater crisis,[1] and the
director Peter Brook (1925–) is now celebrated as one of the greatest
living directors.[2] Since his production of *the CIVIL warS* in 1984, the
highly acclaimed American director Robert Wilson (1941–) has directed
his theatrical works of art in Germany.[3] New impulses also came from
France, for example with Johann Kresnik's (1939–) ballet *Ulrike Meinhof*
(1990), which was modeled on Bernard-Marie Koltés's (1948–1989)
Roberto Zucco in 1990.[4] One year before the Wall came down, many eyes
looked to Moscow, where the production of Michail Schatrow's (1932–)
Die Diktatur des Gewissens (The Dictatorship of Conscience, 1988)
nourished hopes of political change.[5] International influence was noted
in April 1992, when the critic Judith Herzberg enthusiastically announced that a theater group from Akko in Israel would perform a play

during the festival "Jüdische Lebenswelten" in Berlin.[6] Later in the same year, the play *Vermummte* (The Masked, 1992) by the Israeli Ilan Hatsor (1970–) was performed with great success.[7] During the war in Kosovo, the strong interest in foreign theater[8] shifted to the Serbians Dejan Dukovski[9] (1969–) and Biljana Srbljanowic (1970–),[10] whose plays were warmly received as firsthand analyses of the paradoxes of war.[11]

Inadequate Dramatic Writing?

As for German drama, critics constantly called its achievements into question, since they believed that playwrights indulged in self-referential and postmodern prattle that was understandable only to the authors themselves. In this vein, one critic mocked the self-pity and the self-centered poetry that mixed personal and political issues.[12] As a result, Michael Rutschky subsumed a whole range of plays under the heading heavy historical rubbish:[13]

> Jajaja. Der *Sound* ist entschieden ein gehobener. Das Poesie und Symbol-wollen ist unverkennbar. [. . .] Ja, es ist alles ganz schrecklich. Flatterstu-dien, Mythogenese, Männ/Weiblichkeit, Subjektivi/Modernität. Adorno hat mal geschrieben, die besten Gedanken seien die, welche sich selber nicht verstehen. [. . .] Also wird die beschissene Sozialisation monumental versymbolisiert und verpoetisiert, Scheitel und Arsch, unverheilte Tragö-dien, Blutstropfen, nicht größer als die Weltkugel, schlabber.[14]

These observations notoriously fueled the "theater crisis" that has been hotly debated over the last twenty-five years. Is German theater of the post-1968 generation unable to address the burning problems of German politics? Are there no talented playwrights? Did the state's generous funding of the theater stifle all political criticism? Has the art of theater lost its beauty, thus remaining merely a superficial sequence of meaningless effects?[15] The answer to all of these questions is, in fact, "no," and this book aims to provide an overview of the development of political theater in Germany, showing that politically committed theater never ceased to exist, despite the fact that it was overshadowed by theater dominated by the will and whims of the director.

In 1997, the critic Günther Rühle looked back on the twentieth century and concluded that of all modern and postmodern plays, only those of Anton Chekhov (1860–1904) would endure. And, he sighed, even the much-performed Chekhov was tarnished by contemporary productions, such as a staging by the director Christoph Marthaler, which, according to Rühle, lacked humanity and creativity.[16] Does this confirm the verdict of Harold Pinter (1930–) — one of the most influential British playwrights of the twentieth century — who asserted that Germany has not produced a single good playwright in the last thirty years? Peter von Becker, one of Germany's most important critics, does not believe so, and wittily reminds the readers of *Theater heute* that the end of culture, literature, and art — which are usually lumped together — is largely mourned by those who are over forty-five — and male, he hastens to add. According to him, grieving over the death of literature has become the profession of a handful of culturally interested critics, who have effectively stifled many a creative initiative in the past twenty years. He sums up this paradoxical situation with the words: "So brütet das Ei über der Henne, so üben Totenkläger den Vatermord."[17]

When I embarked on this project, it seemed that the plays written in the 1980s and 1990s had played only a minor role in the political landscape of German society. A closer look, however, proves just the opposite. In spite of the conservative shift in society in 1983 following the landslide victory of the Christian Democrats under Helmut Kohl, who was to remain chancellor until 1998, political drama has still continued to comment on, criticize, and even condemn current developments. With hindsight, it can be said that the ongoing complaints about the presence of inertia among playwrights[18] are not justified. Many playwrights were not merely concerned with the self-referential aspects of their writing,[19] and they actively engaged in political debates. The playwright Ludwig Fels (1946–) for example, believes that theater must engage in political discourse and draw attention to the lower end of society in order to stir the audience out of its complacency. According to him, theater is still the fourth power within the state, and a means of enlightening people. In an interview conducted in 1983, he claims that theatre must oppose a society dominated by money. Moreover, he complains that the young generation, which he calls "techno-zombies," exposed themselves uncritically to B-films that glorify violence.[20]

In the 1980s, the persistent attempt to produce politically relevant theater led to an amazing variety of plays, ranging from the critical *Volkstheater* to the postmodern pastiche. In response to social movements such as feminism, the green movement, and peace campaigns, playwrights expressed their concern at the politics of the Kohl government. As the armaments race continued, levels of unemployment rose, and the Christian Democrats advocated a "normal" Germany that should repress the Nazi past, playwrights did not tire of staging their criticisms. In the GDR, censorship and the rigid politics of the socialist dictatorship rendered political criticism more difficult,[21] yet Volker Braun (1939–) and Christoph Hein (1944–) serve as outstanding examples of continuing opposition. Looking back on his difficult position as a writer in the GDR, Hein stated that he saw himself as a chronicler of his age.[22]

The Predominance of Classic Playwrights

To attract large audiences, managers resorted to classic playwrights who they believed would lure to their houses a reliable supply of regular theater-goers. Goethe, Büchner, and Schiller were performed to full houses, yet their approach to politics was radically updated and modernized. Shakespeare was staged so often that he has become *the* classic "German" playwright in the perception of many Germans, and new productions by the *Berliner Schaubühne* or *Volksbühne* have become necessary for the culturally interested. Critics saw many stagings as an expression of the director's opinion on contemporary politics. In Heiner Müller's (1929–1995) production of *Hamlet* at the *Berliner Ensemble* in 1990, for example, the ghost of Hamlet's father was dubbed with Stalin's voice. Peter Zadek's production of *Hamlet* in 1999 alluded to the war in Kosovo,[23] and in 2001, Nicolas Stemann's version in Hanover portrayed Claudius and Gertrud as ultramodern politicians.[24] While this is not to criticize the reception of Shakespeare, these trends show that productions of the classics contended successfully with contemporary German drama.

As early as 1987 the playwright Klaus Pohl polemically stated that in view of the boredom that oozes out of the endless repetition of classic dramas, he had a right to contribute.[25] In the same vein, Klaus Völker blamed managers for not promoting promising playwrights. Instead of staging contemporary plays, theaters went for the safe bet, and opted for the classical repertoire. Rubbing salt into the wound, Völker said that theaters should "Dramatikerbegabungen aus der Enge des Experimentiertheaters [. . .] befreien."[26] Assuming that the classics were given more play than contemporary playwrights, why should we concentrate on modern German theater at all? The answer is simple: the plays that were performed often simply reflected the directors' tastes. It must not be forgotten that many directors had emerged from the 1968 generation, and had meanwhile found a comfortable place in the culture industry. The theater programs do not always reflect the quality of contemporary drama, and Michael Buselmeier even goes so far as to claim that "grand old men" such as Peter Stein, Claus Peymann, and Peter Zadek stifled any possible emergence of new young talent who might challenge them.[27] In short, if political German drama was performed less frequently than one might have expected, it was not due to its quality, but rather revealed the taste of directors and managers:

> Oft ist aus Theaterkreisen zu hören, die Schriftsteller taugten nichts
> mehr oder seien vom Fernsehen gekauft; es gäbe keine jungen deut-
> schen Autoren zu entdecken und keine spielbaren neuen Stücke. Ich
> habe eher den Eindruck, die meisten Dramaturgen sind achtlose, über-
> lastete Leser. Intendanten lassen ihre Studios veröden, spielen nur was
> man anderswo auch spielt [. . .][28]

However, there are exceptions, such as the director George Tabori
(1914–), who produced political plays by lesser-known playwrights, such
as Harald Mueller (1934–)[29] and Gaston Salvatore (1941–).[30] It is the aim
of this book to shed light on the neglected and despised contemporary
playwrights to show that they constitute a strong and committed response
to political developments of the 1980s, and cannot be dismissed as the
authors of trivial or mediocre plays. As the plays of the 1980s were often
treated unfairly by theatre critics, this overview reevaluates the playwrights'
achievements in successfully commenting on and criticizing political issues.

In the 1980s, Herbert Achternbusch (1938–) and Franz Xaver
Kroetz (1946–) reacted to this dilemma by becoming directors themselves, in order to make sure that their views were heard. It is paradoxical
that while lesser-known playwrights faced difficulty in being staged at all,
those who were famous, such as Kroetz, became disenchanted with the
uncritical, subservient attitude of stage managers.[31]

Another icon of the theater scene was the playwright and director
Heiner Müller, who was the most influential figure in East German theater
in the postwar period. Although he could not reconcile himself with a
freshly reunited Germany, he continued to produce plays, mainly using
classic playwrights in order to express his pessimistic views, for example
Bertolt Brecht's (1998–1956) *Der Aufhaltsame Aufstieg des Arturo Ui* (*The
Resistible Rise of Arturo Ui*, 1941) in 1995.[32] Despite the fact that Heiner
Müller, Einar Schleef, Frank Castorf and Peter Zadek remained influential,
a new generation of directors began to emerge from the shadows, such as
Christoph Marthaler, Anna Viebrock, and Thomas Ostermeier.[33]

Twenty Years of Crisis

Although there has been much debate about the "crisis" of the theater,[34]
this book will show that such a perception is a little short-sighted, for
playwrights have contributed to a lively and politically committed theater
scene. "Die Leiche lebt," as Michael Merschmeier states,[35] and the debate about the "famous invalid," the theater, can be interpreted as part
of the self-flagellation so common among German intellectuals. As audiences steadily declined in size,[36] and subsidies were cut, many theaters

were faced with the threat of closure, the most famous example being that of the *Schiller-Theater* in Berlin in 1993. However, the preservation of regional variety in German theater was a necessity, and both left- and right-wing politicians expressed their will to support a lively theater scene that included lesser-known venues.[37]

In a speech given on the occasion of the 150th anniversary of the *Deutsche Bühnenverein* in 1996, Roman Herzog, then president of Germany, emphasized the importance of maintaining a diverse theater landscape that should be allowed to thrive untroubled by financial problems.[38] He pointed out that public spending on culture did not exceed one percent of the total federal budget, and that cuts would not make any real difference to the public budget. However, he made it clear that most theater venues failed to be sufficiently consumer-orientated, and demanded that theaters take better care of their customers, for example by working more closely with schools. Moreover, he found it absurd that theaters close for a two-month holiday over the summer, and suggested that cafés and restaurants be opened inside the theaters to attract more people and to make them a hub of interest for the public.

The question seemed to be whether the theater should pursue an "elitist" path, or make concessions to the potential theater audience. This controversy was highlighted in a discussion between managers and directors in 1998,[39] which was published by the journal *Theater heute*.[40] In the course of the debate, Frank Castorf defended the autonomy of a highly subsidized theater that is not dependent on ticket sales, and compared his associative, postmodern style to a Trojan horse that was intended to stir spectators out of their complacency. In contrast, Volker Hesse outlined the financial problems of the *Theater am Neumarkt* in Zurich, making it clear that in order to survive, the theater must take into account the tastes of its audience. In the same vein, Ulrich Khuon underlined the need to produce a program broad enough to appeal to all kinds of audiences. Thomas Ostermeier went even further, maintaining that theater should once again become more comprehensible to the general public. He stated that the battle between directors trying to top one another's stagings only leads to productions riddled with arcane ideas that render them incomprehensible. At a time when subsidies were cut back and audiences were fleeing in droves, the theater was to shun its elitist aims.

On another occasion, Frank Baumbauer, the successful managing director who took over the *Kammerspiele* in Munich in 2001, underlined the importance of recognizing regional differences. In an interview, for example, he pointed out that a Swiss audience could not relate to Heiner

Müller, whereas a north German spectator might find the Bavarian *Volkstheater* rather farfetched.[41]

Well aware that his approach is somewhat old-fashioned, Ostermaier believes that theater should enlighten its spectators.[42] It is therefore rather surprising that he tries to educate his audiences by producing highly controversial plays, such as Mark Ravenhill's (1966–) *Shopping and F***ing* or Sarah Kane's (1971–1999) *Blasted*.[43] He maintains that German theater could benefit from this type of British theater, as it combines shock effects with realistic psychology, thereby forcing the audience to reconsider its set opinions.[44] The British theater aside, Ostermeier also promoted promising young German playwrights. His production of Marius von Mayenburg's (1972–) *Feuergesicht* (Fireface, 1999), for example, gained international acclaim.[45]

The Generation Change: New Topics, Hybrid Forms

It is not surprising that a new generation of playwrights emerged at the same time as a crop of new, young directors. Both groups were interested in addressing burning problems of contemporary Germany, such as right-wing radicalism and racial attacks; they also looked at other, less dramatic but nonetheless socially significant issues, such as mass media, the role of "modern" women in the light of feminist theory, and terrorism. Although there was no prominent social movement that could provide playwrights with new ideas, as Thomas Ostermeier pointed out in an interview,[46] the theater used this opportunity to present political topics once again through a realistic theater. This meant the end of postmodern collages that had often tried to reveal and explain the mechanisms of word-wide political injustice in just three hours. Playwrights such as Dea Loher (1964–), Theresia Walser (1967–), Oliver Bukowski (1961–), and Roland Schimmelpfennig (1967–), to name but a few, focused on the private sphere and showed the impact of politics on real characters. The slogan "Das Private ist politisch," once used by feminists in the 1970s, has become the new maxim of drama writing. Bukowski depicts the problems of a united Germany from a personal angle, and the "Mauer im Kopf" is alluded to only in a subtle manner. While Rolf Hochhuth's (1931–) *Wessis in Weimar* still uses the stage as a courtroom to take the West Germans to trial for looting the east, Bukowski restricts his criticism to the subtext, providing a fascinating picture of an inner-German culture clash.

In a similar manner, Schimmelpfennig and Walser concentrate on the local social environment of their characters. Despite the fact that their plays are not realistic, they offer lucid analyses of society through the lens of the grotesque and absurd. Walser's hugely successful *King Kongs Töchter* (King Kong's Daughters, 1998) depicts the grim reality of an old people's home with grotesque overtones, and Schimmelpfennig's *Push Up 1–3* (Push Up 1–3, 2000) embellishes competition in corporate business with absurd twists. The tendency of playwrighting in this period is to move away from the postmodern collage and to hark back to traditional forms, such as expressionism, surrealism, theater of the absurd, and Brecht's theater of alienation.

Although topics such as terrorism and neo-Nazism remain at the core of German drama, it is significant that these issues are now presented from a personal viewpoint. Loher's *Leviathan* and Marius von Mayenburg's (1972–) *Feuergesicht,* for instance, do not feature orgies of violence, but rather offer a psychological profile of the terrorists. In the same vein, neo-Nazism is presented as a problem that can affect everyone, while Oliver Czeslik's (1964–) and Gundi Ellert's (1951–) portrayals of skinheads and neo-Nazis provide insight into the twisted minds of people who are not demons, but could be anyone's neighbor.

Kitsch Again?

In an evaluation of current trends in contemporary drama, one critic pointed out that with the exception of Oliver Bukowski and René Pollesch (1962–), today's playwrights "had nothing to say."[47] However, she continued to remark that the void is masked by carefully crafted kitsch, as is seen in Roland Schimmelpfennig's plays. In the same vein, Theresia Walser and Marius von Mayenburg were dismissed as trivial playwrights, for they allegedly neglect the content of their writing, and instead dally with forms. Such criticism clearly underlines the difficult position from which young dramatists must start out. The aim of this book is, therefore, to emphasize the importance of contemporary drama, and to take its function as a critical institution within the state seriously, providing valuable insights into contemporary Germany. Against the backdrop of political developments since 1980, this sample of plays will offer an overview of fascinating dramatic responses to politics.

Using the years 1989 and 1990 as a natural landmark of both German history and German literature, the book is divided into two main parts: first, the discussion of plays from the 1980s and the last years of the two German states; second, the analysis of plays of the 1990s and the wide range of different aesthetic responses to the new political problems in a unified Germany.

Notes

[1] Peter Becker, "Der berühmte Unbekannte — ein Molière der Middleclass?" *ThJ* (1987), 27–38.

[2] See, for example, the reviews by Dorothee Hammerstein, "Über allen Wipfeln ist Brook," *Th* 1 (2001): 12–15 (on *Hamlet*); Dorothee Hammerstein, "Nicht viel Platz zum Spielen hier," *Th* 52 (2002): 24–27 (on Brooks production of Churchill's *Far Away*).

[3] Erika Fischer-Lichte, *Geschichte des Dramas 2* (Tübingen: Francke, 1990), 284.

[4] Michael Merschmeier, "Der Gesellschaftstanz. Johann Kresnik oder Ein Lobpreis der politischen Choreographie," *ThJ* (1990), 76–79; see also Michael Wildenhain, "Fleischerhaken, postmodern. Michael Wildenhain contra Johann Kresniks *Ulrike Meinhof*," *ThJ* (1990), 80–81.

[5] Henning Rischbieter, "Zeitgeschichte vor dem Tribunal der Bühne," *Th* 3 (1988): 2–3.

[6] Judith Herzberg, "Arbeit macht frei. Ein Theater — und mehr," *Th* 4 (1992): 4–7.

[7] Ilan Hatsor, "Vermummte," *Th* 7 (1992): 41–47.

[8] See, for example Klaus Dermutz, "Drama Europa. Zukunftsvisionen und Erinnerungsfragmente aus 20 Ländern — Ein Bericht," *Th* 8 (1996): 25–31.

[9] Dejan Dukovski, "Das Pulverfaß," *Th* 7 (1996): 45–50; Franz Wille, "Vielleicht ist irgendetwas im Wasser. Dejan Dukovskis *Das Pulverfaß*, ein Gastspiel des jugoslawischen Schauspiels Belgrad bei der Bonner Biennale," *Th* 7 (1996): 41–44.

[10] The play *Belgrader Trilogie* was published in *TdZ* 5/6 (1998), 85–97; the play *Familiengeschichten. Belgrad* was published in *Th* 1 (1999): 61–71; see also the review by Franz Wille, "Trautes Heim, Mord allein? — die deutsche Erstaufführung von *Familiengeschichten. Belgrad* am Hamburger Schauspiel," *Th* 1 (1999): 58–60.

[11] "'Wer soll denn das sein, das serbische Volk?' — Ein Gespräch mit Biljana Srbljanovic über Jugoslawien, Milosevic und das Leben in Belgrad," *Th* 1 (1999): 52–60.

[12] Michael Merschmeier, "Das Herzstück fehlt. Wie Theater Gegenwartsdramatik behandeln und die Dramatiker Gegenwart," *ThJ* (1987), 39–44, here: 39.

[13] Michael Rutschky, "Theater? Nein danke," *ThJ* (1987), 54–57.

[14] Rutschky, "Theater? Nein danke," *ThJ* (1987), 57.

[15] In 1995, the critic Franz Wille demanded that theater should return to enlightening its audiences, and that the theater of Friedrich Schiller should be revived, see Franz Wille, "Moderne — ein Teufelspakt. Überlegungen zur gegenwärtigen Theaterkunst," *ThJ* (1995), 34–43.

[16] Günther Rühle, "Veränderungen," *Th* 12 (1997): 72.

[17] Peter von Becker, "Das nächste Finale. Phantome des Abschieds — kurze Anmerkungen zur jüngsten Debatte um Kultur und Kritik," *Th* 4 (1997): 1.

[18] "Neue Stücke in der neuen Saison: Autoren schildern ihre Situation," *ThJ* (1980), 5–10.

[19] In a speech given at the *Münchner Kammerspiele*, the director Ernst Wendt stated: "Es ist aber, was wir in den Künsten betreiben, seit langem die Perfektionierung eines Systems der Austauschbarkeit von ästhetischen Spielmarken. Valeurs, Effekte, Reize, und Anti-Valeurs, Anti-Effekte, Anti-Reize werden zu immer neuem Patch-Work aneinandergeflickt; [. . .]" He thus concluded that theater should redefine itself by abandoning these superficial effects in order to return once again to a true theater. Quoted in *ThJ* (1983), 109.

[20] Ludwig Fels, "Festschrift wider das Leichenbegängnis," *ThJ* (1983), 13.

[21] Ernst Schumacher, "Da war doch was, aber was? Was bleibt?" *BZ*, 20 September 1997.

[22] "Die alten Themen habe ich noch, jetzt kommen neue hinzu. Gespräch mit Sigrid Löffler (März 1990)," in *Christoph Hein. Texte, Daten, Bilder*, ed. Lothar Baier (Darmstadt: Luchterhand, 1991), 37–44, here: 38.

[23] Franz Wille, "Der Fürst regiert. Peter Zadek inszeniert *Hamlet* und entdeckt Shakespeare als vorausschauenden Europa-Politiker," *Th* 7 (1999): 6–9.

[24] Franz Wille, "Shakespeare kann schwimmen," *Th* 4 (2001): 6–9.

[25] Klaus Pohl, "Das Problem des Kostüms im Zeitstück," *ThJ* (1987), 64–66, here: 66.

[26] Klaus Völker, "Die Dramatiker sind die ungeliebten Kinder der Theater," *ThJ* (1987), 60–61.

[27] Michael Merschmeier, "Wenn wir Jungen erwachen . . . ," *ThJ* (1996), 40–51.

[28] Michael Buselmeier, "Mörderspiele, Märchenspiele," *ThJ* (1987), 58–59, here: 58.

[29] See the reviews by Joachim Kaiser, "Schrecklich dynamisches Totenfloß," *SZ*, 1 December 1986; Sigrid Löffler, "Von Zombies und Affen," *profil*, 9 December 1986.

[30] See also Sibylle Fritsch, "Grenzgänger," *profil*, 22 February 1988; Karin Kathrein, "Im Niemandsland verirrt," *Die Presse*, 11 March 1988; Michael Merschmaier, "Götzendämmerung," *Th* 4 (1988): 18–20.

[31] Franz Xaver Kroetz, "Bitte, lieber Gott," *ThJ* (1998), 82–83, here: 82.

[32] Peter Laudenbach, "Panik in jedem Augenblick," *BZ*, 6 June 1995.

[33] The generation change is discussed in Franz Wille, "Im Kreml brennt noch Licht," *ThJ* (1999), 46–60.

[34] H.-Dieter Jendreyko, "Es geht um die Wahrheit des Augenblicks," Peter Iden (ed.), *Warum wir das Theater brauchen* (Frankfurt am Main: Suhrkamp, 1995), 83–87; Peter Iden, "Theater ist Utopie," in Peter Iden (ed.), *Warum wir das Theater brauchen* (Frankfurt am Main: Suhrkamp, 1995), 15–20; Merschmeier, "Das Herzstück fehlt," 38.

[35] Michael Merschmaier, "Das Herzstück fehlt," 39.

[36] See the table in Franz Wille, "Am Mut hängt der Erfolg oder das Debakel mit dem Schauspiel," *Th* 10 (1996): 1–2, here: 1.

[37] Walter Wallmann, "Theater als Ort des utopischen Gegenentwurfs," *ThJ* (1986), 60; Vera Rüdiger, "Gegen eine kulturpolitische Subventionspolitik," *ThJ* (1986), 61; Gerhart Rudolf Baum, "'Subvention' ist das falsche Wort," *ThJ* (1986), 61; Peter

Glotz, "Plädoyer für ein populäres Theater mit Niveau," *ThJ* (1986), 63; Volker Hassemer, "Mehr Geld muß sein, trotzdem sollen die Theater sparen — und sich auf neue Publikumsbedürfnisse einstellen," *ThJ* (1986), 65–66; Otto Schily, "Theater ist notwendiger Luxus — Kunst kann sich nur im freien gesellschaftlichen Wettbewerb entwickeln," *ThJ* (1986), 67.

[38] Roman Herzog, "Kultur. Das Pfund — mit dem wir wuchern," *Th* 7 (1996): 1–5.

[39] Participants were Frank Castorf, manager of the *Volksbühne* in Berlin; Volker Hesse, then manager of the *Theater am Neumarkt* in Zurich; Ulrich Khuon, then manager of the *Staatstheater* in Hanover; and Thomas Ostermeier, then manager of the *Baracke des Deutschen Theaters* in Berlin.

[40] "Auf der Suche nach dem Trojanischen Pferd. Ein Theater Heute-Gespräch mit Frank Castorf, Volker Hesse, Ulrich Khuon, and Thomas Ostermeier," *ThJ* (1998), 24–38.

[41] "Das System Baumbauer. Der erfolgreichste Theaterleiter der Neunziger und neue Intendant der Münchner Kammerspiele über sein neues Haus, alte Strukturen und große Pläne — im Gespräch," *Th* 6 (2001): 1–2.

[42] "Ich muss es einfach versuchen. Interview with Thomas Ostermeier," in *Th* 5 (1998): 26–30, here: 30.

[43] In his obituary for Sarah Kane, Ostermaier emphasizes the authenticity and sincerity of her plays; see Thomas Ostermaier und Marius von Mayenburg, "Klarheit und Schärfe," *Sp*, 5 March 1999, 205.

[44] Petra Kohse, "Die Welt ist zersplittert, aber das Individuum ist ganz. Interview with Thomas Ostermeier," in Therese Hörningk, Bettina Masuch, and Frank M. Raddatz (eds.), *TheaterKulturVision* (Berlin: Theater der Zeit, 1998), 63–65, here: 64.

[45] See the chapter on Marius von Mayenburg.

[46] Eva Corino and Roland Koberg, "Wir können nicht alles aus uns selbst schöpfen. Thomas Ostermeier im Gespräch über Revolte und Repolitisierung, Wölfe und Weiterbildung," *BZ*, 21 September 2000.

[47] Frauke Meyer-Gosau, "Das Politische kehrt zurück — es weiß nur noch nicht genau, wie. Kleiner Rundflug über zeitgenössische dramatische Versuche, gesellschaftliches Unglück zu beschreiben," *Th* 10 (2001): 42–52, here: 49.

Part I: The 1980s

1: Outcasts

AFTER THE WILD PROTESTS against the government led by the Greens and the women's movement in the 1970s, the 1980s were dominated by political inertia. In 1982, the Christian Democrats won the parliamentary election (*Bundestagswahl*), and Helmut Kohl was to become chancellor for the next sixteen years. This landslide victory revealed a neoconservative current in German society that viewed the future with optimism. (*Fortschrittsoptimismus*). In contrast to the Greens' apocalyptic visions of a nuclear desert, the conservatives refused to let their lives be spoiled by sorrow, and were eager to paint a positive picture of the German state.[1] The Christian Democrats' antidote to the allegedly unconstructive tendencies and dissecting philosophy (*Zersetzungsarbeit*) of the political left was to embrace new technologies and to advocate a free market economy.[2] As money matters topped the political agenda, German society allegedly fell prey to the cutthroat competitiveness of capitalism, and Theo Sommer lamented that a self-serving mentality had spun out of control.[3] Simultaneously, the Social Democrats struggled with the new shape taken by society, and found themselves short of answers with which to meet the needs of a highly industrialized, wealthy society.[4]

Four years into Helmut Kohl's chancellorship, however, a general fatigue with politics and political parties was noted. According to opinion polls in 1986, voters showed decreasing loyalty to any particular party, and the percentage of non-voters increased.[5] Kohl gradually expanded his power within the Christian Democrat party, and made sure that any critical opponents within the party, such as Kurt Biedenkopf or Heiner Geissler, were removed from the highest ranks of the party hierarchy.[6] In contrast, it may seem rather strange that Kohl was not perceived to be an intellectual challenge, and his insistence on the fact that everything was "wunderbar" became a running joke.[7] However, his strategy of staying in power was so successful that the Christian Democrats were eventually dubbed a "Kanzlerwahlverein."[8] Even before Germany was rocked by the huge party finance scandal surrounding Kohl in 1999,[9] the conservatives were believed to be manipulated by their mighty chairman Kohl.[10]

The Social Democrats reacted with helpless anger to this conservative U-turn in German history in the 1980s. However, it did not suffice to accuse the government of ignoring the urgent problems that arose from the social changes of computerized society.[11] Scandals surrounding high-ranking politicians further undermined the confidence of intellectuals, and many became convinced that Germany had developed into a state for the rich and powerful.[12] Although much talked-about in the media, the lower end of society slipped from the agenda of both politicians and intellectuals. While critical voices warned of the disastrous effects of uninhibited individualism,[13] commercial reasoning proved to be stronger. Because of the economic slowdown of the early 1980s, the number of Germans out of work and receiving welfare payments steadily increased.

Statistics show that the rate of unemployment rose from 3.8 percent in 1980 to 7.5 percent in 1982, and 9.1 percent in 1984.[14] The percentage of people living on less than the amount they would receive from social welfare rose steadily, and in 1983 roughly 4.3 percent of the population received less income than the minimum benefit.[15] Moreover, many people hid their low social status by not claiming welfare benefits, considerably distorting the figures (*verdeckte Armut*). The poor, the homeless, and the jobless become marginalized, and are not integrated into social life, a problem addressed in Franz Xaver Kroetz's play *Bauern sterben* (The Death of the Peasants, 1985).

Since the government did not address the growing economic problems, an increasing number of people were disappointed in politics and politicians. As opinion polls of the early eighties showed,[16] people grew tired of politics and politicians.[17] It is hardly surprising that playwrights advocate the cause of those at the lower end of German society. The new *Volkstheater*, particularly, (re-)emerged in the form of bitingly critical plays, engaging in the debate about the down-and-outs of German society.[18] In the 1980s, the *Volkstheater* was used by playwrights such as Ludwig Fels (in *Lieblieb* [Beloved, 1986]), Franz Xaver Kroetz, and Kerstin Specht to criticize the violence that is inflicted on the poor, women, the mentally handicapped, and foreigners. Despite the fact that Herbert Achternbusch appears to mock the *Volkstheater*, he still uses its critical potential to show that a narrow-minded "Bavarian chauvinism" can be problematic.

Mocking the Critical *Volkstheater*: Herbert Achternbusch's *Frosch* (1981)

In his play *Frosch* (Frog), the Bavarian playwright Achternbusch mocks the pattern of the new critical *Volkstheater*,[19] coloring the typical perspective of the outcast with a good deal of comedy.[20] His plays are not always comical; in *Susn* (1979) he presents an alcoholic (Susn) and in another play, *Kuschwarda City* (1980), he presents an average citizen who adjusts to the circumstances ("kuschen"), even though this leaves him mentally unbalanced.[21] As a playwright, however, Achternbusch adopts the attitude of the nonconformist jester, who mocks the theater and film business by openly declaring that he merely writes for money. In a letter to the journal *Theater heute* he presents his play *Frosch* as follows:

> Ich habe diese Woche einmal geschrieben, was so war (Das 10. Kapitel des entstehenden Buches *Das Haus am Nil*). Es wird für Sie viel zu lang sein. Kürzen können Sie nicht. Falls es Ihnen nicht zu lang ist: Bei dem erwähnten Theaterstück handelt es sich um *Der Frosch,* das ich kürzlich geschrieben habe, dem erwähnten Film *Der Neger Erwin,* den ich demnächst drehe.[22]

Frosch premiered in August 1982 in Bochum, where it was a flop.[23] On the occasion of Achternbusch's fiftieth birthday, the play was staged at the *Münchner Kammerspiele* in November 1988, this time with more success.[24] In *Frosch,* the underdog protagonist is a frog, and what he suffers from most of all is that he can no longer drink beer.[25] As the Frosch is (or was) a drinker — another critical comment on the *Neue Volkstheater* — he forgets what is like to be human, and as he regards beer-drinking as his only means of communication, he is now completely out of touch with the world.[26] Yet his "misery" is presented in an ironic manner, so that throughout the play, one can never quite be sure whether he really is a frog or whether he simply has a hangover. The title of the play is also a pun on the frog prince, but the kiss by the blond woman Susn does not make him human again. Ironically, he combs her hair, yet is depressed about the fact that she cannot return the favor. Still, the two become lovers, and form a rather odd couple.

Although Achternbusch uses ingredients of the *Volkstheater,* such as dialect, local settings, lower-class characters, poverty, and problematic relationships, he employs them merely in order to unmask them as ridiculous.[27] He uses both the stylized Bavarian dialect and the typical *Volkstheater* settings,[28] such as the beer-garden, to underpin the local picture, but combines them with farcical and absurd features, breaking the frame of the *Volkstheater* style. In some ways, Achternbusch follows in the tradition of Horváth, who intended to destroy the traditional *Volkstheater* and its illusions by parodying it.[29] Like his forerunner, Achternbusch uses elements of the traditional *Volkstheater,* but dismantles the kitsch associated with it, as, for instance, when a band plays bad Bavarian folk music. Moreover, in a similar way to Horváth's plays, the characters do not speak dialect, but rather High German tainted by dialect. The best example is the smart-aleck Erich, for the more he tries to sound sophisticated, the more ridiculous he becomes.

Unlike Horváth, who underlines the gap between the conscious and the subconscious, destructive layers of the personality by means of a subtle picture, Achternbusch takes the irony a little further until the genre itself becomes ridiculous. In *Frosch*, for example, this psychological conflict is made concrete by the fact that Frosch takes refuge in his pond, and the surface of the water symbolizes the border between the conscious and the subconscious. Achternbusch knows very well that this simplified picture is in some ways laughable, and does not hesitate to laugh at himself, such as when Frosch explains that an artist is necessarily simple-minded. In making this statement, he distances himself from this oversimplified view, yet at the same time exploits its comic potential.

Achternbusch therefore both cites and dismantles the critical *Volks-stück* through comedy, for example, when the four sit in the beer-garden of the famous Andechs monastery, knocking back their "Maß," their liter glasses of beer. In the background, a band with frog-like masks plays bad Bavarian music. Other than this, Erich bosses his girlfriend around, while Frosch sips his beer, hiding his face behind a human mask:

> ERICH   Ich kann denken, und kann dann meine Gedanken herunterholen, herunterbiegen wie einen Ast, das ist menschlich, so wird das Denken rund. Die Gedanken der Tiere gehen ins Weltall, so wie bei ihm.
>
> *Er weist auf den Frosch hin.*
>
> FREUNDIN   Ja, und ist das etwas?
>
> ERICH   Das ist auch etwas, nur nicht menschlich. Das ist genauso etwas. Aber du redest wie ein schlecht eingestelltes Radio. Wenn du 3 Halbe Bier hast, redest du wie ein schlecht eingestelltes Radio! Weil das ist die Wahrheit, das man etwas besser einstellt. Weil die Leute nutzen die Wahrheit nicht![30]

Unfortunately, Erich fails to sound sophisticated and his girlfriend is not impressed, and the comic potential of the quotidian Bavarian idiom is used to unveil Erich's silly chauvinism. The "Froschmann," the "diver," renders the German depth of meaning ridiculous, since he literally sits deep below the water surface without having the slightest clue as to what is going on around him. It is therefore not surprising that Frosch often simply reiterates what he is told. Although the play focuses on the viewpoint of a small animal, thereby showing life "aus der Froschperspektive," it is not overtly critical and tedious, but voices social criticism more indirectly, playfully gibing at small talk.

Death in the City:
Franz Xaver Kroetz's *Bauern Sterben* (1985)

Kroetz's play *Bauern Sterben,* which premiered at the Deutsches Schauspielhaus in Hamburg in December 1985, is often seen to be the expression of a personal crisis after his having left the German Communist Party.[31] Indeed, he was deeply disappointed that the political landscape had taken on a more conservative appearance since the Christian Democrat Helmut Kohl had become chancellor in 1982. In his play *Furcht und Hoffnung in Deutschland* (Fear and Hope in Germany, 1982–83),[32] which Kroetz wrote in immediate reaction to the increase in poverty, he had pitted the rising unemployment rate against the welfare state. Due to the conservative turn in Germany, capitalist policies were gaining ground, and *Bauern sterben* shows how they wipe out a whole family, destroying the "natural" way of life. *Bauern sterben* opens in the kitchen, a typical Kroetzian setting, where the family gathers round the stove.[33] However, the situation is far from homey, because the family quarrels about whether the farm should be modernized until the violence escalates and the parents are killed. Predictably, the siblings walk away and look for a better life in the city. However, they cannot find a job, suffer from hunger, fall prey to alcoholism, prostitution, and madness, and eventually flee the city, only to freeze to death on the graves of their ancestors.

Bauern Sterben is a play about the lives of disadvantaged working people, expressing Kroetz's desire to effect changes for their benefit, in accordance with the Socialists' aim to improve the lot of the worker and to achieve social equality. It simply disagrees with ruthless modernization and technological progress, and points to the urban-rural division, for industrialization has damaged traditional ways of life, causing social problems, and bringing with it alienation. Emigration to the city completely severs ties with the old life, and this lack of orientation can only spell disaster for the individuals concerned. *Bauern Sterben* expresses the dark contemporary trauma of a rootless life, reflected in the siblings' flight to the city and back home.[34]

Kroetz sees himself in fundamental opposition to the young and successful manager generation that emerges in the early 1980s. His play depicts the lower end of society, criticizing social inequality. During an interview for the journal *Theater heute,* however, Kroetz vented his frustration regarding the influence of the artist: "In dieser Scheißrepublik haben wir Dichter Null-Stellenwert. [. . .] Die Wirkungslosigkeit ist so groß, daß ich mich oft in den Arsch beißen könnte."[35] According to him, the artist is of no importance, has no status, and has no political influence. However, his words could have been tactical in nature, for Kroetz's success would be impossible without the funding and support of West Germany's political institutions.[36]

Bauern sterben is a compilation of loosely related scenes, or a "dramatisches Fragment," as the author describes it. It consists of fourteen scenes, has a coherent plot, and, in the original version, also a prologue, which is omitted in the High German version.

In line with the *Volkstheater*, Kroetz employs dialect to depict the language and the thought processes of the rural working-class.[37] His characters speak a dysfunctional language that portrays their inability to communicate, and the dialogue breaks down under the impact of the verbal violence that the characters inflict on one another.[38] Instead of trying to understand one another, they use language as a weapon, trying to cause pain with it.[39] This becomes evident at the beginning, when the father is bleeding to death from wounds underneath his arms, even into the milk they are going to sell, yet he refuses to admit it. In order to remove the blood from the floor, the family calls for the grandmother to clean it up, but she has died unnoticed in front of the television. Nonetheless, she is held responsible for being smelly:

TOCHTER   Putz, Großmutter, putz. *(Großmutter sitzt gaffend, still vor einem kleinen Fernseher.)*

TOCHTER   *(schreit)* Kannst nicht hörn! *(Sie geht zur Großmutter.)* Stinken tut sie. Die stinkt, daß man umfalln könnt, so stinkt die.

VATER   Weil sie eine alte Sau ist, eine alte. Die war immer schon eine alte Sau.[40]

This dialogue shows how low the standards in the family already are, and that empathy is an unknown word. Due to her blind rage, the daughter does not even realize that her grandmother has already died. The evils of modernization, such as television, have already begun to creep into their home, spelling death for the grandmother. This indicates that the previously valued independence of the farmer has been undermined by the media-borne influence of the global village.[41] Instead of being buried, the dead grandmother sits, full of worms, in the kitchen, and the only emotion shown by the family, who squabble over the remote control, is jealousy.

Despite its naturalist setting, *Bauern sterben* has strong surreal overtones. In act I, scene 2, for example, the daughter has a miscarriage, and puts the baby into the womb of the dead grandmother whom she is about to prepare for the funeral. Kroetz makes it clear that life and death are closely intertwined; the stillborn baby is also symbolic of the hopeless future. The next scene, the funeral, is also eerily unreal, for, instead of a mass, the audience witnesses the slaughtering of Jesus, a symbol that foretells the impending doom of the two siblings. In act 2, which is modeled on the stations of the cross (*Kreuzweg*), five "Zeichen am Weg" symbolize not only the end of religion, but also dehumanization and the evils of modern technology. Here, Kroetz draws on the mystery plays of the Middle Ages, during which the last hours of Jesus were remembered. In contrast to the pilgrims in the *Kreuzweg*, however, the girl and her brother do not stop to think or pray, but race past the signs in order to forget them quickly. They come across five different people during their journey: a Green farmer who is desperately trying to prevent his farm from being taken over by an electrical company, an unemployed man, a terrorist, a religious person who warns them that ignoring God will result in disaster, and a woman holding a baby in her arms. Due to malnourishment, the woman has no milk, and her breasts are bitten and bleeding, an image that presents a victim of the bleak city. However, the pair ignore this, for they believe that the city and technology (even nuclear power plants) hold blessings for them. Loss of religious faith and alienation go hand in hand, and in an outbreak of madness, the brother later smashes both the crucifix and the legs of the Christ figure, an act reminiscent of the killing of Jesus. Afterwards, he tries to make amends for his act of blasphemy by carving a niche for an altar, and donating blood to the crippled Christ figure. In a similar way to his father, he flees reality and bleeds himself dry, selling his blood to a firm in order to make a living.

The accommodation they find when they reach the city is still under construction, and lacks warmth and individualism, as the apartment complex is the result of a highly rationalized society.[42] The decay and disorder inside the apartment mirrors the siblings' disturbed minds, and to make it look like home again, the brother empties bags of soil onto the floor, and tries in vain to grow vegetables inside the flat. The modern metropolis leads to a lack of individual identity and alienation from the fruits of labor. Despite all his efforts, the brother adopts the patriarchal attitude of his father, asserting that he owns his sister.[43] As the play progresses, their lack of identity becomes apparent, as does their unhappiness, for the two try to recreate their previous life, yet simply end up enduring further degradation and humiliation. Even their repentance comes too late, since their parents have long been dead and buried when they arrive home. As their home is destroyed and they have nowhere to go, they collapse on their parents' graves, and freeze to death in the falling snow.

Impossible Relationships: Ludwig Fels's *Lieblieb* (1986)

Fels's play addresses a topic that is most important to him, namely the spiritual and emotional crippling of outcasts who are unable to cope with a cold and frightening world. In an interview, Fels, a former factory worker, points out that literature can help to cope with the alienation at work:

> Und diese Erfahrungen sind dann wieder einsetzbar, wenn man selber schreibt, *gegen* die Monotonie der Arbeitswelt. Damit kann man diese Entfremdungen, unter Umständen, in Schach halten.[44]

For Fels, writing comes from personal experience,[45] and he is above all concerned with creating real characters, for example in *Soliman* (1991), which is modeled on the real-life character Angelo Soliman who lived at the court of Joseph II in eighteenth-century Vienna.[46] The play shows how the black man Soliman is systematically humiliated, for he is merely regarded as an exotic being on display.[47] In the same vein, *Lieblieb* explores the workings of a perverted human spirit and psyche, and at the same time, unveils the emotional wounds and frailty of his characters. *Lieblieb* premiered in Darmstadt in June 1986 (director: Jean-Claude Kuner), where it received a fairly bad press, as Kuner reduced the play to a simple black-and-white melodrama.[48] A few days later, the play was performed in Cologne, directed by Wolfgang Trautwein, this time with greater success.[49]

The emotional backbone of the play is the impossible relationship between the unemployed alcoholic Rudi Brada, who is likely to have caused the death of his wife Hilda, and the mentally ill Rosina Zarik, who has just been released from a mental asylum. Both are desperate for true love, but are unable to give true affection, as they are preoccupied with their own pasts. While the depressed Rosina has lost track of her real self and is dependent on tranquilizers, Brada cannot but think of his dead wife Hilda, whom he still loves. He allegedly buried her in the bathtub, where he now grows a few flowers, a grotesque idea that also unmasks him as a lunatic. Although Brada and Rosina long for a better future, their hope renders them slaves of their own minds. The relationship between the two is unequal, as Brada addresses her with the condescending "du," whereas Rosina respectfully sticks to the formal "Sie." What is more, Brada does not miss any opportunity to insult her, and calls her an old, ugly and disgusting hag who is too unattractive even to be raped.

At the beginning, the audience sees Brada practicing chatting up a woman, right in front of the gate to the mental asylum. When Rosina appears, he talks to her, taking her first to the cemetery where his wife's grave really is to be found, then to the nearest pub, where he buys her drinks and persuades her to come back to his apartment. Not quite in possession of her wits, Rosina thanks him for his kindness, but before she can say any more, he starts hitting her and forces her to sleep under the bed. For the next two days, he locks her up, giving her alcohol instead of food, and violence instead of affection. As he is short of money, he arranges for his friend Vanka to sleep with her, so that he will get some money to buy alcohol. During these two days, Rosina is beaten, raped, burned and most cruelly insulted by men who regard her simply as an object of their desires. In the end, Brada throws her out, and Rosina staggers back to the asylum, accompanied by a chorus of patients who make fun of her despair.

Despite the play's focus on the psyche of its characters, *Lieblieb* is not strictly realistic, as the action is accompanied by surreal dream-plays. During these interludes, both Hilda and Brada's parents return to life and talk to him, rendering his disturbed psychological condition visible. Parallel to this, the apparitions of patients and doctors from the asylum continue to haunt Rosina, mocking her frailty. The function of these grotesque interludes is to highlight the emotions of the characters, such as Brada's despair over Hilda. Dressed in a bloodstained coat, she rises from her grave in the bathroom to console and soothe the mind of her former husband. In a scene fit for a horror film, Brada and the dead Hilda hug and kiss on the bed, while his dead parents make dirty remarks about Brada's first night with Hilda. It is only during Hilda's apparitions that Brada becomes softer, but his brain is too soaked with alcohol and self-pity to allow him to overcome his grief permanently. Like a little child in his mother's wardrobe, he kisses Hilda's clothes that still hang in his flat.

In contrast to other new *Volkstheater* plays written after 1960, speech in *Lieblieb* is not limited to the dysfunctional set of expressions that would be typical for people at the lowest end of the social scale. As far as language is concerned, Fels returns to the expressionist style that Else Lasker-Schüler (1869–1945) employs in her play *Die Wupper* (The River Wupper, 1909), combining restricted means of expression with highly poetic passages.[50] In an emotional scene, Brada grieves for his wife, watering the flowers in the bathtub with beer and his tears, when a chorus of patients in white coats appear and begin to sing as they rhythmically kick against the tub:

Durch unsere Augen weht ein schwarzer Wind
und der Herrgott schreit im Meer
wir wissen daß wir ohne Heimat sind
der Tod winkt uns zu wie ein trauriges Kind
wir gehören zum verlorenen Heer.

(Von seinem Weinen wacht ROSINA auf. Sie sieht das Kreuz und sagt angstvoll "Guten Tag." BRADA kriecht zu ihr. Sie streichelt sein nasses Gesicht. Das wird ihm zuviel, er stößt ROSINA grob an den Kopf; sie fällt in ihre alte Lage zurück.)

ROSINA   Ich brauche morgen ein anderes Gesicht.

BRADA   Kriegst du! Kriegst du alles! *(Er trinkt wieder aus der
          Bierflasche. Kratzt sich. Spitzt die Lippen. Fährt mit
          seinem Zeigefinger wie mit einem Penis dazwischen.)*
          Wurst und Durst! *(Brada schweigt lauernd.)*

ROSINA   Ich heiße Rosina.[51]

In this passage, the grief that is concealed by Brada's aggressive demeanor is voiced by the chorus of men, as the alcoholic is unable to express his true feelings. His only means of communication is dumb violence or self-pity. Rosina is scared and does not know how to handle the situation, so reverts to a polite greeting, like an obedient little child. Although Brada longs for tenderness and affection, and crawls close to her, he brutally rejects her attempt to console him, thus also punishing himself. In order to hurt Rosina instead of himself, however, he turns his aggression against her and scares her with offensive gestures and rude remarks. His tastes are elemental and crude, and his manner is brusque and violent. As Rosina's mind is broken, she is unable to react sensibly, and replies with stock phrases, telling him her name, as if it were their first encounter.

The task of living and coping with the situation demands the very utmost of Rosina's resources, but sadly her feeble efforts are in vain. Looking back on her life, she realizes that it has mainly consisted of men abusing her. Yet her memories are so painful that she cannot remember the details of each humiliation. As she is used to being the passive object, she quickly internalizes the doctors' advice, rebukes and meaningless chat, and repeats it like a magic formula when she is afraid of Brada.

In the morning, when Brada leaves to go to the pub, she talks to herself as if a doctor is present, reporting her problems and asking for help. But her own thoughts and initiatives were replaced by other peoples' will so long ago that all her attempts not to cry are futile. However, the doctor is merely an apparition who plays with her hopes and fears, and then disappears the very moment Brada enters and beats her. She finds she is unable to scream, hit back, or even defend herself despite attempts to do so. Rosina is the perfect victim, ready to obey Brada's absurd orders. When he forces her to prepare breakfast, a typical ritual of female subjection, the scene becomes even more absurd, for at first Rosina can only find various sorts of alcohol. Even the coffee she makes is immediately poured into the gutter. Disgusted and hungry, she begs for bread, but Brada forces her to drink beer instead.

In a world where such insanity is the norm, mental and physical survival is virtually impossible. Both characters escape their fate by choosing fantasy over reality: Brada continues to drink and is already waiting for the next woman, while Rosina flees to the mental asylum to be given tranquilizers.

Xenophobia: Kerstin Specht's *Lila* (1989–90)

Specht's second play *Lila* is set in a small village in the south of Germany where villagers are shaken by the news that one of the local lads, Sieg-fried, is going to marry Lila, a Philippine girl.[52] Her arrival triggers a series of hostile events, causing the conservative population to protect their closed community. On the surface, the play tells the story of a few years in the lives of a handful of small-town people; below the surface, however, it is a sharp and lucid attack on the cruelty of ordinary people.[53] In *Lila*, a rural idyll becomes a nightmare scenario for a young girl.[54] It was first staged at the *Städtische Bühne Nürnberg* in December 1990, directed by Hansjörg Utzerath.

As in *Lila*, a woman is also at the core of her earlier play *Amiwiesen* (American Funfair, 1989), in which the playwright focuses on the situation of women from a different angle. Through the long monologue of *Amiwiesen* the audience learns that the servant stabbed her employer to death in order to run away with his child, describing a woman who is desperate for a child, since she cannot bear one herself. *Amiwiesen* shows that old-fashioned role models are still strong, and that a woman without offspring is not considered to be of value.[55]

In the tradition of the *Volkstheater*, Specht's *Lila* employs dialect in order to paint a more realistic picture of the narrow-minded nature of her characters.[56] The language, however, is still much closer to High German than to dialect, perhaps because a strict phonetic transcription would exclude a large proportion of a German audience, who would not otherwise be able to follow. The stylized dialect also avoids specific localization of the subject matter, as Specht intends her plays to be a mirror of society at large.[57] Yet there are enough local overtones to paint a lively picture of a quiet, pious, and nationalist village in no-man's-land in Lower Franconia, close to the former German-German border.[58] It is the local dialect that creates the feeling of being at home, and a strong sense of being a legitimate member of the village community. It is unfortunate that Lila does not speak a single word of German, let alone the Franconian dialect. It is telling that she has been given a simple German nickname, indicating that nobody cares about her real one. As she is unable to communicate verbally, she is restricted to a mute and passive existence, and is the ideal target for the villagers' insecurities. Whereas the women see her beauty as a potential threat to their marriages, the men lust after her as an object for their sexual desires. This also holds true for her prospective husband, Siegfried, who boasts about her exotic appeal when he presents her at the pub like a prize animal.

In the first half of the play, Specht describes the arrival of the newcomer Lila and her rejection by the villagers. The conflict with Siegfried's mother escalates after the wedding, and he decides to move to the city. As his father cannot forgive his wife for chasing his son out of the house, their marriage deteriorates rapidly, and he begins to drink and beat his wife. As he sides with Lila, the mother sets fire to the house during the night, and Hanna, their gentle and deaf daughter, is killed in the blaze. In the second part, the father becomes a ragged recluse who is mourning for his daughter. Living in the dilapidated barn next to the site of the former house, he refuses not only to rebuild the house but also to sell the land. Although the village around him is experiencing a modernization boom, he looks forward to dying.

In the end, Siegfried and his family arrive, but not to help him. On the contrary, Siegfried urges his father to sell the land so that he and his family can pay their debts. Still, his father refuses to accept a place in Siegfried's flat, and will have to be put in an old people's home. Chauvinistic as he is, Siegfried blames Lila for their tight financial situation, and his confidential remark "you know how women are" become his last words, as Lila kills him with a stone. This is an act of violence that implicitly tells us what she must have silently endured during the past few years. As Specht points out, her figures are not only victims, but also aggressors, thus reversing the pattern of sufferance of typical *Volkstheater* characters.[59] In the last scene, Lila consoles and caresses Siegfried's father, trying to soothe his grief. At last, she shows her true colors, since the color lilac represents the women's movement. Ironically, she is the only one who is able to feel empathy for others, despite being a Protestant stranger. Finally, the two outcasts are reunited, and the father dies quietly with his head in her lap.

Specht describes the small world in short, precise scenes that take place either in the kitchen of the Kratzke family, in the local pub, or at the local rifle club (Schützenverein). It should be noted that all three locations are symbolic of a very conservative Germany. Usually, local rifle clubs are notorious for their extremely conservative tendencies, particularly with respect to women, who are banished to the kitchen, where they forever bake cakes, as does the mother in *Lila*. She very readily succumbs to men's expectations of the ideal housewife. She is therefore the perfect example of a non-emancipated woman who dedicates her life to the "three Ks": Kinder, Kirche, and Küche.

In accordance with the new *Volkstheater*, *Lila* provides a vivid insight into the customs of common people, showing their everyday routine and unveiling the outward coziness as mere facade. In the kitchen of the Kratzke family, we see the mother kneeling on the wooden floor, trying to clean it with a hairpin. Not only is she obsessed with cleaning, but she is also very organized, as the clock signals that dinner is ready. Of course, she regularly attends holy mass, and is extremely concerned about the mixed marriage. Anxious not to be the cause of rumors, she is annoyed by Lila's arrival and the fact that people gossip. Whereas the father assumes a positive and open-minded attitude, the mother is convinced that "those" longhaired young people are all on drugs. True Christianity does not involve loving a stranger, but of obeying laid-down rules. As Lila is not baptized, the mother hates her, and she tries to hurt the girl whenever possible. Under the pretext of demonstrating how to make dumplings, for example, she quickly dunks Lila's hands into the hot dough, deliberately burning her. To the mother's anger, Lila is consoled by Hanna, who puts her arm around Lila's shoulders. After the wedding, she throws the pregnant Lila from a deckchair in the garden, because she dares to wear a bikini. This reveals the hypocrisy of the mother, who believes herself to be a good Christian, yet is filled with hatred for everybody: she despises her daughter Hanna, whom she considers ugly and dull; she looks down on her husband, whom she finds weak and effeminate; and she condemns Lila, whom she perceives as a black witch who has cast a bad spell on the village.

Convinced that Lila is the carrier of dangerous diseases, Seiger, a member of the rifle club, urges the priest not to follow the normal liturgy during the wedding, but to omit the holy communion, so that the community does not have to share a wine glass, a fear which is a telling example of his narrow-minded mentality.

Lila is alienated and oppressed by cultural violence in several respects.[60] Because the villagers believe that their own culture is better, they think that Protestantism, male domination, white skin and the command of the German language is enough to make them superior. As Lila lacks all of these allegedly positive features, she is marginalized, oppressed, and alienated from her own cultural background. Lila remains an exotic stranger, a rare bird amongst the locals, her only purpose in life being to add some excitement to Siegfried's life. Yet he also violates her human rights; first, he abuses her as a sex object who is expected quietly to fulfill his wishes; second, Lila experiences discrimination in the sense that Siegfried reduces her to a beautiful possession that is to be put on show. Only toward the end of the play does she revolt against this cultural violence through an act of direct aggression. In killing Siegfried with a stone, the underdog Lila becomes superior, at least temporarily.

As the unemployment rate rose, xenophobia increased and the Kohl government introduced a conservative trend, West German playwrights rediscovered the critical *Volkstheater* of the 1950s, which became an important vehicle for social criticism. However, this form is often varied, and the playwrights assembled in the chapter *Outcasts,* for example, each use the *Volkstheater* in their own way. In *Bauern Sterben* (1985), Kroetz depicts the doomed attempt of two siblings who make a break from their parents, and move to the city. Dialect in Kroetz's plays typically plays an important role in expressing the frictions between "Heimat" and hidden conflicts within society, exposing the invisible border between socially acceptable behavior and subconscious aggression. In *Lila* (1989), Kerstin Specht uses the Franconian idiom to add another dimension to social conflicts, namely xenophobia, for the Philippine girl Lila becomes the victim of an ultra-conservative community in a small town. An abused woman is also at the center of Ludwig Fels's *Lieblieb* (1986), a play that employs no dialect at all, and features an elaborate language reminiscent of expressionist plays to portray the destructive relationship between the alcoholic Branda and Rosina, a mentally ill woman. It is worth noting that in the 1980s, feminist issues were also brought up by male play-wrights, a development that indicates that people's attitudes had already changed and the feminist movement had not been as fruitless as many women had thought. Herbert Achternbusch's *Frosch* (1981) is rather different, for he seemingly mocks social problems, yet picks up on people's narrow-mindedness and the gloomy seriousness of *Volkstheater* style. Achternbusch provides a metatheater that serves as a mocking commentary on both form and content of the *Volkstheater.*

Notes

[1] Johannes Gross, "Die Misere der öffentlichen Gefühle. Oder Trübsinn würzt den Genuß des Wohlstands," *FAZ*, 1 March 1980.

[2] Claus Leggewie, "Der Geist denkt rechts. Wo Politik vorgedacht wird: Ein Streifzug durch die konservativen Denkfabriken der Bundesrepublik," *Z*, 16 October 1987; Claus Leggewie, *Der Geist steht rechts. Ausflüge in die Denkfabriken der Wende* (Berlin: Rotbuch, 1987).

[3] Theo Sommer, "Ein Abgrund der Doppelmoral," *Z*, 21 May 1993.

[4] Ralf Dahrendorf, "Das Elend der Sozialdemokratie," *Merkur* 12 (1987), 1019–38.

[5] Christian Graf von Krockow and Peter Lösche (eds.), *Parteien in der Krise? Das Parteiensystem der Bundesrepublik und der Aufstand des Bürgerwillens* (Munich: CH Beck, 1986).

[6] Geißler's plans to "air out" the offices of the party are outlined in his book: Heiner Geißler, *Zugluft. Politik in stürmischer Zeit* (1990) (Munich: Goldmann 1998).

[7] See, for example, Ria Endres, "Die Theater-Krise läßt mich kalt," *ThJ* (1987), 62–63, here: 62.

[8] Warnfried Dettling, *Das Erbe Kohls* (Frankfurt am Main: Eichborn, 1994).

[9] In July 2001, his wife Hannelore committed suicide, an act officially believed to be due to her suffering from an allergy to light, yet her death was tarnished by the scandal that overshadowed her husband's chancellorship. Her devastation was depicted in a short play by Dea Loher, "Licht," in Dea Loher, *Magazin des Glücks* (Frankfurt am Main: Verlag der Autoren, 2002), 9–28. It was premiered at the *Thalia Theater* in Hamburg in October 2001.

[10] See the articles on Kohl's 10th year as Chancellor, which highlighted Kohl's confidence and the party's loyalty: Stephan-Andreas Casdorff, "'Der Kerl steht und steht.' In Bonn feiern 3000 Gäste Bundeskanzler Helmut Kohls zehnjähriges Amtsjubiläum," *SZ*, 2/3/4 October 1992; Thomas Wittke, "3000 feierten die 'ersten zehn Jahre.' Schäuble lobte Kohl ohne Lobeshymnen — Weizsäcker fand keine Lücke im Terminkalender," *Generalanzeiger*, 2 October 1992; Claus Gennrich, "Die Gefühlsanspannung, die den Regierungswechsel vor zehn begleitete, ist nurmehr zu ahnen," *FAZ*, 1 October 1992; Klaus Dreher, "'Irgendwie haben wir uns an ihn gewöhnt.' Helmut Kohl: Hauptdarsteller, Regisseur, Drehbuchautor und Souffleur in Personalunion," *SZ*, 5 October 1992.

[11] Horst Kern and Michael Schumann, *Das Ende der Arbeitsteilung? Rationalisierung in der modernen Produktion* (Munich: CH Beck, 1984), 44–46.

[12] Herbert Riehl-Heyse, "Jedem das Seine, mir das meiste," *SZ*, 20/21 February 1993.

[13] Hermann Scheer, "Die 80er Bewegung und ihre ideologische Zukunftsblindheit," in *Bildung Macht Verantwortung. Welche Zukunft für die Bundesrepublik*, eds. Frithjof Hager, Gerold Becker and Jürgen Zimmer (Leipzig: Reclam, 1994), 176–85.

[14] See the statistics in Bundeszentrale für politische Bildung, ed., "Arbeitslose, offene Stellen und Arbeitslosenquoten im früheren Bundesgebiet 1950 bis 2000," in *Datenreport 2000* (Bonn: Bundeszentrale für politische Bildung, 2002), 97.

[15] Rainer Geißler, *Die Sozialstruktur Deutschlands* (Opladen: Westdeutscher, 1996), 183.

[16] See the table "Die Entwicklung des politischen Interesses," in Statistisches Bundesamt (ed.), *Datenreport 2002* (Bonn: Bundeszentrale für politische Bildung, 2002), 599.

[17] This was referred to as "Politikverdrossenheit," see Hildegard Hamm-Brücher, "Wege in die und Wege aus der Politik(er)verdrossenheit," in *Bildung Macht Verantwortung. Welche Zukunft für die Bundesrepublik?*, eds. Frithjof Hager, Gerold Becker and Jürgen Zimmer (Leipzig: Reclam, 1994), 188–95.

[18] For an excellent overview of the development of the critical *Volksstück* after 1945, see Hugo Aust, Peter Haida and Jürgen Hein, *Volksstück. Vom Hanswurstspiel zum sozialen Drama der Gegenwart* (Munich: CH Beck, 1989), 316–44.

[19] On some general features of the new critical *Volkstheater* see Susan Cocalis, "The Poetics of Brutality: Toward a Definition of the Critical Volksstück," *Modern Drama* 24 (1981), 292–313.

[20] For Achternbusch's use of comedy with respect to his play *Sintflut* (1983), see Gillian Pye, *Approaching Comedy in Contemporary German Drama* (New York: Edwin Mellen, 2002), 323–51. Pye discusses Achternbusch's use of the comic potential, analyzing his anarchic potential in the context of absurdist drama. According to her, Achternbusch's comedies combine an existential absurdity with deep metaphysical implications.

[21] Stefanie Carp, "Vom Unglück der beschißnen Unterdrückung und vom Zorn darauf. *Susn* und *Kuschwarda City* von Herbert Achternbusch in Bochum uraufgeführt," *Th* 12 (1980): 21–22. On the form of the monologue in Achterbusch's plays, see Anne Betten, "Der Monolog als charakteristische Form des deutschsprachigen Theaters der achtziger Jahre: Anmerkungen zu Thomas Bernhards und Herbert Achternbuschs dramatischer Schreibweise," *Cahiers d'Etudes Germaniques* 20 (1991), 37–48.

[22] Quoted in "Neue Stücke in der neuen Saison — Autoren schildern ihre Situation," in *ThJ* (1980), 4–8, here: 4.

[23] Heinz Klunker, "Der *Frosch* in Bochum," *Th* 8 (1982): 22–23.

[24] Thomas Thieringer, "Herbert Achternbuschs Entsetzensherrliche Alpträume," *Th* 11 (1988): 6–8.

[25] The importance of beer in Achternbusch's plays is discussed in Rembert Huser, "Fremdwort Bier," *Zeitschrift für Deutsche Philologie* 114 (Supplement) (1995), 129–57.

[26] Sebald sees parallels to Kafka's *Die Verwandlung*, because the helpless frog is extremely sensitive and completely dependent on the human beings around him; see W.G. Sebald, "Achterbuschs theatralische Sendung," in *Patterns of Change: German Drama and the European Tradition*, ed. Dorothy James and Silvia Ranawake (New York, Bern, Frankfurt am Main, Paris: Lang, 1990), 297–306, here: 304. However, I would not agree with the claim that he is treated cruelly, because Susn still loves him, and even takes him out for a drink.

[27] On the new *Volkstheater* after 1945, see Hugo Aust, Peter Haida, Jürgen Hein (eds.), *Volksstück. Vom Hanswurstspiel zum sozialen Drama der Gegenwart* (Munich: CH Beck, 1989), 316–45.

[28] On the concept of "Heimat" in the *Volksstück*, see Johannes G. Pankau, "Figurationen des Bayrischen: Sperr, Fassbinder, Achternbusch," in *Der Begriff "Heimat"*

in der deutschen Gegenwartsliteratur, ed. Helfried W. Selinger (Munich: Iudicium, 1987), 133–47.

[29] Ödön von Horváth, "Gebrauchsanweisung," in *Materialien zu Ödön von Horváths Kasimir und Karoline,* ed. Traugott Krischke (Frankfurt am Main: Suhrkamp, 1973), 103–7.

[30] Herbert Achternbusch, "Frosch," in Herbert Achternbusch, *Die Einsicht der Einsicht. Theaterstücke* (Frankfurt am Main: Fischer, 1995), 101–140, here: 131.

[31] It is striking that many reviews point out parallels between the play and Kroetz as an artist. See, for example Elisabeth Fischer, "Kroetz stellt seine Wunden aus," *SZ,* 11 June 1985; Benjamin Henrichs, "Kroetz voll Blut und Wunden," *Z,* 14 June 1985; Peter von Becker, "Die Stadt, das Land und der Tod. Kroetz und Achternbusch inszenieren Kroetz und Achternbusch in München," *Th* 7 (1985): 22.

[32] Franz Xaver Kroetz, "Furcht und Hoffnung in Deutschland," in Franz Xaver Kroetz, *Furcht und Hoffnung in Deutschland. Nicht Fisch nicht Fleisch* (Hamburg: Rotbuch, 1997), 1–112.

[33] On the recurring topic of "Heimat" in Kroetz's work, see Michael Töteberg, "Ein konservativer Autor. Familie, Kind, Technikfeindlichkeit: traditionsgebundene Werte in den Dramen von Franz Xaver Kroetz," in *Franz Xaver Kroetz. Materialien,* ed. Otto Riewohldt (Frankfurt am Main: Suhrkamp, 1985), 284–96, here: 268.

[34] Moray McGowan, "'Die Stadt ist der Metzger': The Crisis of Bavarian Peasant Identity in Franz Xaver Kroetz's *Bauern Sterben,*" *German Studies Review* 19 (1996), 30–31.

[35] Franz Xaver Kroetz, "Interview," in: *Franz Xaver Kroetz. Bauern Sterben. Materialien zum Stück. Programmbücher des Deutschen Schauspielhauses Hamburg,* ed. Peter Zadek (Reinbek: Rowohlt, 1986), 160.

[36] Moray McGowan, "Sprache, Gewalt und Gesellschaft," *text & kritik* 57 (1978), 37–48, here: 37.

[37] Günter Rühle, *Theater in unserer Zeit 2* (Frankfurt am Main: Suhrkamp), 153.

[38] Kroetz, quoted in Hellmuth Karasek, "Kroetz Franz Xaver oder: Die Sprache funktioniert nicht," *ThJ* (1973), 76.

[39] McGowan, "Sprache, Gewalt und Gesellschaft," 43.

[40] To facilitate comprehension, the High German version will be quoted here: Franz Xaver Kroetz, *Bauern Sterben,* in Franz Xaver Kroetz, *Bauern Sterben. Der Weihnachtstod. Weitere Aussichten.* Stücke 6 (Hamburg: Rotbuch, 1999), 57–104, here: 66.

[41] Moray McGowan, "Die Stadt ist der Metzger," 17–34, here: 33.

[42] Michelle Mattson, *Franz Xaver Kroetz: The Construction of a Political Aesthetic* (Oxford: Berg, 1996), 157.

[43] Male anger when the male role as the breadwinner is threatened is a common Kroetzian theme, see Ursula Hassel, "'My home is my castle': Zur Familiendarstellung in den Dramen von Franz Xaver Kroetz," *Das zeitgenössische deutschsprachige Volksstück,* eds. Ursula Hassel and Herbert Herzmann (Tübingen: Stauffenburg, 1992), 177–92, here: 188.

[44] Horst Scharnagl, "Vom Fabrikarbeiter zum Berufsschriftsteller. Ein Gespräch mit Ludwig Fels," *Neue Rundschau* 97/1 (1986), 28–40, here: 28.

[45] Wend Kässens, "'Schreiben ist auch ein Stück Selbstzerstörung.' Ein Gespräch mit dem Autor Ludwig Fels," *Th* 10 (1991), 27–31, here: 31.

[46] Ludwig Fels, "Soliman," in Ludwig Fels, *Soliman: Lieblieb* (Frankfurt am Main: Verlag der Autoren, 1991), 7–76.

[47] The play was premiered in September 1991 at the *Volkstheater* in Vienna, yet the production was criticized because of the poor acting, see Jörg W. Gronius, "Ein Mohr im Menschenzoo," *Th* 10 (1991): 30.

[48] Verena Auffermann, "*Alltagshölle Alemania*," *Th* 6 (1986): 41–42.

[49] Werner Schulze-Reimpel, "*Lieblieb* in Köln," *Th* 6 (1986): 42.

[50] Fels, who started his career by writing poetry, explains that this technique allows him to complement the insufficient means of dialogical expression with a dense and symbolic language. See the interview "Eine Liebesgeschichte in umöglichen Verhältnissen," *Th* 6 (1986): 40.

[51] Ludwig Fels, "Lieblieb," in Ludwig Fels, *Soliman. Lieblieb* (Frankfurt am Main: Verlag der Autoren, 1991), 77–138, here: 92–3. See also the print in *Th* 6 (1986): 43–50.

[52] Kerstin Specht, *Lila. Das glühend Männla. Amiwiesen.* Drei Stücke (Frankfurt am Main: Verlag der Autoren 1990), 7–50. Subsequent references to this work are cited in the text using the abbreviation *L* and page number.

[53] In view of the rejection of the foreigner, Specht's play follows the pattern of Sperr's *Jagdszenen in Niederbayern* (1966) and Fassbinder's *Katzelmacher* (1968). See also Thomas E. Bourke, "'Der muß weg!' Ausgrenzungsmuster in den neuen kritischen Heimatstücken des süddeutschen und österreichischen Raums," in *Das zeitgenössische deutschsprachige Volksstück*, eds. Ursula Hassel and Herbert Herzmann (Tübingen: Stauffenberg, 1992), 247–60.

[54] Mario Stumpfe, "MundART-Realismus. Dramatische Texte zum Spielen," in *Stück-Werk 1* (Berlin: Internationales Theaterinstitut, 1997), 114–17, here 114.

[55] The play was premiered at the *Kammerspiele* in Munich in November 1990, where it was warmly received, see Renate Schostack, "*Schwarze Ballade, kühle Kunst*," *Th* 12 (1990): 40–41.

[56] Thomas E. Bourke, "Kerstin Specht and the *Critical Volksstück:* a New Voice in a Seasoned Genre," in *The Individual, Identity and Innovation,* eds. Arthur Williams and Stuart Parkes (Frankfurt am Main: Peter Lang, 1994), 133–47, here: 135.

[57] Ingrid Seidenhafen, "'Meine Figuren sollen keine Opfer sein.' Die oberfränkische Dramatikerin Kerstin Specht über ihre neuen Stücke," *Abendzeitung*, 25/26 August 1990.

[58] Peter von Becker, "Letzte Nachrichten aus dem deutschen Niemandsland," *Th* 1 (1990): 28–30.

[59] See Ingrid Seidenhafen, "'Meine Figuren sollen keine Opfer sein.' Die oberfränkische Dramatikerin Kerstin Specht über ihre neuen Stücke," *Abendzeitung*, 25/26 August 1990.

[60] On the concept of cultural and structural violence, see Johan Galtung, "Violence, Peace and Peace Research," *Journal of Peace Research* 6 (1969), 167–91; Johan Galtung, "Cultural Violence," *Journal of Peace Research* 27 (1990), 291–305.

2: Green Issues

IN THE LATE 1960S, only local protest groups addressed the issue of water and air pollution. Following the report by the *Club of Rome* in 1972, however, which pointed out that economic growth had to be limited if the environment was to be saved, people became aware of the global dimension of environmental destruction. The conclusion was shocking and simple: economic growth would eventually destroy the earth. Similarly, workers in the big cities felt increasingly alienated by industrialization, pollution, and the building of motorways and ugly suburbs. The fact that hardly any green areas survived in cities led to a certain degree of claustrophobia for many, which left young people longing for a romantic and more humane environment.[1]

As early as the 1970s, the feeling of environmental crisis became stronger, for it was believed that the "Atomstaat" Germany would lead its population to an environmental disaster, if not straight into nuclear war.[2] Following a sharp rise in oil prices after the oil crisis of 1973, the German government looked for other potential sources of energy, and envisaged that in 1985, fifteen percent of the country's energy would come from nuclear power plants. At the same time, other ways of saving energy were discussed and funded by the state.

While the plans for nuclear power plants continued, an increasing feeling of uneasiness emerged. As early as 1956, the Ministry for Nuclear Energy (Atomministerium) had spoken of a "Strahlenangstpsychose."[3] In the same year, the journal *Atomwirtschaft* mentioned the psychological distress that the fear of a nuclear accident or war had already produced among the population.[4] Well into the 1970s, however, the media seldom adopted a critical attitude towards the nuclear industry, and the authorities registered with astonishment that protest movements were beginning to form in clusters around the planned sites of nuclear power plants.[5]

Meanwhile, environmental protection groups were founded across the country, and began to voice their protest. The two most prominent examples of these protests were the demonstration, lasting three years, against the nuclear power plant planned in Whyl, and, in 1977, the violent clashes during the protests against the nuclear reprocessing plant in Brokdorf, a scenario that forms the background of Florian Felix Weyh's (1963–) play *Fondue* (Fondue, 1988). The remarkable thing about these so-called *Bürgerinitiativen*, however, was that they were no longer solely supported by students, but were backed by many local protesters, including farmers, teachers, and simply worried parents, all of whom were demonstrating against the impending destruction of their personal environment.[6]

In the late 1970s, the first local Green and "alternative" party lists were formed, and some, such as those in Berlin, enjoyed considerable success.[7] The establishment of a national Green party followed in 1980. In 1983 the Greens were represented in the *Bundestag* for the first time, and were able to force Kohl's conservative CDU/FDP government to take environmental issues seriously.[8] It soon became clear that the "alternative" MPs represented the will of a considerable section of the population, at least in ecological matters.[9] Although the conservative government had turned pale green, as it were, by spending huge sums of money on compensation for the destruction of the environment and the prevention of further ecological damage, these policies left much to be desired. A major point of criticism was that in 1983, after four years of parliamentary debate, the NATO-*Doppelbeschluß* (1979) was finally enforced, meaning that the divide between the Eastern and Western blocs deepened, and the arms race proved to be more important than the concerns of the peace campaigners. Pershing missiles were installed in small towns such as Mutlangen in the Swabian mountains. This measure caused an ongoing quarrel between the government and peace campaigners that was to last for years, since it nourished fears that a nuclear war could be triggered by mistake.[10]

In the early years of protest in the 1980s and then again after the accident at the nuclear power plant in Chernobyl in 1986, the fear of creeping environmental destruction increased, and debate raged over the desirability of abolishing nuclear power and weapons. It is interesting that many thinkers were concerned with its psychological and political consequences rather than the effects nuclear war would have on nature. Harald Mueller's *Totenfloß* (Raft of the Dead, 1986), which is set in a nuclear desert, presents us with a group of crippled and mentally-ill characters who try to survive in a devastated environment.

In contrast to earlier plays such as Friedrich Dürrenmatt's (1921–1990) *Die Physiker* (*The Physicists*, 1962)[11] or Heinar Kipphardt's (1922–1982) *Die Sache Robert J. Oppenheimer* (*In the Matter of Robert J. Oppenheimer*, 1964),[12] the focus of attention now shifted from the perspective of the scientist to that of the man on the street. This phase of the peace movement was accompanied by a wide range of "apocalyptic" literature, such as Anton A. Guha's *Ende* (End, 1983)[13] and Jonathan Schell's *Das*

Schicksal der Erde (Fate of the Earth, 1982), both of which imagined life after nuclear war.[14] Many of these scenarios speak of personal fear, and intend to evoke a feeling of angst in the reader.[15] In the mid-eighties the possible relapse into primitivism and tyranny was a potent vision, and was taken up in *Totenfloß,* where those who are contaminated by radioactivity are oppressed by those living in the low-emanation zones.

Nuclear Deserts:
Harald Mueller's *Totenfloß* (1986)

Mueller began writing *Totenfloß* in 1984, in response to a writing competition on the topic of environmental destruction. The first version was staged in Oberhausen near Cologne, and the journal *Theater heute* celebrated it as "play of the year." Despite this success, Mueller reworked the play, and the revised version premiered in November 1986 at the *Kammerspiele* in Munich. George Tabori's production highlighted the fact that the characters became more humane the more they suffered, and in a letter to the actors, he pointed out that *Totenfloß* was above all a lesson in love and care for others.[16] What Mueller liked about this particular staging was the fact that it not only honed in on the dark sides of the play, but also brought out despair through comedy:

> Wenn ein sterbenshungriger Mensch einen anderen auffressen will und dann bemerkt, daß der andere aufgrund chemischer Verseuchung nicht mehr eßbar ist, woraufhin der andere sich entschuldigt, so ist das komisch.[17]

By the time *Theater heute* published the final version in July 1986, reality had caught up with the playwright and his chosen topic. On 26 April 1986, an extremely serious accident took place at the nuclear power plant in the Ukrainian town of Chernobyl in West Russia, where one of the four reactors melted and caught fire, polluting vast stretches of Russia and causing radioactive fallout that was measurable thousands of miles away. Inspired by Orwell's and Huxley's dark visions of a dictatorship in an alienated society, Mueller adds a political element to the possible effects of nuclear radiation. According to him, dictatorship would be the logical form of government in a radioactive desert that would leave millions of people homeless and desperately searching for food and shelter.[18]

In 1987, the play was translated into fifteen languages and performed at more than twenty theaters throughout West Germany.[19] It received glowing reviews, partly due to the fact that the debate about radioactive contamination was the focus of widespread public interest at the time.[20] Mueller's play can be seen as part of the huge peace movement of the mid-eighties supported by protesters of all ages, but especially by middle-aged Germans who feared for the future of their children and grandchildren.[21]

In *Totenfloß*, the only things that show where huge cities used to stand are holes in the ground; large fires of every color indicate the locations of former industrial sites, oil lakes replace water reservoirs, and the sky is overcast with toxic clouds. The ground is covered with nuclear waste and corpses, and at the rear of the stage a high wall prevents the outcasts from returning to the safe low-emanation zones.

Four creatures who vaguely resemble disfigured human beings desperately try to survive in the atomic desert: Checker, a bossy yet very anxious chauvinist; the mad old man Kuckuck who sings the songs of the dead birds; the docile human clone Itai; and the girl Bjuti, who is as mutilated as her name suggests. A feeling of existential angst prevails, as they are afraid to touch food, drink water or even come close to one another, as they might receive further doses of radioactivity, and the very will to survive turns them into cruel brutes who cannot refrain from cannibalism. As they are too infected by radioactivity to be allowed in the privileged zones, a large waste-disposal machine, the so-called "Tam-Tam," dumps them into the devastated landscape. As the name of the machine alludes to the beating of a drum, it clearly denotes the extent to which the German community has relapsed into primitive barbarism, the four people being not only outcasts, but also living rubbish.

During the first half of the play, the four people fight each another, whereas they develop a kind of friendship in the second part. With the help of a raft found by Bjuti, they start to float down the chemically polluted river Rhine. This is clearly a cynical inversion of the leisure cruises that Kuckuck constantly raves about, and their doomed journey is overshadowed by decay, for example in the slow death of Itai, who suffers immense pain in his body. Finally, Bjuti and Checker, now stripped of his rubber protection, and displaying a vividly red skin, approach Xanten. However, they find themselves outside a high wall guarded by military forces. In deep resignation, they give up and let the raft drift into the open sea, succumbing to death.

The title *Totenfloß* also harks back to Edgar Allan Poe's story *The Narrative of Arthur Gordon Pym of Nantucket* (1837),[22] which ends with the terrible death of a handful of people in a canoe out at sea, dying of thirst, for they have nothing to drink. Mueller adapts the story for the late twentieth century, combining it with the fear of nuclear fallout. The journey in *Totenfloß* leads nowhere, since the landscape is completely devastated wherever the characters go, and the clean city of Xanten, which they reach in the end, is barricaded and refuses to let them in. Xanten, the place where Siegfried, the hero of the *Nibelungen* myth was born, introduces another topic that the playwright Heiner Müller typically associates with being German, namely the warring of everyone among themselves (jeder gegen jeden).[23] The increasingly senseless slaughter of the *Nibelungen* is echoed by the fact that the people drifting down the (polluted) river Rhine are by no means brothers in arms, so to speak, but fiercely fight against each other. The absurdity of the relationship between the four characters is also modeled on Beckett's (1906–1989) *Waiting for Godot* (1948).[24] The "Überlebensmaschine," Checker, bosses Itai around, a human clone strongly resembling the character Lucky in *Waiting for Godot*, who is forced to act at Pozzo's whim. Like Beckett, Mueller focuses on the comic aspects of existential despair, yet the setting of Mueller's play wipes out any positive potential from the start. At the beginning of *Waiting for Godot*, Vladimir and Estragon theoretically have the choice of leaving and starting anew, and in the same vein, the characters in *Totenfloß* are also pathetic in their despair. When faced with Checker's pathetic speeches or Kuckuck's madness, audiences react with laughter and embarrassment towards a display of a character's spleen under inhumane conditions. In Mueller's play, the tendency toward existential "nonsense," which is also central to Beckett's plays,[25] is gradually overshadowed by the disastrous effects of the radioactive fallout. Mueller's nuclear desert turns the void inside the characters into an overwhelming existential angst. In *Totenfloß*, the dream of a better life in Xanten corresponds to the waiting for Godot, and eventually all hopes are disappointed, leaving Checker and the mutilated girl Bjuti to face death. By combining Beckett's play with the sinister twists of Poe's narration, Mueller's apocalypse expresses the existential fear of a nuclear catastrophe, one which was shared by many peace campaigners and members of the environmental movement in the 1980s.[26]

The language is as mutilated as the contaminated beings, as is evident when Checker lectures Itai on radioactivity. His speech consists of a mixture of English phrases, invented words and colloquial German that reflect the disintegration surrounding him:

> Schon mal besser getrickt, eh? Body, dein rechtes Leg ism Arsch Überhaupt der ganze Body. Totally! Zuviel Cadmium drauf. Checker hatn Blick für das. Shit wird inne Nieren gespeichert. Ab nullkommafünf PPM biste ex. Kalk haut ab ausm Knochengewebe. Du wirst kleiner. Schrumpfung des Skeletts. Dazu Blutarmut, Atemnot, Lunge kaputt. Da glotzte aber, hahaha — [. . .][27]

Unable to form grammatically correct sentences, he is forced to communicate through both dysfunctional language and sheer violence. Checker talks about himself in the third person, desperate to distance himself from the weak person that he really is, which he hides behind a facade of aggressive, punk-like language.

Mueller's *Zeitstück* is an outstanding example of dramatic literature that reveals how strong the fear of a nuclear accident was. However, it contains more than the mere description of the actual horrors, for it shows that once nature is destroyed, it is no longer desirable to be alive. The physical and psychological damage would be unbearable in such a situation, and radioactivity would eventually return mankind to a society that resembles the Stone Age. Mueller makes it clear that the effects on humankind would be three-fold: the destruction of nature, the decay of the human psyche, and the end of a peaceful democracy.

"Strahlenangstpsychose" and Small Talk: Florian Felix Weyh's *Fondue* (1988)

Weyh's first play *Fondue* depicts an evening in an apartment in which peace protesters have gathered for dinner a few weeks after the disaster at the nuclear power plant in Chernobyl in the Ukraine. As the play progresses, we learn that the five young left-wing intellectuals are waiting for their friend Eduart, who is delayed because of a demonstration against the planned nuclear power plant in Brokdorf. *Fondue* premiered in May 1988 at the *Freie Volksbühne* in Berlin, where it was warmly received.[28] It is the first part of a trilogy on politics in contemporary Germany, which also includes *Ludwigslust* (1990),[29] and *Stirling. Das Glück der Bewegung* (Stirling. Lucky (Social) Movements, 1992). These plays depict the failure of the new social movements such as the environmental movement or the peace campaigners.[30] Harking back to the bleak style of Rainer Werner Fassbinder's (1946–1982) plays of the late 1970s,[31] Weyh presents us with characters who do not have names, but are numbered from one to six. It is only from the annotations at the end of the script that the reader finds out who the characters are. They are generally frustrated left-wing peace campaigners who were traumatized in their childhood, but have made compromises to adapt to German society.

The form of the play, which is described as an "oratorio for six characters in fifteen chants and nine interludes," draws on Peter Weiss's (1916–1982) famous documentary play about the Holocaust, *Die Ermittlung* (The Investigation, 1965),[32] also an oratorio. However, the theme of Weyh's play is not the Holocaust, but the violent clashes between the police and demonstrators that took place in the 1970s. With the exception of Eduart, the characters simply make sympathetic noises, but do not actively participate in the actions of the violent splinter group, the "Autonome." In *Fondue*, the harmless and cool party-talk of those who are allegedly politically engaged is depicted and criticized, and their commitment is in fact revealed to be sheer hypocrisy. As Weyh pointed out, he was attacking the post-1968 generation for being passive and inert:

> Die Abrechnung ist erstmal eine mit meiner Generation. Und das ist kei-ne Abrechnung von außen, sondern ich gehöre da ja auch rein. Ich will mich nicht ausnehmen. Aber es hat doch Gründe, warum wir so tatenlos sind. Na gut, es gab die Friedensbewegung, die hat sich ganz schnell ver-suppt. Bei der Volkszählung ist schon überhaupt nichts mehr passiert. Ich glaube, daß meine Generation antizipiert hat, daß es keinen Sinn hat, ir-gendetwas zu tun, im politischen Raum zu handeln, weil die APO-Generation gezeigt hat, daß beide Möglichkeiten scheitern: sowohl die Revolte als auch der berühmte Marsch durch die Institutionen.[33]

In a similar manner, *Fondue* portrays the conflict between the active fighter Eduart and a group of intellectuals who merely sit and talk. At the end of the play, Eduart realizes that he is alone, and that both the peaceful and aggressive ways of protesting against the politics of the state are fruitless.

At the beginning of the play, Eduart does not shy away from fighting with the police, and on the first evening, he arrives late and worn out, with three pairs of human ears in a carrier bag. Dumbstruck, the group press Eduart for an explanation, which he gives with reluctance. After a while, it becomes clear that his aim had been to give the German police a bad press for their unnecessary cruelty. In doing so, he had dressed up as a policeman and, in front of the cameras, cut three of his friends' ears off who had volunteered to sacrifice themselves for the "good cause." His explanations, however, are rather sketchy and it is therefore possible that he may actually have attacked the police instead. Strangely, Eduart does not have any scruples, either with regard to not telling the truth, or with regard to others' health. He is generally convinced that one is justi-fied in fighting the police with all means, and he despises the other char-acters for having adapted to the German state. In contrast, the other five are too undecided and plagued by doubts to participate actively, but are content to harbor Eduart. Throughout the play, the group's contribu-tion to the peace movement is cynical and shallow philosophical com-ments, ranging from the radio-active contamination of strawberries after the accident at Chernobyl to dying forests:

6	Etwas habe zu geschehen, war unsere Einschätzung nach dem Unglück. Etwas Neues, das dem Ausmaß unserer Angst entspricht. [. . .] Ich wartete vergeblich auf eure Ideen. Daraufhin begann ich mir andere Bundesgenossen zu suchen. [. . .]
1	Das ist nicht recht, Eduart.
4	Wir haben dich immer gedeckt.
2	Zumindest innerlich an deinen Leiden partizipiert.
1	Du berufst dich auf unser Vertrauen.
4	Ohne uns bist du ein Einzeltäter.
2	Politisch ohne Lobby.[34]

As the group refuses to support him, Eduart takes more radical measures which are paradoxically intended to prevent any further escalation of violence. However, it is rather doubtful whether peace could result from a war-like strategy. In the passage cited above, it becomes also evident that the group maintains a fairly hypocritical position, for they allegedly support Eduart's aims, yet are too afraid to help him actively.

Despite the weaknesses of Weyh's *Zeitstück*, which originate in the fact that it is rather bound to the spirit of the late 1970s and early 1980s, the play is a good example of the climate that reigned among intellectuals at that time. In depicting the typical dialogues of apartment-mates, it offers valuable insight into the pseudo-intellectual debates that did not lead to anything constructive. *Fondue* demonstrates the extent to which thirty-year-olds were stuck in fruitless debates that frequently mixed philosophical bites of thought with cynical prattle. Against the backdrop of the "Strahlenangstpsychose," Weyh's play highlights the conflicts in which many half-hearted supporters of the peace movement found themselves.

After the serious accident at the nuclear power plant in Chernobyl in 1986, Harald Mueller's *Totenfloß* (1986) hit the stage at a time when nation-wide protests against the civilian use of nuclear power had reached their height. However, when Florian Felix Weyh's *Fondue* (1988) premiered in 1988, critics objected that such a "Zeitstück" should have been produced sooner. Nonetheless, *Fondue* received considerable attention, for it pitted a disillusioned post-1968 generation against a violent peace campaigner.

Although the destruction of the environment features as a side-issue in other plays, such as Kroetz's *Bauern Sterben* or Volker Braun's *Die*

Übergangsgesellschaft, it is striking that very few playwrights focus specifically on green issues, especially if one takes into account the huge importance of the green movement in the 1980s. As a recently published volume on the relation of literature and ecology points out, the depiction of environmental destruction in drama is scarce, and apart from the dramas discussed in this book, only the works of the Austrian Elfriede Jelinek treat this theme in any depth.[35]

Notes

[1] John Ardagh, *Germany and the Germans* (London: Penguin, 1995), 533–63.

[2] Karl-Werner Brand, Detlef Büsser, and Dieter Rucht, *Aufbruch in eine andere Gesellschaft. Neue soziale Bewegungen in der Bundesrepublik* (Frankfurt am Main/ New York: Campus, 1986), 28–29.

[3] Joachim Radkau, *Aufstieg und Krise der deutschen Atomwirtschaft 1945–1975* (Reinbek: Rowohlt, 1983), 98.

[4] See Hugo Freund's essay in *Atomwirtschaft* 3 (1956), 119, quoted in Dieter Rucht, *Modernisierung und neue soziale Bewegungen* (Frankfurt am Main/New York: Campus, 1994), 444.

[5] Hans M. Kepplinger, "Die Kernenergie in der Presse. Eine Analyse zum Einfluß subjektiver Faktoren auf die Konstruktion von Realität," *Kölner Zeitschrift für Soziologie und Sozialpsychologie* 40 (1988), 659–83, here: 665. According to Kepplinger's findings, the intellectual climate changed radically in 1973, and until 1986 most newspaper articles adopted a negative attitude towards nuclear power plants.

[6] For a detailed overview of the development of the environmental social movement, see Winfried Kretschmer and Dieter Rucht, "Beispiel Wackersdorf: Die Protestbewegung gegen die Wiederaufbereitungsanlage. Gruppen, Organisationen, Netzwerke," in *Neue soziale Bewegungen in der Bundesrepublik Deutschland,* eds. Roland Roth and Dieter Rucht (Frankfurt am Main/New York: Campus, 1987), 134–63.

[7] Lutz Mez, "Von den Bürgerinitiativen zu den Grünen," in *Neue soziale Bewegungen in der Bundesrepublik Deutschland,* eds. Roth and Rucht, 263–76.

[8] After the post-Chernobyl anxiety, the Green party's fortunes improved dramatically, as they increased their share of the vote in the parliamentary elections of January 1987 from 5.6 to 8.3 percent, winning forty-two seats: see Ulrich von Alemann, *Das Parteiensystem in der Bundesrepublik Deutschland* (Opladen: Leske + Budrich, 2000), here: 63.

[9] Since then, the Greens have been an unconventional but established force in federal and local politics. Despite the disappointing result of the West German Greens after the "Wende" in the parliamentary elections of 1990, due to their unpopular opposition to reunification, the party has recovered, and since 1998 has formed part of the government coalition with the Social Democrats.

[10] Even the Bundespräsident at that time, Carl Friedrich von Weizsäcker, warned that the armament race was a short-sighted measure that would endanger the world: see Carl Friedrich von Weizsäcker's speech at the *Evangelische Akademie Tutzing* in March 1982, *Z,* 26 March 1982.

[11] Friedrich Dürrenmatt, *Die Physiker* (Zurich: Diogenes, 1962).

[12] Heinar Kipphardt, *In der Sache J. Robert Oppenheimer* (Frankfurt am Main: Suhrkamp, 1964).

[13] Anton A Guha, *Ende. Tagebuch aus dem Dritten Weltkrieg* (1983) (Frankfurt am Main: Fischer, 1985).

[14] Jonathan Schell, *Das Schicksal der Erde. Gefahr und Folgen eines Atomkriegs* (Munich: Piper, 1982).

[15] Günther Anders, *Die Antiquiertheit des Menschen* (Munich: CH Beck, 1980), 14.

[16] "Im *Totenfloß* sind alle Personen durch Verseuchung von Körper und Seele verkrüppelt und gesunden in dem Maße, wie sie ihre Menschlichkeit entdecken.": see George Tabori, "Wir sind keine Götter. Brief an die Schauspieler vom *Totenfloß*," in George Tabori, *Betrachtungen über das Feigenblatt* (Frankfurt am Main: Fischer, 1993), 203–6.

[17] Harald Mueller, "In unsern Augen spiegelt sich der Abgrund," *ThJ* (1987), 72–77, here: 75

[18] "'Der Dramatiker muß den Instinkt für Mord besitzen.' An interview with Harald Mueller conducted by Peter von Becker and Michael Merschmeier," *Th* 7 (1986): 1–17, here: 2.

[19] Michael Merschmeier, "Todesreigen auf dem großen Fluß. Über Harald Muellers End-Zeitstück *Totenfloß* und die ersten sieben Aufführungen in Basel, Düsseldorf, Stuttgart, Krefeld-Mönchengladbach, Tübingen, Heidelberg und München," *Th* 1 (1987): 19–27.

[20] See Joachim Kaiser, "Schrecklich dynamisches Totenfloß," *SZ*, 1 December 1986; Sigrid Löffler, "Von Zombies und Affen," *profil*, 9 December 1986; Michael Merschmeier, "Todesreigen auf dem großen Fluß," *Th* 1 (1987): 26. As a glance at recent theater programs shows, *Totenfloß* is still one of the most performed plays to date; it was produced, for example, in Wiesbaden in April 2000, see Felix Koch, "Schiffbruch ohne Palmen," *taz* (Hamburg), 17 April 2000.

[21] Ulrike C. Wasmuht, "Die Entstehung und Entwicklung der Friedensbewegung der achtziger Jahre, in *Neue soziale Bewegungen in der Bundesrepublik Deutschland*, eds. Roland Roth and Dieter Rucht (Frankfurt/New York: Campus, 1987), 90–133, here: 110–12.

[22] Edgar Allan Poe, "The Narrative of Arthur Gordon Pym of Nantucket," in Edgar Allan Poe, *The Complete Poems and Stories 2* (New York: Alfred A. Knopf, 1951), 721–854, here: 848–52.

[23] Heiner Müller, "'Deutschland spielt immer noch die Nibelungen.' Interview mit Urs Jenny and Helmut Karasek," *Sp* 19, 1983, 196–207.

[24] Samuel Beckett, "Waiting for Godot," in Samuel Beckett, *Complete Dramatic Works* (London: Faber & Faber, 1986), 7–88.

[25] See, for example, the analysis by Wolfgang Iser, "Counter-sensical Comedy and Audience Response in Beckett's *Waiting for Godot*," in *Waiting for Godot and Endgame. Contemporary Critical Essays*, ed. Steven Connor (London: Macmillan, 1992), 55–70, here: 66.

[26] As early as 1980, the Senate Committee on Foreign Relations commissioned a study of the possible effects of a nuclear war on the US and the Soviet Union, an undertaking which revealed how serious the threat of a nuclear war had become, see Office of Technology Assessment, Congress of the United States (ed.), *The Effects of a Nuclear War* (Montclair: Allanheld, Osmun & Co, 1980), here: 139. The aims of the analysis were to assess how many people would be killed and how many people would be disabled. Moreover, it predicted what areas would suffer the most from excess pressure, radioactive fallout, and fire damage.

[27] Harald Mueller, "Totenfloss," *Th* 7 (1986): 35–46, here: 36.

[28] Michael Merschmeier, "Ganz Ohr. Florian Felix Weyhs Dramatiker Debüt: *Fondue* an Berlins Freier Volksbühne," *Th* 6 (1988): 34–35.

[29] Florian Felix Weyh, "Ludwigslust," in *TheaterTheater. Aktuelle Stücke 1*, eds. Susanne Wolfram and Uwe B. Carstensen (Frankfurt am Main: Fischer, 1991).

[30] Florian Felix Weyh, "Stirling. Das Glück der Bewegung," in *TheaterTheater. Aktuelle Stücke 3*, eds. Susanne Wolfram and Uwe B. Carstensen (Frankfurt am Main: Fischer, 1993).

[31] See, for example, Fassbinder's play *Preparadise sorry now*, which depicts a nightmare scenario of murder and abuse, in which most of the characters only feature as numbers or abbreviations: Rainer Werner Fassbinder, *Preparadise sorry now* (Frankfurt am Main: Verlag der Autoren, 1982).

[32] Peter Weiss, *Die Ermittlung* (Frankfurt am Main: Suhrkamp 1964).

[33] Weyh in an interview with Karin Hagemann, "Mit Staatsknete politisches Theater machen, ganz cool," *Th* 6 (1988): 34–35, here: 34.

[34] The play *Fondue* is available on the internet as a free download from Weyh's website: www.weyhsheiten.de/Fach4/fondue.pdf.

[35] Sieglinde Klettenhammer, "'Das Nichts, das die Natur auch ist.' Zur Destruktion des Mythos 'Natur' in Elfriede Jelineks *Die Kinder der Toten*," in *Literatur und Ökologie*, ed. Axel Goodbody (Amsterdam/Atlanta: Rodopi, 1998), 317–39.

Although the destruction of the environment forms the backdrop of Heiner Müller's *Verkommenes Ufer Medeamaterial Landschaft mit Argonauten* (1983), it is perceived to be symbolic of the situation of the intellectual in a dictatorship; see Heiner Müller, "Verkommenes Ufer Medeamaterial Landschaft mit Argonauten," in Heiner Müller, *Herzstück* (Berlin: Rotbuch Verlag, 1983), 91–101. For a discussion of Müller's text, see Heinz-Peter Preußer, "Naturzerstörung als Epiphänomen des Geistes. Von Heiner Müllers *Philoktet* zu *Verkommenes Ufer Medeamaterial Landschaft mit Argonauten*," in *Literatur und Ökologie*, 271–97.

3: The Memory of the Holocaust

WITH THE FIFTIETH anniversary of Hitler's seizure of power approaching, West Germany faced numerous commemorations in the early 1980s. At memorial sites and former concentration camps, but also on television and radio, people were reminded of the disastrous years of National Socialist terror, its origins and its consequences.[1] Television series, such as Claude Lanzmann's *Shoah*, sparked off new and old debates about the Holocaust.[2]

As the aim of the newly elected Kohl government was to revive the conservative spirit of the 1950s, the so-called *Adenauer-Ära*, named after the first chancellor of the FRG, it clearly signaled a neoconservative turn in politics. Speaking of a new "Stunde Null," Kohl maintained that the conservatives' success in the parliamentary elections of 1983 was the beginning of a new era of wealth and prosperity.[3] In the same vein, the fact of being German was expected to become "natural" and "normal," and Germany's past freed from its "criminal" undertones.[4] During a speech in Israel on 25 January 1984, Kohl employed the phrase "Gnade der späten Geburt," thereby absolving the younger generation from any responsibility for the Nazi past.[5] In the *Express*, Alfred Dregger maintained that Germany ought finally to emerge from the shadow of Hitler and Auschwitz,[6] and according to Franz Josef Strauß, the Germans should practice the "aufrechte Gang."[7] Conservative politicians such as Alfred Schikel generally aimed to decriminalize the German past:

> Statt sich mit der Vergangenheit auseinanderzusetzen und die streckenweise kriminalisierte deutsche Geschichte unbefangen aufzuabeiten, um das eigene geschichtliche Herkommen zu klären, demonstriert man für den Umweltschutz, besetzt Häuser oder protestiert in sogenannten Friedensmärschen gegen die Politik der Regierung. [. . .] Es wird daher mannigfaltiger Anstrengungen unserer Historiker, Pädagogen und Politiker bedürfen, um den Deutschen wieder einen natürlichen und unbefangenen Zugang zu Geschichte, Staat und Vaterland zu ermöglichen.[8]

Parallel to this, right-wing extremism and right-wing radicalism became institutionalized,[9] but also, in addition to these efforts to institutionalize right-wing extremism, physical violence and aggression became more visible on the streets.[10] In view of increasing economic problems, asylum seekers and foreign workers were blamed for the shortage of jobs. The first important event was the bomb attack at the "Oktoberfest" in Munich in 1980, which was carried out by Gundolf Köhler, a member of the right-wing organization "Wehrsportgruppe Hoffmann." Thirteen people were killed and 213 severely injured. The following years saw a flare-up of right-wing violence, against both people and inanimate objects.

Since the 1980s, playwrights have not only produced large quantities of material dealing with the German mass murder, but they have also tackled this sensitive and traumatic period of more recent German history, in order to counteract the common tendency to gloss over the Nazi past, taking a critical stance towards the popularity of right-wing radicalism and violence. Once again, their aim is to dismantle the myths of the neo-Nazis in order to show how their falsified historiography distorts history and offends its victims.[11] In opposition to the revisionists, who try to belittle the Holocaust and even deny that it ever happened,[12] thus indirectly justifying right-wing violence, playwrights such as Heinar Kipphardt, George Tabori, Thomas Strittmatter (1912–1994), and Volker Ludwig (1937–) address the multi-faceted Nazi crimes from a variety of angles. Heinar Kipphardt's play *Bruder Eichmann* (Brother Eichmann, 1982/83) focuses not only on the Eichmann trial in Israel in 1961, but also contrasts it with contemporary fascist tendencies. Tabori's farce *Mein Kampf* (My Struggle, 1987) presents us with a fictional encounter between the young Hitler and a Jew, Schlomo, in Vienna, during which the image of the politician Hitler is thoroughly deconstructed. Thomas Strittmatter's *Viehjud Levi* (Cattle-Dealer Levi, 1982), written in the style of the new *Volkstheater,* tells the fate of a Jew in a small village after 1933. The director of the *GRIPS-Theater,* Volker Ludwig, produced a pedagogical play for the young, a musical production of *Ab heute heißt du Sara* (From Today on Your Name is Sara, 1989), that successfully adapted Inge Deutschkron's novel *Ich trug den gelben Stern* (I Wore the Yellow Star). Despite the Conservative government's attempt to present Germany as a "normal" state that should be allowed to bury its Nazi past, playwrights strongly opposed this tendency and revived the collective memory by "staging the Holocaust."

"The Banality of Evil": Heinar Kipphardt's *Bruder Eichmann* (1983)

Even before it was first staged, this long-awaited drama received some media attention, with *Theater heute* publishing a few extracts of the play. Yet the high expectations for *Bruder Eichmann,* which was published after

Kipphardt's death, were soon to be disappointed when it premiered on 21 January 1983 in the *Residenztheater* in Munich. As the theater critic Peter von Becker pointed out, the play was far too melodramatic to portray the National Socialist mass murderer Eichmann appropriately.[13]

Eichmann haunted Kipphardt's mind throughout his life, and as early as 1965 he wrote a play about him entitled *Joel Brand. Die Geschichte eines Geschäfts* (Joel Brand. The Account of a Deal, 1965).[14] In *Bruder Eichmann* (1983), the playwright sets out to show how an average young man from Solingen becomes an important administrator in the genocide of European Jews.[15] The action takes place in Eichmann's prison cell, after the Nazi criminal was caught by the Israeli police in May 1960 in Buenos Aires. He was flown to Israel nine days later, and brought to trial in 1961.[16]

The documentary drama *Bruder Eichmann* is based on the recorded interrogation that Captain Avner Less conducted with the prisoner before the trial.[17] Kipphardt is also familiar with the book by the Reverend Hull, who had long conversations with Eichmann, in order to try and effect his conversion back to Christianity.[18] In *Bruder Eichmann*, the trial itself, during which Eichmann sat in a separate glass booth, is omitted, because Kipphardt is more concerned with the private thoughts of the criminal. Critics, however, have often criticized Kipphardt for violating the principles of the documentary drama by changing the original material too much. He embellishes the relationship between Eichmann and Chass, his interrogator, for example, which in reality was anything but cordial.[19] Several years later, these accusations were reconstructed in a meticulously detailed comparison of the original material with Kipphardt's text. In his detailed analysis, Hanuschek looks closely at a plethora of sample passages, revealing that Kipphardt only changes or shortens minor points in order to make the drama work. To criticize Kipphardt for adapting the material to his purpose would, according to Hanuschek, be pernickety.[20] By contrast, Barnett argues in his meticulous analysis of the play that Kipphardt deliberately corrupted documentary reliability in his "meta-play" in order to show how information is distorted as a result of capitalist power structures.[21]

What sparked off a heated debate was not so much the depiction of Eichmann, as five scenes that are interspersed between the two acts of the play. They consist of twenty-two segments in a variety of styles: verse form, narration, documentary scenes and short sketches, all of which cover a kaleidoscope of political injustice from the Second World War to 1982, the year of Kipphardt's death. The common focus of these scenes is the parallel drawn between the Holocaust and the violation of human rights all over the world. To achieve this, the interrogation is juxtaposed with pieces about the nuclear bomb in Hiroshima and the war in Vietnam, narrations of torture from political prisoners in Italy and Germany, and accounts of the raiding of Palestinian ghettos, as well as with an interview with Israel's defense minister at the time, Ariel Sharon. Kipphardt's aim is to uncover what he calls the "Eichmann attitude," the legacy of National Socialist thinking in present-day society; a feature which the singer Wolf Biermann describes as "Der alltägliche Faschismus."[22] The word "brother" underlines the similarities between the Nazi criminal and the man on the street.[23] The introduction of the parallel scenes serves to illustrate the extent to which the contemporary world is still pervaded by evil and injustice. It is paradoxical that, despite Kipphardt's sincere desire to protest against the escalation of violence in the postwar world, he involuntarily scales down Eichmann's crimes, with the result that they appear to differ only in degree, not in kind, from the crimes of other politicians.[24] Although it is not new, the provocative comparison of the Holocaust with more recent crimes generates the main controversy that surrounds the play.[25]

The critics' reaction has generally been one of anger and disappointment, mainly because Kipphardt gives way to melodramatics. This is especially evident in the second part, when Eichmann sends letters to his wife, meets her, and talks to the Reverend Hull and the latter's wife.[26] The playwright's intention is, however, to provide insight into the heart and mind of the *Obersturmbannführer*. The cross-examination in *Bruder Eichmann* displays Eichmann's inner world. Adolf Eichmann is found to be an alarmingly normal person devoted to his duties, a so-called pen-pushing murderer (*Schreibtischmörder*), rather than a diabolic creature.[27] Bearing in mind Hannah Arendt's famous phrase, the "banality of evil," *Bruder Eichmann* can be seen as a portrayal of a hollow man, or an Everyman.[28] Kipphardt shows that the monstrous nature of Eichmann's personality lies in his willingness to adapt to different situations and to keep his head down.[29]

Throughout the play, Eichmann pretends not to remember names, dates, places, and figures, so that Chass, his interrogator, is forced to prompt him. In general, Eichmann avoids giving clear answers, and never gives his opinion on the extermination of the Jews. According to his own account, he only played a minor role in the "final solution" (*Endlösung*), and he denies having ever given orders at all.[30] In his view, his function was mainly to supervise the concentration camps, not to run them. When confronted with the atrocities, he claims to be too sensitive to have even looked at the dead closely, let alone to have taken part in the gassings:

EICHMANN	[. . .] Wir hatten nie, nie, nie etwas mit der Tötung zu tun, wir hatten mit der Konzentrierung zu tun und daß die Züge bereitgestellt wurden, daß sie dorthin kamen, wo es befohlen war.
CHASS	In die Gaskammern der Vernichtungslager!
EICHMANN	Es wurde ja nicht alles getötet, Herr Hauptmann, was arbeitsfähig war, zur Arbeit.
CHASS, *schreit*	Halten Sie Ihren Mund! Halten Sie Ihren Mund! Halten Sie Ihren Mund! — Entschuldigung, meine Familie — Entschuldigung.
EICHMANN	Schrecklich! Es ist doch alles ganz schrecklich! —
CHASS	Sie lügen! Sie heucheln! Sie winden sich heraus! Wenn es nach Ihnen ginge, dann wäre niemand, niemand, dann wäre nur Hitler zur Verantwortung zu ziehen und der hat sich vergiftet.[31]

The passage shows that although Eichmann pretends to be completely ignorant, he occasionally slips and reveals his true colors, such as when he refers to the Jews in the technical language of the Nazis, the offici-alese which compared people to things. Even when Chass loses his temper — the only time during the play — and openly accuses him of being a hypocrite, Eichmann displays a naive innocence. Like his real-life counterpart, the stage Eichmann is above all eager to record his version of events on tape for the sake of posterity, as he expresses concern about the fact that the youth of Germany feel guilty about the Nazi crimes.[32] All in all, the play paints a picture of a cunningly cautious, creepily harmless, and superficially well-mannered man. As the mass murderer is presented to us as a man under heavy guard, he becomes the victim who excites a certain degree of empathy from the spectator.[33] Involuntarily, the audience develops sympathy for the man[34] who ensured that the cremating ovens always remained hot, a point that is heavily criticized in most reviews.[35]

Criticism has often been voiced that Eichmann is pictured in a favorable light, particularly in the second part; for example, when he is portrayed as a loving husband and caring father who is concerned about the welfare of his children. Facing execution, Eichmann gains even more in stature when he heroically faces death and even refuses the black mask. Like a romantic hero, he dies for his ideals. In the first production in

Munich, the leading actor fell into this trap, portraying Eichmann in such a heroic manner that he lost contact with the reality of the petit bourgeois bureaucrat-murderer.[36]

New-Old Anti-Semitism:
Thomas Strittmatter's *Viehjud Levi* (1982)

Viehjud Levi, the central character of the play, is modeled on an authentic Jew who lived in the village of St. Georgen in the Black Forest before the Second World War, the same little village in which Strittmatter was born.[37] He modeled the character of the Jew on tales and stories that he had overheard as a child, trying to bring the late 1930s, the years of the impending Shoah, back to people's minds. In a letter to school children he wrote:

> Als Kind (und immer noch) habe ich mir gerne Geschichten angehört und wollte gerne herausfinden, wie es beispielsweise in der Nazi-Zeit war. Dazu habe ich die Geschichten mit meiner Phantasie und mit geschichtlichen Fakten vermischt, so ist mein erstes Theaterstück *Viehjud Levi* entstanden. Also keine reine Phantasie, keine bloßen geschichtlichen Fakten, sondern ein Gemisch davon.[38]

In *Viehjud Levi,* he weaves scattered pieces of information into a coherent pattern of xenophobia.[39] It is a conventional and realistic play in the style of the new *Volkstheater,* which shows how hate and envy can hover close to the surface of normal village life, ready to break through at any time. Although National Socialism is never directly referred to, and Hitler, the SS and other such notorious terms are not mentioned, the threat of Nazi terror is always present. Instead of exhausting his audience with tedious moral talk, Strittmatter subtly creates an awareness of the "normality" of Nazi terror. *Viehjud Levi* shows that it is above all the desire to live "in peace" that made National Socialist terror possible. Without becoming explicit, the play raises the question as to whether our frame of mind is really so different nowadays.

Like Ödön von Horváth (1901–1938) in his *Volkstheater* plays, Strittmatter contrasts the happy rural idyll with the destructive tendencies concealed behind the peaceful facade of village life.[40] At the time, Horváth was concerned with presenting the *Volkstheater* as a parody, dismantling it as kitsch. Similarly, *Viehjud Levi* highlights the gap between the conscious and the unconscious through long pauses, silences, and an emphasis on noises and smells. In addition, Horger's harmless, yet careless and not so innocent remarks about Jewish nature cause a feeling of uneasiness, such as when Horger rebukes the Jew for citing the Bible only when it suits him. Both Horger and Levi playfully pick up on Jewish stereotypes at first, but the very wording shows the deep-rooted nature of anti-Semitism. Horger's language is also a mirror of his soul, and of his hidden distrust, such as when he calls Levi a witty scoundrel.

Strittmatter's realistic yet sparse setting, along with his focus on the credulity of the characters, underlines his belief that the true story of the Holocaust is not only to be found in statistics and documents. *Viehjud Levi* shows how anti-Semitism permeated every aspect of daily life. Strittmatter condemns the naivety of the common people and their lack of resistance, and by dramatizing the ruined life of one victim, he identifies the guilt of a whole people, instead of simply that of a handful of politicians.

The play was first staged at the *Theater der Altstadt* in Stuttgart in December 1982, and the production's unpretentious staging was well-received.[41] In 1999, it was successfully turned into a film (director, Didi Danquart), which immediately won several prizes at film festivals in Berlin, Potsdam, and Jerusalem. It was celebrated as a masterpiece that unveils the terrifying normality of the National Socialist pogroms with an almost Brechtian concision.

Viehjud Levi opens in a warm, dark stable belonging to the peasant Horger, where Levi and Horger are jocularly haggling over a cow that Levi is about to buy. Although the men are talking business, they get on well together, and Horger invites Levi to stay for a meal. This time, however, they cannot agree on a price, and Levi leaves in order to continue the bargaining some other day, singing joyously. The peasant is thoroughly upbraided by his wife for not having sold the cow, as they are poor, and dependent on Levi's goodwill. In the next scene, Levi brings a pig to the village pub, where he meets some friends who help him unload it in return for a few beers. As the scene shows, Levi is at first fully integrated into the everyday life of the villagers. Yet the next time he drinks beer in the local pub, he learns that Horger has already sold the cow to the train company.

After four years, the train company is back to repair the tunnel nearby to provide a regular train service. Although the reason for the repairs is not directly mentioned, the audience is all too aware of the symbolism of trains. The arrival of the railway workers reminds us of the enforcing of the "Nürnberger Rassengesetze" of 1938, which, among other things, forbade any contact with Jews. Slowly but inevitably, public opinion turns against Levi. Horger is not quite aware of the seriousness of the threat, and continues to be friendly to Levi. He even makes a feeble effort to protect him when the local Nazis turn against the Jew and force him to sing National Socialist songs. In the third pub scene, Strittmatter hints at the Nazi slogan, "Wo man singt, da laß dich ruhig nieder. Böse Menschen haben keine Lieder," a saying that quickly became an "Ur-German" proverb despite the fact that it had only just been created by Goebbels to prevent people from thinking when they were together.[42] Strittmatter, however, turns this proverb against the Nazis, who were of course living proof of the reverse. Although, or rather because, Levi does not know their songs, he is the better person. After Horger tries to help him, the train company refuses to buy the former's goods, on the grounds of a "Jewish smell." In the end Levi is found dead, with a bullet in his head. In the final scene, three speakers read out historical documents that speculate about the nature of the killing. However, the question of who murdered the Jew is not important for Strittmatter, as it is the community as a whole that is responsible for Levi's death. Moreover, it is not only the Jew who is killed, but also the peasant Horger, who later dies in a train tunnel under mysterious circumstances. A few years later his wife dies too, in a fire, whereas others in the house are rescued. Their deaths are not shown on stage, but are reported, in order to complete the picture.

Strittmatter deliberately avoids the grand gesture, which would indicate that "we have put Hitler behind us" once again. The simplicity of *Viehjud Levi* negates the all-too-common attempt to show that denazification has turned the Germans into enlightened beings. Instead, the style is humble and low-key, and excludes grandeur of any sort. The play has at its very core the common people, who become guilty because they are too lazy to object, and too busy with their own concerns. It is their passivity that is to blame, combined with the fear that their lives could fundamentally change. Even when Levi is humiliated and attacked in their presence, the villagers quickly adapt to the new circumstances. Strittmatter's play is not concerned with the major historical events, as he believes that history consists of the millions of stories that happen around us.

The Young Hitler in Vienna:
George Tabori's *Mein Kampf* (1987)

Tabori's farce *Mein Kampf,* first produced at the *Burgtheater* in Vienna in 1987, was a huge success, although it makes no attempt to actually recreate the Holocaust.[43] That is to say, the five-act play does not replicate a ghetto or concentration camp on stage. Although based on Hitler's stay in Vienna before the Second World War, the play has no firm historical date; the year is simply given as "19 . . ." As it is set in a shelter for homeless men in the "Blutgasse," it only alludes to the Holocaust within the structure of an independent plot.

Lobkowitz, a jobless cook, and Schlomo Herzl, a street trader, live together at "Frau Merschmeyer's Männerheim" in Vienna, when one day Hitler knocks on the door. Schlomo is writing a book entitled "Mein Kampf," which will never be finished. Hitler is going to apply for the Academy of Arts, but, like his real-life counterpart, will be rejected. Throughout the play, Schlomo tries to protect and educate Hitler, whom he likes, but, as we all know, Hitler does not reciprocate his affection. In act 5, Hitler demands Schlomo's book in order to make a few "amendments," and in the following fight the hen Mizzi is slaughtered.

Tabori's play, which takes place before Auschwitz (but includes the historical truth of mass murder), draws on both literary and Christian traditions.[44] In act 3, Tabori alludes to Goethe's *Faust* (1790) through the appearance of Gretchen, who accuses Schlomo of murdering Jesus Christ. However, it is not Faust who is selling his soul to the devil, but Hitler. The play ends with a triumphant Hitler, who leaves in the company of Frau Tod, the personification of death, only to return as her death angel in the wake of a looming apocalypse. The structure of *Mein Kampf* also intertwines both Paschal and Easter, since the play begins on Thursday, and ends on the eve of Passover. This marks the slaughter of Mizzi, who symbolizes the paschal lamb. However, the biblical pattern is reversed, since Tabori turns the advent of the prophet Elijah, who brings about the resurrection of the dead, into the ascension of the anti-Messiah Hitler.

Tabori's farcical style rebels against the solemnity and emotionalism of the modern conception of the Holocaust, and by doing so helps to keep the events alive.[45] As a Jew, he can present the Holocaust as a farce, but whether such a style should be permissible has been the subject of much discussion.[46] For Tabori, the use of farce is the only remaining artistic way of expressing a history that has itself largely become farcical.

In his portrayal of Hitler and Schlomo, Tabori uses the well-known stereotypes of Hitler and a Jewish figure, but he distorts them. It is particularly the portrayal of Hitler that takes full advantage of his stereotypical image, for Tabori uses a caricature of Hitler, exploiting elements of the historical figure. Yet it should be noted that it is the Jew Schlomo who, at the beginning of act 2, decides that Hitler's appearance is neglected, and should be radically changed. Whereas the real Hitler was extremely anxious that he be dressed correctly, the Hitler figure in the play is fairly unkempt.[47] As Schlomo is fond of Hitler, he begins to mother him, but it is not surprising that his efforts are in vain. Despite the fact that Schlomo is the wittier of the two, Hitler and his henchmen finally take over.

Tabori's Hitler remains fairly true to the historical Hitler, although Tabori exaggerates the historical truth, making Hitler into a farcical figure. In his first study of Hitler, for example, Ian Kershaw points out that he had strong hypochondriac tendencies that he liked his quack doctor to tend to.[48] After a walk through Vienna, the stage Hitler pretends to suffer from a heart attack, then he asks "krächzend" what the symptoms of the "galoppierende Schwindsucht" are. Tabori lets him play-act the *malade imaginaire,* unmasking him as hypochondriac who, in a theatrically exaggerated manner, believes himself to be facing death. When the hen Mizzi walks in his direction, Hitler interprets this as a symbol of death.[49] Tabori parodies the distorted romantic worldview of a paranoid person, for placing Hitler on stage as a human being with mood swings and health problems belittles the historical cult.[50]

The Jew Schlomo Herzl can be seen as a mixture of the Zionist Theodor Herzl, King Salomo and the wandering Jew, as the name indicates. However, despite the absurdity of Hitler, the Jew still ends up as the loser. Throughout the play Schlomo is the wittier and intellectually superior of the two, but he is nonetheless as much of a joke as Hitler, and he is described as a man who philosophizes rather than acts. Although he intends to write a book called "Mein Kampf," it contains only one sentence, which reads like the happy ending of a fairytale. In the context of the doom that Hitler is about to inflict on the Jews, this fairytale ending is both wishful thinking and a cynical reminder that more than six million people were killed by the Nazis. Tabori does not cast Schlomo as the heroic victim, and it is not he, but the hen Mizzi, who is killed by Hitler and his henchman Himmlischst, a remake of the Reichsführer-SS Heinrich Himmler. As Schlomo refuses to hand over his book, the hen is slaughtered, and in a breathtakingly swift performance by the pseudo television-cook Himmlischst, served as an aromatic stew:

HITLER [. . .]   *Er bewegt sich rasch, die anderen bewegen sich mit ihm, sie umzingeln Mizzi in einer Ecke, Federn fliegen, ein letztes Gackern und Himmlischst taucht auf, den gerupften Vogel, strangulierten Leichnam, in den Händen baumelnd. [. . .] Himmlischst läßt Mizzi in die Bratpfanne auf dem Ofen fallen, zaubert Salz, Pfeffer, Butter und Semmelbrösel herbei. Bald beginnt Mizzi zu brutzeln.*

HIMMLISCHST   Ich serviere Ihnen heute Hühnerkotelett Mizzi in delikater Blutsauce auf Wildart. Um das Brustfleisch von Hühnern wie Koteletts

> zuzurichten, legt man das Huhn auf den Rücken,
> schneidet das Fleisch oben beim Flügel ein,
> durchtrennt die Gelenke, faßt den Flügel fest an
> und reißt mit ihm die halbe Brust heraus. Dasselbe
> macht man auf der anderen Seite, zieht nun die
> Haut vorsichtig vom Fleisch und hackt die
> unteren Flügelglieder ab. Dann klopft man das
> Fleisch wie Koteletts und brät die ausgelösten
> Schnitzelchen in Butter mit Speck und Majoran.
> [. . .] (*MK,* 199–200)

In the context of the impending doom of the Holocaust, the symbolic enactment of torture and death creates an apocalyptic atmosphere. While Schlomo cringes and sobs helplessly in a corner, Hitler and his followers prepare for the genocide to come, as Frau Tod comes to take them with her as her henchmen. Like the Jewish people, Schlomo fails to see the writing on the wall, stubbornly refusing to believe in Hitler's mad racist theories. *Mein Kampf* expresses Tabori's anxieties concerning the increase in right-wing radicalism. As he pointed out in his speech for the Büchner-Preis in 1992, published in the November issue of Theater heute, he "could smell gas again."

Theater for the Young: Volker Ludwig and Detlef Michel's *Ab heute heißt du Sara* (1989)

This play, devised for a teenage audience, is centered on the young Jewish girl Inge Deutschkron, who survived the Holocaust because she changed her identity and was hidden by friends. It is written by the two most famous authors of the acclaimed GRIPS-Theater in Berlin: Volker Ludwig, whose real name is Eckart Hachfeld, and Detlef Michel, who wrote the songs. Ludwig started as a cabaret writer, and switched to theater for children and teenagers in 1968, and GRIPS has its origins in the "Theater für Kinder im Reichskabarett" in Berlin, which Ludwig founded in 1965. In 1972, Ludwig changed its name to GRIPS and has managed it ever since.[51] GRIPS is famous for its first-rate productions for both children and adults, which are, according to Ludwig, more than entertainment:

> Ich würde nie ein Stück schreiben können, das man nur um der Unter-
> haltung willen aufführt, sondern ich hab [*sic*] da ein Publikum, das etwas
> braucht und etwas Bestimmtes erwartet. Mir wäre die Zeit zu schade,
> wenn ich nicht eine bestimmte "message" hätte — oder wie man das
> nennt — , wenn ich nicht wüßte, damit kannst du etwas erreichen.[52]

Ab heute heißt du Sara is based on the autobiographical report by Inge Deutschkron entitled *Ich trug den gelben Stern* (1978).[53] Deutschkron, who emigrated to Israel after the War, was herself involved in the preparations for the premiere on 9 February 1989. The production was positively received, especially because local elections in the same year showed that right-wing parties were on the increase.[54] Due to its success, the production was taken up by more than thirty German playhouses.[55]

Ludwig and Michel transform the autobiographical account of the young, courageous Inge into a fast-moving historical drama. In typical GRIPS manner, they insert several songs that not only summarize the scenes but also add an element of joy and entertainment. Because of this, the play takes on the character of a revue rather than being a moralistic and tedious lesson in history.

In thirty-three "pictures," the play describes the struggle of Inge and her mother during the Nazi rule of terror in Berlin. As a well-constructed play, it tells the story in a straightforward manner, preserving the linearity of time and providing the audience with characters in the traditional sense. It follows the aims of the GRIPS-Theater, which, as its director Volker Michels points out, are to develop the self-confidence of children and to show that society can be changed.[56] This critical approach to society is clearly due to the influence of Brecht, as the GRIPS-Theater teaches recognition of the world as one which can be changed. Nonetheless, there are some basic differences, as GRIPS rejects the parable play that is typical of Brecht, and the youth theater is also less interested in the method of "Historisierung." On the contrary, *Ab heute heißt du Sara* does not employ the *Verfremdungseffekt* in order to create a distance between the action on stage and the audience, but presents past events as if they happened now.

The young and self-confident Inge is the perfect example of an ideal figure with whom a young audience can identify. From the start she is described as independent, critical, and confident, and despite the fact that her environment changes rapidly after 1933, she preserves her critical spirit. Her father is a potential victim in a double sense: first, he is a Social Democrat and second, he is Jewish. In the play it becomes clear that by that time most Jews felt like Germans, as they had been completely assimilated into their country of birth. Her father waits until after the so-called "Reichskristallnacht" of 1938, by which time it is almost too late to emigrate, before leaving for Britain. The play shows how the Deutschkrons try to adjust to the new situation at first, for example by burning dangerous evidence and moving house. The father then loses his job, as Jews are no longer allowed to teach. However, Martin Deutschkron clings to the hope that he was fired because of his Socialist beliefs and not because of his religion. The Gestapo naturally searches for him, and once, when they knock on the door while Inge is at home alone, she just manages to warn him not to come home. Other than this, the play shows how Inge's private life changes. She courageously helps another Jewish girl who is almost beaten up by two young Nazis:

1. HJLER   Haben wir dir nicht gesagt, daß du unsere Gegend nicht mehr verstänkern sollst? *(Sie will ausreißen, der 2. HJLER stellt ihr brutal ein Bein, so daß sie hinfliegt.)*

2. HJLER   Ausreißen willse, die feige Judensau. Mann, und ich hab jetzt Judenschleim am Stiefel! Los — ablecken, du Schwein! *(Er zieht ihren Kopf an den Haaren über seine Stiefel, daß sie schreit. Aus dem Hintergrund kommt INGE — jetzt 13 —)* Leck ab! *(Der erste HJLER tritt dem Mädchen kräftig in den Hintern. INGE rennt von hinten auf ihn zu, tritt ihn, daß er hinfliegt, und geht sofort mit Fäusten auf den überraschten zweiten HJLER los.)*

INGE   Ihr feigen Schweine, ihr![57]

In the end, she manages to free the girl, yet Inge herself also suffers from discrimination, such as when she has a new Jewish identity card made and is forced to take on the name Sara. After the November pogrom of 1938, "Reichskristallnacht," the situation becomes increasingly dangerous, especially for her father, who finally decides to emigrate. As no country lets in entire families, he is forced to leave his family behind. After this, the family is expropriated, and mother and daughter go underground until the end of the war, helped by many German friends. Above all, the play is intended to offer a good example for the young, and Inge is portrayed in the best possible light in order to serve as a good example for resistance.

The early 1980s saw a wave of anniversaries and commemorations, which refreshed the painful memory of the Nazi past. Inspired by these public events, and as a counterbalance to the conservative turn in German politics after the *Bundestag* elections in 1983, playwrights portrayed the fates both of the often unknown victims and their perpetrators. Thomas Strittmatter's *Viehjud Levi* (1982), for example, depicts the fate of a local Jew in a small town in the late 1930s, who becomes the victim of the increasingly hostile villagers around him. Volker Ludwig's *Ab heute heißt du Sara* (1989) focuses on the brave struggle of Inge, a Jewish girl who manages to survive the Third Reich in Berlin. In contrast to

Ludwig and Strittmatter, however, George Tabori and Heinar Kipphardt present us with the most notorious criminals, Hitler and Eichmann. Heinar Kipphardt's *Bruder Eichmann* (1982) combines documentary material of the Eichmann trial in 1961 with a kaleidoscope of scenes which illustrate fascist tendencies in modern politics. Tabori's farce *Mein Kampf* (1987) takes place before the Holocaust, yet refers to it indirectly, as it features a doomed encounter between the young Hitler and a Jewish bookseller, Schlomo Herzl, in a shelter for the homeless in Vienna.

Notes

[1] On the changing face of memorial sites of the Holocaust, see Angela Genger, "Gedenkstätten für Deutschland. Trauer — Dokumentation — Begegnung," in *Täter — Opfer — Folgen. Der Holocaust in Geschichte und Gegenwart,* Heiner Lichtenstein and Otto R. Romberg (Bonn: Bundeszentrale für politische Bildung, 1997), 255–64.

[2] Werner Bergmann, *Anti-Semitismus in öffentlichen Konflikten. Kollektives Lernen in der politischen Kultur der Bundesrepublik 1949–89* (Frankfurt am Main/New York: Campus, 1997).

[3] Rainer Gries, Volker Ilgen, and Dieter Schindelbeck, *Gestylte Geschichte. Vom alltäglichen Umgang mit Geschichtsbildern* (Münster: Westfälisches Dampfboot/PRO, 1989), 129–34.

[4] With hindsight, Leinemann pointed out that Kohl's chancellorship was largely characterized by "banality" and "boredom," see Jürgen Leinemann, "Die verkörperte Entwarnung. Der Kanzler Helmut Kohl," *Sp,* 17 May 1999, 214–19, here: 215.

[5] The term was coined by the commentator Günter Gaus and later adopted by Kohl.

[6] Alfred Dregger, "17. Juni — sein Sinn gerät in Vergessenheit," *Express,* 11 June 1981.

[7] Franz Josef Strauß's speech in Hof, that was published under the title: "'Mehr aufrechten Gang,'" *Frankfurter Rundschau,* 14 June 1987.

[8] Alfred Schikel, "Der Deutsche und sein Vaterland," *Bayernkurier,* 12 May 1982.

[9] See Richard Stöss, *Rechtsextremismus im vereinten Deutschland* (Berlin: Friedrich-Ebert-Stiftung, 2000), 52–61. On 26 November 1983, the right-wing party *Die Republikaner* (Reps) was founded in Munich, and after some quarrels was finally taken over by the former SS-member (and also former journalist of the Bavarian broadcasting house) Franz Schönhuber. After Schönhuber came out as a former Nazi with his book *Ich war dabei* in 1982, he was fired by the *Bayerische Rundfunk.* Up to then, he had produced a very popular program. In January 1989, the Reps won 7.5 percent of the votes for the *Berliner Abgeordnetenhaus,* a success which helped to promote the party nationwide. This result caused quite a shock among moderate politicians, even more so because the Reps won 7.1 percent of votes at the European elections in June of the same year; since then they have been an established party in several *Länderparlamente,* such as Baden-Württemberg, where they held 10.9 percent of the votes in 1992. On 5/6 March 1987, another right-wing party, the

Deutsche Volksunion (DVU), was founded by the media mogul Gerhard Frey, who backed his party's electoral campaigns with enormous sums of money. In 1987, the largest of Frey's papers, the *Deutsche Volkszeitung,* had a print-run of 100,000, and served as a platform for playing down Nazi crimes and discriminating against foreigners. Overall, however, the Reps emerged as the more popular party.

[10] For the following, see Marcus Neureither, *Rechtsextremismus im vereinten Deutschland* (Marburg: Tectum, 1996), 32–33.

[11] On the glorification of the Third Reich in the legends of today's right-wing extremists, such as the "war as holy mass," the "pure blood," and the "Aryan origin" of the German people, see Rüdiger Sünner, *Schwarze Sonne. Entfesselung und Missbrauch der Mythen im Nationalsozialismus und rechter Esoterik* (Freiburg im Breisgau: Herder, 1999).

[12] See, for example, Karl Heinz Roth, "Revisionistische Tendenzen in der historischen Forschung über den deutschen Faschismus," in *Die selbstbewußte Nation und ihr Geschichtsbild: Geschichtslegenden der Neuen Rechten,* eds. Johannes Klotz and Ulrich Schneider (Cologne: PapyRossa-Verlag, 1997), 31–64.

[13] Peter von Becker, "Heinar Kipphardt's letztes Stück: Ein fataler Text. Kein Bruder Eichmann," *Th* 3 (1983): 1–3.

[14] Heinar Kipphardt, "Joel Brand. Die Geschichte eines Geschäfts," in Heinar Kipphardt, *Theaterstücke 2* (Cologne: Kiepenheuer & Witsch, 1981).

[15] Typed note in Kipphardt's papers, dated 12 March 1982. First published in *ThJ* (1982), 56.

[16] For a general interpretation, see Carl Steiner, "Heinar Kipphardt, *Robert Oppenheimer* and *Bruder Eichmann:* Two Plays in Search of a Political Answer," in *Amerika! New Images in German Literature,* ed. Heinz D. Österle (New York: Peter Lang, 1989), 199–211.

[17] The minutes of the interrogation that Kipphardt used were published in the same year in Jochen von Lang (ed.), *Das Eichmann Protokoll* (Berlin: Severin & Siedler, 1983).

[18] William L. Hull, *Kampf um eine Seele. Gespräche mit Eichmann in der Todeszelle* (Wuppertal: Verlag Sonne und Schild, 1964).

[19] Glenn R. Cuomo, "*Vergangenheitsbewältigung* Through Analogy: Heinar Kipphardt's Last Play *Bruder Eichmann,*" *The Germanic Review* 64.2 (1989), 58–66, here: 61

[20] Sven Hanuschek, *"Ich nenne das Wahrheitsfindung." Heinar Kipphardts Dramen und ein Konzept des Dokumentartheaters als Historiographie* (Bielefeld: Aisthesis Verlag, 1993), here: 317. As Hanuschek cites many parallel passages, the reader is also able to make up his own mind on the issue of rewriting history. Hanuschek demonstrates, for example, that the passage where Chass (Less) loses his temper is still very close to the transcript of the interrogation. He also reminds the reader that Kipphardt did not keep Less's name because Kipphardt's intention is to underline the parallels between the thinking of Chass and Eichmann (see *Bruder Eichmann,* 314–16).

[21] David Barnett, "The Holocaust and Documentary Metadrama. Heinar Kipphardt's *Bruder Eichmann,*" in *Jews in German Literature since 1945: German-Jewish Literature?,* ed. Pól O'Dochartaigh (Amsterdam-Atlanta, Rodopi, 2000), 587–98; David Barnett, "Documentation and its Discontents: The Case of Heinar Kipphardt," *Forum for Modern Language Studies* 37.3 (2001), 272–85.

[22] Glenn R. Cuomo, "*Vergangenheitsbewältigung* Through Analogy: Heinar Kipphardt's Last Play *Bruder Eichmann*," *The Germanic Review* 64.2 (1989), 58–66, here: 58.

[23] As Onderlinden suggests, Kipphardt's title is probably inspired by Thomas Mann's self-critical remark about the similarities between himself and "Bruder Hitler"; see Sjaak Onderlinden, "Geschichte auf der Bühne. Die Gattung des dokumentarischen Dramas und ihre Innovationsfähigkeit: Dieter Fortes *Luther/Müntzer* und Heinar Kipphardts *Bruder Eichmann, Neophilologus* 77 (1992), 256–74, here: 266.

[24] Florian Rommel, "Funktion und Problematik der Analogieszenen: Zu Heinar Kipphardts *Bruder Eichmann*," *Fußnoten zur Literatur* 38 (1996), 107–14.

[25] See the short commentary by Paul Kruntorad, "Der Streit um Heinar Kipphardts *Bruder Eichmann:* Stellungnahme von Avner Less, Paul Kruntorad, Johannes Schütz und ein Quellenvergleich," *Th* 4 (1983): 69.

[26] *Sp* also warns against the sympathetic depiction of Eichmann that appeared in *Sp* shortly after the premiere in "Vor Eichmann wird gewarnt," *Sp*, 31 January 1983, 160.

[27] As Hanuschek points out, *Bruder Eichmann* puts less emphasis on the historical character Eichmann and highlights the "banality of evil." See Sven Hanuschek, *Heinar Kipphardt* (Berlin: Morgenbuch, 1996), 86.

[28] Hannah Arendt, *Eichmann in Jerusalem* (New York: Viking Press, 1963), 276.

[29] According to the East German director Alexander Stillmark, these characteristics made it possible to achieve a very strong effect. See his account of the staging of the play in Alexander Stillmark, "Heinar Kipphardt's *Brother Eichmann*," in *Staging the Holocaust*, ed. Claude Schumacher (Cambridge: Cambridge UP, 1998), 254–66.

[30] On the problematic issue of Eichmann's "clear" conscience, see Christoph Leirer, "Das Gewissen und die Selbstverklärung der Haltung: Zu Heinar Kipphardts *Bruder Eichmann*," *Fußnoten zur Literatur* 38 (1996), 93–105.

[31] Heinar Kipphardt, *Bruder Eichmann. Schauspiel und Materialien* (Reinbek: Rowohlt, 1986), 53.

[32] Arendt, *Eichmann in Jerusalem* (New York: Viking Press, 1963), 242.

[33] Anat Feinberg-Jütte, "The Appeal of the Executive: Adolf Eichmann on Stage," *Monatshefte* 2 (1978), 203–14, here: 209.

[34] Lothar Pikulik, "Heinar Kipphardt: *Bruder Eichmann* und Thomas Bernhard: *Vor dem Ruhestand*," in *Deutsche Gegenwartsdramatik 1*, eds. Lothar Pikulik, Hajo Kurzenberger and Georg Guntermann (Göttingen: Vandenhoeck & Ruprecht, 1987), 141–91, here: 153.

[35] Among the critics who mention this dangerous sympathy for Eichmann are Rose-Marie Borngässer, "Theater der Heuchelei: Heinar Kipphardt's *Bruder Eichmann* in München," *W*, 24 January 1983; Georg Hensel, "'Kein Mensch wie jeder andere': *Bruder Eichmann*," *FAZ*, 24 January 1983; Hans Lamm, "*Bruder Eichmann:* Heinar Kipphardt's letztes Stück in München uraufgeführt," *Neue Jüdische Nachrichten*, 4 February 1983, 4; Horst Köpke, "Wir sind alle Eichmann? H. Kipphardt's letztes Stück uraufgeführt," *Frankfurter Rundschau*, 24 January 1983; Wolfgang Johannes Müller, "Selbstdarstellung des Adolf Eichmann: Kipphardts letztes Stück am Residenztheater," *Bayernkurier* 34, 29 January 1983, 12–13; Hans-Dietrich Sander, "Eichmann als Welttheater: Zur Uraufführung des letzten Stückes von Heinar

Kipphardt in München am 21 Januar 1983," *Deutsche Monatshefte für Kultur und Geschichte, Politik und Wirtschaft* 34 (1983), 33–34.

[36] Von Becker, "Heinar Kipphardts letztes Stück: Ein fataler Text," 2.

[37] An anecdotal approach to Strittmatter can be found in Volker Michael, "Thomas Strittmatter und St. Georgen im Schwarzwald," in *Spuren* 56 (Marbach: Deutsche Schillergesellschaft, 2001), 1–16.

[38] Gunna Wendt, *Der Tod ist eine Maschine aus Eis. Annäherung an Thomas Strittmatter (1961–1995)* (Munich: A-1-Verlag, 1997), 13.

[39] See Strittmatter's introductory remarks to the play, in Thomas Strittmatter, *Viehjud Levi* (Zürich: Diogenes, 1992), 8–9. Subsequent references to this work are cited in the text using the abbreviation *V* and page number.

[40] See Ödön von Horváth, "Gebrauchsanweisung," in *Materialien zu Ödön von Horvaths Kasimir und Karoline*, ed. Traugott Krischke (Frankfurt am Main: Suhrkamp, 1973), 103–7.

[41] Gerhard Stadelmaier, "Nix isch passiert!," *Th* 3 (1983): 4–6.

[42] From my own experience I must admit that, sadly, this proverb is still deeply ingrained in the minds of many older Germans who do not know where it stems from.

[43] Sibylle Fritsch, "George für alle," *profil,* 11 May 1987; Michael Merschmeier, "Wien nach der Wende," *Th,* July 1987, 4–7; C. Bernd Sucher, "Schlomo und Adolf im Blutgassen-Asyl," *SZ,* 8 May 1987; Erik G. Wickenburg, "Einen Gott für mich und einen für dich," *W,* 8 May 1987.

[44] Tabori's play *Jubiläum* follows a similar pattern: the dead Jews leave their graves in order to remind the audience of their individual fates; George Tabori, "Jubiläum," in George Tabori, *Stücke 2* (Munich/Vienna: Carl Hanser, 1994), 49–86.

[45] Anat Feinberg, *Embodied Memory — The Theater of George Tabori* (Iowa: Iowa U P, 1999), 249.

[46] Terrence des Pres, "Holocaust Laughter?" in *Writing and the Holocaust,* ed. Berel Lang (New York: Holmes & Meier, 1988), 216–33.

[47] See Joachim Fest, *Hitler: Eine Biographie* (Berlin: Bastei-Lübbe, 1973), 41.

[48] Ian Kershaw, *Hitler* (London: Longman, 1991), 165.

[49] George Tabori, "Mein Kampf," in George Tabori, *Stücke 2* (Munich/Vienna: Carl Hanser, 1994), 142–203, here: 181. Subsequent references to this work are cited in the text using the abbreviation *MK* and page number.

[50] Birgit Haas, *Das Theater des George Tabori. Vom Verfremdungseffekt zur Postmoderne* (Frankfurt am Main: Lang, 2000), 142–47. See also: Sandra Pott, *"Mein Kampf—* Farce oder theologischer Schwank," in *Theater gegen das Vergessen. Bühnenarbeit und Drama bei George Tabori,* eds. Hans-Peter Bayerdörfer and Jörg Schönert (Tübingen: Max Niemeyer, 1997), 248–69, here: 254.

[51] "Dreißig Jahre jung: Grips. Volker Ludwig im Gespräch mit Ingeborg Pietzsch," *TdZ* 7/8 (1999), 52–55, here: 52.

[52] Ellen Brandt and Stefan Fischer-Fels, "Kinder- und Jugendtheater aus dem Geist des Kabaretts," in *Stück-Werk 2* (Berlin: Kinder und Jugendtheaterzentrum in der Bundesrepublik Deutschland 1998), 104–8, here: 108.

[53] Inge Deutschkron, *Ich trug den gelben Stern* (Cologne: Wissenschaft und Politik, 1978).

[54] Michael Merschmeier, "Von Herzen klug sein . . . ," *Th* 3 (1989): 21–25.

[55] "Das Ende der Kinderstücke? *Th*-Gespräch mit dem Autor und Grips-Kopf Volker Ludwig," *Th* 1 (1996): 37–40, here: 40.

[56] Volker Ludwig, "Womit beschäftigt sich GRIPS?," in GRIPS Theater Berlin, *Was ist GRIPS?* (Berlin: Alexander Verlag, n.d.).

[57] Volker Ludwig/Detlef Michel, "*Ab heute heißt du Sara,*" *Th* 3 (1989): 42–57, here: 44.

4: The Decay of the GDR

IN OCTOBER 1949, one month after the founding of the Federal Republic, the German Democratic Republic (GDR) was founded. This move cemented the final division of East and West, which had been presaged by the introduction of two different currencies in 1948.[1] From the very beginning, the GDR, as the Socialist state that was modeled on the Soviet Union, suffered from serious economic problems as a result of the damages and ravages caused by war. While the West soon prospered, thanks to generous financial help from the United States and the other western allies, the GDR had a bad start. The East suffered much due to exploitation by the Russians, who dismantled much of their industry and took it back to Russia.[2]

Although the state economy recovered in the 1960s and 70s, the situation began to deteriorate again in the early 1980s. Despite all efforts of the SED (*Sozialistische Einheitspartei Deutschlands*) to convince its citizens of the prosperity of the state, the economic problems returned with a vengeance. People generally remained skeptical of a state that had to fence in its population with the help of barbed wire, watchtowers, mined land strips, and self-triggering automatic guns. By the time the Wall came down in 1989, a total of almost 200 people had been killed in their efforts to escape. The lack of freedom to travel proved to be one of many elements of the GDR regime that drove the GDR populace to despair, a fact that is dealt with in Volker Braun's *Die Übergangsgesellschaft* (Society in Transition, 1982).

In the late 1970s and early 1980s, opposition groups began to form. Under the auspices of the protestant church, which defined itself as an independent church within the state, peace protesters, environmentalists, and human rights activists began to organize protest groups.[3] It should be noted, however, that following the brutal clampdown on the workers' uprising in 1953 and the harsh treatment of dissidents by the SED, the GDR never knew a genuine mass movement as such.

A peace movement, in which protests were organized against military instruction at schools, sprang up as early as 1978. In the same year, Robert Havemann, who was later expelled, wrote an open letter to Brezhnev, asking him to stop nuclear rearmament. The beginning of the

1980s saw a rapid increase in the number of groups protesting for nuclear disarmament. The environmental movement, which grew out of the peace protest, became dedicated to the fight against the impending doom of the *Waldsterben,* the pollution of the rivers, and the destruction of the countryside — issues that were also addressed by the poet Heinz Czechowski.[4] It reached its height in 1983, becoming the hub of dissidents' circles, which, during the second half of the decade, set up an environmental library in East Berlin, and a network called *Arche,* as well as encouraging the founding of new local groups. To use the term of the Ministry of Security, these groups were all regarded as the "innere Feind," and were constantly surveilled and persecuted, and often brutally silenced by way of imprisonment.

At the beginning of the 1980s, the economic and environmental situation worsened, a fact which forms the backdrop of Volker Braun's *Die Übergangsgesellschaft,* which is set in a polluted landscape. During its tenth party rally in 1981, however, the SED continued in its attempt to convince its people of the efficiency of the system. Despite this, the impending bankruptcy of the GDR was by no means a secret to Western politicians, who by that time were giving generous support to the GDR by way of large loans. Instead of focusing on real problems, the party reacted to the situation by stepping up its ideological indoctrination. During the rally, the head of state, Erich Honecker, enforced his personality cult in his speeches, whilst Willy Stoph, chairman of the *Ministerrat,* read out the new five-year plan. Above all, the meeting signaled continuity, which meant that the severe, centralized conformity imposed by the SED was not even touched upon. This is also at the center of Georg Seidel's (1945–1990) play *Jochen Schanotta* (1985), for Seidel presents us with a teenage boy who wants to be different, yet is mercilessly crushed by a totalitarian society. The party maintained its monopoly on wisdom and truth, and launched a clampdown on the culture industry by banning books, films, and certain types of music.[5] This situation is portrayed in Braun's *Die Übergangsgesellschaft,* where reformers question the rigid structures of Socialist society by harking back to old revolutionary ideals. However, even the attempt, realized as a collective dream, to imagine a positive utopia is eventually stifled by a harsh clampdown on the dissidents. The play ends with an arson attack on the house of the protagonist Wilhelm, an image which was symbolic of the call for a change.

In 1982, the GDR faced a serious economic crisis, as it had reduced the number of imported goods in favor of increasing its exports, a measure which was intended to pay off some of the GDR's enormously large debt to the West. As a result, the Socialist state became dependent on further Western credit. In addition, a rise in consumer demand led to serious bottlenecks in the supply of vital goods, and defense expenditure placed such a burden on the state that it was struggling to survive. The GDR population had long been used to material shortages and wasteful overproduction due to poor infrastructure and cumbersome distribution. These resulted in either the unavailability of goods and long waiting periods or the large-scale delivery of shoddy products at the wrong time of year. In 1987, the waiting time for a car, for example, was from 12.5 to 17 years, depending on the make.[6] All in all, the deterioration of the economy provided cause for growing political unrest. Although the GDR tried to maintain a facade of stability, an ever-increasing number of citizens emigrated to the West; and, in 1984 alone, more than 35,000 people moved to the Federal Republic. Although the playwright Thomas Brasch (1945–2001) had emigrated as early as 1976, he vented his anger about the overbearing Socialist state in his play *Lieber Georg* (Dear Georg, 1980), where the poet Heym becomes the victim of an environment that is dominated by an overbearing father figure.

In March 1985, Mikhail Gorbachev became the leader of the Communist Party in the Soviet Union: the former hard-liners were replaced by an open-minded politician with a will for reform. His aims were two-fold: to break up and relax the rigid governmental structures (*Perestroika*) and to create a democratic society (*Glasnost*). The leadership of the GDR, however, deliberately ignored this call for change, instead clinging tightly to the principles of centralism and hegemony. Even when Gorbachev called for the socialist party to adopt a self-critical attitude, during his opening address of the SED's eleventh party rally, Honecker responded with unaffected ignorance. At this meeting, more than any other, the triviality and irrelevant nature of the speeches revealed the extent to which the GDR leader had already become detached from reality. The leading SED functionaries proved to be out of touch with reality, and they claimed for example that the standard of living in the East was considerably higher than that of West Germany. In his successful play *Die Ritter der Tafelrunde* (The Knights of the Round Table, 1985), Christoph Hein presents us with an allegory of this situation.

In order to maintain its dictatorship, the SED resorted to intimidating its population by strengthening the powers of the dreaded Ministry of Security (*MfS, Staatssicherheit, Stasi*); this is depicted in Klaus Pohl's (1952–) *Karate Billi kehrt zurück* (Karate-Billi Comes Home, 1991/93).[7] In February 1985, the head of the MfS, Mielke, issued a severe warning to all potential dissidents, threatening to punish enemies of the state (*Staatsfeinde*) as harshly as possible.[8] Everybody was aware of the immense power of the organization, which employed roughly 85,000 official and

108,000 unofficial informers, who spied on practically every gathering,[9] tapped telephone lines, and followed every move of citizens who were suspected of disloyalty to the regime. As some of the work of the MfS was deliberately conspicuous, this inevitably resulted in a collective "surveillance trauma," to which even top members of the party succumbed, since they were aware that their every step was being watched.[10]

In increasingly distancing itself from the progressive Soviet Union, the GDR effectively dug its own grave. A number of measures taken by the SED only further highlighted its will to continue to pursue its old course. In 1988, for example, the critical Soviet journal *Sputnik* was banned due to its open criticism of Stalin, stating that he had helped bring Hitler to power.[11] In the same year, the authorities refused to release the Soviet film *Repentance,* which had been filling the cinemas in the USSR. To top it all, the GDR awarded the *Karl-Marx-Orden* to the brutal dictator of Romania, Nicolae Ceausescu. This measure dampened all hopes of democratic reform, at the same time provoking political protest. While protesters began to voice their discontent,[12] many leading party functionaries, together with the geriatric Politbüro, continued to opt for oppression and a more efficient surveillance system in order to stifle social and political unrest.[13] As this was exactly the situation that Hein had depicted in *Die Ritter der Tafelrunde,* the play was received enthusiastically and celebrated for its lucid prediction of the developments during the Velvet Revolution in 1989.

Skating on Thin Ice:
Thomas Brasch's *Lieber Georg* (1980)

Thomas Brasch, the son of Jewish émigrés, was born in Yorkshire, England, and moved to East Germany when he was two years old. From 1968, he was constantly at odds with the GDR authorities and was even briefly imprisoned in 1968, because he had distributed leaflets criticizing the Soviet invasion of Czechoslovakia.[14] In 1976, he successfully applied for permission to emigrate to West Germany. His first play *Rotter* was staged in Stuttgart in 1977 (director, Christoph Nel), and depicts the petit-bourgeois Rotter, who has political beliefs tailored to the prevailing circumstances.[15] After a successful career during the National Socialist dictatorship, he quickly changes his political beliefs in order to become the model socialist citizen. Brasch's third play, *Lieber Georg,* centers on the problematic situation of the writer in a dictatorship; Heym, the central character of the play can therefore be seen as a mask for Brasch himself. Since 1980, Brasch has written several more plays, among them

Frauen. Krieg. Lustspiel (Women. War. Comedy, 1989), set in the First World War.[16] His focus, however, has been on writing film scripts, such as *Engel aus Eisen* (Angels of Iron, 1981), many of which focus on the period of National Socialism. Other than this, Brasch has also translated many Shakespeare plays into German, contributing to a more contemporary approach to the classical playwright. In her memories of Brasch, who died of a heart attack in November 2001, Barbara Honigmann, a good friend of his, noted that he had never adapted to mainstream politics, and had always remained a frank critic of social injustice.[17]

In February 1980, Brasch's collage *Lieber Georg* premiered in Bochum, where it received acclaim for embracing a concise style reminiscent of poetry,[18] in which the postmodern pastiche replaced the dialogues.[19] Art lives on art, is Brasch's credo, and he refers back to Georg Büchner, in whose plays he detects the fears of the individual in the face of dawning materialism.[20] *Lieber Georg* is a soliloquy in which the other characters only exist in the schizophrenic mind of the poet. Although the central character is called Heym, the play is not a strict biographical reconstruction of the life of the expressionist poet Georg Heym (1887–1912). It is rather, as the title suggests, addressing the dead poet, and an attempt to come to terms with the past. Because the poet is surrounded by ice, alluding to the inhumanity and rigidity of the Cold War period, he drowns after breaking through the thin ice, a symbol of the precarious situation in which the GDR writer found himself.

The play suggests that the lives of both the real Heym and his fictional counterpart, an alias for Brasch himself, are in many respects similar. Whilst Heym lived in the Prussian monarchy of Wilhelm II, Brasch grew up in an authoritarian socialist dictatorship, in which his father was an important party functionary.[21] The highly problematic relationship between father and son is featured right at the beginning of *Lieber Georg*, when Heym's father forces his son to carry him on his shoulders. Although Heym is about to collapse under his father's weight, he cannot get rid of him. The political allegory is taken even further, for the father refuses to tell his son where they are going. In his father's eyes, Heym is a living failure who stutters, wets his bed, and, to top it all, writes useless poems instead of "signing death warrants":

PAPA   Lachhaft! Mit deinen Gedichten wisch ich mir
                                                 den Arsch
            Jawohl den Arsch Weiter jetzt Los und halt die
                                                    Fresse
            Ins Gerichtsarchiv werd ich dich stecken In den
                                                     Staub
            Und dann mit dem Säbel ein paar Ausrufezeichen
            auf die Backen Das ist Lyrik Vorwärts jetzt
HEYM   Wohin Papa wohin Die Richtung
PAPA   Die geht dich einen Dreck an[22]

The overbearing father is symbolic of both the time before the First World War and the political oppression in the GDR. *Lieber Georg* addresses the role of the intellectual under the yoke of socialist censorship. Heym is skating on thin ice, likely to drown any minute, an image which expresses the frailty of his existence. Furthermore, both the real poet and his fictional counterpart live in dangerous times: a war was looming on the horizon of Wilhelm's Germany, and Brasch's character fears a Third World War. In their attitudes towards war, however, the real Heym and Brasch differ considerably. Whilst the expressionist wished for a war to clear the atmosphere and bring out the best in man, thereby forging the "Neue Mensch," Brasch is afraid of a nuclear war. In the post-script of *Lieber Georg*, he accuses members of parliament of endangering peoples' lives. This shows that Brasch shared the worries of many Europeans in the late 1970s and early 1980s, when there was no sign of an end to large-scale armament on both sides of the Wall, and in 1979, a NATO resolution envisaged the stationing of more Pershing II missiles in Germany.

Surrounded by this overbearing military power, Brasch's Heym retreats into the private sphere. As all protests against the structures of power are futile, he asks his best friend Balcke to smack him in order to keep him from talking, thereby censoring himself. This alludes to a decree issued by the *Schriftstellerverband* of the GDR in 1975, in which the writers succumbed to the power of the state, and announced that they would exercise self-control:

> Die Mitglieder des Schriftstellerverbandes der DDR anerkennen die führende Rolle der Arbeiterklasse und ihrer Rolle in der Kulturpolitik. Sie bekennen sich zur Schaffensmethode des sozialistischen Realismus. Sie treten entschieden gegen alle Formen der ideologischen Koexistenz und das Eindringen reaktionärer und revisionistischer Auffassungen in die Bereiche der Literatur auf.[23]

This meant that the writers accepted the severe limitations that were placed upon them. What is more, they promised to keep literature clean from any non-socialist influence, and to praise the assets of the socialist state. The readiness of GDR writers to censor themselves, even before the intervention of the state, had been criticized by Christa Wolf as early as 1974.[24] In *Lieber Georg,* the metaphor of the muted and mutilated poet is carried even further, when Heym's tongue is cut off by Balcke, who wears the mask of a Chinese dictator. The character Heym, deprived of his primary means of communication, becomes a victim of the political system. Since he refuses to stay quiet in times of oppression, or, as Volker Braun once put it, "to sit on his tongue,"[25] he is silenced by others.[26]

The play is characterized by the clash of two opposing spheres, namely the private world and the political world: because of the violence inflicted on him by his father and his best friend Balcke, Heym retreats into the private sphere for shelter, and, in contrast to the characters around him, is largely passive, a victim of circumstances. *Lieber Georg* presents the psychological and physical damage caused by an overbearing state that has adopted the role of the father-figure. The poet Heym, who acts as a mask for Brasch, proves unable to fend off the voices that torment his brain, and as a result he becomes mentally ill. Due to the oppressive regime, all his efforts to become a normal citizen fail and his ego collapses, leaving him amidst a cacophony of confused voices.

Between the GDR and a Hard Place: Volker Braun's *Die Übergangsgesellschaft* (1982)

Written in 1982, and first staged at the *Bremer Theater* in 1987,[27] Braun's play was not allowed to premiere at the *Maxim-Gorki-Theater* (director, Thomas Langhoff) in East Berlin until six years later, in 1988. Like Christoph Hein's *Die Ritter der Tafelrunde* (1985), the play benefited from the changes that began to take place in the GDR in 1988/89, when *glasnost* finally made its way into East German playhouses.[28] Together with Hein's play, it became one of the most successful plays of 1988/89, and in less than a year it was performed more than 100 times at the Maxim-Gorki-Theater alone. Within the context of the "Wende," critics read it as an indicator of the crumbling Socialist dictatorship in the GDR.[29] During an interview in 1988, Braun himself admitted that the events that were taking place in the GDR pointed towards a change of direction in society.[30] However, it must be remembered that when Braun wrote the play in 1982, neither the rise of Gorbachev, the end of the Warsaw Pact, nor the peaceful revolution of 1989 was anywhere in sight.

The historical background to the play is the GDR of the early 1980s, where both economic and ecological problems were already beginning to appear.[31] *Die Übergangsgesellschaft* portrays the stagnation of the GDR with respect to the individual, politics and the environment.[32] Braun criticizes the abuse of power that results in the oppression of individuality, the destruction of nature, and the oppression of man by man.[33] The title of the play, indicating a society in transition, is paradoxical, as the situation is rather characterized by inertia. In Marxist thinking, however, the term "society in transition" was wholly relevant to the GDR (and other states of the Warsaw Pact), because "Übergangsgesellschaft" refers to the phase in which capitalism has been overcome, but communism, the utopia of an equal society, has not yet been achieved. The GDR was therefore an example of a reform that ground to a halt before equality had been achieved.[34] As a consequence, many GDR citizens realized that they had fought "at dawn" only to find themselves in an "age of dusk," an age of decline. The GDR had been established according to the Soviet model; it soon became clear that Socialism with a human face would remain a more and more unattainable prospect, and that real communism would be postponed until doomsday. Marxist ideology was distorted and reshaped in order to fit the strict leadership of the *Sozialistische Einheitspartei Deutschlands* (SED), yet the gap between Socialist politics and Marx's concepts widened.[35] In order to justify its policies, the SED constantly maintained that according to Marx, the working class needed an élite as a guide to achieving communism, a role the SED thought it could fill.[36] The fact that both Marx and Engels had always underlined the necessity of a critical spirit was regarded as "staatsgefährdend" and therefore secretly discarded.[37]

In *Die Übergangsgesellschaft*, all the characters appear trapped in their everyday lives under the Socialist dictatorship, regardless of whether they are conformists such as Walter, Franz and Olga, or dissidents like Wilhelm, Mette, Frank, and later Irina. More problematically, the writer Anton stands between the two parties.

At the beginning the audience sees an old garden with a polluted river that gives off fumes, and a veranda half-covered by waste. This image of an impending environmental disaster is later undercut by the distant but continuous sound of a siren, caused by a fault in the electric current. As the catastrophic damage to the environment by the GDR's heavy industry became obvious in the 1980s, ecological problems formed a focus of protest. In fact, half of all river mileage was unsuitable for bathing, let alone drinking, and many lakes were biologically dead.

At the beginning of *Die Übergangsgesellschaft*, all the characters except Wilhelm, the central character, are sitting in the middle of the polluted garden, wrapped in cling film. It is as if the wrapping might help to keep them fresh, a graphic image that is mirrored by the fact that the beginning is a long quotation taken from Chekhov's *The Three Sisters* (1901). It is therefore made clear that the situation is not only artificial, but also absurd.[38] As in Chekhov's play, everybody complains that the total inertia that surrounds them stifles all initiative. They are bored to death by the hopelessness of their situation, and see no reason for being alive. Wilhelm, however, who distances himself from the interlude, refuses to listen and, with covered ears, makes sarcastic comments. At the end of this mini-drama, he announces the end of their short performance, a remark which highlights the pessimistic tone of the opening scene, because it also alludes to the political aspect of the play, the decline of the GDR. According to Wilhelm, the game is already over, in other words, the dream of a just Socialism is already dead.

This becomes evident in the character Anton, a writer who feels helpless and blind, like an unborn child who is trapped in the womb of his overbearing mother, the GDR, although he is supposed to represent the intellectual élite of his country. As he lacks any real experience, his texts are based on hearsay. He adheres so strongly to authority that he even censors his own works in order to please party functionaries — a paradoxical situation which was, in fact, typical of the status of the writer in the GDR.[39] Like these dissidents, Anton is a problematic figure, as he is torn between criticism and self-restriction.

The oppressive climate is further emphasized by the driver Franz, who is really an informer for the Ministry of Security (*Ministerium für Staatssicherheit, Stasi*). It is therefore not surprising that he unexpectedly breaks out of the bushes and checks to see whether a spy is sitting under the table in Wilhelm's house. As Franz is unable to find written evidence of Wilhelm's thoughts, the revolutionary simply mocks the young informer:

> WILHELM [. . .] Du mußt es im Kopf haben, im Kopf. Hier steckts. Da schau nach. Ereignisse, Daten. Übriggebliebene Personen . . . Mumien. Theaterleichen. Die Bühne voll. *Lachanfall.* Das Stück, das die Zensur überlebt hat . . . und nun sich selbst verbietet. Das Elend. Die Hoffnung. Das Elend. *Hält sich die Augen zu.*[40]

Apart from making a fool of the young driver, his mockery alludes to past events that he has witnessed during his long life. As an old revolutionary and advocate of democratic Socialism, Wilhelm therefore remains unimpressed at Franz's display of power, although he is still under house arrest. In Wilhelm's view, the revolution of 1919 and its aftermath resemble a play; what remains, however, is an empty stage covered with dust and filled with zombies.[41] He considers the November revolution to be a drama which did away with censorship only to forbid potentially positive outcomes, with the result that misery outweighs hope. As a result, Wilhelm constantly deplores the fact that the communist revolution ended in Socialist dictatorship.

Although the hardliner Walter clamps down on any attempt to break free, the play ends in turmoil. Eventually, Irina breaks out of her docility and sets the house on fire, a symbolic deed, because Socialism was often referred to as a common house under one roof, in which everybody would find shelter and protection. Walter tries to save it, but nobody else helps him, so Wilhelm's body remains inside and burns with the house. However, not only the revolutionary Wilhelm, but also the student's scripts, referred to as "das Diktat," turn to ashes. Olga's remark is highly ambivalent, because her concern for the scripts could also mean that dictatorship is now under attack, and that revolution is finally taking place, a view which Braun expressed in a interview, saying that the end is potentially a good beginning.[42]

Call for Change: Christoph Hein's *Die Ritter der Tafelrunde* (1985)

It took four years for Christoph Hein's "endgame" on socialism, written in 1985/86, to be published by the West German theater journal *Theater heute* in 1989. In the GDR, a printed version was not available until 1990. As the play was interpreted as a harsh criticism of the geriatric members of the *Politbüro,* the city council of Dresden intervened to halt the production at the *Schauspielhaus Dresden,* but rehearsals began without official permission, and on 12 April 1989 the play was performed in front of a selected audience.[43] As the parallels to the GDR are obvious in the plot, it is not surprising that party functionaries feared the critical potential of the play. However, the premiere ran quietly, and the Ministry of Culture and Science gave the go-ahead for the play to be performed throughout the GDR. Almost a year later, on 3 March 1990, the play premiered at the *Staatstheater Kassel* in West Germany.

Whereas reactions were rather cautious and muted because of the play's political content in the GDR, the West German media read it as a swan song for the GDR state.[44] Hein's depiction of the "Tafelrunde," the disillusioned knights, and their failure to find the Grail, quickly became symbolic of the dismembering of the GDR, because it was performed during the hectic events of 1989. This view was enhanced by various productions that invited audiences to engage in political debate about events in the GDR. Soon the play became a forum for political discussion. Reviews even equated figures in the play directly to SED representatives, stating that the play depicted Honecker, Mielke and Krenz.[45] Yet Hein himself refuses to see *Die Ritter der Tafelrunde* merely as an allegory of the GDR. During an interview in 1990, he insisted on the vagueness of the mythical context, claiming that he never referred to a specific historical framework.[46] Reception of Hein's play is therefore divided: while some critics argue that Hein wrote an allegory of the GDR,[47] others see it as a more general depiction of the petrifaction of Socialism in the mid-eighties.[48]

Hein's insistence that the criticism in his play is of a more general nature is reminiscent of an earlier play called *Merlin oder Das wüste Land* (Merlin or The Waste Land, 1979–81) by Tankred Dorst (1925–).[49] In *Merlin*, Dorst took up the Parzival myth and adapted the saga about the knights of the Round Table for our modern times. His central aim was to show that a waste land of intolerance and violence lurks below the glossy appearance of the so-called civilized world.[50] Like Hein, Dorst also highlighted the importance of the scene in which the young knights rebel against Arthur. While Dorst's *Merlin* presents the end of European civilization,[51] In *Die Ritter der Tafelrunde*, it is Parzifal who vents his frustration with the following words:

> Das alles ist so lange her, daß es fast nicht mehr wahr ist. Und der hochberühmte Gral! Als Kind habe ich mir vor Ehrfurcht eingeschissen, wenn ihr von dem Gral erzähltet. Ich glaubte, es sei wunder was Groß-artiges. Dabei wißt ihr überhaupt nicht, was das ist. Kein Mensch ver-mag zu sagen, was das ist: der Gral.[52]

Whilst the myth ends with the battle of Salisbury, Hein's Artus quietly hands over his power to Mordret, an ending that suggests that the political stand-still may be overcome. Despite its allusions to the GDR, the play remains relatively vague, and only its reception during the events of 1989 trans-formed *Die Ritter der Tafelrunde* into a play about the end of the GDR.

Against the backdrop of the Parzival myth, Hein creates a play about a handful of old, weary knights and their wives who gave up on the quest for the Grail, which can be seen as a symbol of socialist utopianism. It is a criti-cism of the gerontocratic *Politbüro* and its hardliners, whose Grail turns out to be an illusion, just as real socialism never existed. Instead, the state was ruled by a highly privileged élite of party functionaries. In the GDR, censor-ship and oppression continued to silence all public debate, even after Gor-bachev announced the end of the Brezhnev doctrine, introducing *glasnost* and *perestroika*.[53] Although Artus is often identified with Erich Honecker, the leader of the GDR,[54] his tolerant and open-minded nature resembles Gorbachev more than the hardliner Honecker.

In a speech before the tenth *Schriftstellerkongress* in 1987, Hein had already voiced his discontent: "Die Zensur ist überlebt, nutzlos, paradox, menschen- und volksfeindlich, ungesetzlich und strafbar."[55] In the play, it is the young knight Parzival who revolts against censorship, intending to spark off a public debate about the appalling state of the "Tafelrunde." *Die Ritter der Tafelrunde* is a quiet play with undertones of resignation, as Parzival's biting comments force the knights to recognize the extent to which they have wasted their lives.

As there is little action, the play is rather static, and expresses stagnation and slow decay.[56] It is set in the banquet hall of Artus's castle, beginning with breakfast and ending after dinner, and the main lines of conflict run between the generations, between the sexes, and between the private and the public. Because both the fictional and the real Politbüro are out of touch with reality, nobody realizes that public opinion turned against the Round Table long ago, and that people view it as a committee of fools, idiots, and criminals.

Artus's empire is falling apart, a process of decay that is symbolized by the fact that one table leg of the Round Table is loose and the carpenters refuse to mend it. Moreover, the enchantment of the magic table and the free chair is removed by both Jeschute and Parzival. While Jeschute uses it as a normal breakfast table and even sits on the free chair (the Siege Perilous), Parzival covers it with his papers while working on his journal.[57] After all, it is only wood, as Mordret states. The table becomes a symbol of the state in which socialism is to be found: inert, rigid, aged, and a potential fire hazard — one that may provoke violent clashes on the streets. Although the table-leg broke years ago, nobody dares complain to the workers, not even Artus himself, because he is afraid of them, as Orilus remarks. In the end, the symbol for Socialism is taken to a museum, as it is only fit for historical studies.

The generational conflict that played an important role in the reawakening of a critical spirit during the last five years of the GDR has its parallel in the play, for Parzival and Mordret[58] oppose Keie and Orilus.[59] Parzival, who represents the citizens' initiatives in the GDR that began to form in 1985,[60] is a young rebellious spirit who revolts against the rigid structures of the Round Table, advising Keie to open his eyes to reality instead of following age-old hopes. Keie, however, accuses Parzival of being a traitor because he challenges belief in the Grail;[61] this is an allusion to an article which Mielke, the head of the *Stasi,* published an article in *Neues Deutschland* in 1985, in which he openly threatened potential dissidents.[62]

Although Hein attacks the (Socialist) utopia, it is interesting that he clings to the idea of a reformed Socialism, even after the Wall has come down. During the "Wende," he continued to believe that the GDR could be transformed according to Socialist ideas.[63] In an article in *Neues Deutschland* on 2 December 1989, for example, he expressed his hope that true Socialism would finally be realized. Paradoxically, Hein himself was unable to abandon the political utopia, and during 1989, he maintained the myth of the Socialist Grail that he had earlier dismantled in *Die Ritter der Tafelrunde*.

Puberty and Dictatorship: Georg Seidel's *Jochen Schanotta* (1985)

Georg Seidel's play *Jochen Schanotta* offers insight into everyday life in the GDR, particularly with regard to the problems of the teenage generation.[64] It premiered in 1985 at the *Berliner Ensemble* in East Berlin, and in order to avoid censorship, texts by other authors were inserted into Seidel's play.[65] The West German staging of *Jochen Schanotta* took place in Switzerland, at the *Basler Theater*. However, the playwright, who died from cancer at the age of forty-five in 1990, is hardly known in the West. In 1988, Seidel's "Märchenkomödie" *Königskinder* (1978) eventually premiered at the *Deutsche Theater* in East Berlin. Modeled on Georg Büchner's (1813–1837) play *Leonce und Lena* (1838), Seidel's comedy about two kings and their siblings living in a highly symbolic setting close to a border gained the critics' acclaim.[66] By contrast, *Jochen Schanotta* is written in a realistic style, and tells the story of the rebellious pupil Schanotta, who openly protests against the oppressive system of both school and state. As a result, he is expelled from school, and as he is denied the option of reintegrating in another school, he takes refuge in his girlfriend's bedroom. But it is not long until she tires of his lying supine on her bed, and she throws him out. Now homeless, he returns to his mother, and is finally forced to join the military forces.

Through Schanotta's memories, the audience learns how the conformist education system stifles any incentive to be creative. One day at school, they are asked to paint birds, but instead of being allowed to draw an outline themselves, the pupils are provided with a uniform silhouette, and are even reminded that they must religiously stick to the outline. The symbol of freedom, the bird, is coerced into a rigid structure, thereby preventing any freedom of thought from an early age.

Schanotta's outspoken revolt against this mental inertia that systematically crushes the younger generation means that other schools also refuse to take him on as a pupil. As two teachers point out in an interview with him, they do not need a potential troublemaker, as this would call into question their own obedience. The maxim is to keep one's head down at all costs. However, Schanotta is different, and he refuses to submit himself to the tyrannical system:

> [. . .] es muß funktionieren, irgendwie muß alles funktionieren, lerne auch funktionieren, das Leben geht weiter. Fortschritt habt ihr gesagt, wir haben Fähnchen geschwenkt. Frieden habt ihr gesagt, wir haben nicht nur Fähnchen geschwenkt. Es fand statt, alles nach Plan — und ihr habt uns Hoffnung auf Freiheit gemacht. Ihr habt uns betrogen. [. . .][67]

In this monologue addressed to his teacher, Körner, Schanotta gives a lucid interpretation of the oppressive atmosphere in the GDR. Enthusiasm and commitment are encouraged, but only if they are strictly in line with the Communist party.[68] In his depressing analysis of the situation, the student stresses his view that the Socialist state reduces young people to passive spectators whose role consists of applauding. Schanotta, whose real father ran away before he was even born, finds himself under the thumb of a dictatorship that has taken on the role of an overbearing father-figure.[69]

Eventually, however, the outcast Schanotta, who at first resembles the Brechtian character *Baal* (1919), succumbs to the powerful dictatorship and joins the army. As nonconformists are denied the necessary elements of a decent life, such as a job and a flat, he resigns himself to his fate. In the last scene, we learn that he has started drinking, refuses to eat and has become silent. He withers away so quietly that after his leave, his mother wonders whether he has ever been to visit her at all. For her, it is only the nice boy Schanotta, the well-adjusted child, who counts, and she tries to repress the unpleasant truth about her grown-up son.

But Schanotta is not the only one who suffers from burdensome government regulations. His girlfriend Klette, for example, works in a steel factory, where she performs the same hand movement a thousand times per day. Sadly, she becomes so numb that she no longer objects to her dull workplace, and instead simply turns her music up to full volume when she returns from work. The monotonous work also quells the thoughts of the workers Franz and Rudi, who sink into a state of utter indifference. As Socialism reduces them to complete passivity, they become alcoholics.[70] However, their language is littered with allusions to the political situation, such as when Franz talks about a friend who is fascinated by the way in which metal slices form on the top of steel pikes before they break and crumble. This is clearly a powerful metaphor for the stagnation of the GDR, where faces and names changed, yet the rule of the Socialist party abides. Rudi talks about a film on television, where two men sit in a room for two hours, drinking alcohol, until the door finally opens. This image not only reflects his own miserable situation, but also alludes to the collective trauma of the GDR population regarding travel restrictions. It is obvious that he would seize the first opportunity to leave the waiting room, the GDR, through any available loophole. Yet his brain is so saturated with alcohol that he no longer notices the parallels to his own life.

The play portrays everyday life in the GDR in the mid-eighties, when the economic, political, and environmental crisis was becoming increasingly visible. *Jochen Schanotta* depicts a handful of common people for whom life has lost practically all meaning, because time seems to grind to a halt. Instead of creating progress and the hope of a better future, the Communist utopia proves to be a straightforward lie. Feeling betrayed, the common people sink into a state of depression and passivity: Schanotta succumbs to the state, Klette to her monotonous work, and the workers to their artificial alcohol-induced paradise.

In the GDR, playwrights opposed the politics of the Socialist party that had become increasingly rigid following the heated debates concerning the expatriation of the songwriter Wolf Biermann in 1976. Despite a clampdown on dissenting intellectuals, playwrights continued to criticize the shortcomings of Socialism. After his emigration to West Germany, Thomas Brasch vented his anger concerning the stifling conditions in the GDR in his postmodern pastiche *Lieber Georg* (1980). The play shows how a writer named for the expressionist Georg Heym is systematically crushed by an overbearing father-figure, and becomes the victim of an intolerant society. Against the backdrop of a polluted environment, Volker Braun's *Die Übergangsgesellschaft* (1988) presents a clash of views between idealist reformers and dedicated followers of the Socialist dictatorship. The play ends with their house, which is also symbolic of the GDR state, being burned down, and it can therefore be interpreted as a call for revolution. Georg Seidel's *Jochen Schanotta* (1985) concentrates on the psychological impact of an education system that aimed to form the perfect Socialist citizen. The play takes a rather pessimistic view, for Schanotta's revolt against the overbearing education system proves to be in vain. Although it was written in 1985, Christoph Hein's *Die Ritter der Tafelrunde* (1985) is still commonly believed to be *the* play of the "Velvet Revolution" of 1989. Due to its delayed stagings in 1988 and 1989, Hein's portrayal of a group of senile knights prattling on around a broken round table was interpreted as a verbal attack on members of the *Politbüro*. With hindsight, it can be said that despite, or rather because of, the rigidity of politics in East Germany, playwrights never stopped commenting on and criticizing political developments during the 1980s. The difference was, however, that writers in the GDR seemed to sense that a change would be taking place in the foreseeable future, while writers in the West were largely concerned with social movements, ignoring the possibility of a political change that could unite the two states again.

Notes

[1] For the details of the currency reform, the Berlin conflict, and the politics in East and West after 1945, see Christoph Kleßmann, *Die doppelte Staatsgründung. Deutsche Geschichte 1945–1955* (Bonn: Bundeszentrale für politische Bildung (also published by Vandenhoeck & Ruprecht in Göttingen, 1991), 188–93.

[2] For the following, see Hermann Weber, *Die DDR 1945–89* (Munich: Oldenburg, 2000, 3rd revised edition); Manfred Jäger, *Kultur und Politik in der DDR* (Cologne: Edition Deutschland Archiv, 1995).

[3] See Gerda Haufe and Karl Bruckmeier (eds.), *Die Bürgerbewegungen in der DDR und in den ostdeutschen Ländern* (Opladen: Westdeutscher Verlag, 1993), 10–28.

[4] For an analysis of Czechowski's "Ökolyrik," see Ian Hilton, "Heinz Czechowski. A Paradise Lost," in *Literatur und Ökologie*, ed. Axel Goodbody (Amsterdam/Atlanta: Rodopi, 1998), 101–22.

[5] Matthias Judt (ed.), *DDR-Geschichte in Dokumenten* (Berlin: Chr. Links, 1998), 299.

[6] Matthias Judt (ed.), *DDR-Geschichte in Dokumenten*, 140.

[7] As the play was written and staged after 1989, it will be discussed in the chapter "Reflections on German Reunification" of this book.

[8] The warning was published on 7 February 1985 in the state-owned newspaper *Neues Deutschland*.

[9] Jens Gieseke, *Die DDR-Staatssicherheit. Schild und Schwert der Partei* (Berlin: Bundeszentrale für politische Bildung, 2000), 86.

[10] Johannes Raschke, *Zwischen Überwachung und Repression — Politische Verfolgung in der DDR 1971 bis 1989* (Opladen: Leske + Budrich, 2001), 26.

[11] Matthias Judt (ed.), *DDR-Geschichte in Dokumenten* (Berlin: Chr. Links, 1998), 355.

[12] "Rockmusiker und Liedermacher fordern öffentlichen Dialog. 18. September 1989," *Der Morgen*, 18 October 1989.

[13] Matthias Judt (ed.), *DDR-Geschichte in Dokumenten* (Berlin: Chr. Links, 1998), 361.

[14] "Thomas Brasch," in *Wer war wer in der DDR*, eds. Bernd-Rainer Barth, Christoph Links, Thomas Brasch, Helmut Müller-Enbergs, and Jan Wielgohs (Frankfurt am Main: Fischer, 1995), 93–94.

[15] For an interpretation of *Rotter,* see Monika Schmitz-Emans, "Thomas Brasch: *Rotter,*" in *Deutsche Gegenwartsdramatik 1,* eds. Lothar Pikulik, Hajo Kurzenberger, and Georg Guntermann (Göttingen: Vandenhoeck & Ruprecht, 1987, 7–40.

[16] Thomas Brasch, *Frauen. Krieg. Lustspiel* (Frankfurt am Main: Suhrkamp, 1989).

[17] Barbara Honigmann, "Wie viele sind wir eigentlich noch? Erinnerung an Thomas Brasch," *Th* 12 (2001): 34–36. Looking back, another friend recalls an incident when Brasch opened the window of the car and shouted "Polizeistaat," as they passed the *Rummelsburger Gefängnis* in Berlin; see Hanns Zischler, "Der ferne Freund," *Th* 12 (2001): 37.

[18] Henning Rischbieter, "Aus dem Kopf auf das Eis. Warum inszenieren Karge/ Langhoff den *Lieben Georg* so?" *Th* 3 (1980): 18. The Swiss premiere took place in August and was also warmly received; see Christoph Müller, "Der *Liebe Georg* am Zürichsee," *Th* 8 (1980): 63.

[19] Andrezj Wirth, "Vom Dialog zum Diskurs — Ein Versuch über nachbrechtsche Theaterkonzeptionen," *Th* 1 (1980): 16–19.

[20] Thomas Brasch, "Es ist alles still (1978)," *Spectaculum* 63 (1990), 256–57, here: 257.

[21] "Horst Brasch," in *Wer war wer in der DDR,* eds. Bernd-Rainer Barth, Christoph Links, Thomas Brasch, Helmut Müller-Enbergs, and Jan Wielgohs (Frankfurt am Main: Fischer, 1995), 93.

[22] Thomas Brasch, "Lieber Georg. Ein Eis-Kunst-Läufer-Drama aus dem Vorkrieg," *Th* 2 (1980): 15–19, here: 15. For autumn 2002, a book is scheduled: Thomas Brasch, *Lieber Georg. Rotter. Lovely Rita* (Frankfurt am Main: Verlag der Autoren, 2002).

[23] Minutes of the VII Schriftstellerkongreß, reprinted in Manfred Jäger, *Kultur und Politik in der DDR* (Cologne: Edition Deutschland Archiv, 1995), 165.

[24] Christa Wolf, *Lesen und Schreiben. Neue Sammlung* (Darmstadt und Neuwied: Luchterhand, 1980), 84.

[25] Volker Braun, *Unvollendete Geschichte* (Frankfurt am Main: Suhrkamp, 1979), 78.

[26] It should not be forgotten that in the second half of the 1970s, many writers such as Wolf Biermann were expelled from the GDR due to their liberal attitudes; see *Biermann und kein Ende — eine Dokumentation zur DDR-Kulturpolitik,* eds. Dietmar Keller and Matthias Kirchner (Berlin: Dietz, 1991).

[27] The play was received favorably: see Ludwig Zerrull, "Drei Schwestern von gestern und heute. Zur Uraufführung von Volker Brauns *Übergangsgesellschaft* samt einer Tschechow-Lesung in Bremen," *Th* 5 (1987): 21.

[28] Heinz Klunker, "Am Ende kein Tapetenwechsel, ein Tapetensturz!" *Th* 4 (1989): 42–46, here: 46. Klunker points out the passionate reaction of the audience during the second GDR staging in Dresden to what he calls a "Frustrations-Endspiel."

[29] In West Germany, the beginning of *glasnost* in GDR theater was received with great enthusiasm; see for example Sibylle Wirsing, "Stadtparktäter, Volksfeinde und Gralsritter. Notizen zur Spielzeit 1988/89 und zur theaterpolitischen Situation in der DDR," *ThJ* (1989), 81–83.

[30] "Die Kunst als Streit der Interessen. Volker Braun über Politik und Ästhetik, im Gespräch mit Peter von Becker und Michael Merschmeier," *ThJ* (1988), 29–33, here: 30. Braun underlines that people do not dare believe that the GDR is going to change.

[31] Through Wilhelm's remark on GDR politics the play is definitely anchored in GDR society: *Die Übergangsgesellschaft (1982), in Volker Braun, Gesammelte Stücke. Zweiter Band* (Frankfurt am Main: Suhrkamp, 1989), 103–32, here: 105.

[32] In contrast to Constable-Henning's interpretation, I read the play as an attempt to portray GDR society, however absurd the form may be. Moreover, Constable-Henning argues that Braun had completely lost touch with his audience, a viewpoint which seems to be a little problematic. See Carol Anne Constable-Henning, *Intertextual Exile. Volker Braun's Dramatic Re-Vision of Society* (Hildesheim, Zurich, New York: Georg Olms, 1997), here: 3, 198, 235.

[33] On the threefold aim of Braun's critical approach see Rolf Jucker, "Von der 'Ziehviehlisation' (1959) zur 'ZUVIELISATION' (1987): Zivilisationskritik im Werk Volker Brauns," in *Volker Braun*, ed. Rolf Jucker (Cardiff: University of Wales Press, 1995), 55–67, here: 56.

[34] For an analysis of the term "Übergangsgesellschaft" with respect to the role of the working class in the GDR see Benno Sarel, *Arbeiter gegen den "Kommunismus." Zur Geschichte des proletarischen Widerstandes in der DDR (1945–58)* (Munich: Schwarze Risse Verlag, 1985), 24.

[35] Hermann Weber, *Geschichte der DDR* (Munich, dtv, 1999), 329.

[36] This was the main argument of the *Zentralkomitee* of the SED that was published on the occasion of the Karl Marx Centenary 1983, *Neues Deutschland*, 1 December 1982.

[37] Marx demanded: "De omnibus dubitandum — everything must be questioned!" a maxim which certainly did not suit the GDR leading élite. See Karl Marx/Friedrich Engels, *Werke* 9 (East Berlin: Dietz, 1960), 17.

[38] Braun repeatedly draws on Beckett's theater of the absurd, as, for example, in his play *Simplex Deutsch* (1972). The second part, entitled "Hans im Glück," is based on *Waiting for Godot*, with the significant difference that Godot himself takes part in the play. See *Simplex Deutsch*, in Volker Braun, *Gesammelte Stücke. Zweiter Band* (Frankfurt am Main: Suhrkamp, 1989), 9–43. Braun mixes quotations from Beckett with slogans taken from the peace movement and the grassroots revolution of the 1960s. The dialogue between the two hippies E and W and Godot indirectly refers to the problems of Socialism. In the end, Godot — who very much resembles a party functionary — takes off his mask and announces that he is not Godot after all, a statement which leaves E and W rather unimpressed.

[39] Sigrid Damm states that many writers became stunted, and that they were politically immature, muted and dependent on regulations. She also realizes that many writers were over-adapted and subjected themselves to political oppression. See Sigrid Damm, "Unruhe," *Sinn und Form* 50.1 (1988), 244–54.

[40] Volker Braun, *Die Übergangsgesellschaft* (1982), in Volker Braun, *Gesammelte Stücke. Zweiter Band* (Frankfurt am Main: Suhrkamp, 1989), 103–32, here: 106.

[41] For example Trotsky, whose name had to be erased from history. This is dealt with in another play by Braun entitled *T.* (written in 1968 as a reaction to the end of the Prague spring), indicating that Trotsky had become a persona non grata in the Communist world because he kept on fighting for radical utopian equality.

[42] "'Wir befinden uns soweit wohl. Wir sind erst einmal am Ende.' Volker Braun im Gespräch mit Rolf Jucker," in *Volker Braun*, ed. Rolf Jucker (Cardiff: U of Cardiff P, 1995), 21–29, here: 24.

[43] Terrance Albrecht, *Rezeption und Zeitlichkeit des Werkes Christoph Heins* (Frankfurt am Main: Peter Lang, 2000), 104–6.

[44] Albrecht, *Rezeption und Zeitlichkeit*, 56–58. See also Max Thomas Mehr, "Eine Zukunft, die keiner haben will," *taz*, 26 Oktober 1989; Hartmut Krug, "Ritter von der traurigen Gestalt," *Th* 7 (1989); Michael Laage, "Der Verlust der Mythen," *W*, 5 March 1990.

[45] Horst Köpke, "Einen Gral gibt es nicht: Bundesdeutsche Erstaufführung von Christoph Heins *Die Ritter der Tafelrunde in Kassel*," *Frankfurter Rundschau*, 5 March 1990.

[46] "'Das Geld ist nicht der Gral.' Aus einer Diskussion mit Christoph Hein und den Schöpfern des Fernsehfilms *Die Ritter der Tafelrunde* nach der Vorauffführung in der Akademie der Künste zu Berlin," in *Chronist ohne Botschaft. Christoph Hein. Ein Arbeitsbuch*, ed. Klaus Hammer (Berlin: Aufbau, 1992), 226.

[47] Bernd Fischer, *Christoph Hein: Drama und Prosa im letzten Jahrzehnt der DDR* (Heidelberg: Carl Winter, 1990), 144; Michael Schneider, *Die abgetriebene Revolution. Von der Staatsfirma in die DM-Kolonie* (Berlin: Elefanten Press, 1990), 85.

[48] Bill Niven, "A play about Socialism? The Reception of Christoph Hein's *Die Ritter der Tafelrunde*," in *"Whose story?" — Continuities in Contemporary German-language Literature*, eds. Arthur Williams, Stuart Parkes, Julian Preece (Frankfurt am Main, Lang, 1998), 197–218, here: 209–10.

[49] Tankred Dorst, *Merlin oder Das wüste Land* (Frankfurt am Main: Suhrkamp, 1981).

[50] Tankred Dorst, "*Antrittsrede*," in Jahrbuch *1983*, ed. Akademie der Wissenschaften und der Literatur Mainz (Wiesbaden: Steiner, 1984), 77–80, here: 79.

[51] "'Das Stück ist wie eine Handschrift,' Interview with Dorst conducted by Klaus Eder and Wolfgang Ruf, "*Die deutsche Bühne*" 56, December 1986, 8–12, here: 8.

[52] Christoph Hein, *Die Ritter der Tafelrunde*, in *Th* 7 (1989): 27–35, here: 28.

[53] However, Neubert points out that the change in the cultural policies of the GDR in the mid-eighties was not due to an incipient liberalization, but originated in an increasing helplessness of the authorities. See Ehrhart Neubert, *Geschichte der Opposition in der DDR 1949–89* (Berlin: Chr. Links, 1997), 533.

[54] Erich Honecker (1912–1994) was the chairman (Generalsekretär) of the leading political party, the SED (Sozialistische Einheitspartei Deutschlands); he also chaired the *Staatsrat*, the collective head of the GDR. He was therefore the head of the GDR regime.

[55] Quoted in Gustav Just, "Er speiste nie an der Tafel der Mächtigen," in *Christoph Hein. Texte, Daten, Bilder*, ed. Lothar Baier (Darmstadt: Luchterhand 1991), 189.

[56] Ingrid Seyfarth, "Palaver am Runden Tisch," *Sonntag*, 15 May 1989.

[57] As Niven argues, this can be seen as an act of bureaucracy, burying socialism in paperwork; Niven, "A play about Socialism?" in "Whose story?" 204.

[58] The sound of the name Mordret could allude to Hans Modrow (1928–), a leading party functionary and chair of the *Ministerrat* in the GDR, who in 1990 formed a "Government for national responsibility" together with opposition groups on 5 February. In 1993, however, he was convicted of election fraud and taken to court.

[59] It has been pointed out that it was especially the younger generation, the twenty-five to forty-year-olds, the generation that had grown up in the GDR, which finally revolted against the system. See Martin Gutzeit, "Widerstand und Opposition in den achtziger Jahren. Von der Formierung der Opposition bis zum Sturz der SED-Diktatur," in *Enquête-Kommission 'Aufarbeitung von Geschichte und Folgen der SED-Diktatur in Deutschland.' Widerstand. Opposition. Revolution 7.1*, ed. Deutscher Bundestag (Frankfurt/M.: Suhrkamp, 1995), 238.

[60] As early as 1985, many informal groups in the GDR provided a forum for the free discussion of issues that were censored by the authorities, for example, peace, women, ecology, the third world, and human rights. The initiative "Frieden und Menschenrechte" especially, which was founded in 1985, marks the beginning of a broader opposition that called for general reform of the GDR. For a detailed description of these developments see Gerda Haufe/Karl Bruckmeier (eds.), *Die Bürgerbewegungen in den ostdeutschen Ländern* (Opladen: Westdeutscher Verlag, 1993), here: 12.

[61] Keie bears traits of Erich Mielke (1907–), who was head of the *Staatssicherheit* (Stasi) and defended his superior position without any scruples. See also: "Erich Mielke. Revolverheld neuen Typus," *SBZ-Archiv* 5 (1954) 10, 149–50, now in Karl-Wilhelm Fricke, *Der Wahrheit verpflichtet. Texte aus fünf Jahrzehnten zur Geschichte der DDR* (Berlin: Christoph Links Verlag, 2000), 456–58.

[62] Erich Mielke wrote: "Wer seine Hand gegen unseren sozialistischen Staat erhebt, bekommt die sozialistische Macht gebührend zu spüren. Gegen Feinde — unter welcher Tarnung sie auch glauben, gegen die sozialistische Ordnung operieren zu können — werden wir auch weiterhin konsequent vorgehen," *Neues Deutschland,* 7 February 1985.

[63] Eckhard Thiele, "Engagiert — wofür? Zu Christoph Heins öffentlichen Erklärungen nach der 'Wende' in der DDR," *text & kritik 111* (1991): 74–80, here: 78.

[64] On Seidel's treatment of everyday life in other plays, see, for example, Anne Kaiser, "Der nicht-alltägliche Alltag: Zur intendierten Wirkung des Dramatischen von Georg Seidel," *Forum Modernes Theater* 12.1 (1997): 54–74. For Seidel's use of the anecdote, see Christian Klein, "Die Anekdote als Moment des Politischen in der Dramaturgie von Georg Seidel," in *Aspekte des politischen Theaters und Dramas von Calderón bis Georg Seidel,* eds. Horst Turk and Jean-Marie Valentin (Berne: Peter Lang, 1996), 421–35.

[65] Detlef Friedrich, "Spröder Dichter, gültiges Werk," *BZ,* 30 September 1995.

[66] Heinz Klunker, "Am Ende kein Tapetenwechsel, ein Tapetensturz!" *Th* 4 (1989): 42–46, here: 43–44.

[67] Georg Seidel, "Jochen Schanotta," *Th* 4 (1987): 48–53, here: 48.

[68] The *Jugendgesetz* of the GDR of the 28 January 1974 reads as follows:

"§ 1 (1) Vorrangige Aufgabe bei der Gestaltung der entwickelten sozialistischen Gesellschaft ist es, alle jungen Menschen zu Staatsbürgern zu erziehen, die den Ideen des Sozialismus treu ergeben sind, als Patrioten und Internationalisten denken und handeln, den Sozialismus stärken und gegen alle Feinde zuverlässig schützen. Die Jugend trägt selbst hohe Verantwortung für ihre Entwicklung zu sozialistischen Persönlichkeiten [. . .]," in Matthias Judt (ed.), *DDR-Geschichte in Dokumenten* (Berlin: Chr. Links, 1998), 218.

[69] In his comments on the play, Seidel underlines the parallels between the two types of relationships. See Georg Seidel, "Die Zeit ist aufgehoben, der Raum ein Labyrinth," *Th* 4 (1987): 46–47, here: 47.

[70] As reports have underlined, the alienation of the workforce in the GDR was a persistent problem; see Martin Kohli, "Die DDR als Arbeitsgesellschaft? Arbeit, Lebenslauf und soziale Differenzierung," in *Sozialgeschichte der DDR,* eds. Hartmut Kaelble, Jürgen Kocka, Harmut Zwahr (Stuttgart: Klett-Cotta, 1994), 31–61, here: 50.

Part II: The 1990s

5: Reflections on German Reunification

FROM THE MID-1980S, Gorbachev's policies of *Glasnost* and *Peres-troika* were a clear sign that the GDR was also ripe for a change.[1] However, Erich Honecker, the first secretary of the GDR since 1971, refused to acknowledge the growing discontent of the East German population, and in fear of losing the hegemony of his party, adopted a tough line against all attempts at reform.[2] On 2 May 1989, Hungary began to tear down the barbed-wire fence on its border with Austria, thus opening a loop-hole for thousands of East Germans to escape. Others took refuge in the West German embassies in Prague and Warsaw, and, after negotiations, were allowed to leave on 4 November 1989. By June, the trickle had become a mass exodus, especially after the brutal clampdown of China on the counter-revolutionary students in Tianenmen Square in Beijing. In July, Honecker stubbornly announced that the Wall would stand for another hundred years.

It is an irony of history that, from 6–8 October 1989, the GDR celebrated its fortieth anniversary with huge military parades and rallies. On the occasion of Gorbachev's visit, people demonstrated for reforms, calling "Gorbi, Gorbi" and were herded together, beaten and imprisoned. It was clear that Honecker chose to ignore Gorbachev's warning that "those who delay are punished by life itself." Despite the disapproval of the leader of the Soviet Union, Honecker clung to his policy of self-congratulation. After the official celebrations were over, demonstrations erupted in several cities, but were brutally suppressed by the police. The turning point was probably the planned mass demonstration of an estimated 70,000 people in Leipzig on 9 October which, despite all fears, took a peaceful course. Although heavy security forces were on guard, they refused to march against the protestors, partly in response to signals from Moscow, but partly because of a joint public appeal by many artists and intellectuals. It is often underlined that the main characteristic of the revolution was its peaceful nature.

Four outstanding events marked the year of the "gentle" revolution in East Germany: Hungary's breaching of the "Iron Curtain" on 2 May (and the mass exodus which followed), the forced resignation of Honecker due to ill-health (and, some argue, because of secret intervention from Moscow), the demonstration of over half a million people in Leipzig and Berlin on 4 November, and the fall of the Wall during the night of 9 November.

Yet, as researchers have pointed out with the benefit of hindsight, the actual fall of the Wall was the result of a misunderstanding.[3] In view of the increase of refugees in Czechoslovakia, Egon Krenz, Honecker's successor, was forced to allow East Germans to emigrate, because the situation at the West German embassy in Prague, which resembled a refugee camp, had become highly embarrassing. While the *Politbüro* was still meeting, its spokesman Günter Schabovski received a note from Egon Krenz saying that private travel to West Germany would soon be possible. In a press conference, Schabovski read out the note, and when asked when the new rule would come into force, he answered with evident confusion "from now on." By 7:00 P.M., one hour later, all press agencies had spread the false news, claiming either that the German-German border was already open or that it would be opened during the night. It was amidst this confusion that thousands of citizens in East and West traveled to various border crossing-points, thus exerting severe pressure on the Eastern frontier police who finally opened the turnpikes. What then followed was often described as the biggest street-party in world history, a situation that forms the background of part 3 of Botho Strauß's (1944–) *Schlußchor* (Final Chorus, 1991). In his farce, Strauß mocks the self-awareness of politicians, who never tired of telling people what a historic moment the end of the GDR was. However, the swiftness of the developments left many people confused, and this is mocked in Herbert Achternbusch's *Auf verlorenem Posten* (Fighting a Losing Battle, 1989). The play picks up on a former soldier of the GDR army who is completely bewildered by the speed with which his environment changes. In contrast, Manfred Karge's (1938–) collage of plays *Mauer-Stücke* (Pieces of the Wall, 1990) presents us with a kaleidoscope of tragi-comical events following the "Wende": for example, an officer who changes his GDR uniform and his identity in the blink of an eye, thus becoming a prime example of the so-called "Wendehals," a person who quickly changes his beliefs according to the political situation.[4]

The party days of October 1989 were inevitably followed by a hang-over. By mid-November 1989, a so-called "Wende in der Wende" had already begun to emerge, as talks of reunification became increasingly dominant. Despite the vehement warnings of East German intellectuals that the GDR would be annexed, the Federal Republic began to take control. Writers Christoph Hein, Volker Braun, Stefan Heym and many others pleaded for the independence and sovereignty of the GDR in order to realize the ideal of a democratic socialism, but this vision of a "third way" was simply ignored. In spring 1990, these intellectuals sobered up to the inevitability of reunification, when subsequently the GDR joined the FRG via article 23 of the West German constitution. In other words; it simply became a part of the West German state. This proved unpopular in the East, and has caused many East Germans to feel marginalized and distraught, a feeling which is expressed in Volker Braun's plays *Iphigenie in Freiheit* (Iphigenia is Free, 1990) and *Böhmen am Meer* (Bohemia on the Sea, 1992). Injustice can be witnessed in many areas, most symbolically by the fact that the joint national anthem is now that of the former West Germany. In view of a collapsing economy — which was partly due to the continuing stream of emigrants — the chancellor of the FRG, Helmut Kohl pressed on with reforms, and on 1 July 1990, the first state treaty was signed, thus completing the monetary union of the two states. On 3 October 1990, reunification was completed; the whole process had been achieved at breathtaking speed. Pitting capitalist West Germans against helpless East Germans, Elfriede Müller's (1956–) play *Goldener Oktober* (Golden October, 1992) paints a dark picture of these months, for it left the former GDR totally devastated.

Waking up to reality, Germans realized that although the Wall was no longer standing, the divide between the two mentalities was continuing to deepen. In mid-April 1990, for example, Theo Sommer, a leading journalist of *Die Zeit,* no longer spoke of the "EinsWerdung" any more, but instead coined the term "Mauer im Kopf." While everyday life hardly changed in the West, East Germans underwent a culture shock.[5] It soon became evident that during the forty years of separation, the two German states had developed two different cultures, symbolized by elements such as the handshake, the attitude towards conflicts, the role of women, and the importance of labor.[6] It proved extremely difficult to find common ground between the two, as each part narcissistically clung to its own values and viewpoints.[7] In brief, the conjugal bliss of the newlyweds quickly turned into a half-destroyed marriage, a problem which also features in Strauß's *Schlußchor.* Moreover, the lack of a frank exchange of opinions rendered the relationship increasingly difficult. A whole set of long-held assumptions and projections collapsed for left-wing intellectuals of the former GDR (and also those of the FRG, as the example of Günter Grass shows).[8]

Well into the winter of 1989, East German intellectuals still hoped that an independent state would be founded on the territory of the former GDR, a state which would this time be true to the real ideals of socialism. Christoph Hein, for example, repeatedly spoke of the historical chance to build a reformed socialist state that would be free from Stalinism.[9] At the demonstration in Leipzig on 4 November, he was still dreaming of a democratic socialist state that would be far better than the caricature of Socialism presented by the GDR, an idea strongly favored by the famous writer Stefan Heym in a speech given on the same day. Heiner Müller, the figurehead of East German theater, adopted a fairly distanced attitude, but he too still hoped for a second German state.[10] As capitalism proved stronger, however, Müller harked back to topics he had covered earlier, and in his collage *Germania 3 Gespenster am Toten Mann* (Germania 3 Ghosts at the Dead Man, 1996), he emphasized the "fascist" nature of reunited Germany.

In view of Kohl's swift actions, a group of intellectuals published a signed petition entitled "Für unser Land" on 28 November 1989, in which they advocated the independence of the GDR in order to prevent both an economic and a moral sell-out.[11] Yet all protests were in vain, and in the end it was Günter Grass (1927–) who cynically stated that the GDR was nothing more than a cheap bargain.[12] This provoked a harsh response from the theater critic Peter von Becker who argued that the GDR was probably the most expensive real estate of all times, hinting at its threadbare economy and its large-scale environmental problems.[13] The economic aspect of reunification and the "colonization" of the East is criticized harshly in Rolf Hochhuth's *Wessis in Weimar* (1993). Hochhuth regarded it as his duty to protest against the "looting" of the former GDR, and presented the downside of the free-market economy.

As many researchers have pointed out, the East-West divide has only deepened with the passing of time. East Germans were developing a feeling of "Ostalgie" (yearning for the East),[14] glorifying former times and playing down the terrors of dictatorship. This is mocked in Christoph Hein's *In Acht und Bann* (Under the Ban, 1999), where a handful of old hardliners are still working on a Socialist constitution, although they are inmates of a mental asylum. The "Ostalgie" was particularly evident among women, who feel deprived of their freedom and their social status. While West Germans widely perceived "Ossis" as lazy moaners unable to solve their own problems, people in the East felt patronized and demoralized by the insensitive behavior of the money-grabbing "Wessis."[15] In *Randow* (1994), Christoph Hein paints a gloomy picture of a Germany in which old communists and neo-Nazis dominate everyday life. In his award-winning tragedy, *Gäste* (Guests, 1999), Oliver Bukowski depicts the doomed efforts of young East Germans to accommodate to the free market at all costs.

In conclusion, it can be said that post-reunification drama centers on problems and traumas that are at the core of the new Germany, namely the clash of two identities, two pasts, two states, two political systems and, finally, two economies. While the Kohl government attempted to fend off criticism of the hastily knitted together "Staatsvertrag," the debate shifted to the aesthetic sphere, as reunification did not allow for the survival of any GDR values or traditions.

The impact of unification on East and West Germans is clearly radically different, and it is thus hardly surprising that most of the "Wende"-plays come from the former GDR, for they reflect the identity crises of Easterners in the face of an overbearing economy. For them the theater is — in accordance with the tradition of the enlightenment — still the fourth power within the state, and at a time when the two states were hastily being patched together, and one was practically destroyed, it became a means of opposition. As any criticism of the political climate was energetically suppressed by Kohl, intellectuals resorted to the stage to make themselves heard. As so often before in German history, the stage became a courtroom in which the political system was to be examined and judged.

Ridiculous Revolutionaries: Herbert Achterbusch's *Auf verlorenem Posten. Eine Revolutionsfarce* (1989)

In 1981, Achternbusch announced in his typically picaresque manner that he would stop writing plays as his royalties would suffice to pay for his retirement.[16] However, he has still not stopped writing plays, and *Auf verlorenem Posten* is another example of Achternbusch's lucid yet deconstructive approach to history. As an immediate reaction to the "Wende" in 1989, especially with respect to the revolution in Romania, Achternbusch wrote his play in three days over Christmas 1989, and also directed the premiere at the *Münchner Kammerspiele* in May 1990. In this farcical approach to the gentle revolution of 1989, Achternbusch presents three nameless East Germans: a couple and the wife's lover on their voyage to Italy, in search of happiness. It contains the most important characteristics of the farce to achieve comical effects: the theme of infidelity and jealousy, the mockery of authorities, and the contrast between high and low style.[17] The play's action, which technically consists of only one scene, follows the principle of association. Consequently, the play breaks away from the traditional constraints of character, psychological motivation, and literary style; it is a montage of a ruined marriage, pseudo-philosophical talk about politics, news reports about the uprising in Romania, the massacre of

Temesvar, and the nativity.[18] In a deliberately contrived construction of a happy ending, the divorced general finally falls in love with a woman called "Das Glück," after a woman who seems to have stepped out of the painting *La Primavera* by Sandro Botticelli.

Despite its disrupted plot, *Auf verlorenem Posten* focuses mainly on the man who claims to have been a general in the artillery. His appearance is rather ridiculous, as he wears Italian designer shoes and drags a toilet roll behind him. He seems rather confused and sick, and Achternbusch presents him as a ridiculous former GDR citizen who has no idea of what is going on. Because of the general's lack of intellectual understanding of the situation and his over-sensitive reaction to sudden political change, he becomes the perfectly stereotypical "Ossi." His discontent with the swift political changes manifests itself through diarrhea and other intestinal problems, so that he constantly farts — a typical device of a farcical play. After forty years of the GDR, he has stomach problems, because subordination has consumed him. Although he is now free, he cannot get used to it, and finds freedom rather frightening — which is a typical reaction of East Germans following 1989. Alluding to the famous episode in Günter Grass's novel *Die Blechtrommel* (*The Tin Drum*, 1959), where a former Nazi chokes on a party sticker that he tries to swallow in fear of the allied troops, Achternbusch's general complains that he cannot seem to put the correct "Akzent" on the things he encounters, because old accents whirl through his body until they resemble a swastika. It is telling that he is unable to rid himself of the party symbols within him, a metaphor for the common belief that the GDR never really enlightened its populace on the Nazi past.[19] His loss of identity leads him to become a "Wendehals," an opportunist. The man sports the clichés that West Germans associated with former citizens of the GDR shortly after the "Wende"; a lack of self-confidence and a lack of political awareness, both of which made Easterners feel useless and overpowered.

In his typically associative manner, Achternbusch adds yet another feature of the "Wende," namely the stream of curious East Germans who visited the West. Here, an East German *Trabant,* the most popular car in the GDR, appears onstage, filled with sixteen East Germans — an open mockery of the fact that after the opening of the border, thousands of people jumped into their cars to see the west. Before they can get out of the car, however, they are pelted with bananas, which they obediently start to eat. This little pantomime is a sarcastic allegory of German-German perception: while the "Wessis" lure the "Ossis" westwards with bananas, the symbol of capitalism, the "Ossis" are characterized as docile idiots who — in the early days — did not object to such insulting treat-

ment.[20] This becomes obvious when an infatuated West German professor comes onstage:

WESTLER　　Nu, schenkt dir keiner eine Banane — kleiner Ossi? Ja,
　　　　　　die Banane ist ein Universum — für euch. Für mich?
　　　　　　Affenfutter. [. . .] Bananen habe ich keine, und mit Geld
　　　　　　kannst du nicht umgehen. Also gebe ich dir einen guten
　　　　　　Rat: Laß das mit den Bananen.[21]

Behaving as impertinently as is expected of him, the Westler insinuates
that the fall of the Wall was caused by the Easterners' longing for bananas, and clearly considers the East Germans to be completely useless
when it comes to money.

The typical mixture of sincerity and nonsense found in Achternbusch's writing also comes to the fore when a messenger reads out the
latest telegram about the revolution in Romania, where Dracula's regime
(namely that of Ceausescu) is being overthrown. The breathless delivery
is once again mixed with farcical ingredients, such as the messenger's
apologies for all the untrue news that he had hitherto expected people
to read. The list of agencies at the end of the telegram is also ironic,
because if read in one go, "mehr/ap/mh/po" translates as "more at the
backside": another clear reference to the problem the audience is already
well acquainted with.

In comparison to other plays about the "Wende," Achternbusch's
farce stands out not only as the earliest approach to the "Velvet Revolution," but also because of its farcical use of "Ossi-Wessi" stereotypes.
Against the backdrop of a ruined marriage — an image commonly used
at the time to depict the difficulties following reunification — the former
East German is portrayed as the ultimate cliché of the allegedly ill-
educated and stupid "Ossi." In accordance with some historians' analyses
of the "Wende," Achternbusch thus insinuates that the collapse of the
GDR was not the result of demonstrations and protest marches held
during 1988 and 1989, but came about because of the bankruptcy of the
GDR and the peoples' longing for capitalism(/consumerism).[22] According to *Auf verlorenem Posten,* the end of the socialist state came about
too rapidly for contemporaries to fully comprehend it — a view which is
also to be found at the core of Botho Strauß's *Schlußchor.*

Achternbusch's comedic stance also differs from the majority of post-
1989 plays, particularly those from the East, because most playwrights
took the negative effects of 1989 seriously. In a different vein, *Auf verlorenem Posten* uses the nativity as a backdrop against which to combine
the cruelty of revolution with biographical problems, i.e. the general's

failed marriage. By depicting the "Wende" as a handful of random events, it plays down the historical importance of 1989. In contrast to politicians who constantly underlined that every moment during that year was "historical," *Auf verlorenem Posten* presents history through the distorting lens of a gross farce.

Stereotypical Views of East and West: Manfred Karge's *Mauer-Stücke* (1989/90)

Karge wrote his *Mauer-Stücke,* a collage of short farcical scenes, in 1989 and 1990; a preliminary version premiered at the *Akademietheater* in Vienna in September 1989 and the play ran at the *Royal Court Theatre* in London in 1990. Through a series of short farcical mini-dramas, the play addresses economic and psychological problems following the "Wende" in a rather stereotypical manner, although Karge's use of irony saves the play from becoming pretentious. In the typical manner of a farce, there are no psychologically motivated characters, and a kaleidoscope of issues replaces the plot. These issues include a squabble in the former Ministry of Security, the "looting" of the GDR, a comical inversion of the Nibelung myth; and a handful of astronauts seeking refuge from a world colonized by Germans.

Besides various former members of the Stasi, who, typical of the farcical style, are both dead and alive; the cast comprises Mary and Joseph; a policeman and his dog; Kriemhild, Siegfried, Hagen, Volker, Gunther and Brunhilde; a radical East German feminist; and a variety of other people undeserving of either a name or a significant role in the collage. Karge thus employs characters merely as stereotypical examples of the Ossi-Wessi division, who act according to popular expectation. *Mauer-Stücke* paints a rather grim picture of the mental disorder of the Germans post 1989, albeit in a superficially ironic manner. In the last scene, "Schwanendreher," the remaining few people have gathered in a space station, the only place that has not yet been invaded by the Germans. Unfortunately, the space shuttle is over-crowded and, foreseeably, crashes into the sea, to the music of Hindemith. Here, Karge expands the East German fear of being colonized into an overblown satirical view of the Federal Republic, thus dismissing the entire debate as plain nonsense.

In the farcical scene entitled "Mauerhund," which is set on the former German-German border shortly after the Wall came down, a former GDR "Grenzpolizist" and his watchdog quarrel about their future duties. While the dog insists on guarding the border, the man quickly adapts to the new circumstances. He slips through a hole in the Wall, only to return dressed in the uniform of the West German police. He thus represents the ultimate "Wendehals," as he exhibits a mixture of cloying self-pity, deep-seated prejudice, and radical egoism.[23] His new hat provides for a comic interlude that alludes to the Geßler episode of Friedrich Schiller's *Wilhelm Tell* (1805). In this particular scene, the Fronvogt Gessler's hat is placed on a stick, and he demands that the common Swiss people greet and respect it as if it were the Fronvogt himself. Against this backdrop, Karge draws on parallels between the West German "rulers," who are equated with the Fronvogt, and the oppressed East Germans. In contrast to *Wilhelm Tell*, however, the "oppressed" Easterners, the underdogs in Karge's play, fail to revolt successfully against the yoke of reunification:

DER HUND	Sag an, Soldat, was hast du auf dem Kopf?
DER SOLDAT	Ich?
DER HUND	Wer denn sonst? Das ist ja ein Hut Und äußerst verdächtig und gar nicht gut
DER SOLDAT	Das ist nie ein Hut. Das ist eine Mütze Die ich so gut Wie schon immer besitze.
DER HUND	Ich warn dich, Soldat, laß diesen Scheiß. Herunter den Hut, oder ich beiß.
DER SOLDAT	Sind Sie von Sinnen, Gefreiter Fritz. Ich sag, Gehorsamsverweigerer sitz.
DER HUND *pariert.*	
DER SOLDAT	Hut oder Nichthut, das ist die Frage. Was ists, was ich auf dem Kopfe trage?[24]

Finally the dog gives in and sees nothing wrong with the newly acquired hat, but the montage of quotations from Schiller and Shakespeare creates more than simple comedy. The fact that Karge imitates the meter of Schiller's play, yet mocks its content, suggests that Karge does not take his characters seriously. He renders ridiculous the complaints of East Germans who claimed that they had been placed under the West German yoke. This is underlined by the farcical elements of the scene, such as the speaking dog, who mocks the self-deploring attitude of the East Germans who perceive themselves as the losers in reunification. It is also ludicrous that a dog should try to educate his owner on how to maintain his integrity. The soldier, however, does not agree with the dog's idea of freedom. He defends his "Wendehals" attitude aggressively, forcing the dog to sit and be silent. In short; Schiller's ideals of freedom of thought and freedom of speech are traded in for something quite different,- subservience, which is also alluded to by the "Mütze" of the East German Michel. In spite of the subconscious tensions, however, the tone remains light and farcical, underlining the comic view of the "Wende." The oscillation between humor and seriousness in this scene is predominantly caused by a clash between a strange post-reunification environment and daily GDR routines into which the man is likely to lapse at any moment. Yet humor does more than simply amuse the audience, for its ironic nature serves several purposes, not the least of which is to save the play from collapsing under the weight of self-pity and self-concern. Ironic humor provides distance, both for the audience, from the characters, and for the characters, from their obsessive concerns.

It is striking how many political cartoons of the time feature the notion of reunification as a marriage of the overbearing, masculine West Germany with the vulnerable, feminine East Germany, an image which is mocked in a scene called "Ostfotze."[25] In a similar manner, Karge playfully uses the Nibelung myth, rereading the model story of the eternal quarrel among the Germans as a parody on the so-called occupation and colonization of the GDR. The play begins with the takeover by the West Germans, who complain about the appalling state of the roads. The reason for their visit of threadbare East Germany is, hardly surprisingly, Gunther's courting of Brunhilde, here an East German waitress. Like his forerunner, the modern Gunther is incapable of satisfying his lover's sexual appetite, and asks Sigi, the eastern "Held der Arbeit," who happens to come along, for assistance. Sigi is easily persuaded to help out, and it is ironic that, metaphorically speaking, the East helps to rape itself. The dull worker is first exploited, then later stabbed while he helps himself to a can of coke, and finally accused of being a Stalinist. Once Siegfried has been killed, the plot develops according to the model story: the women argue and Kriemhild, Siegfried's wife, swears to take revenge. Suddenly, she changes her mind and decides to stay. She travels east and refuses to participate in any further bloodshed. Thus, Karge's Kriemhild becomes the first Wessi to drop out of the money-grabbing capitalist society, a move which can be regarded as a parodistic inversion of the real migration inside Germany after 1989, which typically went west.

The farcical tone of the play presents the "Wende" and its ensuing problems in East and West Germany as a laughable issue that has been blown out of proportion. By means of stereotypes and clichés, Karge mocks the rift that is opening between the East and the West, to show that the Germans take the negative side of reunification a little too seriously. Consequently, the historical background merely provides the raw data, which is presented with mock irony, for example when the "colonizing" of the former GDR is compared to the Nibelung myth. Instead of representing historical events truthfully — like Rolf Hochhuth, for example — Karge introduces a more imaginative approach, combining drama with elements from myths, epics, and science-fiction in order to pick up on the German tendency to worry unnecessarily.

Freedom and Free-Falling:
Volker Braun's *Iphigenie in Freiheit* (1990)

Braun's *Iphigenie in Freiheit,* written between 1987 and 1990, demonstrates the transition from Braun's earlier socialist utopias to his preoccupation with the psychological impact of reunification.[26] The play begins where Goethe's drama ends, namely when Thoas sets Iphigenie free,[27] but with a significant difference. Whereas Goethe celebrated the victory of humanism over revenge and bloodshed, Braun's play is dominated by violence and aggression, indicating the end rather the birth of a humanitarian era. While Goethe's Iphigenie escapes from institutional violence, she now becomes a victim of the new political system.

The four scenes are, technically speaking, a monologue, as none of the voices are identified.[28] In scene 1, "Spiegelzelt," several voices comment on the decline of a state, probably the GDR, and their fear of things to come; in scene 2, "Iphigenie in Freiheit," Iphigenie is set free, yet immediately becomes the victim of her capitalist brothers; scene 3, "Geländespiel," alludes to the scandal concerning the site of the former concentration camp Ravensbrück, on which a supermarket was built; and scene 4, "Antikensaal," describes a world ruined by the evils of modernization.

As *Iphigenie in Freiheit* is a radical postmodern text, explicit stage directions are scarce, and the setting and the characters can only be deduced from the spoken text itself. As the play is not dialogically structured, there is no real communication, and the quotations from plays by Büchner, Müller, Lessing and Goethe add to the bewilderment of the reader.[29] Encapsulated in Iphigenie's, or perhaps Braun's, brain,[30] the citations no longer serve the purpose of enlightening or teaching the audience, and instead, they become nothing more than the intellectual waste of civilization. Language fragments are torn from their original context and pieced together in order to underline the insignificance of speech. Instead of maintaining a single perspective throughout, Braun shifts his ground so that the audience can never be sure whose thoughts are being reproduced onstage. As a result, the opinions of one character are likely to flow and merge with those of another. Although different speakers, like Iphigenie, Orest, and Pylades, can be identified in scene 2, the play rather resembles a couple of voices echoing in somebody's head. Against the backdrop of the "Wende," the monologue expresses the loss of identity of East Germans, and is a self-encounter in front of the mirror, as the afterword suggests.

The West German premiere at the *Kammerspiel* in Frankfurt in 1992 was not well received, but the East German staging in Cottbus later that year was a success, because people could identify with Iphigenie's agony.[31] In the East, the play hit a raw nerve, namely the emotional crisis of the East German individual in the New Germany. Following reunification, people bitterly asked themselves whether they had lived forty years in vain. The official collective identity, the GDR state, was in tatters, and all values and ideals were being questioned from a new perspective. This led to serious disorientation among Easterners, because their individual and collective identities were no longer balanced.[32] It is, indeed, remarkable that in April 1990, 51 percent of former East Germans felt a strong GDR identity;[33] in 1991, the number was still 14 to 16 percent, while 16 percent reported a total loss of identity.[34] In general, the East was particularly apprehensive of the free-market economy; therefore it is not surprising that, in 1991, 65 percent rejected what they labeled an "Ellenbogengesellschaft," a Darwinian society, in which everybody is solely concerned with making a profit.[35]

Iphigenie in Freiheit presents an individual who finds herself in a state of confusion. Overwhelmed by the overpowering West German "brothers" who come to make a quick profit, Iphigenie adopts the role of the victim. She can thus be regarded as a typical example of the East German who experienced reunification as culture shock.[36] After being isolated from the world for forty years, confined, supervised, watched by the police, and told how to behave, Iphigenie does not know how to react to her newly gained freedom:

> Abgesessen
> Hab ich meine Zeit in meinem Lande.
> Wie ich, Genosse. In der Sitzung. LAUT
> BESCHLUSS. Sprich dich ruhig aus.
> Am Trog der Treue. Am Strick des Staats.[37]

As the names of the characters are missing, the lines cannot be allocated to any one character, and interspersed comments and quotations in capitals further disrupt the dialogue. Indeed, the lines take on the shape of an inner monologue by Iphigenie. On the one hand, she accuses herself of having adapted to the police state, yet on the other hand the new developments frighten her. Suddenly free, she feels a bewildering mix of emotions, as her past has become worthless and the future insecure. Similarly, many inhabitants of the *Neue Bundesländer* felt as if they were living in a foreign state, although technically they had not moved.[38] In less than a year a new constitution, a new legal system, a new economy, and a new currency had been introduced. In short: East Germans woke up to a new reality in their own country.[39] As a result, they developed the so-called "Ostalgie," and yearned the allegedly better times of the GDR. Iphigenie finds herself in a similar state of mind, although she is painfully aware that life under a dictatorship has left her with emotional and physical bruises.[40]

With the arrival of her brother she becomes aware that the old order will collapse. Thoas, symbolic of the leadership of the Eastern bloc, is briskly asked to open the iron curtain, and thus the revolution begins. Like the West Germans who arrived to rebuild the economy and administration of the former GDR, Orest and Pylades do not behave tactfully. Having looked carefully at Iphigenie's situation, wondering whether she had a decent life, they contemptuously decide that she will have to learn the capitalist lesson the hard way. Like the insensitive West Germans on their arrival in the East, the money-grabbing men immediately begin to humiliate her, regarding her as an object, a beautiful prize, a whore. As profiteers usurp her home country, Iphigenie associates Orest and Pylades with Hitler's slogan "Heim ins Reich" and for her, freedom means that humanity is thrown overboard.

As scenes 3 and 4 show, colonization brings with it disastrous results, as it destroys history, memory, humanity, and the environment. As soon as the Soviet Union has withdrawn, capitalism, once again associated with Nazi terror, takes control. The scene cuts to Ravensbrück, the site of the former concentration camp, where Antigone is still trying to bury her brother.[41] Today, however, she pushes him through the concentration camp in a shopping-trolley, a symbol which once more underlines the link between capitalism and National Socialism. In view of the powerful GDR doctrine that saw West Germany as merely the successor of the Third Reich, it is interesting that Braun, or one of his various characters, is still influenced by this doctrine. In the new Germany, however, it is not Kreon who prevents Antigone from burying Polynices, but the exceedingly high land prices, which shot up after reunification. This suggests that after the "Wende" even the former concentration camps were just seen as land that could be exploited. In the last scene, the holy grove (of Diana) becomes a runway, another symbol for the destructive power of capitalism. Confused by advertisements and capitalist propaganda, the inhabitants of a formerly prosperous country dig their own graves by working for the capitalist industry. In this nightmarish scenario, cattle are slaughtered, people are sacrificed, and the environment poisoned. A man overwhelmed by his sexual desire for the beauty of money, for the whore called capitalism, is cruelly rejected by the whore. Out of total frustration, he castrates himself with a shovel, showing that capitalism destroys both love and fertility.

The voice that speaks to us throughout the four scenes is that of both the West and the East Germans, and is thus polyphonic: angry and impertinent in the same breath, defensive and aggressive in turns, and necessarily inconsistent. By emphasizing the perspective of the stunned Iphigenie, Braun acknowledges that the task of coming to terms with the new situation will be difficult, if not impossible. If the past was not good, the future will be even worse. At a time of change, language seems inappropriate to her, so she is thrown back on her own thoughts. The single theme that binds all four scenes together is the depiction of Iphigenie, symbolic of the East Germans, the victims of reunification. Their revolt against the GDR was in vain, as they find themselves silenced and humiliated once again. Alongside this view of history, there is another more pessimistic lesson: the play depicts a hostile capitalist world of sheer destruction, pollution, and violence in which any hope for humanity lies buried beneath a layer of concrete.

Mythmaking, Greek Goddesses and Showbiz: Botho Strauß's *Schlußchor* (1991)

Strauß's play *Schlußchor* (1991), written in 1990, premiered at the *Münchner Kammerspiele* in February 1991.[42] It is an attempt to address the moral, social, and psychological issues of reunification, its farcical style akin to earlier plays such as *Kaldewey Farce* (1981).[43] Far from being an epic, narrative account of the events of 1989, *Schlußchor* is, therefore, a highly speculative and ambiguous play. In true farcical style, *Schlußchor* contains neither real characters nor a consistent plot or setting. Although the acts and scenes are not linked by a linear or logical development, the continuous references to the year 1989 bind them together.

The central theme is the making of politics into myths, and the problematic interplay of watching and being watched.[44] Strauß delivers his views on the nature of politics as spectacle through the staging of events at three different places: a photo session, a gala dinner, and a restaurant. Central to all three is the misunderstanding and distortion of historical facts. In part 1, historical events freeze into photographs; in part 2, the troublesome liaison between Lorenz and Delia mirrors the tensions of East and West Germans; and in part 3, the making of history is reflected by the symbolic figure Anita, who tries to falsify historical evidence.

As journalists had reported at the time, the opening of the German-German border on 9 November resembled a massive funfair. Even during the weeks that followed, it was a "Volksfest mit Wildfremden, Umarmungen, fassungsloses Gestammel. Das am häufigsten gebrauchte Wort "Wahnsinn." Und über allem der zähe Duft öligen Zweitaktgemisches und das Rrrörrörrrottöttött der Plastewagen."[45] Photos were taken, and champagne was consumed in large quantities.

In the first part of his play, Botho Strauß explicitly refers to the first days after the fall of the Wall as a "spectacle," during which everything was "great" and "historic." This moment in history had, therefore, to be documented on Polaroid.[46] This is exactly the situation we encounter in part 1, when we see a group of anonymous men and women posing for a group photograph. As in other texts, Strauß adopts a critical view towards photography, insisting that the presence of the photographer provokes a complacent attitude. Because of the photographer's presence, the group is mainly concerned with its appearance. According to them, life makes sense only when you are watched, and as a result, it does not matter who you are; the only thing that counts is one's exterior image.

Everybody stares straight ahead towards the eye of the camera, while a strange conversation takes place concerning their positioning. As they are intent on attaining the perfect image, they are not allowed to turn their heads to look at one another. In order to find out what the person standing beside them is like, they will later have to consult the photograph. Ironically, the group fails to pay attention at the critical moment, despite the fact that the whole point of their gathering was to prove that they were present at the crucial moment, that is, the fall of the Wall. What is more important to them than the act of taking the picture is the fact that they will be able to show it to others afterwards. They display a keen awareness of their own "historical importance," a phrase used so often by the chancellor of the FRG, Helmut Kohl, that the "historical importance" of 1989 became a running joke at the time. In the first few lines of the play, Strauß subtly picks up on this complacency:

M 8 *brüllt* Deutschland!

Stille. Der FOTOGRAF *unterbricht seine Arbeit.*

M 5   Sie wissen, wie das gemeint ist?

FOTOGRAF Nein?

M 5   Sie wissen nicht, was das zu bedeuten hat?

FOTOGRAF   Ich wüßte nicht . . .

M 5   Ach? Das wundert mich nun wieder.

FOTOGRAF   Tja. Damit hatte ich nicht gerechnet.

M 5   Damit hatte *niemand* von uns gerechnet.

F 1   Mit anderen Worten: Sie haben gar nicht abgedrückt?

M 9   Und gerade in *der* Sekunde hätte man sich später gern
             gesehen! (*S,* 15)

Strauß analyzes the German psyche through a highly symbolic tableau, emphasizing the loss of individuality caused by the photographer, who is aiming to shoot the ideal photo, on which the individual faces merge into one. The anonymous "Chor," therefore, expresses a skeptical attitude towards the individual,[47] and in *Paare, Passanten,* Strauß writes:

> Die Identität, nach der man sucht, existiert nicht. Abgesehen von einigen äußerlichen, behördlichen Erkennungsmerkmalen gibt es nichts, was für die Existenz eines zusammengefaßten Einzelnen spräche.[48]

According to Strauß, the presentation of a historical moment through photography wipes out its distinctive features and is therefore bound to lead to biased interpretations. Against the funfair atmosphere of 1989, the play depicts, or rather dissects, the superficial representation of history in the media. Both television and newspapers were keen to celebrate the miraculously peaceful events of reunification. Strauß indirectly refers to the slogan, the "Fernsehrevolution," a term coined after the collapse of the GDR. With hindsight, a number of researchers have pointed out that the role of the media was overrated, a fact which subsequently led to misleading conclusions. First, the excessive echo in the media created the impression that the Wall came down mainly because of the media coverage of the events. Second, it made the spectators believe that they had been involved as eye-witnesses and were thus in a position to understand the events fully. The third and perhaps most important point is that the live broadcasts presented the result of political change as if it were the political change itself. Complex political developments were thus tailored to suit the requirements of television.[49]

Strauß is equally apprehensive of the way in which we shape history, but presents the events from an ironic perspective. In *Schlußchor,* the photographer fails to capture reunification as a fixed moment in German history, indicated by the shout "Deutschland." Viewed through the lens, this historic moment is given an artificial frame, which eventually turns it into a media myth. The group photograph thus becomes a substitute for memory and history.[50]

In the second part, "Lorenz vor dem Spiegel," Strauss portrays an unsuccessful relationship between the architect Lorenz and his client Delia. As the scene opens, we see Lorenz walking through a dark, empty house, searching for the light switch. In doing so, he opens all the doors until he accidentally enters the bathroom where Delia, naked, is drying herself with a towel.

Embarrassed and confused, Lorenz walks out and starts putting up his plans for Delia's new house on the wall of the room next door. Although seemingly marginal, this incident is highly symbolic and of great importance for the whole play, since in this scene Strauß adapts the story of the Greek Olympic goddess Artemis, whose epithet was also Delia, meaning "born on Delos." She was known as the goddess of hunting, who protected the weak, and had dedicated her life to virginity. As a consequence, she killed any mortal who dared to approach her in an indecent manner, Actaeon being one of them. After he had seen her bathing, she transformed him into a stag and had him torn to pieces by her dogs. There are echoes of the myth in *Schlußchor*, although the Greek myth is not only merged with the Narcissus myth, but also modernized.

The intended parallel to Actaeon is compounded with mythical imagery, identifying the naked Delia with the Greek goddess. Yet the mythic theme is slightly modified, because, realizing that he will never win her love again, Lorenz shoots himself in front of a mirror during a banquet. The glimpse he caught of her, "das Versehen," turns into a pessimistic self-consciousness, induced by his hour-long staring into the mirror.[51] Here, Strauß blends two levels of meaning: first, unrequited love and second, Lorenz's suicide as a narcissistic reaction to being rejected.

Against the backdrop of the "Wende," Delia becomes a symbol for the East Germans' proud and hostile reaction that followed the initial euphoria. Like the GDR, Delia is obviously flabbergasted by the sudden opening of the door: the fall of the Wall. It is as unexpected as the call for a change, the call for "Deutschland" in part 1. Written in 1990, *Schlußchor* reflects the difficulties experienced by the peoples of the two states in becoming one again. Like Delia, who refuses both Lorenz's love and physical union, the "Neue Bundesländer" strongly opposed the swiftness and boldness of the reunification process, which was seen as ignoring the feelings of East Germans. This is evident in Delia's hostile attitude, which becomes apparent while they are discussing her prospective new home. The planner Lorenz, who intends to build Delia's new home, can be interpreted as a symbol for the so-called "Architekten der Wiedervereinigung": politicians such as the chancellor, Helmut Kohl, who were keen to complete the German Treaty, the "Staatsvertrag" as soon as possible. In this context, Delia can be seen as a symbol for the East Germans, who felt overpowered and duped by capitalist efficiency. She thus accuses him of having already seen everything by mistake. Interestingly, Delia asks for a glass shelter to protect her from the weather, a request which alludes to the fears and sorrows of East Germans, who felt that, within the free market of the FRG, a social safety net did not exist. It is also symbolic that the shelter should be glass, as it allows one to see both in and out, which means that there is no privacy. His answer echoes the copious complaints of West Germans concerning the costs of reunification. Quite symbolically, Delia asks for protection, whereas Lorenz is concerned with the construction of the so-called new German house.[52]

In the second scene of part 2, the audience sees the foyer of a hall in which a gala dinner is taking place. However, while the party continues inside, our attention is focused on a gathering of people in the foyer whose lives have more or less been a series of failures. Lorenz is desperately trying to contact Delia, who has already got a new partner, but his attempts prove to be fruitless. Around him the partying continues, but he is too concerned with himself to notice. Devastated by her rejection, Lorenz racks his brains as to whether he should have used more appropriate language when talking to her:

> [. . .] Ah, das langsame Gift der Scham zerstört mir meine Muttersprache. Bei jedem Wort, das ich an Delia richte, blinkt im Geist ein Rotlicht auf: Vorsicht, Ausdrucksschwäche! Verfehlter Ton! [. . .] Wäre ich, wie es meiner innersten Verfassung entspricht, ein Zuhausegebliebener, dann sähen sie mich jetzt meinem eigenen Schatten gleich an den Zimmerwänden entlangstreichen und mit spitzer Kohle darauf einen Schlußstrich nach dem anderen ziehen. (*S,* 46)

The passage is littered with references to the failed communication between East and West. Lorenz, for example, wonders whether he should have stayed at home instead of visiting Delia, because this would have been in accordance with his "Verfassung." It is interesting that "Verfassung" is an ambivalent term, meaning either frame of mind or constitution. With hindsight, the term can be seen to refer to the self-critical attitude of many West German intellectuals, who asked whether the GDR should not have been left alone. Moreover, Lorenz talks of drawing the final line with "spitzer Kohle," an allusion to the chancellor, Helmut Kohl, who was only too keen to see an end to the GDR constitution. The liaison between Delia and Lorenz thus veils a political layer of meaning, laden with references to reunification.

The festive atmosphere resembles the events of the opening of the German-German border, an event which ironically is casually indicated by the cryptic exclamation "Deutschland." It is significant, however, that the scene is restricted to the foyer, where the guests pull off their social masks and reveal their real selves in front of a large mirror. As guests keep coming and going, the foyer becomes a thoroughfare, and literally turns into a place of passage. As Thomas Oberender points out, the characters literally remain on the threshold; they are incapable of crossing the border into a new world.[53] Instead of showing the public side of 1989, Strauß concentrates on the private aspects of life.

In the final part, entitled "Von nun an," Strauß unfolds a kaleido-scope of scenes. In a bar, strangers meet and start talking. This part is strongly reminiscent of Arthur Schnitzler's (1862–1931) Der grüne Kakadu (The Green Cockatoo, 1899), a play set in a bar during the French Revolution. Schnitzler has a group of actors perform a revolu-tionary play, ignorant of the events unfolding outside. In a similar way, reunification takes place outside the bar, and is only reluctantly acknowl-edged by the people chatting in the "Vogelkäfig-Bistro," as Anita calls it. However, the meeting of East and West is characterized by cautious-ness; the way in which people in the bar greet one another is therefore rather reserved. As in part 2, the events are announced by the "Rufer," but the people do not seem too impressed; Strauß is mocking the Ger-mans' self-awareness regarding this historic event. Again, he is referring to the "spectacle" aspect of the "Wende" and the ridiculously self-conscious attitude of those who witnessed the fall of the Wall.

It gradually transpires that Anita, the central character of this part, has depicted her father as a glorious member of the Resistance. Yet it emerges that she has falsified evidence or at least left out events that she considered inappropriate for public attention. As Patrick dryly remarks, her father's subversiveness mainly consisted of seducing the wives of high-ranking SS officers. What is more, Patrick reminds Anita that her father died because his amorous adventures were discovered. Realizing that her attempt to present a sanitized version of history has failed, Anita attacks him, yet he insists on the truth.

According to Jürgen Schröder, both Anita and Patrick exemplify a distorted view of history: Whereas Anita stands for the extremely conser-vative view, Patrick is the representative of an exaggeratedly modernist approach.[54] As he does in his text "Anschwellender Bocksgesang" (1993), Strauß abandons the negative influence of the "Vergangenheitsbewältigung" (coming to terms with the past) of postwar intellectuals, as he wants to get rid of the "ugly enlightenment" of his critical age.[55] It is therefore telling that Patrick does not pursue this matter, but leaves Anita with some condescending words, letting her know that nobody is any longer interested in her pseudo-research.

Immediately afterwards, the setting changes to a zoo, where we see Anita standing in front of a bird cage, in the corner of which an eagle hovers. In order to set the bird free, Anita cuts a huge hole in the wire netting and encourages the bird to kill her. As Steffen Damm notes, Strauß inverts the mythical story of part 2 by alluding to another myth, that of Leda and the swan. Leda's beauty was so overwhelming that Jupiter turned into a swan in order to approach her and win her love.[56] Here, this myth is blended with Ovid's account of the female Titan Asterie who was approached by Jupiter disguised as an eagle. According to Damm, the two stories are merged into one. As a symbol of strength, wit and rebirth, the eagle often appears as a heraldic bird.

Yet the eagle in *Schlußchor* does not appear to live up to Anita's expectations, and remains immobile and silent until she loses her temper and calls it a chimera and a wimpy heraldic animal. She accuses it of being an illusion; thus symbolically the German *Doppeladler* is portrayed as hardly more than a delusion, an image for a degenerate, exhausted and decayed republic.[57] As Hensel points out in his review of a performance in Berlin, the eagle becomes a symbol of exhaustion.[58] Following her accusation, the light changes and the eagle sits on Anita's shoulder, as if threatening her. Anita, however, is far from being intimidated, and informs it of the fact that it is merely old, grey and powerless. As a result, it is not Anita, but the eagle who, in the end, is mutilated.

Whether the eagle is symbolic of the lame and sluggish Federal Republic of Germany is debatable. According to Hensel, it is unclear whether the crippled bird symbolizes the beginning of the end of the FRG, or rather the death of the former "Reichsadler," representing monarchist tendencies.[59] The traditional image of the eagle has become meaningless, and it has lost its magical power.

Economic Issues and a No-Man's-Land: Elfriede Müller's *Goldener Oktober* (1991)

Müller's play focuses on the conflict between East and West Germans after reunification, and was premiered at the *Landestheater Tübingen* in April 1991 (director, Dieter Bitterli). In 1990, the playwright spent a year in Berlin to gain firsthand experience of the climate of change in the city. As her play explicitly focuses on the political situation after 1989, she calls it a "Zeitstück."[60] Like many other playwrights of the 1990s, Müller turns her back on the postmodern pastiche in the attempt to revive a politically relevant theater.[61]

In *Goldener Oktober,* the playwright presents us with what she calls the "archeology" of post-1989 Berlin, demonstrating that the dismal and abandoned cityscape in which the play is set affects the characters to a great extent. It is set in 1990 near the former death strip and consists of two parallel sections, each of which is divided into three "Streifen." The first "Streifen" of each part takes place in the hastily refurbished and westernized bar called "New Moskau"; the action then moves to the street, and each section ends in no-man's-land. Against the backdrop of no-man's-land, Müller portrays the early years of failed East-West encounters. Apart from the former concentration camps, the former border is probably *the* most emotionally charged real estate in German history. Up to this very day, the Wall is a symbol of national trauma, and forty years of separation have left an all-too-visible scar.[62] In this vein, Müller depicts the depressive atmosphere of the death strip at the time when the first Western capitalists arrive, hoping to make large profits. Indeed, it was not long after the fall of the Wall that investors became aware of the potential goldmine that existed in the former no-man's-land. It is ironic that for forty years the death strip preserved what is now classified as Berlin's most expensive real estate.[63] The best example of such investment is perhaps to be found in the "battle" for *Potsdamer Platz,* where four firms have created gigantic new commercial centers connected by new underground tunnels.[64] While some praise the new development as a positive step forward for the new-old capital, others remain apprehensive in view of the enormous sums of money that were spent on them.[65] From this setting, the playwright has crafted a skeptical, committed and emotional drama that brings together a number of themes that have since become stereotypes of reunification. These stereotypes include the "rape" of the East by the potent West German state, the colonization of the former GDR, which fell prey to West German money-makers, and finally the view that reunification deprived East Germans of their traditions and turned them into nervous wrecks. The play presents the psychological problems of both East and West Germans after reunification, from the perspective of several individuals. Looking back on reunification, Müller generally paints a dark and gloomy picture:

Die Deformationen von Ost und West treffen sich über einem Abgrund voller Leichen. Da wird weder Gras noch Europarasen darüberwachsen. Obwohl viele unerschrockene Deutsche mit dem Fall der Mauer auch gleichzeitig ihre Ursache mitbegraben wollten, ist sie nicht begraben.[66]

At the end of the play, we witness the complaints of a man who has just been thrown out by his wife; he sums up the situation as follows: "Gequirlte Scheiße im Deutschlandfieber, det wird det neue Nationalgericht."[67] Despite these indications of failure, the official view of reunification remained ostentatiously positive. The chancellor, Helmut Kohl, never tired of praising the positive aspects of unified Germany. His desperate attempt to turn the "gentle" revolution into a success was supported by the media, which initially tried to gloss over the problems, particularly for the East Germans. In *Goldener Oktober*, the idea that unification was merely a "spectacle" is conveyed through its setting: a run-down bar, in which a presenter tirelessly entertains his guests with cheap distractions, such as the harrassed stripper Silke, or the talentless group of singers called the "Plastic-Bomber-Boys." Their function within the play is similar to that of the Greek chorus: they unveil the emotions and attitudes of both guests and staff, revealing, for example, the so-called "Wendehälse," who rapidly adapted themselves to the Western system in order to draw benefit from it:

Der Wendehals fehlt im Verein
Wo ist ein Arsch ich kriech hinein.
Wir sind die Wendehälse und schnattern wie die Gänse im Chor.
Wir sind die Wendehälse und lernen schnell die neue Partitur.

(*GO*, 147)

In an ironic travesty of a popular left-wing song, "Die Moorsoldaten,"[68] the singers reveal themselves as opportunists who have jumped on the bandwagon, and who have learned what to say and what not to say.

Helped by the biting irony of the singers' comments, Müller employs the metaphor of the theater to criticize the events on the "political stage." This is particularly interesting with respect to the year 1990, during which *Goldener Oktober* was written. It is significant, however, that the declining euphoria was reflected with increasing intensity in the political commentaries of television news programs such as *Tagesthemen*. On 5 April 1990, the commentator Ernst-Dieter Lueg thus remarked: "Das politische Drehbuch der Wiedervereinigung kennt nicht nur erhabene Szenen."[69]

Against the backdrop of these doomed "infotainments," we meet the idealist Leo, who refuses to work for the sewage treatment company belonging to his future father-in-law. While they get riotously drunk, the patronizing "Onkel" from the West, Erich, tries to convince the young, idealistic East German, Leo, of the merits of capitalism. We feel that no good can come of this, and we are right: the result is a verbal clash between the two, followed by Leo's splitting up with his girlfriend. Whereas Leo defends his viewpoint, which is that of the exploited and deceived former GDR citizen, the uncle praises the free market. The quarrel turns into an increasingly heated debate, which is secretly recorded by a frustrated young journalist who has just come onstage. The uncle's wife, Margot, is aware of the situation and tries to calm them down, but it is too late. Everyone is listening, and, to make it even worse, the three singers start commenting on the situation by making loud remarks.

The two viewpoints are incompatible: on the one hand, the uncle is convinced that he can make the world a better place by organizing everything according to an efficient, capitalist principle. On the other hand, Leo defends his independence by underlining that he does not even have the chance to build his own future; in his eyes, the GDR has simply been bought up and taken over by the Wessis. However, the "spectacle" nature of this conversation must not be forgotten, an aspect which Leo makes clear when he tells his guests that the "show" is over. This refers to the showy character of political events themselves, for not only was the fall of the Wall constantly monitored by the media, but it was also transformed into a show performed for the media.[70] Similarly, it did not take long for the Wall to be hacked to pieces and exported as souvenirs. The compère constantly repeats "The show goes on," but in contrast to his desperate efforts to make the evening a success, the guests ruin his attempt to present an idealized world by ignoring him. Under a hastily modernized exterior, newly suppressed anger clearly continues to smolder.

At the bar we also find Letty and Harry, two would-be capitalists from the West, who constantly talk about the fortune they intend to make by cheating the so-called "Ossis." They chat up a middle-aged prostitute, Lola, and promise her a fortune, but instead intend to abuse her for cheap porn films. She is not the only victim of the "colonization" of East Germany: the young East German girl Silke, who earns her living as a stripper in the "New Moskau," is harassed by a mentally disturbed West German department store detective. The detective turns out to be a victim of capitalism, whose life is gray and hopeless, and who will finally kill her, just to experience one exciting moment in his life before he commits suicide. All the frustrated detective can think about is the grayness of his own tarnished existence in the department store; he is fed up with the greed of customers, whose aim is simply to steal goods. He is unable to think in any other terms, and his single-mindedness becomes apparent when he refers to love and money in the same way, and loving and stealing become the same thing. In his fantasies, he places Silke in the middle of the department store, posing in all kinds of clothing. Although the thought of her brightens up his life, he does not perceive her to be a real person, but rather a doll. She is there to be admired and looked at, but not because of her personality. Silke becomes increasingly disgusted with him, but he does not listen to her, and instead gently takes her by the throat, a gesture which she mistakes for an affectionate move. In the end he strangles her, then shoots himself. Although several people walk by, nobody notices the dead couple.

The melancholy of the death strip, the deserted no-man's-land between two cities, provides a visual image of the world of those who are left behind by the speed of reunification. Comparing the former GDR with a girl, Müller draws on the metaphor of "marriage," which was soon to become a stereotype of reunification, the media portraying this event as a shotgun wedding between a masculinized West Germany and a vulnerable, feminized East Germany.[71] Both reunification and Silke's relationship are overshadowed by economic and psychological problems, which are expressed in the desolate topography. Müller shows that at that time, the gap between East and West was about to widen, and her play can thus be read as a warning not to overlook the signs of the growing tension.

The *Stasi* and Its Victims: Klaus Pohl's *Karate-Billi kehrt zurück* (1991/93)

Klaus Pohl's post-"Wende" play is the only drama which addresses the burning issue of the *Stasi,* the *Ministry of State Security* (MfS) in the GDR after 1989. The premiere took place at the *Hamburger Schauspielhaus* in May 1991, directed by Pohl himself. Although the play shows how the MfS network continued to work even after the fall of the Wall,[72] the press criticized it for presenting the issue too tamely. Despite this critical reaction, however, the play can be seen as a valuable contribution to the post-reunification debate in Germany and the difficult task of coming to terms with forty years of dictatorship. In fact, the MfS continued to cast its shadow over reunified Germany. Allegations concerning the cooperation with the MfS of East German writers such as Christa Wolf (1929–) and Sascha Anderson greatly damaged their reputations, and sparked off the "Literaturstreit."[73] However, a controversial law passed by the GDR parliament, the *Volkskammer,* as early as 24 August 1990, made personal files accessible to a huge number of former GDR citizens. While they claimed to find this opportunity to dig into their past painful, they also found it a helpful means of coming to terms with the legacy of the MfS.[74] Even the former chancellor, Helmut Kohl, still denies access to his files, as they could not only shed light on his dubious role in the party-funding scandal of 1998, but probably also reveal potentially devastating facts about his cooperation with the GDR. By pitting conspiring former Stasi members against one of its victims, the athlete Billi, Pohl's play takes up the debate concerning who was involved in the murky transactions of the MfS, and to what extent.

The conventional drama is set in the political aftermath of 1989, when the once-successful gold-medal winner, Billi, who has spent thirteen years in a mental asylum, is released and returns to his village in Saxony. For him, however, the past is not over, as he is determined to discover the exact circumstances which led to his detention. In the final scene, when Billi finally persuades the other villagers to put their cards on the table, it gradually transpires that practically everybody had been working for the MfS as informers, albeit unofficial.[75] Out of jealousy of his success and his privileges as an athlete, especially the opportunity to travel, the mayor's wife had started a rumor and produced a forged letter in order to put him behind bars "lawfully." Challenging Nickchen, the mayor, with a butcher's knife, Billi winkles out the truth about the conspiracy, in which even his sister was involved. As the mayor's wife fancied Billi's best friend, and pitied him for always being second, she produced a fake letter in which she claimed to be a girl from abroad whom Billi had once met. Nickchen used the forged evidence to arrest him for attempted "Republikflucht." When Billi was released after six months, he took to drinking, as he was the outcast of the village; not only that, but his career was in tatters. After his second arrest following his supposed misdemeanor after a drinking session, he was taken to a mental asylum in which his sister Greta worked as a doctor — a post she obtained only as a result of passing information on to Urban. Even the local priest, who was at one time her confessor, turns out to have been an informer. The drama thus provides an example of the shady and reckless methods employed by the Stasi, and reveals the extent to which even "normal" citizens were unwillingly caught in the carefully crafted web of the State Security.

The drama opens with the homecoming scene in the local pub, where a few villagers and a banker from the West are waiting for the arrival of the small town sensation, namely Billi. The former informer Urban, the mayor Nickchen, who used to be dubbed "little Ceausescu," and the banker von Stahl have gathered to celebrate Billi's release from the psychiatric asylum. But Billi is too drugged to recognize anyone, let alone the old photographs of himself. It is fairly obvious that he suffers from a mental disorder, as he refers to the allegedly naughty half of his character as the "Affe." Apart from the barmaid Sascha, the villagers treat him like an imbecile, and Billi's sanity seems to have suffered seriously from the long medical treatment.

Klaus Pohl's cynical conclusion points towards the fact that even after 1989, innocent victims of the Stasi continued to suffer in order to prevent the truth from emerging. In fact, the activities of the MfS continued for several months after the opening of the border, because the hardliners refused to believe in a reunited Germany. According to the Bundestag commission which investigated the GDR past, the task of investigators was considerably hindered, as files disappeared or were mostly rendered illegible with black ink, and many were not accessible for reasons of data protection.[76] Nonetheless, the findings are shocking enough. As many testimonies show, people spied on one another, and, having read their personal files, many claimed that they would never dream of trusting their friends again.[77]

Fantastic as Billi's story may seem, reality was often much worse, and the *Stasigefängnis* in Berlin was notorious for the ill-treatment of prisoners. As one witness states, for example, illnesses were often not cured, but used as a means of putting pressure on prisoners, and interrogations took place when people were on psychoactive drugs.[78] In the play, Billi is kept in a similar state, as a deep hole in his chest, through which the doctors "spied out his secrets," is exploited to weaken him mentally and physically:

| BILLI | Da kucken sie immer rein. Da haben sie immer reingekuckt. Was mit dem Affen los ist. Wenn der wild wird . . . müssen sie rechtzeitig kucken . . . So eine Art Guckloch. Warum erzählst du das nicht, Greta? |
| SASCHA *lacht* | Das ist ja richtig zum Gruseln.[79] |

Billi literally becomes the victim of the Stalinist "operation"; and the hole in his chest can be interpreted as a graphic symbol of complete control. Billi's question suggests that Greta is too embarrassed to talk about the physical torture inflicted upon him, as she was also involved in the conspiracy against him, albeit unwillingly. Her superior, Urban, cleverly used her ambition as a device, for he knew that she would owe him a favor after being given a good job. This was typical of the MfS, which played on the weaknesses of its informers; strangely enough, the superior officers often acted as psychologists, offering a shoulder to cry on.[80] It is therefore not unlikely that Greta genuinely wanted the best for her brother, but found herself in the compromising situation of being forced to spy on him. It is no secret that the Stasi took pride in harassing priests into its service, a policy which also features in the play, for the priest Menzel was blackmailed by Urban, and in the attempt to save his reputation he too succumbed to the Stasi.

Although the heritage of the totalitarian regime remains problematic, Pohl insists that the past must not be repressed, as it needs to be dealt with in order to do justice to the innumerable victims of the MfS. Drawing on the example of an athlete, he shows how immense the impact of the MfS really was on everyday life. Practically everybody conspired against Billi, a fact which was too much for him to bear. Based on the example of Billi, "Vergangenheitsbewältigung" is to be found at the very core of the play, and both the priest and the West German banker are implicitly criticized for their attempts to gloss over their pasts.

The Dismembered Socialist Ideology: Volker Braun's *Böhmen am Meer* (1992)

Böhmen am Meer is a post-reunification play that draws on the loss of GDR identity and the yearning for socialism. Written between 1989 and 1992, it is essentially a pessimistic portrait of the world after the collapse of the Warsaw Pact.[81] It premiered at the *Schiller Theater* in Berlin in 1992 and was far from successful.[82]

In the tradition of Ionesco's absurdist "anti-pièces" of the 1960s, Braun presents a play in which words do not necessarily entail sensible actions, and opposing views such as communism and capitalism coincide in final agreement. In ten loosely connected scenes, *Böhmen am Meer* refers to the shattered socialist utopia after reunification by means of theater of the absurd, abandoning coherent narrative, specified settings, and meaningful conversations. Consequently, we encounter ridiculous, clown-like figures instead of characters, while tittle-tattle replaces logical dialogue.

The protagonist, the Czech Pavel, finds himself deprived of his ideological roots, because since the end of the Warsaw Pact he has not been able to define himself in any way other than as a critic of the Soviet-American conflict. The other two central characters are Bardolph, a rich American entrepreneur whose ill-health has turned him into a pessimist, and the Russian journalist Michail, who frantically reads newspapers in order to compensate for forty years of censorship. Although both have had a sexual relationship with Pavel's wife Julia, they are reconciled in the end.

The capitalist Bardolph takes Vaclav, his child, with him, Julia breaks up with her husband, and Pavel is shot during the cannibals' uprising.

Despite the island setting, which would normally be the classic location for a utopian state, the political situation appears quite the opposite. Instead of peace and harmony, Braun depicts a world which has been destroyed by both political and environmental problems. The island paradise of the Bohemian intellectual Pavel turns out to be a utopia in the original sense of the word: it is literally a *u-topos*, a place which does not exist. The fact that Bohemia cannot be equated with any geographical entity resembles the situation in Shakespeare's *The Winter's Tale* in that it simply denotes an undefined political state in Europe.[83] Despite vague references to *The Winter's Tale* and *The Tempest*, Braun's play is highly artificial. It merely uses the literary context to underline the idea that any quest for a utopia is absurd, and at the end of *Böhmen am Meer*, Bohemia and Sicily merge into one when the Sicilian mafia takes control of the island.[84]

As a kind of prologue, the audience encounters six anonymous tourists who are leaving the island in panic. Although the official reason for their flight is an alga causing water pollution, this is not the only problem. From the hectic conversation of the six people it emerges that there is political turmoil:

VIERTER MANN	Die Politik ist das Chaos.
ERSTER MANN	Die Anarchie der Vernunft!
SECHSTER MANN	Noch nie, gestatten Sie, hat sich die Realität
DRITTE FRAU	Wovon sprechen Sie?
VIERTE FRAU	Ich habe mein Plaid vergessen.
SECHSTER MANN	die Realität so rapid
ZWEITE FRAU	Küssen Sie mich
SECHSTER MANN	verändert.[85]

As the absurd conversation shows, political reason is submerged in chaos, because of the rapidly changing political situation. A real exchange of opinions never takes place, as their absurd dialogue is characterized by incoherence and sudden changes of topics. In fact, people do not really seem to understand what is going on. This is obviously modeled on the events of summer 1989, a hectic year which left many people bewildered and stunned, because the pace of events was simply breathtaking.[86] When Bardolph and Michail enter the stage, they find an empty, depopulated space. In the heat of the events of 1989, the dominating conflict between the two hemispheres ended, wiping out the homeland of the East Germans.

Bardolph and Michail follow Pavel's invitation to meet on an island in the Adriatic sea, where Pavel has taken refuge. Both are tired of the East-West division, and decide that these times are over, as indeed they are. As Bardolph suggests, the world will inevitably develop along capitalist lines, and the Russian is too depressed to protest, yet states that he is denied the right to change because he would be accused of being a "Wendehals." After more than twenty years of humiliation, Pavel seeks revenge; however, his expectations are not fulfilled, because Bardolph and Michail grow close. When he sees the old opponents shoulder to shoulder, Pavel begins to despair. He remains intellectually grounded in the spring of 1968 and can comprehend neither the victory of capitalism nor the fact that, according to Bardolph, the East will finally attain the materialist "paradise" of the West.

Pavel's existential confusion in view of the environment that has become foreign to him is expressed in his last monologue in scene 9, where he describes how the stormy changes in history have overturned old values and thus rendered life shallow: Prospero becomes prosperity, and Ariel is transformed into a well-known washing powder. Life lacks its spiritual dimension after capitalism has captured the East, and the speaker perceives freedom to be like free-falling, a fear which took hold of many East-German intellectuals after reunification.[87] It is therefore not surprising that Pavel practically commits suicide by exposing himself to the crossfire of revolution, an act which is also symbolic of his intellectual position.

Braun thus offers a pessimistic outlook of a polluted and unscrupulous world governed by imbeciles like Vaclav, whose linguistic incompetence conveys a lack of intelligence, and whose violence proves his uncivilized character. Whatever the topic, Vaclav's response is either "Perfid" or "Steil," two words repeated so often that they become almost meaningless. Eventually, Bardolph announces that as a dutiful father, he will take Vaclav with him to the capitalist "paradise." In a similar manner to Braun's *Iphigenie*, Vaclav is to learn how to rule the world with money, a mission for which he needs neither brains nor morals. Moreover, he claims that he does not want to be humane and is therefore perfectly suited to follow in his father's footsteps. Again, Braun's contempt of capitalism shines through, for he emphasized in his speech on receiving the *Büchner-Preis* in 2000 that Germany's revolution hit the poor, depriving them of their human rights and causing mass unemployment.[88] Against the backdrop of a looming revolution carried out by unknown dark figures,[89] who are repeatedly connected to the Sicilian mafia, Braun presents the "Wende" and the reunified Germany resulting from it as a violent uprising followed by an anti-utopia in which money rules and weapons speak.

Treuhand, Business, and Deceit:
Rolf Hochhuth's *Wessis in Weimar* (1993)

The main topic of Hochhuth's play is the economic and social injustice he believes the West Germans to have inflicted on the *Neue Bundeslän-der* after reunification. As the subtitle "Szenen aus einem besetzten Land" suggests, reunification is not the result of peaceful cooperation for Hochhuth, but rather a matter of colonization and occupation of the GDR by the West. Even before his play was staged or published, *Wessis in Weimar* sparked off a media debate on the question of whether or not violence, and even murder, can be a justified means of self-defense.[90] Hochhuth himself willfully provoked discussion by sending three scenes to a journal for business managers, *manager magazin*. All three scenes speak of violence: in the first, the manager of the *Treuhandanstalt*,[91] Karsten Rohwedder, is killed; in the second, a member of the Berlin Senate is killed by a letter bomb; and in the third, expropriated heirs set fire to their parents' house. The minister Norbert Blüm attacked Hochhuth for allegedly collaborating with and excusing murderers, and Herta Däubler-Gmelin found his play "disgusting." Even the chancellor, Helmut Kohl, joined in, calling it a warrant for murderers.[92] These vehement reactions proved that Hochhuth had touched on a delicate issue.

In an interview with *manager magazin* he explained his viewpoint in detail. When the interviewers accused him of legitimizing the assassination of Karsten Rohwedder, he carefully corrected them by stating that Rohwedder must have been aware that his actions would ultimately provoke violence: "Daher bleibt ein Meuchelmord zwar ethisch unhaltbar, aber er mußte vorausgesehen werden von jedem, der Geschichte kennt."[93] The playwright's aim is therefore not to excuse violence, but to provide an explanation for it.

The main themes of the play are the unequal East-West relationship, the ruinous actions of the *Treuhandanstalt*, the plundering of the former GDR, and the "occupation" of the *Neue Bundesländer* by the FRG. The ten scenes are constructed in a documentary style, combining Hochhuth's dialogues with reprints of letters, laws, articles, and interviews. Each scene has a long introduction which serves as more than mere stage directions, offering Hochhuth's detailed analysis of the economic and historical background. In fact, these introductory notes read more like a political manifesto than stage directions, but it becomes clear that Hochhuth has a naturalistic setting in mind. It is for this reason that he maintains that *Wessis in Weimar* was premiered only when staged for the second time, on 25 February 1993 at the *Ernst-Deutsch-Theater* in Hamburg, because it followed his concept of a naturalistic play. In contrast, he very much rejected the anti-naturalistic montage of scenes and dialogues of the premiere on 15 February 1993 at the *Berliner Ensemble,* created by director Einar Schleef.[94] In fact, Schleef greatly adulterated the text, inserting additional quotes from Schiller, Brecht and others, with the result that ninety minutes of the performance were not actually Hochhuth's play. After a long quarrel with Schleef, Hochhuth finally gave his consent to the production, on condition that the audience be given a free copy of the play's original text.[95]

Drawing on real examples, Hochhuth accuses West Germany of looting the "bargain called the GDR," by means of the *Treuhand.* This hastily founded institution has, according to Hochhuth, betrayed the East Germans for a second time — after the looting by the Soviet Union after the war — because speculation and the hope of quick money meant that many firms were sold for less than their real value, without regard for of unemployment and social hardship.

In the introductory scene, Hildegard, a law professor, interviews the president of the *Treuhand* in his home, minutes before he is shot. Shortly after the assassination in 1998, terrorists of the Red Army Faction (RAF) declared themselves responsible for his murder.[96] Hochhuth admits that he changed the facts slightly, and instead of his wife, the law professor herself witnesses the president's death in the play. During their conversation, Hildegard accuses him of depriving the former GDR citizens of their individual prosperity, their jobs, and their national wealth ("Volksvermögen") by managing a huge sell-out of the GDR. The president, however, is unaffected by her criticism, because he is deeply convinced that he is doing a good thing by transforming the bankrupt GDR economy into a capitalist system. Of course, the professor sees it differently, pointing out to him that the GDR citizens are being "robbed" for a second time, the first time being the nationalization of private firms by the Communists.[97] Totally outraged, she even calls him the last absolutist autocrat of Europe, who has occupied the weaker state in order to bring about "reform." In her view, it is outrageous that the East Germans are not even allowed to take part in the undertakings of the *Treuhand,* let alone stop some of its transactions. For her it is only logical that he will not survive the injustice he has caused. He defends his policy by stating that many GDR firms were not only bankrupt, but also posed an imminent danger to the environment. Still, Hildegard is not convinced, and demands that the East Germans should be given their "own" land back. Her courtroom-like speech culminates in her accusing him of expropriating the East Germans of their property and selling it back to them. Predictably, the scene ends with the murder of the president.

Scene 6, entitled "'Zu ebener Erde und erster Stock oder: Die Launen des Glücks.' Lokalposse mit Gesang, frei nach Nestroy" focuses on the problems of East German house owners in Berlin whose properties were expropriated and demolished to clear the way for the so-called "Todesstreifen." Too close to the Wall, or to the border, the houses had been in the way of the patrolling soldiers. Now the German state refuses to return them to their rightful owners, declaring that the expropriation had been in accordance with GDR law and can not be overturned.[98] The scene takes place on a flight of steps, immediately before the start of an official reception for a congress of lawyers. A few former house owners in their eighties gather at the bottom of the stairs in order to protest against this injustice. Although they are not invited guests, nobody asks them to leave, and they finally manage to speak to the Federal Minister of Justice, Sabine Leutheusser-Schnarrenberger. It is, of course, highly symbolic that the group of protesters gradually move up the stairs until they reach the landing on the first floor. Here the deprived people at the lower end of the social scale literally revolt against the powerful; the class difference is also emphasized by the strong Berlin dialect of the old people. It is striking, however, that the dialogue is extremely artificial in the sense that everybody talks in long, complex sentences about complicated juristic matters without even once stumbling over the words. Again, it becomes obvious that the characters are merely delivering Hochhuth's view, presenting the house owners as victims and the Minister as an inhuman state official. In contrast to Hochhuth's intention, it is not only the Minister whose German seems strangely detached from the spontaneity of the spoken word, but also the common people. While the Minister recites a letter she wrote to the people (in reality she never met them personally), a woman called Frau Trumpf opposes her with extremely well-structured speech:

> [. . .] halten Sie, seine Kabinettskollegin, für denkbar,
> Frau Ministerin, daß Herr Schäuble,
> als er den Einigungsvertrag aushandelte,
> a 1: auch nur *gedacht* hat an eine Einzelheit
> wie die Mauergrundstücke?
> Und daß er a 2:
> wenn er an sie gedacht *hätte,*
> die soeben von ihnen genannte,
> "Unvereinbarkeit" einer ehmaligen DDR-Anordnung
> mit unserem Grundgesetz —
> als Voraussetzung, diese DDR-Anordnung einfach *aufzuheben . . .*"
>
> (*WiW,*127)

Despite Hochhuth's intention to write a naturalistic play, it becomes obvious from this passage that he produces the opposite effect. It is doubtful whether an old woman in an intimidating environment would talk in such a sophisticated manner, especially when confronted with a high state official. Her argument resembles an official speech rather than mere private talk. Although she is upset, there is no linguistic sign of emotion whatsoever. The dramatic structure finally crashes to the ground under its ideological weight, when "Honecker" enters the stage, justifying the construction of the Berlin Wall. Here Hochhuth underlines the fact that while Honecker was taken to court for his crimes, the Berlin Republic does not question its own illegal policies, namely the confiscation of real estate on the "Todesstreifen." In fact, the elderly people in the play express Hochhuth's own opinion, which he made clear in his interview with the *manager magazin*:

> Nun, es gibt Häuser und Boden. Und da der Kommunismus sie den Einheimischen gestohlen hat, mußte der Westen sie den Einheimischen zurückgeben. Die Ossi-Funktionäre waren die Diebe — die Wessi-Funktionäre sind die Hehler [. . .][99]

In the same vein, the play concludes with a long scene bearing the title "Ossis: Diebe, Wessis: Hehler" set in the Baroque manor belonging to the family of Claus von Stauffenberg, who is known to have attempted to kill Hitler. Under the pretext of shooting a film about manor houses in Thuringia, Professor Roessing and his granddaughter Ruth gain permission to enter the house, although a huge state reception is being prepared.[100] Expropriated by the Communists, the Stauffenbergs hoped to get the house back, but the German government decided to keep it as a leisure home for high-ranking politicians. Gradually Ruth and her grandfather's intentions become clear. While she prepares the interview, Roessing sets the attic on fire. At this point, Hochhuth adds another fictional element, for the fire never actually took place. Here he provides us with another example of what he calls self-defense, for, as he believes, it is hardly surprising that deprived people revolt against their fate. As Ruth points out, the fire is a just means of snatching the manor back from the receivers of stolen goods, whom she believes to be identical with the state. Hochhuth takes his role as a committed playwright very seriously, and he believes that a writer is not only on a political mission, but also has the power to influence historical developments. Moreover, Ernst Jünger (1895–1998), a problematic and disputed writer with regard to the nature of war, is featured as the promoter of the rights of the individual. His novel *Auf den*

Marmorklippen (1939) is praised as the "Magna Charta of Resistance," a dubious interpretation of a highly controversial novel.[101]

Hochhuth clearly believes that theater can change the world by changing people's minds, and thus that theater equals education. Although he explicitly condemns murder, he adopts the role of the provocative and potentially "dangerous" poet.[102] His moralistic play refers more than once to famous writers of the eighteenth century, such as Lessing, Goethe, Voltaire, and especially Schiller.[103] Against the backdrop of Schiller's theater as "moralische Anstalt," Hochhuth's intention can be summed up as follows: *Wessis in Weimar* aims to enlighten the audience by means of a huge compilation of documentary material that is presented as dramatic dialogue. Using his characters as mouthpieces, the playwright forces us to believe in the characters. However, *Wessis in Weimar* is not a genuine platform for an exchange of ideas. In place of offering room for thought, Hochhuth persuades the audience of his central hypothesis, namely that "Ossis" are good, and "Wessis" are bad. This black and white portrayal of East and West reduces the play to a mere vehicle of information, and thus the characters become nothing more than mouthpieces. For this very reason, and for its lack of controversy, it has been argued that it becomes little more than propaganda.[104]

The Wall inside People's Heads: Christoph Hein's *Randow* (1994)

Randow,[105] Hein's first play following the "Velvet Revolution" addresses a wide range of issues, including the rise of right-wing radicalism, racism, the legacy of the Ministry of Security, property speculation, and asylum-seekers.[106] It was premiered in December 1994 at the *Sächsische Staatsschauspiel* in Dresden,[107] and was directed by Klaus Dieter Kirst, who had also directed the famous production of *Die Ritter der Tafelrunde*. Expectations of the premiere were thus high, yet many critics were disappointed, partly because they found the staging too tame, but also because it was thought that the multiplicity of themes had led to a certain superficiality.[108] Others found that the characters lacked psychological depth,[109] and that the language was not realistically devised for each character.[110]

The play centers on the painter Anna Andress, who lives by herself in a cottage in the valley of the river Randow near the German-Polish border. As Anna's house is located in a very beautiful spot of the valley, set apart from the village because it used to be a military training center, several people are trying to take possession of it. Right from the beginning, it is evident that Anna is not at all welcome, for both the local ranger and gamekeeper, Kowalski, and the mayor, Voß, are trying to make Anna sell the house by plotting to poison her dog and killing two asylum-seekers in a nearby field. Her complaints to the authorities are in vain, as the two hardliners from the former GDR despise democratic thinking and make it clear that she has no official support at all. In addition, the men are at odds with a right-wing organization run by the dubious nationalist Fred P. Paul. In the end, Paul obtains the house and transforms it into a training center for right-wing extremists. In letting the neo-Nazi network win, Hein sports theories of a nationwide conspiracy of neo-Nazis.[111] However, recent analyses have repeatedly questioned these views, and make it clear that a network of neo-Nazis does not exist.[112]

The conflict between the problematic heritage of the SED (Sozialistische Einheitspartei Deutschlands) regime and democracy is not only paired with and compared to the conflict between neo-Nazis and the state, but is further watered down by the introduction of private problems. It emerges that Anna is divorced from her husband, who is an alcoholic and a victim of the socialist dictatorship. Having a severe drinking problem, Rudolf cannot look after himself, yet Anna bluntly tells him that she refuses to support an alcoholic any longer. It should be noted, however, that Hein does not simply depict him as a victim of "Wendestress," for we learn that he had always depended on her, even during GDR times. Rudolf is therefore a victim twice over: in the GDR he could not cope with being restricted, and now he is frightened of facing freedom.[113] Moreover, Anna feels alienated from her teenage daughter. Due to the many lines of conflict in the play, each problem can only be sketched in a rather superficial manner, a feature which does little to make the play more dramatic.

According to Hein, life has returned to "normal" five years after the "Wende," albeit in a rather negative way: Paul's organization of neo-Nazis spreads unnoticed, the mayor Weiß is a ruthless "Wendehals" who simply backs the new allegedly "democratic" values after having supported the GDR for many years, and the Border Police officer is an unscrupulous egoist who does not shy away from killing. The only positive character, Anna Andress, is threatened by the deaths around her, and is driven out of her house in panic.

Despite the play's substantial criticism of the Berlin Republic, its depiction of the ever dismal state of the new Germany fails to be convincing, for despite the intertwining of several plot lines, the outcome is predictable. Although political problems erupt in people's private lives, the characters are not believable; similarly, Hein did not employ Brecht's alienation effect. All characters use the same linguistic register, remaining at all times eloquent, and never stuttering or repeating themselves. Parallel to this, the stage directions do not provide additional information about individual features, and the play comes across as a rather dry lesson in contemporary history. Hein subconsciously trades in clichés, yet offers rich material for those interested in cultural images. Although *Randow* is interesting as a text, it lacks a specifically dramatic treatment of the conflicts of reunited Germany.

Looking Back: "Ein Traum, was sonst?": Heiner Müller's *Germania 3* (1996)

Müller began writing his third play based on the theme of Germania in 1994 (published in 1996), and the rehearsals started while he was still working on it.[114] After his death on 30 December 1995, however, the project was postponed, and resumed six months later.[115] The fragment *Germania 3*, published posthumously, is often regarded as a swan song for both Müller himself and reunited Germany. Although his original intention was to focus on Germany's recent past, he found himself unable to forget the Nazi past, which had disturbed him for the majority of his life.[116] He thus wrote *Germania 3*, the title of which harks back to the *Third Reich*, for "Germania" was the name Hitler had assigned to Berlin.[117] It is therefore not surprising that Hitler features as one of the characters, for, according to Müller, only an artistic dialogue with the dead can lead to a better future.[118] However, as this dialogue also implied extensive quoting from other playwrights, Bertolt Brecht's heirs claimed that Müller had violated the copyright, and took the publishing house to court. In 1998, the *Oberlandesgericht* in Munich banned Müller's book, yet the *Bundesverfassungsgericht* in Karlsruhe revoked the decision on the grounds of the freedom of works of art.[119]

Germania 3 premiered in May 1996 at the *Schauspielhaus Bochum*, directed by Leander Haußmann, and opened four weeks later at the *Berliner Ensemble*, directed by Martin Wuttke. The critics were full of praise,[120] and Sibylle Wirsing saw it as an appropriate attempt to emphasize the romantic yet ghostly elements of Müller's play.[121] It conjures up the past, but it bears the unreal features of a dream, or rather a nightmare.[122] The production of the *Berliner Ensemble*, however, was believed to lack the necessary sense of history inherent in Müller's work, for it presented sarcastic shock effects alongside silly gags.[123] In the third successful staging, in Vienna in November 1996, the director Frank-Patrick Steckel presented history against the backdrop of a massive heap of scrap metal and other junk.[124] This image is symbolic of Müller's world view, for he wanted to free historical discourse of the "ideologischen Ramsch des Jahrhunderts."[125] The production at the *Schauspielhaus* in Hamburg in March 1997 (director, Dimiter Gotscheff), passed as an appropriate attempt to stage *Germania 3*, yet critics unanimously considered it to be "unspielbar."[126] One critic pointed out that Müller's *Germania 3* was part of a "Hitler-Welle" on the Berlin stages, since the years 1995 to 1997 also saw Müller's production of Brecht's *Arturo Ui*, with Martin Wuttke playing the main part, and a staging of *Emmy Göring an der Seite ihres Mannes* (Emmy Göring at Her Husband's Side) in the *Maxim Gorki Theater*, which was sold out for months.[127]

Before 1994, Müller had originally planned to write a play about Hitler and Stalin, focusing on the Second World War. However, the actual play concerns the postwar era, and ends in 1961 with the building of the Wall. As the subtitle *Gespenster am toten Mann* suggests, Müller presents a kaleidoscope of perpetrators and victims: soldiers and their women, opportunists and traitors, prisoners and torturers. It expresses Müller's view that the utopian hope of a humane German state should finally be buried. The subtitle also alludes to the novel *Gespenster am toten Mann* (1931), written by Paul C. Ettighoffer, in which the traumatic events of the First World War are described. It refers to the battle of Verdun in 1917, part of which took place on a hill called "Toter Mann," during which a dying soldier, whose physical pain is torturing him out of his wits, foretells the dreadful end of his comrades:

> Sie haben sich soeben mit Handgranaten, mit Gewehren und Spaten bekämpft, dort, in der Luft, über dem Toten Mann. Nun weiß ich, daß mein Ende gekommen ist. Ich muß sterben, Kameraden. Es wird ein großes Sterben geben in unserem Regiment. [. . .] Ja, es wird ein großes Sterben geben; da, da . . . seht ihr nicht, da sind sie wieder. Jetzt sind es Franzosen . . . Sie kommen auf uns zu . . . Alarm! Alaaarm! Gespenster! Gäspänstär!! Gäspänstär am Toten Mann! Alarm! Alaaarm![128]

For Müller, the future holds no positive outlook, and he thus describes how the Germans are tearing both themselves and their enemies to pieces. In an interview with Peter von Becker, he remarked that reunification merely left a void, which East and West Germans alike hastily filled with stereotypes:

> Das Gespenstische ist das Vakuum. Die Utopie ist weg, ein Feindbild ist weg, und jetzt gibt es eine verzweifelte Suche nicht nach Utopien, sondern nach neuen Feindbildern. Das führt zu Süffisanz und Häme. Nicht nur gegen den Osten.[129]

Müller's judgment of the disastrous course of history in *Germania 3* is even harsher than in earlier works, for he had previously considered failure to be a necessary precondition for progress.[130] When faced with the "gentle" revolution and the victory of capitalism, however, Müller's hopes for a better future came to an end, as unified Germany is ruled by money, or, in his words, the "Prinzip Auschwitz."[131]

Germania 3 is a montage of quotations taken from plays by other authors, intertwined with Müller's own interpolations.[132] As he does in earlier works, Müller abandons the structure of the conventional drama, and experiments with collage and montage, thus creating a postmodern pastiche. As early as 1975 he argued that only the fragment suited his view of history,[133] which resembles a heap of material that has collapsed.[134] This montage style enables layers of memory to meet that would otherwise have been separated by centuries. According to Müller, a chronological structure is inappropriate if one's aim is to demonstrate the recurring situations of history.

The pastiche character is evident in the scene "Maßnahme 1956," in which excerpts from Brecht's *Galilei* and *Coriolan* are interwoven with a conversation between the two theater directors Peter Palitzsch and Manfred Wekwerth, and are commented on in an imaginary dialogue between the actresses Helene Weigel and Martha Kilian.[135] While the two "Brecht-Witwen" comment on the *Coriolan* rehearsals, we hear a debate held between the two stage directors, in which Wekwerth tries to avoid Palitzsch's politically risky interpretation, which insists on the parallel between the revolt of the proletariat in *Coriolan* and the workers' uprising in the GDR in 1953. In the end, Brecht's empty steel coffin is carried on stage, and one of the workers is asked to try it for size to see if fits Brecht's stature. In a symbolic act, the worker (called Arbeiter 1) buries himself in the coffin of the intellectual advocate of the poor. In a monologue, however, the worker laconically voices his contempt of the poet, and states that he prefers to have fun, women and beer:

> Es liegt sich gut in deinem Stahlsarg, Dichter.
> Wovor versteckst du dich. Angst vor den Würmern.
> Mach dir nichts draus. Wenigstens lügen sie nicht.
> Sie machen ihre Arbeit nicht so gut wie wir.
> Und vielleicht hast du dich zu lieb gehabt
> Und deine Arbeit. Ich arbeite für Geld.
> Mein Spass heisst Feierabend, Bier und Weiber.
> Jetzt heissts vergessen, was du ihnen wert warst
> Dem oder jenem, Dichter. Der Tod zahlt bar.[136]

The scene concludes with Brecht's voice reading out one of his poems, in which he makes it known that, in view of people's ignorance, he would rather be forgotten. It is symbolic that Brecht, the figurehead of left-wing criticism of capitalism, is finally buried, along with his revolutionary ideals.

As in his first play of the Germania series, *Germania Tod in Berlin* (Germania Death in Berlin; 1956/1971), Müller intertwines layers of time, allowing the dead to meet the living, and conjures up the worst possible image of an idea(l), Germania, which is torn to pieces by the greed for power.[137] In Müller's view, the Germans have always fought one another, and always will. They are unable to find reconciliation because of their relentless thirst for money and blood, an age-old trait expressed in the Nibelung myth, where one murder demands the next.[138] As Müller claims, any revolution will inevitably devour its own children. This is evident in the third part of the scene "Siegfried eine Jüdin aus Polen," in which German soldiers at the battle of Stalingrad eat the bones of their dead comrades. A similar image can be found in *Germania Tod in Berlin,* where a soldier is torn to pieces and eaten by his dead comrades in the scene "Hommage à Stalin 1." Bloodshed breeds bloodshed, and the majority of Müller's characters are obsessed by a disturbing zeal for revenge.[139]

It is therefore hardly surprising that his last play ends in 1961, the year the Wall was built and Socialism turned against its own children. This is depicted in the opening scene of the play, with Thälmann and Ulbricht guarding the German-German border.[140] As Müller points out, 1961 effectively marked the end of the GDR as an idea, and the beginning of an ongoing "Kesselschlacht" in the Soviet Union. In other words, he sees the GDR as the prisoner of a repressive dictatorship in the Eastern bloc. In his eyes, the fate of the GDR became obvious after the so-called "kettle" of Stalingrad, the notorious battle between Hitler's and Stalin's armies, in which Stalin adopted Hitler's tactics of encircling the enemy. It is typical of Müller's view of history that time appears to shrink until parallels between two events become clear, since it should be noted that the GDR had not even been conceived of as an idea at this point.

In *Germania 3,* both dictators appear onstage and, in long monologues, express their personal fears as well as their hunger for power. Both are frank in admitting that they soaked the soil with the blood of their own people, and willingly accepted their sacrifice. In dramatic images, Stalin is confronted with the dead Lenin and Trotsky, and welcomes Hitler as his brother in arms, in comparison to whom he emerges as the savior of his people. Hitler is unaffected by the death of his people, and asks women to dance through the fire in front of the *Walhalla* while he shoots his dog. All in all, Müller makes it clear that neither revolutions nor wars can end in true victory, as they will always demand the sacrifice of the lives and the future of the common people.

It is only in the last scene "Der rosa Riese" that Müller indirectly refers to reunification at all, depicting it as the beginning of an exaggerated German nationalism. The pink giant alludes to a famous washing-powder brand called "Der weiße Riese," as well as the 1950s, when the Germans worked to achieve an economic miracle. However, it also refers to the giants Fasolt and Fafner of Wagner's *Das Rheingold* (1869), who are a dull and clumsy part of the action, and remnants of a glorified mythology. In the context of reunification, the pink giant can be interpreted as a combination of both, thus German dullness personified.[141] Masturbating under an oak tree, *the* symbol of German nationalism, the giant, who calls himself the "death of Brandenburg," laughs about dead parents and their children. He wants to forget the past at all costs, even if this means "über Leichen zu gehen," as the German saying goes. The scene concludes with a quotation by Yuri Gagarin, the first man in space, whose remark is tendered as: "Dunkel Genossen ist der Weltraum sehr dunkel." This reads like Müller's comment on the omnipresence of war and manslaughter in the world.

Müller's attitude towards the "gentle revolution" in the GDR is reserved, and he is careful not to get carried away by overtly positive emotions. He also admits that he had not expected the uprising to happen so quickly.[142] When asked for his opinion on reunification, Müller emphasized that he saw it simply as a "Währungsunion," unity under the rule of money.[143] Moreover, he showed concern that those who had just liberated themselves from the hold of Stalinism tended to overlook the global division between poverty and prosperity.[144] According to him, reunification has produced a vacuum of values, and the only adequate response is thus to continue writing. Whilst other East German authors, such as Volker Braun and Christoph Hein openly succumbed to their personal problems following the "Wende," Heiner Müller's post-1989 identity crisis is more indirect. Other than in the last scene, reunification is more or less ignored in his play, and Müller's problems with the "Wende" are reflected in his stunned amazement at the death of a state in which he always believed, no matter how harshly he criticized it.

"Wessi" meets "Ossi": Oliver Bukowski's *Gäste* (1999)

Gäste is the thirteenth play written by the East German playwright Oliver Bukowski, who has written a total of sixteen plays, seven radio plays, and three film scripts. *Gäste* won him the *Mülheimer Dramatiker-Preis* in 1999, and he is probably the best-known playwright from East Germany. However, Bukowski is not too happy with this label, and states with resignation:

Wenn ich was schreibe, ist das immer "Osten." Der Reflex ist nicht zu
überwinden: Ein Autor kommt aus dem Osten, also schreibt er auch
über den Osten. Hat gar keinen Sinn, dagegen etwas zu sagen.[145]

It is remarkable that all his works have already been already staged and
produced, and that his plays have been translated into more than ten
languages. Bukowski has shown close interest in the events of the
"Wende" and its impact on East German society, and continues this
focus in *Gäste*. The tragedy belongs to a cluster of six plays focusing on
the "gentle" revolution: *Die Halbwertszeit der Kanarienvögel* (The Half-
life of Canaries, 1993), *Londn — L.Ä. — Lübbenau* (1993), *Intercity*
(1993), *Lakoma* (1996), and *Hinter den Linien* (Behind the Lines,
1998).[146] In February 1999, *Gäste* premiered at the *Staatstheater Braunschweig*, a production that was generally considered not to do the play
justice, as it failed to express the East German character of the text.[147] By
contrast, the East German staging, directed by Bukowski's friend Hans-
Joachim Frank, was seen to be much more successful in bringing out the
frailty of the East German psyche.[148] This production took place at the
home of *theater 89* in the small village of Niedergörsdorf in Brandenburg, a few miles south of Berlin, a region which is highly representative
of the hopelessness found in Bukowski's plays. Due to its tremendous
success, the production was soon transferred to a small theater in Berlin,[149] and in April 2000, to the *Hebbel-Theater*.[150] In February 2000, the
Altonaer Theater in Hamburg put on a four-day festival called "Best of
Bukowski," which included another production of *Gäste*.[151] The play was
also shown at the *Volkstheater* in Rostock in January 2001, where the
press praised the production by Alejandro Quintana.[152] Despite his success, Bukowski is committed both to the practical aspects of theater, and
to helping younger, lesser-known playwrights gain prominence. He thus
founded the first German *Uraufführungstheater* (UAT) which is pres-
ently hosted by the *Staatsschauspiel Dresden* and modeled on the *Royal
Court* in London.

In a similar plot to the so-called "Hardcore-Schwank," *Londn —
L.Ä. — Lübbenau*, which ends with the suicide of the Gretschke family
following the failure of their newly opened cocktail bar,[153] *Gäste* depicts
Erich and Kathrin's doomed attempt to run a hotel. This proves symbolic of the East German economy, which has suffered considerably from
the impact of reunification and the subsequent migration of East Germans to the richer Western regions. As a result many people turned to
the service industry in their attempt to make a living.[154] Since customers
failed to appear, many East Germans were left with shattered self-esteem[155]

and huge debt; in *Gäste*, Kathrin eventually commits suicide because she is pregnant with her guest's child. As she is keen to please him and offer good "service," she even sleeps with him, albeit in front of her husband, who is aghast. In the same vein as earlier works, *Gäste* is a realistic play, which focuses on the real problems of the normal citizen. After two decades of postmodern pastiches, Bukowski's plays thus mark the return to a more conventional art form.

Gäste is set in a desolate part of the *Niederlausitz*, a region to the southeast of Berlin,[156] where the bored and desperate inhabitants of the run-down village *Alt-Kreumel* are thrilled at the arrival of their first West German guest. The village is inhabited by the loving couple Kathrin and Erich, who have just finished converting a former stable into a hotel; the sexually frustrated butcher Hagedorn, who says of himself: "Ich bin kein Hengst, ich bin eine Tube Sekundenkleber" (*G*, 65); Äppel-Treitschke, the apple farmer who has resorted to making apple-brandy because his organic apples do not sell; the tart, Jutta, and her demented but beautiful daughter Edith, who finally marries the guest, "Dr." Neugebauer; Frau Stoklosa, the esoteric artist; and the constantly drunk priest Lutz, called "Lulle," who, as is revealed after his fatal fall from a pew, had been sacked by the church years ago.

The play opens with an intimate encounter between Erich and Kathrin, who have happily finished refurbishing the stable, and are excitedly looking forward to their guests. However, their expectations are soon to be disappointed, as reservations are cancelled and visitors stay away. Kathrin becomes depressed, and just when Erich is trying to console her and almost rapes her in the foyer of their hotel, a guest enters. By the following morning, virtually the whole village has gathered to admire their new guest, and each villager is determined to please him:

> *Der Gast sitzt, wird ungeniert angestaunt, versucht freundlich zu bleiben, weiß bald vor Verlegenheit nicht mehr, wohin er sich wenden soll.*
>
> JUTTA (VOM) SCHWANHOF *mutig*   Die Eier. Samt und sonders von Hühnern mit Namen noch. Rotchen. Scharrwanst. Käti. Fötzchen. Und so weiter, sag ich nur. Hühner mit Namen, glückliche Hühner.
>
> GAST *hüstelt*   Ja . . . Schön, daß es das noch gibt, nicht wahr.
>
> ER   Wir sollten den Gast in Ruh sein Essen essen lassen.

WILHELM HAGEDORN   Gegen ein Gespräch in Ehren wird er
schon nichts haben. Konversation ist gestattet.
Wie, darf ich fragen, ist ihr persönliches
Verhältnis zur Mettwurst?

SIE *wieder auf*   Die Eier, das Brot, einen gesunden Appetit
wünsch ich.

GAST *die Stimme rutscht ihm weg*   Da . . . Danke.

beginnt zu essen. Er wird weiter bestaunt und folglich immer nervöser.
[. . .]

EDITH (VOM) SCHWANHOF   *ebenfalls all ihren Mut*
zusammennehmend Sie sind am Ende der KO-
Pilot? *erträgt die mütterlichen Backpfeifen, ohne*
den Blick von ihm zu wenden.

Der Gast hustet, verschluckt sich. Alle springen auf, ihm zu helfen: Ein
Glas Wasser und bis neun zählen/ Einen Obstler sag ich nur, einen
Obstler/ Die Backen blähen, die Bäcken blähen/ Daran ist schon manch
einer verreckt usw. Der Gast wehrt tapfer ab. (G, 63)

In this scene, Bukowski portrays the naive yet friendly manner with
which the villagers make conversation with the guest. Despite the fact
that he feels increasingly uncomfortable in their clumsy company, they
continue to chat to him, thus revealing the small world in which they
live. While the butcher is most concerned about the guest's opinion on
sausages, and Jutta embarrasses herself by adding the personal touch of
naming her chickens, Edith, who is largely in search of a "Ko-Pilot," or
rather, husband, sees him as her savior. It is therefore hardly surprising
that the guest chokes on his food, and in doing so, ironically attracts
even more attention from the villagers.

Despite the weaknesses portrayed above, however, it should be noted
that Bukowski is still on the side of the East Germans. This becomes evident after the guest returns from a tour of the village, during which he was
given several presents. While looking at the various items that the friendly
villagers forced upon him, he makes derisory comments. The string of
sausages around his neck is, in his eyes, a ridiculous attempt to imitate the
customs of Hawaii, and the precious piece of pottery made by Frau Stoklosa, which is supposed to express her most delicate soul, he misuses as a
whistle. He is riotously drunk after drinking apple-brandy, and then insults
his host by referring to the villagers as a rare species, as if he was at the zoo
watching exotic animals: "Begreif euch einer, ihr seid fantastisch! Man
sollte euch einlegen und ausstellen, lange macht's diese Lebensform nicht

mehr" (*G*, 64). From this point onwards, the guest's behavior becomes increasingly impertinent. When he realizes that his hosts are truly devastated by his departure, he humiliates Erich by making him dance for him, and then sleeps with Kathrin. Although he has evidently ruined the young couple's relationship, he marries the beautiful young Edith, because Jutta is keen to get rid of her. In the last scene, Kathrin hangs herself in front of the villagers, as she is too ashamed of her actions.

Bukowski's play depicts a handful of stereotypical East German villagers who are desperately trying to adapt to Western standards, despite the fact that they are unsure of what these may be. Their naive efforts appear both ridiculous and moving, thus expressing the East Germans' deep bewilderment when confronted with capitalism. Bukowski is, however, not only critical of his fellow citizens, but also of the overbearing West Germans, who lack all sense of respect. The guest is therefore symbolic of the typical clichéd "Wessi," who believes that East Germans are ill-behaved, silly little children who have yet to be educated.

Ten Years After:
Christoph Hein's *In Acht und Bann* (1999)

In 1999, the *Nationaltheater* in Weimar asked Hein and the West German writer Gerd Heidenreich (1944–) each to write a comic play on the situation in Germany ten years after the Wall came down. The two plays premiered as a double-bill on 29 April 1999 under the title *Siegfried und Sieglinde*. Yet *In Acht und Bann* is not a play about the Nibelungen, but harks back to the myth of Parzival that Hein had already treated in *Die Ritter der Tafelrunde*. In his second play about the knights of the Round Table, Hein presents a comedy about a few forgotten knights, former GDR politicians, who are not aware that their time is up.[157] Once more, we encounter the hardliners Keie, Orilus, and Lancelot on one side, and Artus and Parzival on the other. The setting is the courtyard of a citadel, which is surrounded by high walls and turns out to be a prison, if not a mental asylum, in which the knights are locked up. In this comedy, Hein playfully highlights the "Ostalgie" of the former party functionaries who find themselves longing for past times.

In order to occupy themselves, Keie, Orilus, and Lanzelot continue working on a new constitution and try to evaluate their present situation. Although Artus's empire is in tatters, the trio discuss a future state, failing to notice that they are accused of committing crimes against humanity and abusing power. Firstly, they quarrel about the distribution of the ministries in their imaginary state, a ridiculous debate, because it turns out that the three knights share twenty-two invented portfolios. Although it remains undecided whether the question of accommodation for members of cabinet should be raised in second or third place on the agenda, there are no objections against an increase in pay:[158]

ORILUS   liest vor Punkt drei: über den unhaltbaren und entwürdigenden Zustand der Unterbringung, Verpflegung und finanziellen Ausstattung der Mitglieder des Kabinetts Keie.

KEIE   Wieso ist das Punkt drei? Vorige Woche war es wenigstens noch Punkt zwei. Und Anfang des Jahres war es sogar monatelang Punkt eins.

ORILUS   Ich weiß nicht. Ich habe die Tagesordnung nicht festgelegt.

LANZELOT   Ich kann auch nichts daran ändern. So steht es im *Kleinen Morus.*

KEIE   Müssen wir uns immerzu nach diesem Handbuch für Volksvertreter richten? Unter Artus haben wir auf den Immanuel Morus gepfiffen.[159]

The debate mocks the meetings of the former *Politbüro* of the GDR and the hot air they produced. It becomes increasingly ridiculous, as the emphasis on formalities makes the agenda look more like the pop charts than the outline for a serious debate. This rather farcical scene also shows that the knights must be out of their minds, as they have not realized that the conditions in prison will not change. It is also interesting that Hein's characters use phrases typical of East German political jargon, which is immediately made ridiculous through the context. Keie, for example, complains that the agenda might confuse the people, and that they as leaders are supposed to present a good example to the common man. Phrases like "giving priority to something" or "preserving values" mirror GDR jargon, the function of which was to emphasize the notion of a well-integrated community.[160] At the end, the trio work out some emergency laws that would allow them to preserve law and order, and if they took over, the people would be silenced immediately, in the name of democracy, of course.

In contrast to Parzival's positive role in the earlier play, *Die Ritter der Tafelrunde,* he is now referred to as traitor, because he told the truth at the trial against the knights. In a conversation with Artus, he insists that he only wanted the best for his state, that he believed in the truth and that, sometimes, treason can be equated with honesty. All in all, he gives a fairly hypocritical impression, even claiming not to have known anything about the crimes committed by the Round Table. It is highly ironic that he reminds Artus of his tears when he learned the truth. Parzival refuses to be held responsible for any injustice, maintaining that he had withdrawn from politics. This is the typical example of an opportunist who immediately changed sides, as Parzival is now trying to become chairman in three important West German firms.[161]

Likewise, Keie refuses to accept any responsibility, just as many former GDR politicians and officials denied any knowledge of the violation of human rights. Orilus also maintains that he was not informed of every detail. This touches on the question of whether collective responsibility for the GDR dictatorship existed, or whether Artus was solely responsible. In reality, most GDR officials saw Honecker to be the ideal scapegoat. Hein implicitly states that a dictatorship cannot be set into motion by one person alone, and that all former GDR citizens are culpable to a certain extent.

It is also telling that Parzival does not interfere in the pseudo-parliamentary meetings, but concentrates on gardening. While the trio meet, he shows a complete lack of interest in political matters. This alludes to the ending of Voltaire's *Candide,* who, after traveling the world in search of justice, decides to look after his garden. In an ironic twist, Voltaire advises the reader that, although there are political issues to talk about, "Il faut cultiver son jardin." Parzival seems to be very much in this frame of mind, as his only concern is the color of the flowers. Gardens and allotments often became the "niche," or the center of one's private circle in the GDR, as this was the one place where one could truly escape from the rigidly politicized GDR society. This obsession with gardening parodies the East Germans' tendency to wallow in their golden memories of the "rosige Käfig," as the GDR state was often known. Even ten years into the new order, Parzifal refuses to acknowledge reality.

All in all, Hein's former members of the *Politbüro* are little more than ridiculous doppelgängers of their real-life counterparts. It can be rightly said that Hein avoids any sentimentality, and instead employs woeful undertones in order to criticize those East Germans who still deny the Socialist dictatorship. This becomes evident towards the end, when a knight in shining armor suddenly appears, but disappears into dust when the nurse Uta touches him. Each knight sees the apparition to be the fulfillment of a dream, and it becomes obvious that the shining knight was merely a chimera. As in his earlier depiction of the *Tafelrunde,* Hein presents the quest for the Grail, the search for a utopia, as a self-betrayal.

The economic and political breakdown of the GDR in 1989, followed by the fall of the Wall and reunification in 1990, had an enormous impact on many people's lives, particularly in the *Neue Bundesländer.* Indeed, the so-called "Velvet Revolution" provoked a variety of responses, ranging from fear and disorientation to mockery and criticism. Among Eastern writers, disappointment with the consequences of capitalism prevailed, together with a general feeling of angst, and the way in which the former GDR had virtually been incorporated into the FRG left many discontented. Similarly, the "colonizing" and "raping" of the often "feminized" GDR was a hotly debated issue. With hindsight, it can be said that most responses have focused on the clash between East and West. Playwrights depict the immediate consequences for the man on the street; the East German anxieties regarding capitalism are pitted against the money-grabbing nature of the "Wessis." Other prominent issues include the problematic legacy of the Ministry of Security, the "looting" of the former GDR, and the discussions over whether or not those who had had property expropriated during the GDR should receive compensation.

Written over Christmas 1989, Herbert Achternbusch's farce *Auf verlorenem Posten* (1989) picks up on one of the "myths" of reunification, namely that the GDR had collapsed because of the mass demonstrations in the GDR during 1988 and 1989. The main character of the play, a former member of the *Volksarmee,* stumbles around in a disoriented fashion, for he is unable to understand fully what is happening in his country. In *Mauerstücke* (1990), a postmodern collage of scenes concerning the gentle revolution, Manfred Karge also takes an ironic view of events following 1989. Reunification is presented as an encounter between the biblical Mary and Joseph, the Nibelungen go east to "rape" a girl in the former GDR, and although they are already in hell, subservient members of the Ministry of Security commit suicide for a second time. In contrast, Volker Braun's *Iphigenie in Freiheit* (1990) and *Böhmen am Meer* (1992) both reflect the author's distress in the new Germany. Set on dystopian islands, both plays feature completely devastated protagonists, Iphigenie and Pavel respectively. Neither is able to adapt to the changed political situation. Braun's plays comment on the disastrous effects of the free market, and yearn for the Socialist state, although Braun had never stopped criticizing it while it existed. Klaus Pohl's approach is more concrete, for *Karate-Billi kehrt zurück* (1991/92) focuses on a victim of the Ministry of Security. It tells the story of the athlete Billi, who was locked away in a mental-asylum following a conspiracy against him. Although the play is set in 1990, it shows how Billi may well unravel the web of lies which date from the GDR, yet is unable to come to terms with the injustice inflicted upon him, and his life is in tatters.

Elfriede Müller and Rolf Hochhuth concentrate on the economic consequences of 1989. In *Goldener Oktober* (1992), which is set in the former death strip in Berlin, Müller depicts a handful of Western profiteers, who shatter Easterners' hopes of a better future. Hochhuth's *Wessis in Weimar* (1993) portrays the "looting" of the former GDR, presenting us with the ruined existences of simple farmers, and house owners who fail to receive compensation although their property was expropriated in the GDR. Hochhuth sees it as his duty to radically defend the cheated East Germans, and paints a clear-cut picture of good "Ossis" and bad "Wessis." Since some of the characters even justify murdering high-ranking officials as a legitimate answer to the politics of the German state, Hochhuth was also criticized for supporting terrorist actions, an accusation which he denies.

Against the backdrop of mythology, Botho Strauß's *Schlußchor* (1991) depicts three issues of the time: the "Mauer-Show," the rape of the East, and the revival of revisionist tendencies. In the first part, the presence of the media is mocked, for this creates a heightened awareness, in which every single small event becomes important. Modeled on the Actaeon myth, the second part features a doomed encounter between a West German architect and an Eastern woman, Delia, whom he surprises naked in the bathroom. He falls in love with her, yet she cannot forgive him, and he eventually commits suicide. Strauß masks the conflict between East and West behind the cloak of mythology, and their failed relationship is symbolic of the political situation. In the last part, a young woman, Anita, attempts to gloss over her father's crimes during the Third Reich, thus becoming the representative of revisionist tendencies.

A few years into reunification, Christoph Hein and Oliver Bukowski began to focus more on everyday life in the Berlin Republic, where the "Mauer im Kopf" continues to exist. Hein's comedy *Randow* (1994), which is set near the Polish-German border, shows that "normality" in Germany today involves the rise of fascist tendencies that are even more fatal if they are paired with old Socialist structures of power. In his tragedy *Gäste* (1999), Bukowski depicts the desperate effort of an East German couple to adapt to the economic changes by opening a hotel. However, their undertaking is doomed from the start, for they lack all professional experience. As they are too eager to please their first guest, a West German, they are mocked and ridiculed as a species that should be saved from extinction in order to provide some amusement for their guests.

In his postmodern pastiche *Germania 3 Gespenster am toten Mann* (1996), Heiner Müller returns to a theme that has haunted him all his life, namely that fascism did not end in 1945, and that both German states were the offspring of a plot by Hitler and Stalin. Despite the fact that he was one of the harshest critics of the GDR, Müller bemoaned the death of the Socialist state, and showed his contempt for the victory of capitalism. In his dialogue with the dead, he thus presents us with a scenario of war, death, and disaster. Through this, he voices his despair, yet also expresses the fact that he feels at a loss with regard to the new Germany, and is unable to contribute new answers.

In his play *In Acht und Bann* (1999), Christoph Hein also looks back, but focuses on Germany's recent past since 1989. Harking back to his *Die Ritter der Tafelrunde,* Hein once again assembles the knights of the Round Table, now inmates of a mental asylum, who cannot give up their megalomaniac dreams of an "ideal" state. At the end of the play, the Socialist hardliners' hopes literally go up in smoke, when a knight in shining armor appears and then dissolves in front of their eyes. In a playful manner, Hein mocks "Ostalgie," the longing for allegedly better times in the GDR, by indicating that a Communist utopia would always fail due to politicians' greed for power.

Post-reunification drama employs many stereotypes that emerged after 1989, and the images of rape, marriage, looting, *Mauer-Show,* and Ostalgie subconsciously found their way into most plays of the time. However, a closer look reveals that the intellectual East-West divide cannot be maintained. In fact, the assumption that the West sees events in a more ironic light does not hold true, in the same way that the deeply wounded East does not adopt a more tragic stance. On the one hand, former GDR writers such as Christoph Hein view the situation with irony. On the other hand, playwrights such as Hochhuth clearly adopt a moralistic attitude, accusing the West of profiteering and arrogance. Yet it must not be forgotten that there are dramatists such as Volker Braun, who still express their personal culture shock through the stage. In conclusion, reunification has led to a psychological sea change that opened up new conflict lines between the two German mentalities, and many "Ossi-Wessi" stereotypes and debates over the Berlin Republic found their way into post-1989 drama.

Notes

[1] For the following, see Stephen Brockmann, "Introduction: The Reunification Debate," *New German Critique* 52 (1991), 3–30; Gerhart Maier, *Die Wende in der DDR* (Bonn: Bundeszentrale für politische Bildung, 1991); Wolfgang Herles, *Nationalrausch* (München: Kindler, 1990); Hermann Weber, *Die DDR 1949–1990* (München: Oldenburg, 2000, 5th edition), 107–20; John Ardagh, *Germany and the Germans.*

(London: Penguin, 1995), 421–34; Dieter Grosser, Stephan Bierling, and Friedrich Kurz, *Die sieben Mythen der Wiedervereinigung* (München: Ehrenwirth, 1991).

[2] Stephen R. Bowers, "Honecker's Legacy," *GDR Monitor* 23 (1990), 39–52, here: 40.

[3] See Hans-Hermann Hertle, "Der Fall der Mauer — Sternstunde einer friedlichen Revolution," *Aus Politik und Zeitgeschichte. Beilage zur Wochenzeitung Das Parlament,* 22 Oktober 1999, 12–19.

[4] After 1989, many hardliners of the former GDR quickly denied that they had had anything to with state security (*Staatssicherheit*). They were called "Wendehälse," after a little bird that can turn its neck right round. See also: John Ardagh, *Germany and the Germans* (London: Penguin, 1995), 437.

[5] Wolf Wagner, *Kulturschock Deutschland. Der zweite Blick* (Hamburg: Rotbuch, 1999), esp. 11–43.

[6] This is analyzed in some detail in Wolf Wagner, *Kulturschock Deutschland. Der zweite Blick* (Hamburg: Rotbuch, 1999), 127–52.

[7] On the psychological problems following reunification, see Alison Lewis, "Analyzing the Trauma of German Reunification," *New German Critique* 64 (1995), 135–60, here: 136.

[8] Andreas Huyssen, "After the Wall: The Failure of the German Intellectuals," *New German Critique* 52 (1991), 109–29, here: 117.

[9] Christoph Hein, "Ich bin ein Schreiber von Chroniken . . . ," *Neues Deutschland,* 2/3 December 1989.

[10] In Müller's view, reunification would be a very sad thing, see "'Nicht Einheit sondern Differenz.' Ein Gespräch mit Patrick Landolt für *Deutsche Volkszeitung/die tat,* 24 November 1989," in Heiner Müller, *Gesammelte Irrtümer 3. Texte und Gespräche* (Frankfurt am Main: Verlag der Autoren, 1994), 37–44, here: 44.

[11] *Neues Deutschland,* 28 November 1989.

[12] Günter Grass, *Ein Schnäppchen namens DDR. Letzte Reden vor dem Glockengeläut* (Frankfurt am Main: Luchterhand, 1990).

[13] Peter von Becker, "Wahns Welt," *Th* 11 (1992): 1.

[14] A bittersweet memory of the GDR and a look at its positive and negative sides from the viewpoint of three old ladies is presented in Einar Schleef, *Totentrompeten 1–4* (Frankfurt am Main: Suhrkamp, 2002). The first part of the tetralogy was premiered in March 1995 in Schwerin, where it was warmly received, see Franz Wille, "Von Pilzen und Menschen," *Th* 4 (1995): 22–25; the second part, "Drei Alte tanzen Tango," was premiered in February in Schwerin, and was praised for its authenticity; see Ernst Schumacher, "Die Geschichte bittet zum Tanz. Das bisher authentischste Wendestück: Einar-Schleef-Uraufführung in Schwerin," *BZ,* 24 September 1997.

[15] On East-West stereotypes, see Wagner, *Kulturschock Deutschland. Der zweite Blick* (Hamburg: Rotbuch, 1999), 153–75; Gerhart Schmidtchen, *Wie weit ist der Weg nach Deutschland? Sozialpsychologie der Jugend in der postsozialistischen Welt* (Opladen: Leske + Budrich, 1997), 341–68.

[16] Herbert Achternbusch, "Theater — Theater nicht," in *Herbert Achternbusch,* ed. Jörg Drews (Frankfurt am Main: Suhrkamp, 1981), 122.

[17] The word "farce" is derived from kitchen language and originally denoted a mixture of spices and other ingredients for fillings; as a genre, it was very popular in the 15th century. On the contemporary stage, it is also characterized by swiftness and quick changes. See also A. Bermel, *Farce. A history from Aristophanes to Woody Allen* (1982) (Southern Illinois: Southern Illinois UP, 2001), 22–29; W. D. Howarth, "From Harlequin to Abu: Farce as Anti-theatre," *Themes in Drama* 10 (1988), 153–71, here: 169; Jessica Milner-Davies, *Farce* (London: Methuen, 1978), 1–24.

[18] See Peter von Becker, "Der wüste Westen," *Th* 5 (1990): 9–13, here: 11.

[19] In the GDR, the Wall was perceived as the antifascist shield, and antifascism was used to legitimize the political system, although it was acted out rather superficially. This unsatisfactory approach to the Nazi past is perceived to have caused a dramatic rise in right-wing extremism in East Germany after reunification. See Marcus Neureiter, *Rechtsextremismus im vereinten Deutschland* (Marburg: Tectum, 1996), 36–38. This view is contested by Walter Friedrich, "Einstellung zu Ausländern bei ostdeutschen Jugendlichen. Autoritäre Persönlichkeit als Stereotyp," in Hans-Uwe Otto and Roland Merten (eds.), *Rechtsradikale Gewalt im vereinigten Deutschland* (Opladen: Leske + Budrich, 1993), 189–99.

[20] The banana topic is also mocked in three short farcical scenes and a comic strip, all published in *Theater heute*. See Andreas Müry, "A Fall of a Banana Peel"; Matthias Messmer and Johanna Martin, "Aufstieg und Fall der Banane"; Wolf-Dietrich Sprenger, "Das krumme Ding oder Ausgerechnet Bananen," *ThJ* (1990), 51–53.

[21] Herbert Achternbusch, *Auf verlorenem Posten. Eine Revolutionsfarce*, in *Theater Heute* 4 (1990), 15–20, here: 17.

[22] See Dieter Grosser, Stephan Bierling, and Friedrich Kurz, *Die sieben Mythen der Wiedervereinigung* (Munich: Ehrenwirth, 1991), 68–78.

[23] On this new East German, see John Ardagh, *Germany and the Germans* (Harmondsworth: Penguin, 1995), 437.

[24] Manfred Karge, "Mauer-Stücke" [1989–90], in Manfred Karge, *Die Eroberung des Südpols. Sieben Stücke* (Berlin: Alexander Verlag, 1996), 129–208, here: 159. Subsequent references to this work are cited in the text using the abbreviation *MS* and page number.

[25] Susan S. Morrison, "The Feminization of the German Democratic Republic in Political Cartoons 1989–1990," *Journal of Popular Culture* (25 April 1992), 35–51.

[26] The premiere at the *Kammerspiel* in Frankfurt in January 1992 was coolly received; see Franz Wille, "Zeitgeistshows: Sinn oder Stuss? Rainald Goetz *Festung* und *Katarakt* in Frankfurt, Volker Brauns *Iphigenie in Freiheit* in Frankfurt und Cottbus," *Th* 2 (1993): 12–17.

[27] Goethe's *Iphigenie auf Tauris* (1786) follows Euripides interpretation of the Greek myth, in which Iphigenie is not sacrificed by Agamemnon, but secretly transferred to the land of the Taurs on the Krim. In the realm of King Thoas, she becomes the priestess of Artemis and is obliged to prepare every intruder for his ritual killing. One day, her brother Orest and his comrade Pylades arrive, only to be given to Iphigenie. In Goethe's adaptation of the myth, she refuses to succumb to the curse of Tantalus, who had predicted that her family would kill one another, but confesses the truth to Thoas. An enlightened king, he allows her and Orest to leave the country.

[28] Wilfried Grauert, "Furor melancholicus auf wüstem Planum; oder, Abschied von der Präzeptorrolle: Zu Volker Brauns szenischem Text *Iphigenie in Freiheit*," *The German Quarterly* 67 (1994), 1–111.

[29] Especially the end of scene 1 is a montage of quotations from Büchner's *Danton's Tod*, Heiner Müller's *Fatzer*-Fragment, Lessing's *Philotas*, and Goethe's *Iphigenie auf Tauris*. Danton's critical attitude towards revolution is molded into: "Das ist sehr langweilig, immer in der nämlichen Rüstung herumzulaufen und die nämlichen Waffen zu ziehn. So ein altmodisches Instrument zu sein, bei dem ein Schlag immer einen Schrei ergibt" (*Iphigenie in Freiheit*, 10). While Büchner's *Danton* originally uses the image of a string producing a sound, Braun transforms this image into an allusion to manslaughter and torture. The last part of scene 1 starts with a quotation from Lessing's *Philotas*: "Glaubt ihr Menschen, daß man es nicht satt wird?" These are the last words of the play, spoken by Aridäus, indicating that war is likely to continue.

[30] With reference to the line "DAS VOLK/ Ich bin Volker" (*Iphigenie in Freiheit*, 7), it has been suggested that the play directly communicates Volker Braun's thoughts, see Carol Anne Constable-Henning, *Intertextual Exile. Volker Braun's Dramatic Re-Vision of Society* (Hildesheim: Olms, 1997), 220.

[31] Franz Wille, "Zeitgeistshows: Sinn oder Stuss? Rainald Goetz *Festung* und *Katarakt* in Frankfurt, Volker Brauns *Iphigenie in Freiheit* in Frankfurt und Cottbus," *Th* 2 (1993): 16.

[32] According to Habermas, the individual needs both the individual and the collective identity in order to socialize. Jürgen Habermas, *Zur Rekonstruktion des Historischen Materialismus* (Frankfurt am Main: Suhrkamp, 1976), 92–126, here: 93.

[33] Zentralinstitut für Jugendforschung Leipzig, ed., *Ergebnisse der DDR-Repräsentativen Meinungsumfrage M5*, 20. www.za-uni-koeln.de/data/ddr-nbl/codebuch/6076cb.pdf. Accessed on 17 March 2003.

[34] Bettina Westle, "Strukturen nationaler Identität in Ost- und Westdeutschland," *Kölner Zeitschrift für Soziologie und Sozialpsychologie*, 3 (1992), 461–88, here: 472.

[35] Elisabeth Noelle-Neumann, "Die Vorzüge der Freiheit stehen nicht im Mittelpunkt," *Frankfurter Allgemeine Zeitung*, 30 September 1991, 13.

[36] The term was coined by Kalvero Oberg, who distinguishes four phases: 1. euphoria, 2. alienation and self-accusation, 3. misunderstandings, 4. communication: learning to live with cultural differences. Iphigenie is probably in the second and third phases, both blaming herself and condemning the West German culture. For the term cultural shock, see Kalvero Oberg, "Cultural Shock: Adjustment to New Cultural Environments," *Practical Anthropology* 7 (1960), 177–82.

[37] Volker Braun, *Iphigenie in Freiheit* (Frankfurt am Main: Suhrkamp, 1990), 7. Subsequent references to this work are cited in the text using the abbreviation *I* and page number.

[38] In a poem of 1991, entitled *Das Eigentum*, Braun describes the loss of his home country and his bitter resentment of the colonization of the GDR, which deprived him both of his past and of his future: "Was ich niemals besaß, wird mir entrissen./ Was ich nicht lebt, werd ich ewig missen./ Die Hoffnung lag im Weg wie eine Falle./ Mein Eigentum,

jetzt habt ihrs auf der Kralle . . . ," in *Von einem Land und vom andern. Gedichte zur deutschen Wende,* ed. Karl Otto Conrady (Leipzig: Suhrkamp, 1993), 51.

[39] Wolf Wagner, *Kulturschock Deutschland. Der zweite Blick* (Hamburg: Rotbuch, 1999), 11.

[40] Wilfried Grauert, *Ästhetische Modernisierung bei Volker Braun* (Würzburg: Königshausen & Neumann, 1995), 194

[41] According to Sophocles' tragedy, Kreon forbade Antigone to bury her brother, who was killed during his attack of Thebes. She regarded this as an offense against the gods, and symbolically cast a few handfuls of soil onto his corpse. As Kreon's soldiers caught her, she was sentenced to death and buried alive.

[42] Reviewed by Gerhard Stadelmeier, "Ode an die Meute. Komödie der Deutschen," *Frankfurter Allgemeine Zeitung,* 4 February 1991.

[43] "Kalldewey. Farce," in Botho Strauß, *Theaterstücke 2* (München: Carl Hanser, 1991), 7–72.

[44] In Strauß's works, the myth is often employed to criticize contemporary historical developments. This is perceived as a general feature of Strauß's writing. See also Christoph Parry, "Der Aufstand gegen die Totalherrschaft der Gegenwart. Botho Strauß' Verhältnis zu Mythos und Geschichte," *text & kritik* 81 (1998), 54–64, here: 55.

[45] Hermann Hillebrecht: "Wahnsinn!" *Göttinger Tageblatt,* 13 November 1989. "Plastewagen" refers to the Trabant.

[46] On the influence of the photographer on the group see also Steffen Damm, *Die Archäologie der Zeit. Geschichtsbegriff und Mythosrezeption in den jüngeren Texten von Botho Strauß* (Opladen/Wiesbaden: Westdeutscher), 1998, 60.

[47] Here Strauß follows writers such as Rimbaud ("Moi, c'est un autre") or Valéry, who, at the end of the nineteenth century, had vehemently rejected the idea of a whole, undivided subject.

[48] Botho Strauß, *Paare, Passanten* (Munich: dtv, 1981), 176.

[49] The "spectacle" aspect of the fall of the Wall and the role of the media are discussed in Rainer Bohn, Knut Hickethier, and Eggo Müller (eds.), *Mauer-Show. Das Ende der DDR, die deutsche Einheit und die Medien* (Berlin: sigma, 1992), 7–9.

[50] See Jürgen Schröder, "Ein Nachwort zum *Schlußchor* von Botho Strauß," in Jürgen Schröder, *Geschichtsdramen. Die "Deutsche Misere" — von Goethes* Götz *bis Heiner Müllers* Germania (Tübingen: Stauffenburg, 1994), 341–51, here: 344.

[51] Thomas Oberender suggests that Strauß regards the "gentle revolution" to be an error, a "Versehen," something that happened by mistake and cannot be taken back, see Thomas Oberender, "Die Wiedererrichtung des Himmels. Die 'Wende' in den Texten von Botho Strauß," *text & kritik* 81 (1998), 76–99, here: 84.

[52] On the importance of the metaphor of the house for the political discourse of 1989, see Wilfried Korngiebel/Jürgen Link, "Von einstürzenden Mauern, europäischen Zügen und deutschen Autos. Die Wiedervereinigung in Bildern und Sprachbildern," in Rainer Bohn, Knut Hickethier and Eggo Müller (eds.), *Mauer-Show. Das Ende der DDR, die deutsche Einheit und die Medien* (Berlin: sigma, 1992) 31–54, here: 43.

[53] Oberender, "Die Wiedererrichtung des Himmels. Die 'Wende' in den Texten von Botho Strauß," *text & kritik* 81 (1998), 76–99, here: 81. Oberender points out that

Strauß's characters are largely undecided, a state of mind which is symbolized by locations such as doorsteps and mirrors.

[54] Jürgen Schröder, "Ein Nachwort zum *Schlußchor* von Botho Strauß," in Jürgen Schröder, *Geschichtsdramen. Die "Deutsche Misere" — von Goethes Götz bis Heiner Müllers* Germania (Tübingen: Stauffenburg, 1994), 341–51, here: 348.

[55] Botho Strauß, "Anschwellender Bocksgesang," *Sp*, 6–8 February 1993: "Von ihrem Ursprung an hat sich die deutsche Nachkriegs-Intelligenz darauf versteift, daß man sich nur der Schlechtigkeit der herrschenden Verhältnisse bewußt sein kann: sie hat uns sogar zu den fragwürdigsten Alternativen zu überreden versucht und das radikal Gute und Andere in Form einer profanen Eschatologie angeboten."

[56] Damm, *Die Archäologie der Zeit. Geschichtsbegriff und Mythosrezeption in den jüngeren Texten von Botho Strauß* (Opladen/Wiesbaden: Westdeutscher, 1998), 137.

[57] Damm, *Die Archäologie der Zeit. Geschichtsbegriff und Mythosrezeption in den jüngeren Texten von Botho Strauß* (Opladen/Wiesbaden: Westdeutscher, 1998), 138.

[58] Georg Hensel, "Vereinigungen da und dort. *Schlußchor* in Berlin, mit Rückblicken nach München," *FAZ*, 6 February 1992.

[59] Hensel, "Vereinigungen da und dort," 1992.

[60] For a very short introduction to Müller's plays, see Eva Pfister, "Von den Schrek-ken der Sehnsucht," in *Stück-Werk 1* (Berlin: Internationales Theaterinstitut, 1997), 79–81, here: 80.

[61] On the re-emergence of political theater in a wider context see Christel Weiler, "Am Ende/Geschichte. Anmerkungen zur theatralen Historiographie und zur Zeitlichkeit theaterwissenschaftlicher Arbeit," in *Transformationen. Theater der neunziger Jahre. Theater der Zeit Recherchen 2*, eds. Erika Fischer-Lichte, Doris Kolesch, and Christel Weiler (Berlin: Theater der Zeit, 1999), 43–56, here: 44.

[62] The Wall is still a burning issue in contemporary Germany. See, for example Josef Joffe, "Die Beton-Blamage. Die Mauer: Grabplatte des Sozialismus und Lektion für die Zukunft," *Die Zeit*, 9 August 2001; on the personal implications and tragedies on both sides of the Wall see Christoph Dieckmann, "Die Lebenden und die Toten," *Die Zeit*, 9 August 2001; on the situation of the intellectuals in the GDR, see Günter Kunert, "Eingemauert im Paradies," *Die Zeit*, 9 August 2001.

[63] For an overview of the gigantic construction projects along the former Wall, see Christian Bahr, *Berlins Gesicht der Zukunft* (Berlin: Jaron, 1998). The book includes old and new photographs of the sites in question, as well as photographs of models of future projects.

[64] For an excellent documentation of the Berlin border before and after the fall of the Wall see Harry Hampel and Thomas Friedrich, *Wo die Mauer war* (Berlin: Nicolai, 1997). For an architectural history of Berlin's most famous venues and places, see Rainer Haubrich, *Berlin. Gestern heute morgen. Auf der Suche nach der Stadt* (Berlin: Nicolai, 1997). For useful teaching material concerning the changing Berlin, see Landeszentrale für politische Bildung (ed.), *Berlin. Europäische Metropole und deutsche Hauptstadt, Deutschland und Europa* 31 (Stuttgart, Reihe für Politik, Geschichte, Geographie und Deutsch, 1995).

[65] See "Berliner Tunnelprojekte — gigantisch und fragwürdig," *Stuttgarter Zeitung,* 12 October 1995; "Am Reichstag: Abrißpläne enthüllt," *Die Zeit,* 14 Juli 1995; "Berlins beste Baustellen," *Sonntag aktuell,* 5 November 1995.

[66] Elfriede Müller, "Warum flutscht das alles so gut durch?" *ThJ* (1995), 152–53, here: 153.

[67] Elfriede Müller, "Goldener Oktober," in Elfriede Müller, *Die Bergarbeiterinnen. Goldener Oktober* (Frankfurt am Main: Verlag der Autoren, 1992), 48. Subsequent references to this work are cited in the text using the abbreviation *GO* and page number.

[68] This information appears in an earlier version of *Goldener Oktober,* published in *Th* 5 (1991): 44–54, here: 52.

[69] Quote taken from Harald Kurz, *Die Wiedervereinigung im Spiegel der 'Tagesthemen' — Kommentare von 1988 bis 1992* (Frankfurt am Main: Peter Lang, 1996), 143.

[70] See for example Rainer Rother, "Jahrestag — Fernsehtag. Der 9.11.89 im TV, ein Jahr danach," in *Mauer-Show. Das Ende der DDR, die deutsche Einheit und die Medien,* ed. Rainer Bohn (Berlin: Sigma-Edition, 1992), 157–74. The TV program of 9 November 1990 reads as follows: "Wer zu spät kommt — Das Politbüro erlebt die deutsche Revolution." Written by Cord Schnibben, directed by Jürgen Flimm and Claudia Rohe, ARD, 9 November 1990, 8:15 P.M.; "'Und wenn die Welt voller Teufel wär.' — Die Lutherstadt Eisleben und die Wende, documentary film by Jürgen Schröder-Jahn," ARD, 9 November 1990, 10:20 P.M.; "'Wer jetzt schläft, der ist tot!' Als die Mauer in Berlin fiel," by Sabine Nawroth and Christhard Läpple, ZDF, 8 November 1990, 9:00 P.M.; "Eine deutsche Geschichte. 'Wir haben die Mauer durchbrochen,'" documentary film by Wolfgang Schwarze and Gitta Nickel, ZDF, 9 November 1990, 10:15 P.M.; "Die Mauer," documentary film by Matthias Walden, Günter Hahn, and Lothar Kompatzki, Nord 3, 9 November 1990, 9:15 P.M.; "November Days," documentary film by Marcel Ophüls, RTL plus, 9 November 1990, 12:15 A.M.

[71] See Susan S. Morrison, "The Feminization of the German Democratic Republic in Political Cartoons 1989–1990," *Journal of Popular Culture* 25 (1992), 35–51.

[72] This prompted one critic to note: "Doch was vor kurzem noch als Schauermärchen aus der Feder eines Wessi-Schreibers gelten konnte, ist von der Wirklichkeit der täglichen Enthüllungen längst eingeholt, womöglich übertroffen." See Rüdiger Schaper, "Die Nacht der wahren Gesichter. Alexander Lang inszeniert *Karate-Billi* in Berlin," *SZ,* 22 April 1992.

[73] See the excellent documentation by Thomas Anz (ed.), *Es geht nicht nur um Christa Wolf. Der Literaturstreit im vereinten Deutschland* (Frankfurt am Main: Fischer, 1995; first edition: München: edition spangenberg, 1991).

[74] Klaus-Dietmar Henke, "Die Staatssicherheit," in Werner Weidenfeld and Karl-Rudolf Korte (eds.), *Handbuch zur deutschen Einheit 1949–1989–1999* (Bonn: Bundeszentrale für politische Bildung, 1999), 721–30, here: 728.

[75] As a recent study shows, the number of MfS "employees" rose from 3,000 in 1950 to more than 90,000 in 1989. See Jens Gieseke, *Die DDR-Staatssicherheit. Schild und Schwert der Partei* (Bonn: Bundeszentrale für politische Bildung, 2000), 86.

[76] Deutscher Bundestag (ed.), *Materialien der Enquete-Kommission zur Aufarbeitung von Geschichte und Folgen der SED-Diktatur in Deutschland,* vol. *7: Das Ministerium für Staatssicherheit, Seilschaften, Altkader, Regierungs-und Vereinigungskriminalität* (Frankfurt am Main: Suhrkamp, 1995), 97.

[77] Deutscher Bundestag (ed.), *Materialien der Enquete-Kommission* 7, 106–7.

[78] Deutscher Bundestag (ed.), *Materialien der Enquete-Kommission* 7, 92–93.

[79] Klaus Pohl, *Karate-Billi kehrt zurück* (Frankfurt am Main: Verlag der Autoren, 1993), 50.

[80] Deutscher Bundestag (ed.), *Materialien der Enquete-Kommission* 7, 71.

[81] There are two versions of the play: The 1992 version dealt with here, and a later version of 1993, in which Braun omits Michail's daughter Raja and the German student Robert. The bibliographical data of the later version is: Volker Braun, *Böhmen am Meer. Texte in zeitlicher Reihenfolge* 10 (Halle: Mitteldeutscher Verlag, 1993).

[82] Wolfgang Fritz Haug, "Endspiele des Postkommunismus? Zu Volker Brauns Stück *Böhmen am Meer,*" *Freitag,* 20 March 1992; Roland H. Wiegenstein, "Gewellte Pappe. Volker Brauns *Böhmen am Meer* uraufgeführt," *Frankfurter Rundschau,* 12 March 1992.

[83] The play is a free adaptation of *The Winter's Tale* with the jealousy subplot included. In Shakespeare's play, King Leontes of Sicily is convinced that King Polixenes of Bohemia rendered Hermione pregnant. Polixenes manages to escape before he is poisoned, and Leontes imprisons Hermione. In jail, she gives birth to a daughter whom Leontes believes to be the offspring of Polixenes. He asks Apollo's oracle, in order to find out the truth, but refuses to believe it. Right afterwards, his son Mamillius dies. Hermione faints and is also believed to be dead. Sixteen years later, Polixenes's son Florizel has fallen in love with Perdita, Leontes daughter, not knowing that she is not a shepherdess. Finally, the truth becomes known and the two kingdoms are reconciled through the marriage of Perdita and Florizel. Moreover, Hermione, who has been declared dead, is brought back to life by supernatural powers. Hermione is restored to Leontes, and the two royal families are finally reconciled.

Unlike in Shakespeare's *The Winter's Tale,* where jealousy consumes King Leontes of Sicily, who accuses his wife of committing adultery with King Polixenes from Bohemia, Pavel does not really seem to care about Julia's past. Also, Shakespeare's play is reversed in the sense that Julia has given birth to a son that is not Pavel's, whereas Hermione is innocent.

[84] Theodore Fiedler has also detected intertextual references with Franz Fühmanns's *Böhmen am Meer* and Ingeborg Bachmann's *Böhmen liegt am Meer.* See Fiedler, "Apocalypse Now? Reading Volker Braun's *Böhmen am Meer,*" *Studies in GDR Culture and Society* 14/15, eds. Margy Gerber and Roger Woods (Lanham: UP of America, 1996), 87–110.

[85] Volker Braun, *Böhmen am Meer* (Frankfurt am Main: Suhrkamp, 1992), 10.

[86] Stephen Brockmann, "Introduction: The Reunification Debate," *New German Critique* 52 (1991), 3–30.

[87] Wolfgang Bialas, *Vom unfreien Schweben zum freien Fall. Ostdeutsche Intellektuelle im gesellschaftlichen Umbruch* (Frankfurt am Main: Fischer, 1996), 106–8.

[88] Volker Braun, *Die Verhältnisse zerbrechen. Rede zur Verleihung des Georg-Büchner-Preises 2000* (Frankfurt am Main: Suhrkamp, 2000), 26.

[89] In view of Braun's critical stance towards reunification, these cannibals could be identified as West German managers who "captured" and "colonized" the GDR in order to make money at the expense of native citizens.

[90] The controversial scene in which Karsten Rohwedder is shot was published by *Sp*, 1 June 1992, 272–75.

[91] An institution founded after reunification to secure the smooth privatization of GDR businesses.

[92] Volker Müller, "Wirbel um *Wessis in Weimar*. Rolf Hochhuths neues Stück empört die deutschen Chefetagen," *BZ*, 29 May 1992.

[93] "Das Bekenntnis. Im mm-Interview: Die kalkulierten Provokationen eines professionellen Dramatikers," *manager magazin* (Hamburg, June 1992).

[94] Ernst Schumacher, "Wirkliche Kunst ist nicht gefällig," *BZ*, 12 February 1993.

[95] Stefan von Bergen, "Bühnen-Polemik um Wiedervereinigung," *Berner Zeitung*, 16 March 1993. Bergen points out that the 260 pages would have to be cut for any staging, because they would provide roughly six hours of performance.

[96] For a discussion of the Red Army Faction, see also the chapter on terrorism in this book.

[97] Rolf Hochhuth, *Wessis in Weimar* (München: dtv, 1994), 25. Subsequent references to this work are cited in the text using the abbreviation *WiW* and page number.

[98] Hochhuth quotes an article from Peter Schmalz in *W*, 15 July 1992: "Doch auf Kosten der Opfer, die damals Haus und Grund für den Grenzbau verloren, will der Staat jetzt einen milliardenschweren Gewinn machen: Die Bundesregierung weigert sich beharrlich, die Mauergrundstücke und ihre früheren Eigentümer zurückzugeben. Die Enteignung werde nicht rückgängig gemacht, da sie nach dem Verteidigungsgesetz und somit nach damals gültiger Rechtslage der DDR erfolgt sei."

[99] Rolf Hochhuth, "Das Bekenntnis. Im mm-Interview: Die kalkulierten Provokationen eines professionellen Dramatikers," in *manager magazin* (June 1992). Quoted in Rolf Hochhuth, *Wessis in Weimar* (München: dtv, 1994), 263–71, here: 267.

[100] Roessing is modeled on Friedrich Carl Jung, the Head of the "Institut für Molekularbiologie" in Berlin. Here, the authenticity of a character is traded for a fictitious figure.

[101] On Ernst Jünger, see, for example: Steffen Martus, *Ernst Jünger* (Stuttgart/Weimar: Metzler, 2001); Helmuth Kiesel, *Wissenschaftliche Diagnose und dichterische Vision der Moderne — Max Weber und Ernst Jünger* (Heidelberg: Manutius, 1994); Thomas Nevin, *Ernst Jünger and Germany. Into the Abyss 1914–1945* (London: Constable, 1997).

[102] Interview with *manager magazin*, 1992.

[103] Bernd Herhoffer, "*Wessis in Weimar*. Hochhuth, Schiller und die Deutschen," in *The New Germany*, eds. Osman Durrani, Colin Good and Kevin Hilliard (Sheffield: Sheffield Academic Press, 1995), 109–27.

[104] David Barnett, "Tactical Realisms: Rolf Hochhuth's *Wessis in Weimar* and Franz Xaver Kroetz's *Ich bin das Volk*," in *'Whose story?' — Continuities in contemporary*

German-language literature, eds. Arthur Williams, Stuart Parkes, and Julian Preece (Berne: Peter Lang, 1998), 181–96, here: 182–87.

[105] Christoph Hein, *Randow* (Berlin: Aufbau, 1994), 13. Subsequent references to this work are cited in the text using the abbreviation *R* and page number.

[106] See Bill Niven, "On Private Utopia and the Possessive Mentality: Christoph Hein's *Randow*," in *Christoph Hein,* eds. Bill Niven and David Clarke (Cardiff: U of Wales P, 2000), 100–16.

[107] Ulrich Hammerschmidt, "Im deutschen Seelengrund," *Th* 2 (1995): 15.

[108] Ernst Schumacher, "Ostwestdeutscher Zerrspiegel," *BZ,* 23 December 1994; Wolfgang Engler, "Froschs Ende," *Die Zeit,* 30 December 1994.

[109] Harmut Krug, "Wessis mit Elan und Ossis ohne Visionen," *Badische Zeitung,* 28 December 1994.

[110] Reinhard Wengierek, "Wenn das Theater der Zeitung nachläuft," *W,* 23 December 1994.

[111] Burkhard Schröder, *Im Griff der rechten Szene. Ostdeutsche Städte in Angst* (Reinbek: Rowohlt, 1997).

[112] Armin Pfahl-Traughber, *Rechtsextremismus in der Bundesrepublik Deutschland* (Munich: CH Beck, 2000), 65–75.

[113] On alcohol abuse in the *Neue Bundesländer* before and after reunification, see Michael Schmitz, *Wendestress. Die psychosozialen Kosten der Einheit* (Berlin: Rowohlt, 1995), 161–74.

[114] The first play is *Germania Tod in Berlin* (1971), which Müller started writing in 1956: Heiner Müller, *Germania Tod in Berlin* (Berlin: Rotbuch, 1977); the other is *Leben Gundlings Friedrich von Preußen Lessing Schlaf Traum Schrei. Ein Greuelmärchen* (Frankfurt am Main: Verlag der Autoren, 1982).

[115] In an obituary for Müller, Peter von Becker complains that in 1995, Müller's plays were buried together with the playwright; see Peter von Becker, "Gespenster am toten Mann. Heiner Müller oder Eine Variation über Vampire, *ThJ* (1996), 108–10.

[116] This was also obvious in Müller's successful staging of Brecht's *Der aufhaltsame Aufstieg des Arturo Ui* (1941) at the *Berliner Ensemble,* where Müller once again focused on Hitler's seizure of power. See Michael Merschmeier, "Die Stimmen über Berlin," *ThJ* (1995), 24–25.

[117] Günther Rühle, "Am Abgrund des Jahrhunderts. Über Heiner Müller — sein Leben und Werk," *Th* 2 (1996): 7–11, here: 11.

[118] Heiner Müller, "Nekrophilie ist Liebe zur Zukunft," in *Jenseits der Nation. Heiner Müller im Gespräch mit Frank M. Raddatz* (Berlin: Rotbuch, 1991), 22–31, here: 31.

[119] "*Germania 3*-Verbot aufgehoben," *BZ,* 27 July 2000.

[120] Peter Laudenbach, "Abschied vom blutigen Jahrhundert," *BZ,* 28 May 1996. Laudenbach praised the unpretentious production, which harked back to the simple devices of the "poor theater" of Jerzy Grotovski.

[121] Sibylle Wirsing, "Der Ausgang der Geschichte. Sibylle Wirsing über Heiner Müllers *Germania 3,* uraufgeführt von Leander Haußmann in Bochum, nachgespielt am Berliner Ensemble," *Th* 8 (1996): 34–37.

[122] Horst Domdey, *Produktivkraft Tod. Das Drama Heiner Müllers* (Cologne, Weimar, Vienna: Böhlau, 1998), 238.

[123] One critic spoke of the "aesthetic insult" of the audience; see Peter Laudenbach, "Gespenster am toten Müller," *BZ,* 21 June 1996.

[124] The fact that the stage was buried under heaps of rubbish hampered the acting, and the production was thus considered to be a little boring; see Thomas Götz, "Im Kosmos immer noch kein Licht," *BZ,* 23 November 1996.

[125] Sigrid Löffler, "Entsetzenskomik auf dem Müllhaufen der Geschichte," *Th* 11 (1996): 8–9, here: 8.

[126] Detlef Friedrich, "Die Spielbarkeit ist noch zu beweisen," *BZ,* 10 March 1997.

[127] Gustav Seibt, "Der Führer privat," *BZ,* 14 April 1997.

[128] Paul C. Ettighoffer, *Gespenster am Toten Mann* [1931] (Gütersloh: Bertelsmann, 1937), 129–30.

[129] "'Die Wahrheit, leise und unerträglich.' Ein Gespräch mit Heiner Müller, von Peter von Becker," *ThJ* (1995), 9–30, here: 14.

[130] Heiner Müller, "Gegen den Zeitgeist. Der Regisseur Fritz Marquardt," in *Kalkfell. Arbeitsbuch für Heiner Müller,* ed. Frank Hörningk (Berlin: Theater der Zeit, 1996), 23.

[131] Interview with Heiner Müller, "Was wird aus dem größeren Deutschland? Fragen von Alexander Weigel," *Sinn und Form* 4 (1991), 665–69, here: 667.

[132] Müller quotes passages from Heinrich von Kleist, *Der Prinz von Homburg;* Friedrich Hölderlin, *Empedokles;* Friedrich Hebbel, *Die Nibelungen;* Bertolt Brecht, *Leben des Galilei* and *Coriolan;* Franz Kafka, *Das Stadtwappen;* Franz Grillparzer, *Die Ahnfrau;* and from his own plays *Philoktet* and *Macbeth.*

[133] Heiner Müller in a letter to the GDR journalist Martin Linzer, in Heiner Müller, *Theater-Arbeit* (Berlin: Rotbuch, 1975), 125. On Müller's technique of fragmentation, see Francine Maier-Schäffer, "'Noch mehr Fragment als das Fragment': Zur Fragmentarisierung in Heiner Müllers Theaterarbeit," in *Aspekte des politischen Theaters und Dramas von Calderón bis Georg Seidel,* eds. Horst Turk and Jean-Marie Valentin (Berne: Peter Lang, 1996), 367–87.

[134] "Ohne Inferno kein Paradies. Worum es Heiner Müller in seinem letzten Stück *Germania* geht — ein Vademecum," *Der Tagesspiegel,* 24 March 1996, 5.

[135] Both directors worked at the *Berliner Ensemble,* where, in the 1950s and 1960s, they staged various Brecht plays, thus opposing the Socialist dictatorships within the feasible limits.

[136] Heiner Müller, *Germania 3 Gespenster am toten Mann* (Cologne: Kiepenheuer & Witsch, 1996), 61.

[137] On *Germania Tod in Berlin,* see Wolfgang Seibel, *Die Formenwelt der Fertigteile. Künstlerische Montagetechnik und ihre Anwendung im Drama* (Würzburg: Königshausen & Neumann, 1988), 183–227, here: 194–202.

[138] On Müller's reinterpretation of the Nibelung myth in the context of Stalingrad, see Joachim Schmitt-Sasse, "Die Kunst aufzuhören. Der Nibelungen-Stoff in Heiner

Müllers *Germania Tod in Berlin,*" in *Die Nibelungen,* ed. Joachim Heinzle (Frankfurt am Main: Suhrkamp 1991), 370–96.

[139] See also: Ernst Wendt, "Ewiger deutscher Bürgerkrieg. Über Heiner Müllers Texte 1–6," *Sp,* 17 April 1978, 260.

[140] Ernst Thälmann (1989–1944) was a communist who was murdered in the concentration camp in Buchenwald; Walter Ulbricht (1893–1973), a political hardliner, was the leader of the *Sozialistische Einheitspartei Deutschlands* (SED) (1950–71) and chair of the *Staatsrat* (1960–71), thus head of the GDR state.

[141] Eke sees parallels between the "Rosa Riese" and the serial murderer and fetishist Wolfgang Schmidt, who murdered five women in the forests near Beelitz; see Norbert Otto Eke, *Heiner Müller* (Stuttgart: Reclam, 1999), 251. This view is supported by Anna Langhoff's play about the murderer Schmidt, *Schmidt Deutschland der Rosa Riese* (1995), commissioned by the *Berliner Ensemble* and written while Müller was still alive.

[142] "'Nicht Einheit, sondern Differenz' Ein Gespräch mit Patrick Landolt für *Deutsche Volkszeitung/ die tat,* 24 November 1989," in Heiner Müller, *Gesammelte Irrtümer 3. Texte und Gespräche* (Frankfurt am Main: Verlag der Autoren, 1994), 37–44, here: 38.

[143] "'Für immer in Hollywood, oder: In Deutschland wird nicht mehr geblinzelt.' Ein Gespräch mit Frank Raddatz für *Lettre International* 24 (1994)," in Heiner Müller, *Gesammelte Irrtümer 3,* 214–30, here: 216.

[144] Heiner Müller, *Zur Lage der Nation* (Berlin: Rotbuch, 1990), 81.

[145] Quoted in Franz Wille, "Reden Sie mal mit einem Penner . . . Drei Fragen an Oliver Bukowski," *Th* 10 (1997): 38.

[146] For a useful if short introduction to these plays, see Jörg Mihan, "Bukowski-Zeit-Stücke," in *Stück-Werk 3,* eds. Christel Weiler and Harald Müller (Berlin: Zentrum Bundesrepublik Deutschland des Internationalen Theaterinstituts, 2001), 20–25.

[147] Matthias Heine, "Hirnlos unter der Spreewaldhaube," *W,* 20 February 1999; Irene Bazinger, "Die Liebe in den Zeiten der Rezession," *BZ,* 3 February 1999.

[148] Barbara Burckhardt, "Wenn der Osten Westen werden will — Hans-Joachim Frank inszeniert Oliver Bukowskis *Gäste* in Brandenburg, Wolfgang Gropper in Braunschweig," *Th* 4 (1999): 58–59.

[149] Irene Bazinger, "Die Zinsen des Glaubens," *BZ,* 8 May 1999.

[150] Detlef Friedrich, "Schöne Schräglagen. Das theater 89 gastiert mit *Gäste* im Hebbel-Theater," *BZ,* 13 April 2000.

[151] Jürgen Serke, "Himmelbewahrer im Scheitern," *BZ,* 12 February 2000.

[152] Detlef Friedrich, "Verrat an Harri," *BZ,* 16 January 2001.

[153] This is one of Bukowski's most successful plays: see "Theater 89. Hausautor Oliver Bukowski: Zwei erfolgreiche Inszenierungen des garstig-einfühlsamen Gegenwartdramatikers," *BZ,* 31 August 2001; "Theater 89. *Londn-L.Ä.-Lübbenau* — Ein Hardcoreschwank in Lausitzer Mundart von Oliver Bukowski," *BZ,* 28 March 2002.

[154] See Martin Diewald, Bogdan Mach, and Heike Solga, "Erfolge und Probleme der ostdeutschen Arbeitsmarkttransformation in vergleichender Perspektive," in *Vom Zusammenwachsen einer Gesellschaft. Analysen zur Angleichung der Lebensverhältnisse*

in Deutschland, eds. Heinz-Herbert Noll and Roland Habich (Frankfurt am Main: Campus, 2000), 107–29, here 120–21; Robert Hettlage and Karl Lenz (eds.), *Deutschland nach der Wende* (München: CH Beck, 1995), 122.

[155] See, for example, Michael Schmitz, *Wendestress. Die psychosozialen Kosten der deutschen Einheit* (Berlin: Rowohlt, 1995), 174–83; Klaus Udo Ettrich, Matthias Huth, and Antje Fischer-Cyrulies, "Veränderungen von Einstellungs- und Persönlichkeitsmerkmalen im höheren Lebensalter und Beziehungen zum Gesundheitszustand im Ost-West-Vergleich — Ergebnisse der ILSE-Studie," in *Deutsch-deutsche Vergleiche. Psychologische Untersuchungen 10 Jahre nach dem Mauerfall,* eds. Hendrik Berth and Elmar Brähler (Berlin: Verlag für Wissenschaft und Forschung, 1999), 70–93, here 91.

[156] Oliver Bukowski, "Gäste," *Th* 4 (1999): 61–68, here: 61. Subsequent references to this work are cited in the text using the abbreviation *G* and page number.

[157] See the chapter on Hein's *Die Ritter der Tafelrunde.*

[158] This is clearly a stab at the German *Bundestag,* whose members are allowed to raise their own salaries.

[159] Christoph Hein, "In Acht und Bann," in Christoph Hein, *Stücke* (Berlin: Aufbau, 1999), 85–128, here: 104.

[160] For the ritual character of communication in the GDR, see the analysis by Ulla Fix (ed.), *Ritualität in der Kommunikation der DDR* (Frankfurt am Main: Peter Lang, 1998), here: XIII.

[161] See Bill Niven, "Christoph Hein's *In Acht und Bann* oder Die Unverbesserlichen," *German Monitor* 51 (2000), 235–53, here: 239.

6: Women in Society Today

IN GERMANY, THE WOMEN'S MOVEMENT came to life in the early days of the student movement, when women began to realize that their male colleagues were not interested in female issues.[1] The 1970s saw a vehement struggle to combat discrimination against women at home, at work and in politics, and German feminists began to oppose the existing legal conditions, such as article 218 of the German Criminal Code,[2] according to which abortion was illegal.[3] By the late 1970s, feminists had established a female counter-culture, and were propagating female values and viewpoints in journals such as *Courage* and *Emma*. Moreover, a close-knit network of institutions and organizations for women in need was set up, comprising *Frauenhäuser*, health centers, cafés, and restaurants, all especially for women.[4]

During the 1980s, the *Frauenbewegung* began to lose its momentum, and as Alice Schwarzer lamented, the increasingly conservative trend within German society[5] was once again glorifying maternity and motherhood.[6] Instead of participating in discussion groups, many women thus bore children and stayed at home.[7] Mainstream journals such as *Brigitte* and *Stern* also began to discuss women's issues, although they sometimes considerably watered down problems. Special columns presented women's issues in easy-to-read articles, juxtaposed with beauty tips, and advice on cooking and household management. Many feminists thus argued that little had changed in practice,[8] a view which features in Gesine Danckwart's (1969–) play *Girlsnightout* (2000).

Although many autonomous groups that offer counseling, homes for prostitutes, and special archives and libraries for women continue to exist today,[9] many women still prefer motherhood to a career.[10] However, feminist scientists energetically debated this return to the private sphere, most notably at a series of public lectures at the *Technische Universität Berlin* in the summer of 1998.[11] These lectures focused on the future of the *Frauenbewegung*, and asked whether the concept of a liberated woman can still be maintained.[12] Playfully picking up on the stereotype of the successful business woman, Roland Schimmelpfennig's *Push Up 1–3* (2000) looks at female top managers and their male and female adversaries. Set in a corporate business, the play offers an ironic insight into the devastated souls of over-emancipated women who cannot reconcile their jobs with their private lives.

Yet the movement largely became institutionalized, and women founded a considerable number of institutes and organizations, such as the *Feministische Interdisziplinäre Forschungsinstitut* in Frankfurt (1983), and the *Verein zur Förderung einer Frauenakademie* in Munich (1984).[13] Many groups are also united under the auspices of the *Deutscher Frauenrat,* the forerunner of which was called into being as early as 1951.[14] In the same vein, Manuela Reichardt organized a theater festival exclusively for women in Cologne in 1980, which aimed to explore the concept of women's theater. As the organizer pointed out, it was simply not sufficient for men to produce plays about women in the belief that this would solve the problem of inequality. In a series of cabarets, improvisations and experimental sessions, the international festival presented a lively feminist culture.[15]

Whereas in the 1970s, Ulrike Meinhof's (1934–1976) play *Bambule* (1970) stood out as the only contemporary play written by a woman, the 1980s saw the emergence of several female playwrights. As early as 1976, Gerlind Reinshagen (1926–) received much critical acclaim for her play *Sonntagskinder* (Sunday Children, 1976), and playwrights such as Gisela von Wysocki, Ursula Krechel (1947–), and Ginka Steinwachs (1942–) made their voices heard. In 1985, Ria Endres's (1946–) *Der Kongreß* (The Conference) criticized the ways in which the culture industry misused women for marketing purposes. At that time, female playwrights insisted on being different, in order to set themselves apart from the theater dominated by men.[16] Painfully aware of this, Ria Endres writes in 1985: "Wir Schriftstellerinnen sind ja alle so *süß!* Und so dankbar! Wir bedanken uns fortwährend, ob unsere Stücke aufgeführt werden oder nicht."[17] Above all, she points out that is rather absurd for women to still be treated differently, as in her eyes, this is in itself discrimination. According to the playwright Gerlind Reinshagen, women want to be accepted for what they achieve, not praised for their female nature:

> Der weibliche Blick: Er ist schneller, leichter umfassender, sagen die einen. Er ist lebendiger, emotionaler, aufrührerischer, die anderen. Ich sage: Es gibt ihn nicht. Nein, auch das ist nicht richtig. Was ich sagen möchte, ist: Wie immer er auch beschaffen sein mag, es soll ihn nicht geben. So wie es den männlichen Blick in einem Kunstwerk nicht geben sollte.[18]

Similarly, the 1990s generation of female writers opted for a gender-encompassing aesthetic. Dea Loher, for example, refuses to support female aesthetics: "Literatur ist für mich androgyn, ich versteh nicht, wie man eine Ästhetik des weiblichen Schreibens überhaupt wollen kann."[19] According to her, a work of art can only be either "good" or "bad," not male or female. Others continued to write and produce plays, sometimes defending themselves in a polemical way.[20] In 1998, the most renowned female directors, Andrea Breth, Katharina Thalbach, Anna Viebrock, Konstanze Lauterbach, and Karin Beyer, to name but a few, moved away from specifically feminist topics in order to criticize society as a whole.[21]

In the same vein, Theresia Walser depicts the situation of women today with distanced irony, in a style that provides scope for the grotesque. Her play *King Kongs Töchter* (King Kong's Daughters, 1996) centers on three female caregivers in their mid-thirties who turn out to be serial murderers. The play, about three frustrated women who accommodate themselves to their working environment in their own way, prompted a heated debate about the situation in old people's homes, and proved that social issues can also be addressed in a non-melodramatic manner.

Despite the advent of young female playwrights such as Loher, a pessimistic attitude prevails in relation to the importance of women in the world of theater and drama. In 2001, the director Brigitte Landes summarized the situation: "Feministischer Aufbruch fand im Theater nicht statt — oder er ist an mir vorbeigerauscht."[22] Other directors, such as Pina Bausch (1940–) and Ariane Mnouchkine (1939–), also respond fairly evasively when faced with the question of a female counter-culture. Mnouchkine thus refers to her work rather in terms of a new approach to acting, thereby avoiding the narrow categorization of a feminist theater.[23]

Although the evaluation of the 1990s *Frauenbewegung* in Germany is fairly pessimistic, Menzel, for example, maintains that the movement has created an awareness of the various manifestations of physical and psychological violence, such as incest, an issue that is at the core of Dea Loher's play *Tätowierung* (Tattoo, 1992). The abused children in Loher's play do not make use of the help that is available, but numerous voluntary workers in women's support centers help women to cope with rape, abuse, and beating. Since the controversy concerning article 218, the need to ensure non-violent and humane conditions for women has been at the top of the feminist agenda.[24] However, the time when feminists presented their issues in an exclusively moralistic manner is over. From a humorous perspective, Kerstin Specht's *Froschkönigin* (Frog Queen, 1998) thus shows the belated liberation of a mother of two children. Through the lens of comedy, Specht looks back to the original motto of the women's liberation movement, and insists that the private must become political, albeit in a humorous manner.

Sexual Abuse: Dea Loher's *Tätowierung* (1992)

Loher's second and hugely successful play,[25] which has meanwhile been translated into seven languages and is performed all over the world, concerns sexual abuse within the family. It was premiered at the *Ensemble Theater am Südstern* in Berlin in October 1992, and in 1993 it was presented as a reading at the Royal Court in London.[26] In 27 short scenes, the bleak and mutilated dialogues of *Tätowierung* depict a dysfunctional family torn apart.[27] The mother, Jule, suffers from allergies and eczema, and expresses her refusal to engage in conversation by wearing a mouth protector, whilst the father abuses the two daughters.[28] As the first victim of his abuse, the older daughter, Anita, manages to escape from home with the help of her boyfriend, Paul. Following this, the father rapes her younger sister Lulu who, like Anita, becomes pregnant with her father's child. The play primarily shows how the psychological effects of physical abuse are burned into Anita's soul like a tattoo.[29] Indeed, Anita is unable to overcome her traumatic memories, and her inability to enjoy a healthy sex life means that she quarrels with her husband Paul. In the end, Anita even threatens him with a shotgun. The shadow of her overbearing and abusive father continues to haunt her adult life.

In the second scene, entitled "Heim," the audience learns that, despite the father's efforts to gloss over his perversion, the family home is a trap akin to a nightmare. During their meal, he rants about abortion and is terribly concerned that somebody might make his daughters pregnant. Yet he clearly has double standards, because it is he who ruins his daughters' future; not only does he rape them, but he does not even take any precautions against pregnancy.

Anita does not seek help, but keeps everything to herself. She suffers in silence while she lies awake at night, frightened that her father might appear at any moment:

> [. . .] Zeit
> mich schlafend zu stellen
> Daliegen
> steifern
> stockbeinig
> zumachen alles
> Er merkt es
> Ich bin sicher
> daß er was merkt
> Meine Muskeln sind alle angestrengt

so lasse ich mich auseinanderreissen
wie ich da liege
wenn nur das eine Mal kommt
wo er mir zuviel tut
dann schnappe ich zusammen
wie ein Messer[30]

Stiff with fear, Anita awaits her torturer, her own father, who forces her into an unnatural commitment. It is no surprise that the girl is afraid of becoming mad, losing control, and attacking him. Yet the father takes every opportunity to prove to his offspring that his perverted desires are justified. He even twists the things his daughters learn at school to his own advantage. When Anita tells him about the growing AIDS problem in Africa, for example, her father unashamedly makes up a story about black men sleeping with their daughters. This, he maintains, is common practice in Africa, and according to him, it is a good ancient custom. The father clearly sees nothing wrong with violating women's rights, and in his opinion, his daughters are merely objects of his pleasure. However, he acts in a rather jealous and overprotective manner, for example, by forbidding them to cycle in the summer, as such behavior would only awaken primitive male instincts. Yet in reality, he is talking about his own subconscious lust for them.

Anita does not suffer alone; her sister Lulu also behaves in a self-destructive manner, cutting herself with a knife and threatening to carry out an abortion on herself with her own hands. Her mother's negative example has rubbed off on her: pretending to be plagued by an allergy, Jule scratches herself until she bleeds. The only possible reaction to an overbearing father and husband appears to be self-mutilation.

Although Jule knows what is happening to Anita, she keeps quiet and refuses to see the truth. When she searches Anita's wardrobe and comes across extravagant pieces of underwear, Jule convinces herself that there is nothing wrong with it. Even when Anita catches her looking at her underwear, Jule is unable to communicate, and quickly covers her mouth. The weak and helpless mother thus only makes the situation worse; later, when Anita is about to leave, she begins to hurt herself in order to put pressure on Anita to stay.

With the help of a young man, Paul, the older daughter finally manages to free herself from her father's grip to a certain extent. Despite Paul's honest attempts to help her get over such dreadful experiences, Anita is unable to forget them. Although he accepts her father's child as his own, the girl is still deeply affected, and physical violence becomes a stain on her soul that will not wear off. Again, the short sentences and the mutilated language express the inner devastation of those involved: neither the victims nor their perpetrator are capable of wringing coherent sentences out of their souls. The violence her father has planted in Anita's mind is, sadly, destructive; when her younger sister Lulu begs her to help her to escape from her father, Anita refuses point blank.

In short, dramatic scenes, Loher depicts a doomed family, and presents a web of fatal psychological torture. Nevertheless, the play is more than a simple documentary drama, for it bears the traits of a tragedy. *Tätowierung* highlights a timeless issue, one which is only too often ignored in society.

Old People's Homes:
Theresia Walser's *King Kongs Töchter* (1998)

Walser's third play *King Kong's Töchter* is set in an old people's home, where Berta, Carla, and Meggie, three women in their thirties, look after a handful of elderly people. As the title suggests, the three caregivers are more like monsters, since they murder the elderly residents, but the play's wit and humor makes *King Kongs Töchter* an enjoyable read. Walser, who herself worked in an old peoples' home for a year, presents the gruesome reality through rapid, witty dialogue portraying the frustration and hidden anger of both staff and residents in a grotesque manner. When asked whether her play focused more on the absurdity or the inhumanity of life, she answered:

> Es ist ein hartes Stück, und ich glaube nicht, dass human der richtige Ausdruck dafür ist. Die Pflegerinnen stehen ja gerade unter dem Druck eines Humanitätsanspruchs, der sich in ihrer konkreten Arbeit gar nicht mehr einlösen lässt, der ihrer täglichen Erfahrung widerspricht.[31]

As early as 1997, Walser was presented as a promising new playwright,[32] due to her play *Kleine Zweifel* (Little Doubts, 1997) that features a murder in the night, and *Das Restpaar* (The Last Couple, 1997) which depicts the hopeless situation of two female actors who apply for a job at a run-down theater.[33] In 1998, Walser was voted best new playwright by the journal *Theater heute;* in 1999 *King Kongs Töchter* was play of the year; and in November 2000, Walser was invited to Edinburgh as *Writer-in-Residence.*

The play premiered at the *Theater Neumarkt* in Zurich in September 1998, and the press celebrated it as the beginning of a new style of writing.[34] The production by Volker Hesse was a huge success, because it highlighted the grotesque humor of the play.[35] *King Kongs Töchter* has become one of the most performed plays in Germany, and the *Kammerspiele* in Munich staged it in June 1999, but the press considered the production by Antoine Uitdehaag to be overacted and exaggerated.[36] October 1999 saw a performance at the *Deutsche Theater* in Berlin, but critics found the production too stale.[37] The play also attracted considerable international attention,[38] for the *Royal Court* presented a reading in London in November 1999,[39] as did the *Traverse* in Edinburgh in October 2000.

The production at the *Schauspielhaus* in Frankfurt in May 2000, and the ensuing public debate between the actors and several managers of old people's homes, also sparked off a debate about the difficult working environment of caregivers and nurses. With fatal incidents becoming ever more common at old peoples' homes,[40] the debate raised the question as to how long it would be before the grotesque situation depicted in *King Kongs Töchter* would eventually become reality.[41] However, the topic is, sadly, not as far-fetched as it seems; in 1989, the case of four caregivers at an old people's home in Lainz (Austria) shocked the public, when it came to light that they had murdered forty-one elderly people. Under the pretext of sparing the residents a miserable life, the caregivers had drowned their victims in the bathtub.[42] In Great Britain, the general practitioner Harold Shipman was convicted of killing fifteen of his elderly patients with lethal injections in January 2000: he allegedly killed more than 215 people in twenty-seven years. The judge's comment on the way Shipman faced the relatives and walked away without any suspicion falling on him was that it would be dismissed as "fanciful" if depicted in a work of fiction.[43]

In contrast to the rather depressing setting of *King Kongs Töchter*, the play takes a comical view of the events in the home, and it is only halfway through the play that the audience learns that the caregivers are serial murderers. What is more, the three women do not only kill the elderly, but then make them up as Hollywood stars, the choice of the model actor being dictated by the calendar. This becomes evident when they reminisce about past death days:

BERTA   Ah ja, da sage ich nur mal 12. Juli, Herr Friedrich als Clark Gable auf der Badematte, deine Idee.

CARLA   Gut Berta, wie stehts mit Frau Wacker, 17. März, Rita Hayworth im Pelzmantel, deine Idee.

BERTA   Dann wär da noch der 9. August, Carla, Herr Franz als Fred Astaire auf der Treppe, auch ein ziemliches Pfui Teufel.

CARLA   Immer noch besser als Frau Franz, 10. Oktober, Ginger Rogers.[44]

In this passage, Walser portrays the disrespectful conversation of care-givers, an attitude that helps them to endure the daily routine of washing, feeding and cleaning. Despite their age they are cynics, and Berta maintains that she is glad to be able to smell the all-pervading odor of urine, for this tells her that she is still alive. Although they play it down, the three women are weary of being what they call the "Seniorendompteuse" of the senior citizens (*K,* 12) and during a rare moment of weakness, Berta confesses that she hates her hands, since they remind her of her job, even when she is at home. In view of the ever-present decay surrounding them, however, the women rejoice in their youth and are glad to be alive. As they believe death to be such an unimportant phenomenon, they decide to dress and make up the dead as famous Hollywood actors, thus making it more glamorous. Indeed, the clash between the shiny world of film stars and the ugly corpses mocks the glossy world of the celebrities, who are now dead despite their fame. At the same time, it presents the foolish yet understandable longing to be important and to live forever.

When the play opens, the lesbians Berta and Carla are enjoying themselves with some olives and a bottle of champagne, neglecting their duties. It is therefore not surprising that they are not on good terms with Meggie, who is left with the majority of the cleaning up. Meggie, however, tries to make the best of the situation, and is suspected of having a sexual relationship with Herr Pott, one of the residents. This is not really a secret, as Herr Pott keeps repeating the lines of a poem he has written called "Die Fünfuhrmorgenvögel,"[45] and calls Meggie his sexy Marilyn. Here, Walser touches on a largely taboo issue, namely the sex life of old people, which is often considered to be non-existent. In *King Kongs Töchter,* however, the mentally disturbed old people rant about their desires in a touching manner, since their words reveal how lonely and neglected they really are. When Frau Greti, for example, hopes for a new man in her life, who will touch all the previously untouched parts of her body, the longing of a young girl's soul trapped in an old body shines through the surface of the old hag. Although the residents are old, they still feel young inside, as their feelings and opinions have not changed, and it is only too understandable that Herr Pott refuses to accept his age. He considers it embarrassing, since he always feels disoriented, talks nonsense, and smells, a bodily state that causes him a good deal of distress. Carla cruelly mocks the way he speaks, and on one occasion forces him to take out his teeth, thus leaving him to mumble unintelligibly. Moreover, the play shows the various ways in which the old people succumb to their daily routine on their way to death, a phenomenon which becomes evident in little remarks repeated daily. After tea, for example, Herr Albert always states that another day is "beheaded," a remark prompting Herr Pott to note that, as always, there will not be a film with Judy Garland on television that evening.

Alongside these more serious undertones, the play also presents the funny but sad flirtations between Frau Greti and a young electrician, Rolf. When she sneaks away into town, she is picked up by the homeless Rolf, and is flattered into believing that he fancies her, although he is really only after her credit card. While Rolf drinks one beer after another, Frau Greti makes him take off his shoes and socks, and hers too, and fantasizes about dancing with him. In this moving scene, behavior that would be considered absolutely normal for a young girl suddenly becomes despicable, thus leaving the elderly woman trapped in her solitude. Towards the end of the scene, however, reality catches up with the two, for Rolf steps in some excrement, and Frau Greti is pleased to see him humiliated.

The confusion in the home reaches its peak in the middle of the night: Frau Tormann is murdered and dressed up as Mae West, Rolf sleeps with Frau Greti, after which he is seduced by Meggie, who later pays her regular visit to Herr Pott. In the hours of the early morning, Rolf is accidentally killed by Herr Nübel while trying to repair the light in the dining room. His death, however, is commented on with the same phrases as usual, and the confused Herr Nübel introduces himself with his well-known "großes N und kleines übel." For the old people life goes on, and, not realizing that Rolf is dead, they complain that he is a safety hazard, since they might trip and fall over him. Although Frau Tormann was to celebrate her eightieth birthday that day, she is already forgotten. Frau Albert now sits in her wheelchair, and the prattle continues.

King Kongs Töchter offers an alternative to the critical and melodramatic approaches to this sensitive topic by mixing black humor with sadness, thus presenting a very critical portrait of the situation in old people's homes, but one masked by a jocular tone. Since Walser refuses to write realistic drama, she has the freedom to present the murderers and their victims in an outrageously funny manner. Against the backdrop of the senseless tittle-tattle of old people, who mostly reiterate their favorite phrases, yet can also be direct and cruel to one another, Frau Greti points out that at least Frau Albert will only need one shoe after having her leg removed. Walser thus presents us with the exaggerated absurdities of a day-to-day routine to which every caregiver can probably relate, yet avoids any melodramatic overtones.

Hope and Black Humor:
Kerstin Specht's *Froschkönigin* (1998)

In the first part of her trilogy *Königinnendramen* (1998), Specht playfully picks up on Grimm's fairy tale of the princess who kisses a frog, which turns into a king. It premiered at the *Stuttgarter Theater am Depot* in April 1998, and despite the fact that some critics praised its wit, it was not a great success.[46] In Specht's comedy, however, the king is already human and his only royal feature is his surname: König. The play opens when this young man, Stefan König, happens to knock at the kitchen door in the middle of the night, at the very moment that a woman is about to commit suicide. His car has broken down and he needs some water for the radiator, but because the water supply has been cut off, he cannot sort out his car, and similarly the woman cannot swallow an overdose of sleeping pills. Herr König seems to be oddly at home in this situation, and they begin to chat and become friendly. Charming as he is, he becomes her lover, convinces her that her children are unbearable brats who should be no longer catered to, and makes her see life from a different point of view. She wins back her self-confidence, and finally runs away with one of the wealthy clients of her new fortune-telling business. Although it is not König she marries, her life changes drastically and she experiences a second awakening. The plot unfolds in fast and amusing dialogues which mirror sloppy family talk, yet are never offensive.

Specht adopts a light and comical approach in this play, although the subject is serious, because the playwright for one knows that the mother's plight has been told so often that a change of tone is needed. Although the playwright seemingly mocks the generational conflict, on a subconscious level it is portrayed in a serious way. And since coincidence drives the highly unlikely plot, it is enjoyable and never boring. Although *Froschkönigin* raises a notorious topic, it avoids an accusatory tone:

Draußen kracht etwas gegen das Gartentor, die Küchentür fliegt auf, Stefan König tritt herein.

KÖNIG   Hallohallo
MUTTER   Kaufe nichts
Keine Behindertenbesen
keine Blindenpostkarten
KÖNIG   Will nur einen Schluck Wasser
Kühler kocht
MUTTER   Nichts zu machen

KÖNIG   [. . .] Die gelben Engel kommen nicht
                 kein Wasser springt aus dem Fels
                 Die Menschheit ignoriert mich
MUTTER   Das Wasser ist abgestellt
Sie hebt ihr leeres Glas hoch.
KÖNIG   Und Sie wollten ihre Pillen nehmen?
MUTTER   Ja alle
                 [. . .]
KÖNIG   Da haben wir ja Glück
                 Daß ich eine Panne hab [. . .][47]

Specht makes full use of the absurd potential of the farce, and the line breaks suggest a fast-moving dialogue. Although the situation could be serious, as the mother suffers from depression and König is not welcome, they talk as if nothing unusual has happened. Both characters are in fact caricatures of clichés. König is the young and energetic lover who easily strikes up a pleasant conversation, and the mother is the depressed, middle-aged woman wanting to die. The time and place of their encounter, and the reason for it, are completely absurd and thus amusing, because Specht mocks the nature of both fairy tales and wishful thinking.

Stefan König gradually persuades the mother not to spoil her children any longer, a move that is far from warmly received by the children. Both son and daughter keep trying to foster their mother's guilty conscience, but she chooses to ignore them. Following the advice of König, who has meanwhile become her lover, she starts a fortune-telling business; the fact that she has never touched fortune-telling cards before goes without saying. Despite an amateur beginning, she has great success, and clients flock to listen to her, much to the anger of her daughter, who feels neglected. Once Herr König is discovered to be a womanizer, the mother runs away with one of her clients, leaving only a videotape behind containing instructions: her once-loved pets lie slaughtered in the fridge, and her daughter is advised to stop picking her nose if she ever wants to find a husband.

Despite its idiosyncratic nature and unlikely twists, *Froschkönigin* is a "Küchenmärchen" with a happy ending. As the action mainly takes place in the kitchen, the play portrays retreat into the private sphere, which has become typical for the *Frauenbewegung* since the early 1980s.[48] The revaluation of family life evidently put the mother in *Froschkönigin* back in charge of the so-called "Three Ks": *Kinder, Küche, Kirche*. Specht also alludes to another phenomenon that reemerged at the time, in which women were associated with the myths of fertility, and mystified as beings who were in close contact with both the earth and nature.[49] *Froschkönigin*, however, addresses both issues through farcical means, as the only "supernatural" power which the mother commands is faked fortune-telling.[50] *Froschkönigin* thus shows that insight and laughter can be reconciled, because if happiness is to be achieved, as the German saying goes, "müssen Kröten an die Wand geworfen werden": old habits must be discarded.[51]

A Dream World:
Gesine Danckwart's *Girlsnightout* (1999)

Despite the fact that Danckwart used to claim that she had no intention of becoming a playwright, she started writing *Girlsnightout* in 1997, finishing it in 1999.[52] This followed a period of experimental theater at a fringe venue called *Theaterdock* in Berlin, where she worked as an assistant, actress and director. At the *Theaterdock,* the main aim had been to deconstruct dramatic texts in a postmodern way. However, this phase ended with *Girlsnightout,* and Danckwart developed her own peculiar style, which is characteristic of all her plays.[53] In a similar way to *Arschkarte* (Ass Card, 2000) and *Täglich Brot* (Daily Bread, 2001), *Girlsnightout* consists of a couple of monologues which reveal the characters' stream of consciousness, yet they could also be several voices in one person's mind.[54] In general, her plays focus on the unhappiness caused by the pressures of a society in which success, beauty, and efficiency are more important than love and understanding.[55] Under the surface of apparently superficial talk, the loneliness and fears of the characters are always perceptible. *Girlsnightout* presents us with an afternoon in the lives of three apartment-mates, who are not able to communicate, although they never stop prattling.

Danckwart's third play, *Girlsnightout,* premiered in 1999 at the *Theater Neumarkt* in Zurich, and the *Schauspiel Hannover* staged it in May 2000, where critics praised it for its witty entertainment.[56] It soon became a successful play, and was also produced at the *Thalia Theater* in Hamburg in January 2001,[57] and the *Sophiensaele* in Berlin in March 2002.[58]

The play has no scenes and is simply divided into two main parts, entitled "1. Wie die Mädchen" and "2. Wie die Frauen." The three characters have no names and are simply referred to as women. Moreover, it is not clear who speaks which lines, and there are no stage directions, thus giving the director the task of setting the play in an appropriate context. As the lines are not allocated to any one character, different versions of the text are possible. Through their conversation, it gradually emerges that the women are apartment-mates who are anticipating an exciting night out.

Although they are together, they rarely address one another directly, and their ranting creates the impression that each of them is wrapped in her own thoughts. Still, they share the same fears: not finding a partner, not being successful at work, and becoming old and ugly. For these women, the perfect moment in time does not seem to exist, since they feel either too young and foolish to enjoy their youth, or too old to be attractive. One of them, who is probably in her mid-thirties, refers to the benefits of being more mature, yet fails to sound truly convincing:

> Ich bin froh, daß es mir jetzt so gutgeht. Und ich glaube, daß es mir immer besser geht, je älter ich werde. Manche Dinge regen mich nicht mehr so auf, und man hat doch auch dazugelernt und weiß, wer man ist und auf was man bauen kann.
>
> Ich werde diesen Sommer nicht mehr verreisen, ich habe einfach keine Zeit, sonst zu mir zu finden. Das verbindet mich mit den Großen dieser Erde, die haben auch nie Zeit.
>
> Ich bin im besten Alter.
>
> Man ist hier vor Überraschungen nicht sicher.[59]

However, the first remark rather sounds as if she had tried to convince herself that this really was true. As similar phrases crop up throughout the play, their discontent becomes increasingly obvious. The longing for better looks, charming boyfriends, and a good job is ever present, yet their desires remain unfulfilled. There does not seem to be a right age for happiness, for none of them are really satisfied with what they have achieved. This passage is also a good example of the non-communicative manner of speaking in the play, for the women do not engage in creative dialogue. Conversation progresses by leaps and ruptures, and sometimes goes around in circles, thereby depicting the characters' inability to abandon their self-centeredness.

The monologic style[60] of *Girlsnightout* creates a dreamlike atmosphere that combines the postmodern pastiche with the monodrama, as the dialogue could just as well be thoughts echoing in someone's mind. Danckwart thus harks back to monodramatic experiments of the early twentieth century, such as those of the Russian psychiatrist Evreinov (1879–1953), who had experimented with a new method of analyzing the mind that allowed the patient to adopt several identities. He also pursued this idea in his dramatic works, such as *The Theatrical Soul* (1912), which expresses his belief that the desire to playact is inherent in everybody.[61] The monodrama is still used in psychotherapy, today mainly with patients who do not respond to other therapies.[62] In this particular form of therapy, the protagonist becomes active as his or her own therapist. Despite the fact that *Girlsnightout* is not psychotherapy, its structure plays with the monodramatic form, criticizing the relapse into "girlism."

Top Girls:
Roland Schimmelpfennig's *Push Up 1–3* (2000)

Schimmelpfennig's plays are typically characterized by an almost surrealistic style that combines narration and dialogue to produce an ironic effect. In *Die arabische Nacht* (Arabian Night, 2001),[63] for example, he presents us with a magic and comic scenario in a block of apartments during a summer night, where couples come together and split up, a man disappears inside a bottle and dies, and a caretaker eventually finds his sleeping princess. Each character seems to exist only in the imagination of another, yet they all exert a subconscious influence on each other. One critic suggested that Schimmelpfennig indirectly paid tribute to both Peter Handke's (1942–) plays and Alain Robbe-Grillet's (1922–) *nouveau roman*. Like Robbe-Grillet, Schimmelpfennig merely alludes to the important moments in life by means of varying similar scenes and motives.[64] However, it could also be argued that Schimmelpfennig takes Brecht's recommendations for actors literally. In order to achieve the *Verfremdungseffekt*, Brecht had advised playwrights to interrupt the action with actors' comments in the third person, and to put parts of the dialogue in the past tense, thereby forcing the actors to distance themselves from their roles.[65] *Die arabische Nacht* premiered at the *Staatstheater Stuttgart* in February 2001, and was produced in the same year in Oberhausen, Hamburg,[66] Leipzig, Mannheim, and Graz, and at the *Berliner Schaubühne* in May 2001.[67] In April 2002, it ran at the *Soho Theater* in London, where the critics praised its combination of magic and suspense.[68] Schimmelpfennig was awarded the *Else-Lasker-Schüler-Förderpreis* in 1997 for his play *Fisch um Fisch* (1994),[69] and since the 2000/2001 season, he has been writer-in-residence at the *Schaubühne* in Berlin.

Schimmelpfennig's ninth play, *Push Up 1–3*, consists of three main parts framed by two monologues by the porters, Heinrich and Maria. Set on the top floor of a huge firm, it presents us with the problems and conflicts of top managers.[70] The first part, *Push Up 1*, premiered in October 2000 at the *Theater in der Basilika* in Hamburg,[71] and in October 2001, the *Berliner Schaubühne* produced the complete play, *Push Up 1–3*. However, reviews were mixed, and while one critic found the play too shallow,[72] another maintained that sex at work was simply not important, and Schimmelpfennig's play was thus negligible.[73] In contrast, the press praised the production at the *Schauspielhaus* in Hamburg in November 2001 under the direction of Jürgen Gosch, because of its lucid analysis of the characters[74] and the brilliant acting.[75] Due to its abstract setting, which placed the characters in a cube of metal bars, the characters only had to take a single step in order to enter their inner, monologic world.[76] An English version of *Push Up 1–3* premiered during the *Third International Playwrights Season* at the *Royal Court* in London, where critics acclaimed it for being a well-structured and apt satire of corporate business.[77]

Each of the three main parts presents us with a pair of opponents: the boss Angelika and her employee Sabine; Robert and Patricia, who are unable to express their feelings; and Frank and Hans, who are contending for a top job within the firm. The interactive scenes alternate with short monologues, in which the characters unveil their real states of mind. As the short flashbacks and flash-forwards are similar to filmic narration technique, they do not disrupt the logical flow of the plot. Instead they provide additional information about the characters' motives, which largely contradicts what they have just said or done.

The first encounter takes place between Angelika, the boss, and Sabine, a slightly younger but apparently self-assured woman. Although Sabine behaves rather aggressively, Angelika tries to calm her down at first, for she likes the idea that they are rather similar in the way they dress and think. What is more, their monologues reveal that both are insecure, sexually frustrated, and overworked. However, Sabine is outraged, for her application for promotion was turned down without explanation, and she is tired of Angelika's subtle display of power. The second part features a conflict between the colleagues Patricia and Robert, and in part 3, Frank, a middle-aged man, and Hans, who is approaching retirement, talk about a promising job in India for which they have both applied. Again, it is not the aggressive Hans who is selected for the post, but the rather lazy Frank, who spends most of his time searching for pornographic Web pages.

In part 2, we are presented with the doomed relationship between Robert and Patricia. From their monologues, we learn that they once had sex in an empty office during a drinks reception in the firm. However, each was too proud to contact the other, and attraction turned into hatred. At the beginning of scene 2.1, Robert contemptuously rejects Patricia's proposal for the new television ad. Unaffected by his criticism, she claims to have quoted certain elements from the first, very successful, video clip, but Robert questions her creativity and dismisses her proposal as a waste of time and money. Although Patricia initially reacts angrily, she suggests that they should talk the matter through over a drink. However, he declines the offer, and in his monologue it becomes clear that he is suffering just as much as she is, and is unable to overcome his pride:

> Diese Frau war wichtig. Diese Frau war eine Sensation —
> *Kurze Pause.* So eine Frau kann man nicht einfach anrufen. Das wäre ein Fehler gewesen, da bin ich mir jetzt noch sicher. Ich wollte nicht, daß sie den Eindruck hat, daß ich es in irgendeiner Weise nötig hätte, mit ihr Kontakt aufzunehmen.[. . .] Ich stand ihr in nichts nach und sie in nichts mir. Sie war so wie ich: Ich war so wie sie, und ich wollte, daß sie das begriff. Wir — sie und ich — gehörten zusammen.[78]

In spite of, or rather because of his feelings for her, he does everything to ruin her professional career from this point onwards. He therefore tries to persuade Kramer that Patricia's idea is worthless. In an unexpected twist, however, it is he who is sacked, while Patricia's new ad is enthusiastically accepted. Although the plot may sound conventional, the structure saves the play from becoming boring. In the case of Patricia and Robert, the play is enjoyable for the spectators, for they know more than the characters, due to the long asides in which the characters reveal their state of mind. As these monologues mirror one another, the audience also enjoys the symmetrical way in which the action is mapped out. Robert's monologue cited above, for example, finds its equivalent in Patricia's thoughts:

> Das hier war zu wichtig. *Kurze Pause.* Und deshalb konnte ich ihn nicht anrufen. Das wäre nicht richtig gewesen. Das wäre ein entscheidender Fehler gewesen, davon bin ich auch jetzt noch absolut überzeugt. [. . .] (*P,* 316)

Although the wording is not exactly the same, the audience will immediately recognize Robert's thoughts. In his typical style, Schimmelpfennig juxtaposes the two mindsets by means of two parallel monologues. In accordance with Brecht's *Verfremdungseffekt,* the characters narrate their experiences and allow the audience to adopt a distanced viewpoint. In contrast to epic theater, however, Schimmelpfennig focuses primarily on personal problems. His theater is, therefore, less concerned than Brecht's with presenting a sociological "experiment"[79] that could serve as a paradigm for society as a whole.

In *Push Up 1–3,* aggression does not pay, and professional success does not result from efficiency, but depends on character. By means of a well-crafted and symmetrically built play, Schimmelpfennig mocks the widespread belief that the career-ladder can be climbed simply through hard work. What is more, *Push Up 1–3* offers some insight into the burnt-out minds of high-ranking employees, for their jobs do not leave them enough time for a decent life. The porters aside, all the characters suffer from loneliness, and are unable to socialize. The competitive work environment puts considerable strain on them, causing depression and unhappiness: Frank is in love with girls on the internet, Hans spends more than four hours a day on his bicycle, Robert and Patricia cannot show their feelings, and finally, Sabine and Angelika are deeply dissatisfied with their (sex) lives. Despite their top positions, all the characters suffer from a society dominated by money.

Following a decade of considerable fatigue concerning the role of women in society, both male and female writers presented their audiences with a fresh approach to the topic. In contrast to the 1970s and early 1980s, when Gerlind Reinshagen and Gisela von Wysocki depicted the battle of the sexes, and insisted that the female view was special, contemporary playwrights refuse to be different, for they regard this to be a form of discrimination. The plays of the 1990s thus depict the shifting position of women in the family and in society, yet no longer match the narrow categories of feminist writing. Dea Loher, one of today's most successful playwrights, completely rejects the notion of a female style, and maintains that works of art should not be divided into male and female, but rather into good and bad.[80] Her play *Tätowierung* (1992) presents us with the problems of incest, and in her characteristic style, she avoids any melodramatic overtones. Indeed, the characters speak a concise, brief, and practically mutilated language that creates the impression of a hostile atmosphere, yet the violence is never really brought to the fore, and hovers instead beneath the surface of small talk.

Towards the end of the millennium, Kerstin Specht and Theresia Walser changed the tone of female writing by presenting women's issues from a humorous viewpoint. In her grotesque satire *King Kongs Töchter* (1998), Walser depicts an old people's home, where three women in their thirties look after a handful of residents. However, the play does not feature the misery and plight of the female caregivers, as one might expect. Although the women are discontented with their lives, they still try to make the best of them. In order to do so, they entertain themselves by dressing up and making up dead residents as Hollywood stars. This appears fairly harmless at first sight, yet it soon becomes clear that the audience cannot identify with the three women, for they are serial murderers, or "monsters," as the title suggests. Although Walser's play is grotesque and does not claim to give an accurate portrayal of reality, it has initiated many debates about the situation in old people's homes today, and has become one of the most performed plays on the German stage. Kerstin Specht's absurd play *Froschkönigin* (1998) is centered on a middle-aged, divorced mother of two children who is tired of living. Again, Specht cites the worn-out stereotypes and overturns them at the same time. The mother's second spring is presented in fast and funny dialogues, which lend a comical touch to the absurd twists of the plot.

Gesine Danckwart's play *Girlsnightout* (2000) offers insight into the thoughts of three women who are about to dress up for an evening out. In three intertwined monologues, Danckwart presents us with the worries and sorrows of women in today's society, for they ponder over their jobs and their partners, and are aware of their sagging bodies. Modeled on Sarah Kane's *Crave* (1998), the play is written in a pensive manner, and the self-reflective comments in *Girlsnightout* produce a feeling of distance in the spectator. In this way, the audience is given the role of the listening counselor, and *Girlsnightout* can thus be described as a triplex monodrama, in the course of which the women analyze their lives.

It is interesting that Roland Schimmelpfennig's *Push Up 1–3* (2000), which is set on the top floor of a corporate business, adopts a politically correct attitude towards women. In this well-crafted and symmetrically built play, we are presented with conflicts between top managers and employees that are also battles between the sexes. In *Push Up 1–3*, both men and women are in fact victims of a dehumanized competition raging among high-ranking employees, for they sacrifice their private lives and happiness in order to pursue their careers. Although it could be argued that this is nothing new, Schimmelpfennig's way of presenting these conflicts make them intriguing to follow. He unfolds fascinating frictions inside characters by combining dialogues and monologues that symbolize the contradiction between the public and the private person. Using Brecht's thoughts on the *Verfremdungseffekt*, Schimmelpfennig contrasts dialogues in the present tense with asides in the past tense. In accordance with Brecht, the characters thus step out of their roles, yet the effect does not destroy the fictional surface of the play. In fact, the monologues resemble a voiceover, a filmic narration technique, thus offering extra information that does not deconstruct the flow of events.

As far as the new image of women in contemporary society is concerned, it is evident that a generation change has gradually taken place. Playwrights have called for an end to a theater dominated by a moralistic depiction of the disadvantaged woman, replacing it with funny and witty approaches to this topic.

Notes

[1] Marie Th. Knäpper, *Feminismus — Autonomie — Subjektivität. Tendenzen und Wiedersprüche in der neuen Frauenbewegung* (Bochum: Germinal Verlag, 1984), 14.

[2] Despite these conservative tendencies, the *Frauenbewegung* sent further shock waves through Germany, when 374 women publicly admitted to having had an abortion. This collective confession was published in the magazine *Stern,* under the headline "Ich habe abgetrieben." See Alice Schwarzer, *10 Jahre Frauenbewegung. So fing es an!* (Cologne: Emma Verlag, 1981), 24. She writes: "Bis dahin hatten Frauen geschwiegen und — gehandelt. Daß sie dies täglich zu Tausenden heimlich taten, begriffen die isolierten Frauen selbst in vollem Ausmaß erst nach dem Eklat der Selbstbezichtigungskampagne. Vom scheinbar privaten Problem wurde der § 218 nun zum Politikum."

[3] Leonore Knafla and Christine Kulke, "15 Jahre neue Frauenbewegung. Und sie bewegt sich noch! Ein Rückblick nach vorn," in *Neue soziale Bewegungen in der Bundesrepublik Deutschland,* eds. Roland Roth and Dieter Rucht (Frankfurt and New York: Campus, 1987), 89–108, here: 93.

[4] Knafla and Kulke, "15 Jahre neue Frauenbewegung," 98.

[5] Claus Leggewie, "Der Geist denkt rechts. Wo Politik vorgedacht wird. Ein Streifzug durch die konservativen Denkfabriken der Bundesrepublik Deutschland," *Z,* 16 October 1987; see also: Claus Leggewie, *Der Geist steht rechts. Ausflüge in die Denkfabriken der Wende* (Berlin: Rotbuch, 1987).

[6] Alice Schwarzer, *10 Jahre Frauenbewegung. So fing es an!* (Cologne: Emma, 1981), 93.

[7] Frauke Haug, "Perspektiven eines sozialistischen Feminismus — 20 Jahre Frauenbewegung in Westdeutschland und West-Berlin," in *Frauenbewegung in der Welt Band 1. Argument Sonderband 150,* ed. Autonome Frauenredaktion (Hamburg: Argument Verlag, 1988), 32–41, here: 36.

[8] In 1991, Birgit Meyer wrote: "Die Frauenbewegung hat keines ihrer Ziele erreicht [. . .] Es ist ihr nicht gelungen, in nennenswertem Umfang gesellschaftliche Macht zu erlangen, um die Ohnmacht von Frauen wirklich spürbar zu verringern. Die Frauenbewegung hat die herrschenden Machtverhältnisse und ihre Spielregeln nicht außer Kraft setzen können, wie sie es einst vorhatte, aber sie hat immerhin für gehörige Unruhe und Verwirrung gesorgt."; Birgit Meyer, "Frauenbewegung und politische Kultur in den achtziger Jahren," in *Die Bundesrepublik in den achtziger Jahren,* ed. Werner Süß (Opladen: Leske + Budrich, 1991), 219–34, here: 228.

[9] Dieter Rucht, *Modernisierung und neue soziale Bewegung* (Frankfurt am Main, New York: Campus, 212.

[10] On the situation of East German women after 1989, see Ingrid Scherzer-Harz, *Freiheit, Gleichheit, Solidarität* (Buxtehude: B. Pusch, 1996).

[11] In practice, women's studies have been introduced at universities to explain sociology from a female viewpoint, such as the study of female language. See Brigitte Brück, Heike Kahlert, Marianne Krüll, Helga Milz, Astrid Osterland and Ingeborg Wegehaupt-Schneider, *Feministische Soziologie* (Frankfurt am Main: Campus, 1997), here: 209–23.

[12] Ines Weller, Esther Hoffmann, and Sabine Hofmeister (eds.), *Nachhaltigkeit und Feminismus: Neue Perspektiven und alte Blockaden* (Bielefeld: Kleine Verlag, 1999), 11. The volume includes several papers that discuss the future of the women's liberation movement with respect to the environment, culture, and economy.

[13] Rosemarie Nave-Herz, *Die Geschichte der Frauenbewegung in Deutschland* (Bonn: Bundeszentrale für politische Bildung, 1993), 96–97.

[14] Dieter Rucht, *Modernisierung und neue soziale Bewegung* (Frankfurt am Main/New York: Campus, 1994), 213.

[15] "Das Theater mit Frauen. Interview with Manuela Reichardt," *Th* 4 (1980): 2–3.

[16] Anke Roeder, "Der andere Blick. Weibliche Präsenz als Provokation," in *Autorinnen: Herausforderungen an das Theater,* ed. Anke Roeder (Frankfurt am Main: Suhrkamp, 1989), 7–26, here: 13–14.

[17] Ria Endres, "Die Theater-Krise läßt mich kalt," *ThJ* (1987), 62–63, here: 62.

[18] Gerlind Reinshagen, "Abbruch des alten Theatergesteins," in *TheaterFrauenTheater,* eds. Barbara Engelhardt, Therese Hörningk, and Bettina Masuch (Berlin: Theater der Zeit, 2001), 111–15, here: 113.

[19] Quoted in Birgitta Willmann, "Kalter Blick auf menschliche Tragödien," *SoZ,* 18 January 1998.

[20] See, for example Dagmar Papula and Norbert Kentrup (eds.), *Frauentheater* (Offenbach: Verlag 2000, 1982).

[21] Karin Uecker, Renate Ullrich, and Elke Wiegand, *Frauen im europäischen Theater heute* (Hamburg: Europäische Verlagsanstalt, 1998), 31–46.

[22] "Feministischer Aufbruch im Theater? Diskussion mit Claudia Bauer, Brigitte Landes und Johanna Schall," in *TheaterFrauenTheater,* eds. Engelhardt et al., 55–65, here: 58.

[23] "Die zweite Haut des Schauspielers. Interview mit Ariane Mnouchkine von Josette Féral," in *TheaterFrauenTheater,* eds. Engelhardt et. al., 182–96, here: 195.

[24] Annette Menzel, "Sexualität und Frauenbefreiung," in *Texte — Taten — Träume: Wie weiter mit der Frauenbewegung,* eds. Inge Baxmann, Edith Laudowicz, and Annette Menzel (Cologne: Pahl-Rugenstein, 1984), 156–70, here: 160.

[25] The highly acclaimed playwright Loher, who was born in 1964 in Traunstein, Bavaria, has won numerous prizes; for example, in 1992, the *Playwright Award* of the *Royal Court Theater* in London; in the same year, the *Goethepreis* of the *Mülheimer Theatertage.* Further honors include the following: in 1993, she was awarded the prize of the *Frankfurter Autorenstiftung;* in 1993/94, she was voted best new playwright by the journal *Theater heute;* and in 1995, she won the *Fördergabe* of the *Schiller Gedächtnispreis.*

[26] Sandra Umathum, "Unglückliche Utopisten," in *Stück-Werk 3,* eds. Christel Weiler and Harald Müller (Berlin: Zentrum Bundesrepublik Deutschland des Internationalen Theaterinstituts, 2001), 101–5, here: 101.

[27] Sascha Löschner, "Dea Loher: Verletzte Sprache," in *Stück-Werk 1* (Berlin: Internationales Theaterinstitut, 1997), 71–73, here: 72.

Thomas Joningk's play *Täter* (1999) also takes up the issue of sexual abuse and places it in a wider social context, including lawyers and social workers. The play was published in *Th* 2 (2000): 58–68, and was premiered at the *Deutsche Schauspielhaus* in Hamburg in December 1999. However, the reviews of the premiere and later productions were rather mixed; see Andreas Schäfer, "Mit dem Maschinengewehr auf Quallen," Berliner Zeitung, 13 December 1999; Franz Wille, "Neue Sorgen hat das Selbst," *Th* 4 (2000): 4–11.

[28] Alexandra Ludewig, "Dea Loher," *Forum Modernes Theater* 2 (2000), 113–24.

[29] Sandra Umathum, "Unglückliche Utopisten," in *Stück-Werk 3*, eds. Christel Weiler and Harald Müller (Berlin: Zentrum Bundesrepublik Deutschland des Internationalen Theaterinstituts, 2001), 101–5, here: 104.

[30] Dea Loher, "Tätowierung," in Dea Loher, *Olgas Raum: drei Stücke* (Frankfurt am Main: Verlag der Autoren, 1994), 65–144, here: 74.

[31] "'Die Schärfung der Stimme ist nur in der Mehrstimmigkeit möglich.' Ronald Richter im Gespräch mit der Autorin Theresia Walser," printed in the program for the production at the *Staatsschauspiel Dresden* on 30 December 1999; also available on the Internet; see www.mythenmaschine.de.

[32] Franz Wille, "Pseudonym? — Da hätte ich Thea Wacker genommen," *Th* 11 (1997): 35–37.

[33] Both plays were published in one volume: Theresia Walser, *Kleine Zweifel. Das Restpaar* (Frankfurt am Main: Verlag der Autoren, 1997). For a short overview of Walser's plays, see Thomas Irmer, "Virtuose Sprachwelten verlorener Gestalten," in *Stück-Werk 3. Arbeitsbuch*, eds. Christel Weiler and Harald Müller (Berlin: Zentrum Bundesrepublik Deutschland des Internationalen Theaterinstituts, 2001), 148–50.

[34] Franz Wille, "Illusionen von Glück und Theater. Volker Hesse führt in Zürich *King Kongs Töchter*, das neue Stück von Theresia Walser zum Erfolg und rettet das Theater vor der Wirklichkeit," *Th* 11 (1998): 76–79; Joachim Johannsen, "Alter zu Sperrmüll," *W*, 28 September 1998.

[35] Richard Reich, "Der Tod ist ein Termin," *BZ*, 10 October 1998.

[36] Christopher Schmidt, "Todesengel im Streichzoo," *BZ*, 22 June 1999; Franz Wille, "Vorbereitungen fürs Sterben," *Th* 8/9 (1999): 23–25.

[37] Roland Koberg, "Drei Damen vom Kill," *BZ*, 19 October 1999; Matthias Heine, "Hollywood jenseits der Bettpfanne," *W*, 19 October 1999.

[38] The *Düsseldorfer Schauspielhaus* production (director, Patrick Schlösser) also traveled to the *International Theatre Festival* in Warsaw in May 2000, where Angieska Kaczynska produced a Polish version, *Córki King Konga*. Franz Marijenen directed a staging at the *K.V.S.-Theatre* in Bruges in January 2000; the *Schauspielhaus Graz* staged it in October 2001; and in June 2002, a Catalan version premiered at the *Theater Festival* of Sitges in Spain.

[39] Carola Dürr, "Vom Tragischen ins Komische. Neue deutsche Dramatik am Royal Court Theater in London und Mark Ravenhills neuer Reißer," *W*, 19 November 1999.

[40] See, for example, Michael Mielke, "Der Tod stand schon im Raum," *W*, 5 November 1996. The article describes how a nurse was taken to court because an old woman died from asphyxiation.

[41] The debate at the *Schauspielhaus Frankfurt* was documented by Walter Paul, director of the old people's home *Heilandsgemeinde* in Frankfurt, see http://www.seniorentreff-msp.de/Theater.htm.

[42] Werner Mück, *Österreich. Das war unser Jahrhundert* (Vienna: Kremayr & Scheriau, 1999), 172–73.

[43] Helen Carter and David Ward, "Britain's worst serial killer: 215 dead but we still don't know why," *G*, 20 July 2002. The journalists report on the inquiry that followed Shipman's conviction.

[44] Theresia Walser, *King Kongs Töchter* [1998] (Frankfurt am Main: Verlag der Autoren, 1999), 17. Subsequent references to this work are cited in the text using the abbreviation *K* and page number.

[45] "Vögeln" is a colloquial word for having sexual intercourse.

[46] Franz Wille, "Sie kann auch anders. Die neue Mutter in Kerstin Spechts *Die Froschkönigin* und in der Stuttgarter Uraufführung," *Th* 4 (1998): 52–54, here: 53.

[47] Kerstin Specht, *Die Froschkönigin*, in Kerstin Specht, *Königinnendramen* (Frankfurt am Main: Verlag der Autoren, 1998), 7–82, here 9–10. Subsequent references to this work are cited in the text using the abbreviation *F* and page number.

[48] See the chapter on the *Neue Frauenbewegung* in *Aufbruch in eine andere Gesellschaft. Neue soziale Bewegungen in der Bundesrepublik*, eds. Karl-Werner Brand, Detlef Büsser, and Dieter Rucht (Frankfurt and New York: Campus Verlag, 1986), 141

[49] Alice Schwarzer writes: "was einst als Erweiterung gedacht war, ist heute eher erneute Einengung: Da wird gependelt statt diskutiert, die Göttin beschworen statt politisch gehandelt." in Alice Schwarzer, *10 Jahre Frauenbewegung. So fing es an!* (Cologne: Emma, 1981), 109.

[50] What is more, Specht returns to both the new and the old *Volkstheater*. These are two genres which reflect the split within German thinking after the *Third Reich,* because, as the traditional and entertaining *Volkstheater* had been abused by the National Socialists, a highly artificial and intellectual new *Volkstheater* was created by playwrights such as Franz Xaver Kroetz, Felix Mitterer, and Fitzgerald Kusz. For the *Volkstheater,* see Hugo Aust, Peter Haida, and Jürgen Hein, *Volksstück. Vom Hanswurstspiel zum sozialen Drama der Gegenwart* (Munich: C.H. Beck, 1989), 316–44.

[51] Franz Wille, "Sie kann auch anders. Die neue Mutter in Kerstin Spechts *Die Froschkönigin* und in der Stuttgarter Uraufführung," *Th* 4 (1998): 52–54, here: 54.

[52] On Gesine Danckwart and her latest play *Täglich Brot,* see Eva Berendt, "Die höchste Schmerzstufe," *Th* 6 (2001): 52–55.

[53] On the occasion of the production of *Täglich Brot* at the *Sophiensaele* in Berlin, a critic interpreted Danckwart's mono-dialogues as theater of the absurd; see Cosima Lutz, "Die marginalen Leben Dagmars, Margas und Marquardts," *W*, 1 June 2001.

[54] Susanne Kunckel, "Dialoge in der dritten Person," *W*, 24 June 2001.

[55] Tom Mustroph, "Lebensformen ausprobieren," in *Stück-Werk 3*, eds. Christel Weiler and Harald Müller (Berlin: Zentrum Bundesrepublik Deutschland des Internationalen Theaterinstituts, 2001), 38–41.

[56] Ronald Meyer-Arlt, "Zurüstungen für einen unsterblichen Abend," *Th* 6 (2000): 42.

[57] "Vergnügliches Gequassel über Gott und die Welt," *Mopo*, 22 January 2001; "Die Mädels sind hier aufgeweckt," *W*, 22 January 2001. Overall, the staging was warmly received because of its accurate, yet funny, portrayal of the problems of the three women.

[58] The production was received with some apprehension, partly because there was not enough action, partly because of its topic, which was not considered to be interesting enough to fill an evening, see Tom Mustroph, "*Pläne fürs Leben*," *Taz*, 14 March 2002; Eva Corino, "Plüschrosa Geheimnisse," *BZ*, 14 March 2002.

[59] Gesine Danckwart, "Girlsnightout," in *TheaterTheater. Aktuelle Stücke 10*, eds. Uwe B. Carstensen and Stefanie van Lieven (Frankfurt am Main: Fischer, 2000), 105–32, here: 126. Subsequent references to this work are cited in the text using the abbreviation *G* and page number.

[60] It also resembles the structure of Sarah Kane's play *Crave* (1998), which has been a great success in Germany; *Crave* is published in Sarah Kane, *Complete Plays* (London: Methuen, 2001).

[61] Sharon M. Carnicke, *The Theatrical Instinct: Nikolai Evreinov and the Russian Theater of the Early Twentieth Century* (Frankfurt am Main: Lang, 1991).

[62] Barbara Erbacher-Farkas and Christian Jorda, *Monodrama* (Vienna: Springer, 1996).

[63] *Die arabische Nacht* was premiered at the *Staatstheater Stuttgart* in March 2001, and was received with some apprehension, for the production lacked inspiration; see Silvia Stammer, "Der Teppich hebt nicht ab," *Th* 4 (2001): 44–46. A later staging in Leipzig, which set the action in a doll's house, was warmly received; see Franz Wille, "Komm, süßer Schlaf," *Th* 4 (2001): 45.

[64] Andreas Schäfer, "Triumph der Normalos. Ein Versuch über den Dramatiker Roland Schimmelpfennig," *BZ*, 12 May 2001.

[65] Bertolt Brecht, "Kurze Beschreibung einer neuen Technik der Schauspielkunst, die einen Verfremdungseffekt hervorbringt," in Bertolt Brecht, *Werke. Band 22.2: Schriften 2. Große kommentierte Berliner und Frankfurter Ausgabe*, eds. V. W. Hecht, J. Knopf, W. Mittenzwei, and K.-D. Müller (Berlin/Weimar/Frankfurt am Main: Suhrkamp, 1993), 644–47, here: 642.

[66] The staging was received with some apprehension due to the fact that it rather resembled a radio play; see Susanne Oberacker, "Sehnsüchte und Träume im Keller der Mietskaserne," *Mopo*, 23 April 2001.

[67] Ulrich Seidler, "Spuk im Hochhaus," *BZ*, 23 May 2001; Eva Corino, "Konfirmandendrama," *BZ*, 28 May 2001.

[68] The play was warmly received and described as a combination of the "tale-spinning Scheherazade of Arabian Nights crossed with Hitchcock," see Michael Billington, "Arabian Night," *G*, 30 April 2002.

[69] For a brief introduction to Schimmelpfennig, see Tom Mustroph, "Der Vielseitige," in *Stück-Werk 3*, eds. Christel Weiler and Harald Müller (Berlin: Zentrum Bundesrepublik Deutschland des Internationalen Theaterinstituts, 2001), 133–37.

[70] In recent years, there has been a growing interest in the working environment, see the plays by Urs Widmer, *Top Dogs* (Frankfurt am Main: Verlag der Autoren, 1998); Gesine Danckwart, "*Täglich Brot*," *Th* 6 (2001): 56–60; Dea Loher, "*Der dritte Sektor*," *Th* 5 (2001): 54–66.

[71] Brigitte Scholz, "Vom Clinch in die Chefetage," *Mopo*, 4 October 2000.

[72] Ulrich Seidler, "Auf einmal war es wichtig," *BZ*, 12 November 2001.

[73] Matthias Heine, "Der Schuh des Moneymakers," *W,* 12 November 2001.

[74] Brigitte Scholz, "Grandios," *Mopo,* 21 December 2001.

[75] Monika Nellissen, "Sie küssten und sie schlugen sich," *W,* 1 December 2001. The only flaw was that *Push Up* was presented as a double bill with Schimmelpfennig's *Vor langer Zeit im Mai,* which was simply considered to be too much for one evening; see Karin Liebe, "Brav im Körbchen," *taz,* 1 December 2001.

[76] See the comparison of the two stagings in Berlin and Hamburg by Barbara Burckhardt, "K.O.-Prinzip im Wohlstandsdrama," *Th* 1 (2001): 46–49.

[77] Michael Billington, "Push Up," *G,* 12 February 2002.

[78] Roland Schimmelpfennig, "Push Up 1–3," in *TheaterTheater. Aktuelle Stücke 11,* eds. Uwe B. Carstensen and Stefanie von Lieven (Frankfurt am Main: Fischer, 2001), 289–340, here: 318. Subsequent references to this work are cited in the text using the abbreviation *P* and page number.

[79] See Bertolt Brecht, "Über experimentelles Theater," in Bertolt Brecht, *Werke. Große kommentierte Berliner und Frankfurter Ausgabe. Vol. 22.1, Schriften 2,* eds. V. W. Hecht, J. Knopf, W. Mittenzwei, and K.-D. Müller (Berlin/Weimar/Frankfurt am Main: Aufbau and Suhrkamp, 1993), 540–56.

[80] Quoted in Birgitta Willmann, "Kalter Blick auf menschliche Tragödien," in *SoZ,* 18 January 1998.

7: Terrorism in Germany

TERRORISM IN THE 1970S in Germany looked very different from the terrorist attack of 11 September 2001 on the World Trade Center in New York.[1] Whereas the 2001 attacks originated in religious and nationalist beliefs, the German left-wing terrorists acted like Marxist revolutionaries whose "war" aimed to overthrow the German government from within, with little or no support from the people.[2]

In 1967, at the same time that the students' movement was beginning, several small Marxist and extreme-left splinter groups were also being founded. Neo-Marxist groups, such as the Rote Armee Fraktion, the Bewegung 2. Juni, and the Revolutionäre Zellen, greatly influenced the political scene in Germany, particularly during the 1970s. Unlike the student movement itself, these groups did not concentrate on social, university, feminist, and pacifist issues. Rather than trying to change German society through "der lange Marsch durch die Institutionen," that is, through legal protest, these militant groups resorted to violence. The most important and notorious of these groups was the Red Army Faction (Rote Armee Fraktion; RAF), also known as Baader-Meinhof-Gruppe. In her play *Leviathan* (1993), Dea Loher presents us with the dilemma of Marie, a character who draws on Ulrike Meinhof. Focusing on the beginnings of terrorism, Loher depicts a Marie who decides to use violence only because she is convinced that there are no legal ways to change the "fascist" West German state.

In the light of neo-Marxist beliefs, the accepted concepts of the state and the social economy appeared outdated and unjust in the late 1960s.[3] They were dismissed as an artificial facade, behind which large-scale manipulation was believed to be at work. As the alleged restraints of the consumer society were subtle, criticism focused on the secret constraints which, it was believed, originated in the governing elites.[4] Although the members of the RAF were, paradoxically, children of the well-fed and educated middle class, the group waged a war against the state in order to voice the protest of the lower classes.[5] They hoped that through terrorist action they would be able to jolt the working class into action, and thus function as a catalyst for the Marxist revolution.[6] They regarded the state authority to be a new form of fascism, for the state as such was rejected as an offshoot of the Third Reich.[7] The main aim was thus to destroy the state, which they believed to be exploiting the people.[8] However the terrorists ignored two facts: first, that the majority of the population did not feel at all oppressed; and second, that the political murders produced the unwelcome effect of widespread disgust and disapproval among the masses.[9]

Under the leadership of Andreas Baader and Ulrike Meinhof, the Red Army Faction began its protest against "imperialism" and "Konsumterror" with an arson attack on a department store in Frankfurt. Baader was arrested, but two years later, on 14 May 1970, he escaped from prison with the help of journalist Ulrike Meinhof, hitherto the editor-in-chief of the respected left-wing magazine *Konkret*. During the liberation of Baader, however, a policeman was accidentally killed. In the following two years, the Red Army Faction continued its clandestine fight against the state. In a series of bank robberies that supplied the group with the necessary money to buy weapons, shoot-outs with the police took place. However it took two more years, and a nationwide search, before the first generation of terrorists could be arrested: Baader, Meinhof, Jan-Carl Raspe, Holger Meins, and Gudrun Ensslin were all put into various high-security prisons. But their sentencing did not end the problem, for a new generation of terrorists stepped in to continue the "anti-imperialist struggle." Meins died in a hunger strike, and Meinhof committed suicide.[10] In 1977, an attempt to free the prisoners through the taking of hostages failed, and the three remaining prisoners died in prison. An official inquiry concluded that cause of death was suicide, although unofficial allegations of murder have persisted since then. In his play *Born in the R.A.F.* (1999), John von Düffel (1966–) takes a comedic stance towards these events, in that we see the events from the viewpoint of a child-prodigy whose misbehavior stifled his parents' will to commit further crimes.

The terrorist activities reached their height in the so-called "Deutsche Herbst" in 1977, when the RAF kidnapped and killed several politicians and high-ranking bankers and state officials. Moreover, they hijacked a Lufthansa plane in order to further pressure the German government into releasing the prisoners, but in a surprise attack, a special unit of German police managed to overwhelm the terrorists. Although most of the terrorists were imprisoned by this point, a third generation took over, and so the actions of the Red Army Faction entered a third phase: between 1986 and 1991, the group murdered four more top managers and state officials, among them the boss of the Treuhandanstalt, Karsten Rohwedder. This murder also figures in the opening scene of Rolf Hochhuth's *Wessis in Weimar* (1993).[11] It was only in 1998, in a document posted to the British news agency *Reuters* on 20 April, that the group officially declared that it would discontinue its activities.[12]

Although the *RAF* was not the only extremist group in Germany, no other series of events terrified and paralyzed West Germany to this extent, and at no other time did the state react so harshly. Parliament passed amendments to the *Grundgesetz*, the basic constitutional law of West Germany, which provided the government with extraordinary powers with which to handle emergency situations. In order to provide means for legal action, several new laws were passed, such as the "Notstandsgesetze" in 1968, which, among other things, legalized the tapping of telephones, and the opening of terrorist suspects' mail,[13] and the so-called "Extremistenbeschluss" in 1972, which excluded extremists from certain professions[14] — a law that also affected the playwright Franz Xaver Kroetz, for example, for he was a member of the *Deutsche Kommunistische Partei* at that time. Another law was the "Anti-Terror-Gesetz" in 1978 that allowed courts to penalize people for participating in, recruiting for, or aiding groups identified as terrorist.[15] Written before September 11, Oliver Czeslik's (1964–) play *Gaddafi rockt* (Gaddafi Rocks, 2000) presents us with a suicide bomber who belongs to one of the Muslim terrorist groups in Germany. It portrays the absurd reasoning of a disturbed man who is not only going to kill himself, but indulges in the sadistic pleasure of murdering innocent people at the same time. Marius von Mayenburg's *Feuergesicht* (Fireface, 1999), however, focuses on a different kind of terror, namely the violent attacks committed by students. In a series of short scenes, the play shows how a frustrated teenage boy turns into a terrorist who commits arson attacks and finally murders his parents.

The terrorist attacks in New York and Washington in September 2001 shattered the feeling of security and safety throughout the western world, not only in the USA.[16] It is thus not surprising that immediately after the terrorist attacks on the twin towers in New York in September 2001, the German government issued two more packages of laws. The so-called "security package I" (*Sicherheitspaket I*) — that had been prepared before the 2001 attacks — abolished religious freedom for clubs (*Vereine*), in order to prevent foreigners in Germany from developing terrorist activity under the veil of harmless club activities. Moreover, in addition to the provisions of the "Anti-Terror-Gesetz" of 1978, it is now forbidden to be a member of a terrorist group that is based abroad.[17] In November 2001, Otto Schily, the Home Secretary, launched an initiative for a second, heavily criticized package of laws concerning the security checks of the border police, the registering of particulars of potential criminals, and the aim to establish a database in order to enable a smooth and fast exchange of important data in the event of a "Rasterfahndung."[18] Asylum seekers and immigrants are also to be closely inspected, and issued with a tamper-proof (*fälschungssicher*) passport; suspects who hover around public places, airports, or other such sensitive areas, are to be monitored by electronic equipment. The second batch of laws, which was approved by the *Bundestag* on 20 December 2001, has often been criticized for going too far. As numerous scholars have pointed out, the legal situation poses a threat to the privacy of the average citizen.[19] Others have underlined that it is the duty of the state to provide a framework that best secures the freedom and safety of every citizen.[20]

The *Rote Armee Fraktion*:
Dea Loher's *Leviathan* (1993)

Dea Loher's play *Leviathan* is based on the true story of Ulrike "Marie" Meinhof who became the intellectual mouthpiece of the Red Army Faction. The play premiered at the Ballhof in Hanover in 1993, and the Royal Court in London staged a reading in the same year. It tells of the internal struggle experienced by Ulrike Meinhof, the respected and well-known journalist and editor-in-chief of the journal *Konkret* from 1960–64.

As Meinhof's political views become increasingly radical, she and her husband, Klaus Rainer Röhl, who owned the journal, quarreled, and Ulrike left her family. In Berlin, she worked as a freelance journalist, produced the critical TV documentary program *Panorama,* and wrote a TV-drama called *Bambule.* In 1969, she ended her work for the journal *Konkret,* and on 14 May 1970, she helped free the terrorist Andreas Baader. Generally, Meinhof is seen as the logistic mastermind of the action, during which three people were severely injured. This event is generally seen to be the birth of the *Baader-Meinhof-Gruppe.* In June of the same year, Meinhof took refuge in Jordan, together with other terrorists, in order to receive training from the Palestinian guerilla.

The play depicts the two ways in which young Germans reacted to the unsatisfactory nature of the German state in 1968: Whereas Ulrike Meinhof ("Marie"), Andreas Baader ("Karl"), and Gudrun Ensslin ("Louise") choose terrorism, Christiane advocates patience and "the long march through the institutions" in order to change society for the better. *Leviathan* focuses on a turning point in Meinhof's life: the choice between continuing the intellectual protest and turning to radical terrorism. In an interview, Loher states her view that it is too narrow-minded to judge Meinhof's intentions simply through the events of 1977, when left-wing terror in Germany reached its height: "Außerdem finde ich es bis heute falsch, wenn die ganze Geschichte der RAF nur aus der Perspektive von 1977 geschrieben wird und man das, was vorher war und sich auch anders hätte entwickeln können, nicht mehr sieht."[21] As the title *Leviathan* suggests, the play focuses on the nature of the state. With her title, Loher harks back to Thomas Hobbes, who wrote *Leviathan*, his treaty on the nature of the state, in 1651. Hobbes had encountered strong criticism from the outraged clerics who disapproved of Hobbes's state set up by man. In Hobbes's view, the state must be entrusted with power in order to prevent everybody from fighting against everybody else. Despite the fact that the individual loses some of his natural rights, the state guarantees security and safety. In Loher's play, however, the state becomes a threat to the rights of the individual Ulrike Meinhof, who claims that the German state restricts her freedom. The story of the leviathan in the version of Herman Melville's *Moby Dick* (1851) influenced the thinking of the Red Army Faction: it is known that in order to fool the prison guards, Gudrun Ensslin borrowed aliases for the terrorists from Melville's novel: Ahab was the assumed name for Andreas Baader, Starbuck stood for Holger Meins, and Bildad for Horst Mahler, to name but a few.[22] It thus becomes clear that the terrorists saw their actions as a hunt for evil, the leviathan that, according to them, represented the German state.

Although Loher is the first playwright to address the issue of the Red Army Faction, left-wing terrorism had previously featured in several films, such as *Die verlorene Ehre der Katharina Blum* (The Lost Honor of Katharina Blum, 1975, director, Volker Schlöndorff); *Die bleierne Zeit* (The Two Sisters, 1981, director, Margarethe von Trotta); and *Stammheim* (1986, director, Reinhard Hauff).

As in *Die bleierne Zeit*, terrorist actions appear only peripherally in Loher's play; what is important is the arguments on which they are based. Unlike Trotha's film, however, which depicts the debates between the sisters Gudrun and Christiane Ensslin after Gudrun's imprisonment in a high-security prison, Loher presents us with the dilemma facing the nascent terrorist Marie.[23] As Marie (Meinhof) is responsible for the severe injuries of a prison guard, caused when she helped to free Karl (Baader), there seems to be no going back for her.[24] The sixteen short scenes all take place in Christine's flat, to which Marie fled in order to hide from the police. The audience learns from their conversations that 10,000 marks have been offered as a reward for her arrest. Frightened, confused and scared, yet oddly determined, Marie decides to go underground and continue her violent struggle. In the end, she and Karl take a plane to Palestine, in order to train for guerrilla war: This is where Baader, Meinhof, and Ensslin, the first generation of the Rote Armee Fraktion, actually went to learn terrorist tactics from June to September 1970.

Marie compares the state to a monstrous system, a kind of leviathan, alluding to several scandals about the withholding and falsifying of information that had shaken the German media, such as the *Spiegel* affair in 1962. At the same time, the Axel Springer publishing house, usually associated with the tabloid newspaper *Bild*, was allegedly at the center of a witch-hunt against the leaders of the students' movement.[25] As protesting students insisted, the assassination of their charismatic leader, Rudi Dutschke, in 1968, was a result of *Bild's* aggressive anti-student propaganda.[26] Moreover, even twenty-five years after the War, Germany was rocked by scandals concerning its Nazi past, such as the discovery that the governing Christian democrat chancellor, Kurt Georg Kiesinger, had been an active member of the NSDAP (Nationalsozialistische Deutsche Arbeiterpartei) since 1933.[27]

Marie experiences strong feelings, and is torn between motherly longing and revolutionary reasoning. Although she misses her children and her husband, she feels obliged to sacrifice personal happiness for the greater cause, the Marxist revolution.[28] Like her real-life counterpart, Marie blames herself for being too soft, and for failing to act. Contrasting Marie's strangely unemotional, monologue style with her effort to come to terms with being a terrorist, Loher reveals a rift between Marie the terrorist and Marie the mother. The repetitive, dreamy language highlights the fact that she is still in a state of shock. Despite this, she denies herself any love or affection when her husband comes to see her. All his efforts to make her come back and turn to legal means of protest, such as publishing articles in his journal, are in vain. Marie is determined to sacrifice her life for the revolution.[29]

In the late 1960s, it was commonly believed that democracy in Germany was imperiled, if not doomed to failure, and because intellectuals accused the West German state of fostering fascist tendencies, even extreme violence seemed justified. Marie believes that she is right to protest violently against the alleged monopoly of the tabloid press and the machinations of the government. According to her, terrorists must wage a guerrilla war rather than leaving the battle to those who are restricted by the power of the state:

> Der Krieg geht weiter
> die Verfassung wird geändert
> die Notstandgesetze verabschiedet
> der Protest eingemeindet
> Nein
> Die Zeit der Diskussionen ist vorbei. (*L*, 157)

The Germans who do not want to be enlightened must therefore be forced to recognize the evils of the state. In Marie's eyes, war against the upper classes, or "Klassenkampf" against the privileged, is the only solution.

With the benefit of hindsight, Dea Loher addresses the principal dilemma facing *Red Army Faction* terrorists: should there be a tedious, long-term protest against the West German state, or should there be a violent neo-Marxist revolution. *Leviathan* offers insight into Marie's fears and hopes, showing that terrorism can originate in frustration, and in a moment of total desperation, Marie claims that her entire life has been a lie. Based on the example of Ulrike "Marie" Meinhof, the play shows how good intentions can have disastrous results, both at the personal level of the family and in the wider context of the state.

Smoldering Anger:
Marius von Mayenburg's *Feuergesicht* (1998)

The play *Feuergesicht* had its origins in a final examination at the *Berliner Hochschule der Künste*. It earned Mayenburg the *Kleist-Förderpreis für junge Dramatiker* and made him famous almost overnight. After an unsuccessful attempt to become an actor, he studied writing in Berlin, worked as an assistant at the *Kammerspiele* in Munich, and now works closely with Thomas Ostermeier at the *Schaubühne* in Berlin.

Like Mayenburg's earlier play, *Haarmann* (1995), which features a mass murderer,[30] *Feuergesicht* unveils the mechanisms of violence behind the mask of normality.[31] The play centers on Kurt, a teenager in an incestuous relationship with his sister Olga. Kurt fails at school, is expelled after setting fire to a classroom, and finally murders his parents in their sleep. Against the backdrop of a petit-bourgeois family, Mayenburg shows that the parents' desire for peace and quiet, and their efforts to ignore their son's abnormal behavior cause Kurt to become a terrorist. While the parents fail to notice what their children are really up to when they are upstairs, or away during the night committing arson attacks, Kurt becomes an incommunicative monster who justifies his love for fire with a twisted version of Heracleitus's (540–480 B.C.) philosophy. As Kurt takes the philosopher's word literally, and his teachers were evidently unable to explain that it would be fatal and short-sighted to interpret the philosopher's words literally, he develops a half-digested pseudo-philosophy in order to justify his acts of arson. The link between madness and visions of fire also harks back to Georg Büchner's portrayal of a disturbed mind in *Woyzeck* (1836/37). In this play, the soldier Woyzeck has visions of red circles before he eventually goes mad as a result of the injustice inflicted on him. His wife is unfaithful, he is treated unfairly in the army and, finally, abused as a guinea-pig for medical experiments. As in *Woyzeck*, the obsession with fire in *Feuergesicht* becomes symbolic of a mental illness, which is the result of failed communication with those around him.

Although the scenes follow one another chronologically, they begin and end abruptly, like those in the so-called "Minutendramaturgie" of the late plays of Rainer Werner Fassbinder.[32] As the "scenes" sometimes only consist of one sentence and are not numbered, and the play is not divided into acts, the plot unfolds very fast. Typically, Mayenburg does not explore the conflicts in every detail, and often leaves the end of a scene open. The deliberately fragmented play offers hardly any stage directions, and leaves a great deal to the creativity of the director.

Feuergesicht premiered at the *Kammerspiele* in Munich in October 1998 and quickly became a national and international success.[33] At Mayenburg's request, Jan Bosse directed the premiere,[34] and while critics criticized Bosse's rather artistic and artificial production, the *Berliner Zeitung* praised its precise psychological profiles.[35] In January 1999, it was staged in Frankfurt an der Oder[36] and Vienna, and in June 1999 at the *Schauspielhaus* in Hamburg, under the direction of Thomas Ostermeier.[37] Reviewers praised this production because of its calm representation of the topic and its brilliant acting.[38] From then on, *Feuergesicht* was also read in the historical context of the 1970s, when terrorism in Germany had reached its height. In addition, a tragic incident in Erfurt in April 2002, where a student had killed sixteen teachers after he had been thrown out of school, proved that Mayenburg's diagnosis was — sadly — not exaggerated.[39] Since the tragedy of Erfurt triggered a heated debate about violence in schools, *Feuergesicht* became one of the most performed plays in Germany[40] and an international success.[41]

The title of the play refers to a key scene in which Kurt deliberately exposes his face to the pieces of smoldering fabric falling from the curtains of a classroom. Instead of retreating from the danger, as one would expect, he masochistically rejoices in the feeling of fire on his skin. This act of self-harm is symbolic of Kurt's insistence on being different by living his life to the extreme, and he claims that only those who burn are alive. It is this naive and simplistic misreading of Heracleitus's views that show the extent to which he is in need of fruitful communication with the world. However, it is due to his aggressive demeanor on the one hand, and the stunned bewilderment of his mother coupled with the full-mouthed tirades of his father on the other, that Kurt sees himself trapped, and burns his bridges behind him.

Feuergesicht depicts the revolt of a teenager against a stifling petit-bourgeois world in which, because the other members of the family choose not to notice the burning rage inside him, he finds no social place Soon, the feeling inside becomes too much, and he sets his environment on fire. At first it is birds and rubbish, then a classroom, a factory, and eventually himself. Indeed, Mayenburg's play is an example that warns that parents' negligence and lack of interest can drive their children further and further away from them, until they eventually become terrorists and murderers.

When the play opens, the family is gathered round the kitchen table, quarreling. Kurt is disgusted, for he has just stepped in his mother's blood in the bathroom; his mother refuses to apologize, and the father calls an end to the meal. Here the main conflict is already established, namely Kurt's reluctance to accept that hormones are raging inside him, and that his desire to retreat into his mother's womb is pointless. Both he and his mother recall his birth, yet from a different perspectives. While Kurt secretly longs for protection, his mother remembers that it was painful, and she felt as if he had grabbed her insides and refused to let go. Indeed, it is the feeling of being torn between affection and hatred for his mother that drives Kurt insane. In a typical teenage paradox, the longing for love manifests itself in a violent rejection of the beloved. However, the fact that he chooses fire as his means of expression reveals a disturbed mind.

His confusion grows when his sister Olga mocks his awakening sexuality, and eventually sleeps with him. Their incestuous relationship, however, plunges the siblings into depression, for they feel abused and empty afterwards, unable to give one another true support. Kurt's frustration increases when Olga, who is like their mother, destroys their intimacy by introducing her boyfriend Paul to the family. Foreseeably, the boy vents his anger by perfecting his skills in building bombs, yet even this passes practically unnoticed. His parents turn a blind eye to his activities, and defend him even when he burns Paul's clothes.

Although the play portrays a classic family drama, it does not follow a realistic style, either with respect to the language or to the structure. The characters are not defined by their individual way of speaking, but use a rather sophisticated language:

OLGA   Ich will schlafen.

KURT   Schlafen gibts nicht mehr. Wir müssen jetzt wach sein.
        Wir schmelzen uns zusammen und detonieren hier über
        den Matratzenrand.

OLGA   Wirst du nie satt?

KURT   Satt gibts auch nicht mehr. Wir müssen brennen und
            uns verschleudern. Ich will mich an dir zerpulvern.[42]

As this passage shows, Kurt's image-laden sentences sound strangely distanced and inappropriate in this situation, for he simply wants to have sex. The conversation also portrays Kurt's narrow-minded view of the world, revealing that he is unable to think in terms of anything other than metaphors of fire. Even coming close to his sister bears a violent undertone of burning, detonating, and exploding. These images sound fairly normal in a sexual context, yet the problem is that Kurt cannot change his frame of mind, regardless of where he is. Since he is unable to grow emotionally close to anyone, he masks his desires behind a language reminiscent of expressionist plays. In *Feuergesicht,* however, the quest for the "neue Mensch" fails. Although Kurt tries to believe that his views will make the world a better place, his actions reveal the megalomania of a child who has grown up too quickly.

Fact and Fiction:
John von Düffel's *Born in the R.A.F.* (1999)

The monologue *Born in the R.A.F.,* premiered in March 2001 in Osnabrück, presents us with the confession of a teenage boy who grows up in Ireland[43] and Germany as the son of two notoriously famous Red Army Faction terrorists, Andreas Baader and Gudrun Ensslin. The play mixes fact and fiction, using German terrorism of the 1970s as a foil, yet presenting it as ridiculous, for the events are seen from the perspective of a jester-like boy who depicts the past as a farce:

> Gudrun wohnte exakt in Ulrike Meinhofs Haus. Gudruns Leben und Arbeiten verlief in genau denselben Bahnen wie das der Meinhof. Was für Beweise will man mehr: Gudrun war Ulrike Meinhof. Und die permanenten Fahndungsmißerfolge der Polizei erklärten sich schlicht und ergreifend aus der Tatsache, daß nach zwei Personen gefahndet wurde, obwohl es in Wirklichkeit nur eine einzige gab: Meine Mutter war Ulrike Meinhof *und* Gudrun Ensslin.[44]

In an ironic manner, the boy tells the Generalbundesanwalt (Chief Federal Prosecutor) that he was the youngest terrorist in the IRA, yet involuntarily hindered its activities to a considerable extent by organizing its members, a very German undertaking. Ironically, he becomes the "Führer" of the other children, and tells them to smash the glass windows of English telephone booths. It goes without saying that the boy insists on speaking his mother tongue, thus forcing the other children to learn German.

In the tradition of Tristram Shandy or Oskar Matzerath, the child-prodigy is an artifact, a super-human child, and his lucidity and reason allow him to comment on the world, thereby ironically distancing himself from it. It is not surprising that the three-foot high know-it-all takes control not only of his friends, but also of his parents. Indeed, he does not tolerate an English word in his hearing, thus forcing his parents to return to Germany, since they are unable to communicate with their friends.

The image of the stereotypical terrorist is dismantled, as the parents are described as disorganized, petit-bourgeois, and more or less unable to buy a bus ticket. It is clear that von Düffel is attacking the way in which the Red Army Faction members were demonized in the media at the time, presenting them as not human. This becomes evident when the boy mentions the black-and-white photographs of terrorists that were displayed on posters all over Germany, stating that they all looked alike. Von Düffel is alluding to the fact that most of these photographs convey the image of the unkempt and dangerous criminal, thus calling into question the purpose of the terrorist hunt. According to the boy, however, the aim of the police was to scare the man on the street, and to create the impression of being in control of the situation. In *Born in the R.A.F.,* the German efficiency in hunting down criminals is constantly mocked, such as during a stop-and-search procedure, when the police fail to notice that the passports are faked. However, this does not serve the purpose of playing down the terrorist attacks themselves, but rather criticizes the clampdown on terrorists. With an ironic wink to the reader, the boy states that this incident caused him to quell terrorism in his own family.

In order to do so, he keeps his parents busy with his homework, ruins their attempts to relax on a Sunday, and pretends to be ill if they want to go out. Baader and Ensslin, however, act like average parents, and *Born in the R.A.F.* presents us with their complete failure to organize terrorist activities, which is caused not least by their utterly conservative child. Due to their help, their son soon becomes the best-prepared pupil of the entire school, and it is rather ironic that his homework — done by two hunted terrorists — is copied by his schoolmates. Von Düffel thus inverts the usual approach to terrorism in several ways, since he focuses on the boy and thus mocks the viewpoint of the man on the street, for the boy is a model student and the advocate of an organized, crime-free state.

The monologue of the jester-like boy mocks psychological approaches to terrorism, and picks up on debates about terrorism that typically maintained that during their childhood, the highly intelligent Red Army Faction members were so neglected that they resorted to violence.[45] In *Born in the R.A.F.,* however, the boy looks after himself, and prevents his parents from pursuing their subversive activities. Although von Düffel employs the perspective of the jester-like boy who intends to make the world a better place by enforcing an iron discipline, he implicitly questions this over-organized, military family. The playwright thus criticizes the police mentality of the Germans, who supported the nation-wide hunt for the *Red Army Faction* for rather dubious reasons.

Monologues of Madness: Oliver Czeslik's *Gaddafi rockt* (2000)

The subtitle of this play, "Trance and Monologue," indicates its form, which is simply one man's monologue, interrupted by the distant laughter of a girl and police announcements over a megaphone. It therefore never becomes clear whether the monologue is a dream or reality.[46] This man is really a middle-aged German called Werner Mittgross, who is obviously mentally ill, and pretends to be a Muslim who is fighting the holy war of the Islamic world. *Gaddafi rockt* is set in a public place, perhaps a theater or café, and because Mittgross turns out to be a suicide bomber, the people, which means in this case the audience, are threatened. Czeslik deliberately leaves the ending open for the audience to decide whether the bomb explodes or not.

In 2001, *Gaddafi rockt* was presented as a *szenische Lesung* at the *Neue Theater Halle,* at the *Schauspielhaus Graz* and at the *Schaubühne Berlin.* The text was also presented by the *German theater abroad* in New York and the *Theater Hollandia* in Amsterdam in 2002.

In *Gaddafi rockt,* the man begins by counting the number of people in the audience in order to see how many his bombing will kill, before expressing his satisfaction that everybody is nicely dressed. He is convinced that the destruction he will cause will recreate the world, and he calls his act a "work of art" that complies with his vision of beauty. Obviously out of his wits, he says that rubble and dismembered corpses are beautiful. Yet his aims and the reasons for his actions are rather dubious, not only because he is a terrorist, but also because he is a fake Muslim. As he is a German, his anti-Semitism seems to be more important than his rapidly adopted religious beliefs, for, as it turns out, he only joined the "holy war" ten days before.

Despite the fact that the situation is eerily threatening, particularly in view of the events during the siege of a Moscow theater in October 2002, his simplistic beliefs in the materialistic rewards of the "holy" terrorist war are laughable. Since the attacks on New York in 2001, researchers have pointed out that the equation of martyrdom and paradise is based on a very narrow interpretation of the Koran.[47] For Mittgross, however, the prospect of having plenty of young girls at his disposal seems to be more important than the "holiness" of his actions. It gradually emerges that he is in love with a beautiful young girl, Susanne, who ended their relationship and made him feel worthless. His act of terrorism is a way of turning his death into a theatrical spectacle, in an attempt to glorify it with confused religious objectives.[48]

The personal aspect becomes stronger towards the end of the play, when Mittgross laments the fact that Susanne rejected him and that he is hardly more than an "asshole":

> ich bin moslem — ja
> hinterhältig, feige und grausam!
> ich war in luxor und in algerien.
> ich bin der ayatollah des wahnsinns!!
> ein gespenst geht um in europa.
> hört ihr es? seht ihr es? riecht ihr es?
> ich bin das opium, das lsd, das ecstasy im namen allahs.
> ich bin lockerbie, ich bin saddam.
> gaddafi rockt in mir über den gräbern von luxor.
> intifada, intifada, intifada! (*GR*, 104)

This passage shows that Mittgross believes he is an embodiment of all terrorists. In a fit of megalomania, the mentally disturbed man rants about the evil of terrorism that haunts the world. What is most disturbing is that he enjoys it. Yet his confused speech also reveals that he is not a committed member of any specific group, and that he does not really have any political aims. His interest lies solely in the act of terror itself. Moreover, he accuses the Muslims of being cowardly and cruel cheaters, and it thus becomes clear that he is exploiting the *intifada* as a weird pretence to justify his actions.

In a manner reminiscent of the theater of the 1970s, Czeslik's actor addresses the audience directly,[49] and forces the spectators to question their passive role.[50] *Gaddafi rockt* plays on this involvement of the audience, yet reminds one that this situation could be abused for a perversely lethal attack, mixing reality and theater performance.[51] In the light of the kidnappings, hijackings, and bombings that take place around the globe in the name of God, the audience could feel uncomfortable, hoping that the action onstage really *is* a play. Despite this, the action is purely fictional, and the weakness of the play is its highly artificial situation, which renders it difficult to take the action seriously.

Aggression and its consequences play an important role in the depiction of terrorism, which is two-fold: the re-evaluation of the wave of terrorism in Germany in the 1970s, and the portrayal of the terrorists' psyche. With respect to the latter, Dea Loher and John von Düffel look at the terrorism of the Red Army Faction in different ways. Dea Loher's *Leviathan* (1993) depicts the inner struggle of the terrorist Ulrike Meinhof after the first arson attack on a department store in Frankfurt. It retraces Meinhof's painful choice between changing the state by means of violence, and opposing it within the bounds of legality. While Loher approaches the subject seriously, von Düffel's *Born in the R.A.F.* (1999) takes a comedic stance. Von Düffel presents terrorism from the viewpoint of a three-year-old smart-aleck who is determined to quell terrorism at its origin, namely within the family. In a mock-ironic monologue, the child makes a public confession of his parents' allegedly unlawful past, and describes how he organized them until they were unable to commit any further crimes. The real terrorist in this play is thus the child, who turns his parents' lives into hell. *Born in the R.A.F.* wittily challenges common assumptions, such as that the public witch-hunt for the terrorists in the 1970s was useful. Moreover, the child prodigy rejects the stereotype of cold-blooded murderers, insisting that his parents were normal petit-bourgeois citizens, in another stab at the media, which was only too willing to demonize terrorists.

Marius von Mayenburg's internationally successful play *Feuergesicht* (1999) also centers on a boy, yet it could hardly be more different. In a style that combines brusque and laconic dialogues with expressionist language, a sequence of short scenes portray a boy unable to come to terms with his awakening sexuality, who develops a distorted view of the world that is largely inspired by the philosopher Heracleitus. As he unable to relate to anyone, the boy develops his own twisted philosophy, and insists that everything that burns is alive. As communication with his parents and sister fails, he turns to committing arson attacks, is expelled from school and eventually murders his parents.

In a fast-moving monologue, Oliver Czeslik's *Gaddafi rockt* (2000) presents us with the confession of a suicide-bomber. As Czeslik wrote this play before 11 September 2001, it does not include historical knowledge of the terror attacks, but focuses on the insane logic of the terrorist's mind. In *Gaddafi rockt*, Czeslik paints the picture of a man who does not kill for political reasons, but rather for sadistic pleasure, and for the simple reason that he has a broken heart and is incapable of maintaining long-term relationships with women. In an age of increasing violence, the need to tell stories and analyze social experiences is stronger than ever, and this necessity is demonstrated by the plays discussed above, which shed some light on the origins and developments of terrorism.

Notes

[1] Bruce Hoffmann, *Inside Terrorism* (London: Victor Gallancz, 1998; second, revised edition 2001), 276–82.

[2] Irving Fetscher, *Terrorismus und Reaktion* (Frankfurt am Main: Europäische Verlagsanstalt, 1977), 49.

[3] Capitalism and its negative influences were strongly criticized, especially at universities, for example by Herbert Marcuse in his book *Der eindimensionale Mensch* (Darmstadt/Neuwied: Luchterhand, 1967). Yet it should be pointed out that Marcuse did not support terrorist views.

[4] Peter Waldmann, *Terrorismus. Provokation der Macht* (Munich: Gerling Akademie Verlag, 1998), 87–88

[5] These ideas were fairly fashionable at the time; see Hans-Jürgen Krahl, *Konstitution und Klassenkampf. Zur historischen Dialektik von bürgerlicher Emanzipation und proletarischer Revolution* (Frankfurt am Main: Suhrkamp, 1971). Above all, Krahl strongly opposed the "Notstandsgesetze," and prophesied the end of democracy in Germany.

[6] Tobias Wunschik, *Baader-Meinhofs Kinder — Die zweite Generation der RAF* (Opladen: Westdeutscher Verlag, 1997), 44.

[7] Gerhard Wisniewski, Wolfgang Landgreber, and Ekkehard Sieker, *Das RAF-Phantom* (Munich: Droemersche Verlagsbuchhandlung, 1992), 15.

[8] Butz Peters, *RAF Terrorismus in Deutschland* (Munich: Knaur, 1991), 130.

[9] Irving Fetscher, *Terrorismus und Reaktion* (Frankfurt am Main: Europäische Verlagsanstalt, 1977), 32–41.

[10] Stefan Aust, *Der Baader-Meinhof Komplex* (Goldmann: Munich, 1998), 303–5; 632–36.

[11] See the discussion of the play in the chapter on reunification.

[12] Together with a critical introduction by Eckhard Jesse, the document is published in *Extremismus & Demokratie* 11 (1999), 127–45.

[13] For example, an amendment to article 87a enables the state to use the armed forces in the event of an extraordinary threat to the democratic republic from within, if the two chambers of government, the *Bundestag* and *Bundesrat,* so wish. Article 80a regulates the procedures in a "state of tension" (*Spannungsfall*), which again have to be formally acknowledged by the *Bundestag.*

[14] On 28 January 1972, under the chancellor Willy Brandt, the Social Democrats decided to exclude political extremists from the civil service. This is laid down in article 4, paragraph 1(2) of the "Beamtenrechtsrahmengesetz."

[15] Article 129 and 129a of the Criminal Code provide for the imprisonment of leaders of terrorist groups for up to ten years.

[16] This loss was especially expressed by the slump in transatlantic air travel, which went down by a third; see "Anschläge erschüttern Flugverkehr," SPIEGEL-ONLINE, 23 November 2001.

[17] Thus article 129 of the Criminal Code was completed with an amendment called 129b. See also: Berthold Meyer, "Die innere Gefährdung des demokratischen Friedens. Staatliche Terrorismusabwehr als Balanceakt zwischen Sicherheit und Freiheit," in *Ground Zero — Friedenspolitik nach den Terroranschlägen auf die USA,* ed. Österreichisches Studienzentrum für Friedensforschung (Münster: Agenda-Verlag, 2002). The article is available on the Internet under the following address: www.uni-kassel.de/fb10/frieden/themen/Innere-Sicherheit/meyer.html; the book is scheduled for 2002.

[18] Yet it should be noted that in February 2002, the Federal Court (*Landgericht*) of Wiesbaden forbade a systematic, computer-aided search (*Rasterfahndung*) for members of Islamic groups in Hesse, as no terrorist attack was perceived to be imminent. In the same vein, the *Rasterfahnung* was forbidden in Berlin at the end of January 2002. See also: *FAZ,* 8 February 2002, 4.

[19] Ralf Bendrath, "Von 'Freiheit stirbt mit Sicherheit' zu 'Keine Freiheit ohne Sicherheit'? Über die Umwertung des Staates und das 'Grundrecht auf Sicherheit,'" *antimilitarismus information* 12 (1997), 11–23.

[20] Dieter und Eva Senghaas, "Si vis pacem, para pacem. Überlegungen zu einem zeitgemäßen Friedenskonzept," in *Eine Welt oder Chaos?* ed. Berthold Meyer (Frankfurt am Main: Suhrkamp, 1996), 247–59, here: 250.

[21] "Ich kenne nicht besonders viele glückliche Menschen. Ein Gespräch mit Dea Loher über das Leben, das Schreiben und ihre Stücke," *Th* 2 (1998): 61–65, here: 65.

[22] See Stefan Aust, *Der Baader-Meinhof Komplex* (Goldmann: Munich, 1998), 286–89.

[23] Sandra Umathum, "Unglückliche Utopisten," in *Stück-Werk 3,* eds. Christel Weiler and Harald Müller (Berlin: Zentrum Bundesrepublik Deutschland des Internationalen Theaterinstituts, 2001), 101–5, here: 104.

[24] On 14 May 1970, Ulrike Meinhof, Ingrid Schubert, and Irene Goergens helped Andreas Baader escape from prison.

[25] On the opposition outside the government see, for example, Pavel A. Richter, "Die außerparlamentarische Opposition in der Bundesrepublik Deutschland 1966–1968," in *1968 — vom Ereignis zum Gegenstand der Geschichtswissenschaft,* ed. Ingrid Gilcher-Holtey (Göttingen: Vandenhoeck & Ruprecht, 1998), 35–55, here: 39–40.

[26] See Hans-Jürgen Krahl, *Konstitution und Klassenkampf. Zur historischen Dialektik von bürgerlicher Emanzipation und proletarischer Revolution* (Frankfurt am Main: Suhrkamp, 1971), 45.

[27] Manfred Görtemaker, *Geschichte der Bundesrepublik Deutschland* (Munich: CH Beck, 1999), 484.

[28] Dea Loher, "Leviathan," in Dea Loher, *Olgas Raum. Tätowierung. Leviathan* (Frankfurt am Main: Verlag der Autoren, 1994), 145–229. Subsequent references to this work are cited in the text using the abbreviation *L* and page number.

[29] Although it does not feature in the play, it is important to note that Ulrike Meinhof committed suicide in prison in 1977.

[30] *Haarmann* was premiered belatedly in Hanover in March 2001, and was celebrated enthusiastically; see Barbara Burckhardt, "Armer Mörder," *Th* 4 (2001): 46–47.

[31] For an overview of Mayenburg's works, see Sandra Umathum, "Die Hölle sind immer die anderen," in *Stück-Werk*, eds. Christel Weiler and Harald Müller (Berlin: Zentrum Bundesrepublik Deutschland des Internationalen Theaterinstituts, 2001), 106–8.

[32] For an analysis of Fassbinder's *Preparadise Sorry Now*, see Wolfgang Seibel, *Die Formenwelt der Fertigteile. Künstlerische Montagetechnik und ihre Anwendung im Drama* (Würzburg: Könighausen & Neumann, 1988), 157–82, here: 169.

[33] It was, for example, staged at Regensburg and Ingolstadt, where it was warmly received; see Konstantin, Korosides, "Aus einem ganz normalen Wohnzimmer. Bayern Kritik: Theater Regensburg," *W*, 3 March 2001; Detlef Baur, "Beklemmende Aktualität: Von pyromanischen Terror-Kindern. Schauspiel *Feuergesicht* im Theater Ingolstadt," *W*, 1 October 2001. In May 1999, this production went on tour to the *Contemporary Drama Festival* in Budapest and the *Polish Theater Festival* in Warsaw, and the *Edinburgh International Festival* invited the production in 2002; see Barry Gordon, "Passion burns brightly as sparks fly at Gilded Balloon," *The Scotsman*, 10 June 2002. However, it was claimed that the production was discouraging. In November 1999, it toured to the *Royal Court Theater* in London; see Carola Dürr, "Vom Tragischen ins Komische. Neue deutsche Dramatik am Royal Court Theater in London und Mark Ravenhills neuer Reißer," *W*, 19 November 1999. In February 2001, it was at the *Sydney Festival*, where it sold out completely; see Susan Shineberg, "Der Potsdamer Platz liegt am Pazifik," *W*, 15 February 2001. In July 2001, the director Alain Françon presented the French translation *Visage de Feu* at the *Théâtre de la Colline* in Paris, where it was enthusiastically received; see Dorothee Hammerstein, "Der Fürst spricht: Grausamkeiten zuerst," *Th* 8/9 (2001): 46–49. Indeed, the play attracted considerable international attention, and in December 2001, the Latvian director Oskaras Korsonovas presented his fast and furious version of Mayenburg's play at the *2. Festival für internationale neue Dramatik* at the *Schaubühne* in Berlin; see Eva Corino, "Jetzt sickern sie in die Matratzen!" *BZ*, 15 December 2001; Iris Ayanyali, "Der Theater-Teufel aus Litauen. Oskaras Kursonovas, Off-Regiestar europäischer Festivals, wirbelt durch Berlin," *W*, 23 November 2001.

[34] Reinhard Wengierek, "Eintracht führt zum Weltbrand. Marius von Mayenburg triumphiert mit *Feuergesicht* über das junge Drama," *W*, 12 October 1998. Wengierek especially praises Mayenburg's ability to present violent conflicts in "concise language."

[35] Barbara Burckhardt, "'Lieber tot sein oder besoffen.' Marius von Mayenburg und seine Monsterkinder," *Th* 5 (1998): 51–56; Hans Krieger, "Zur Welt kommen im Brand. Furioses Regiedebüt, tiefgründiges Stück: Marius von Mayenburgs *Feuergesicht* in München uraufgeführt," *BZ*, 12 October 1998.

[36] Friedemann Krusche, "Weltbrand im Familienkessel. Münchens Kammerspiele und das Kleist-Theater Frankfurt/Oder schauen Monstermacher Marius von Mayenburg ins *Feuergesicht*," *Th* 1 (1999): 24–26.

[37] Franz Wille, "Als alles anfing. Thomas Ostermaier entdeckt in Hamburg Marius von Mayenburgs *Feuergesicht*," *Th* 6 (1999): 6–7. Wille compares the stagings in Frankfurt an der Oder and Munich to Ostermeier's production in Hamburg, which he considers to be the most effective due to its clear-cut aims.

[38] Gottfried Krüger, "Inzest als Spiel von heiler Familie," *Mopo*, 17 April 1999; Kläre Warnecke, "Im Katastrophen-Käfig der Angst. Thomas Ostermeier inszeniert Mayenburgs *Feuergesicht* als Spiel mit den Fatalitäten des Menschseins," *W*, 17 April 1999.

[39] Above all, people raised the question as to how the teenage boy could possibly have hidden from his parents for more than a year the fact that he had been expelled from school, had secretly bought a gun, and cold-bloodedly plotted the mass murder of his teachers; see Susanne Gaschke, "Er kam nicht vom anderen Stern. Robert S. und der Mord als Menetekel: Wo die Familie versagt, helfen weder die besten Schulen noch die strengsten Gesetze," *Z*, 2 May 2002. Gaschke points out that parents cannot shake off responsibility for their children, and thus puts the blame on the family; see also: John Hooper, "Teachers massacred," *G*, 27 April 2002. See also Liane von Billerbeck and Michael Schwelien, "'Mal so richtig aufräumen.' Der Mörder S. und seine Welt: Die Website, die Waffen, die Zeugen," *Z*, 2 May 2002. The authors trace the motives and give a portrayal of Robert Steinhäuser's character. Other pupils remember an incident two years before, when Robert had formed his hand as if holding a gun, and told a teacher "Du bist tot." During Robert's murder spree, this particular teacher was practically executed.

[40] See the ad in the *BZ* for the stagings of *Feuergesicht* at the *Schaubühne am Lehniner Platz*, which read: "Vor dem Hintergrund der aktuellen Ereignisse in Erfurt erhält das Stück eine erschreckende Aktualität," *BZ*, 15 June 2002.

[41] This could also be explained by the fact that mass murders are a tragic but recurrent phenomenon at schools and universities; compare the murder spree of a student in Montreal in 1989 who killed 14 people, the mass murder of five people, plotted by two boys in Jonesboro (Arkansas) in March 1998, and the massacre of twelve students and one teacher by two teenagers in Littleton (Colorado) in April 1999.

[42] Marius von Mayenburg, "Feuergesicht," in Marius von Mayenburg: *Feuergesicht. Parasiten* (Frankfurt am Main: Verlag der Autoren, 2000), 7–70, here: 20.

[43] Due to parallels between the biographies of the boy and von Düffel, critics tend to see the boy merely as a mask for the playwright, who is believed to be uttering his own opinion; see Isabell Jannack, "Der Autordramaturgdozent," in *Stück-Werk 3*, eds. Christel Weiler and Harald Müller (Berlin: Zentrum Bundesrepublik Deutschland des Internationalen Theaterinstituts, 2001), 46–50, here: 48.

[44] John von Düffel, *Born in the R.A.F.* (Gifkendorf: Merlin, 1999), 46. Subsequent references to this work are cited in the text using the abbreviation *B* and page number.

[45] See Irving Fetscher, *Terrorismus und Reaktion* (Cologne/Frankfurt am Main: Europäische Verlagsanstalt, 1977), 28–31.

[46] Axel Schalk, "Vom Voyeur zum Akteur," in *Stück-Werk 3*, eds. Christel Weiler and Harald Müller (Berlin: Zentrum Bundesrepublik Deutschland des Internationalen Theaterinstituts, 2001), 35–37, here: 37.

[47] See Peter Heine, *Terror in Allahs Namen. Extremistische Kräfte im Islam* (Freiburg im Breisgau: Herder, 2001), particularly the chapter "Märtyrer," 31–42.

[48] See a prayer by the so-called "Khomeini von Köln," a fundamental Turkish Islamist, who advocated the idea of a revolution modeled on the example of Iran: "Man muß an die Sache glauben, man muß bis zur Liebe bei ihr gehen. Ein junger Mann liebt ein Mädchen; er faßt eine tiefe Zuneigung zu ihr. Bei Tag und bei Nacht, im Wachen und im Traum ist alles mit dem Traumbild verbunden. Wer an die Bewegung glaubt, sie sich zu eigen macht, der wird ein Gefühl für den Glauben entwickeln, das dieser Liebe entspricht," quoted in Werner Schiffauer, *Die Gottesmänner. Türkische Islamisten in Deutschland* (Frankfurt am Main: Suhrkamp, 2000), 105.

[49] A typical example of this is Peter Handke's early play "Publikumsbeschimpfung" (1966), in Peter Handke, *Theaterstücke in einem Band* (Frankfurt am Main: Suhrkamp, 1992), 7–42, here: p. 17: "Wir machen keine Geschichten. Sie verfolgen kein Geschehen. Sie spielen nicht mit. Hier wird Ihnen mitgespielt. Das ist ein Wortspiel."

[50] Oliver Czeslik, "Gaddafi rockt," in *Aktuelle Stücke 1*, eds. Uwe B. Carstensen and Stefanie van Lieven (Frankfurt am Main: Fischer Taschenbuch Verlag, 2001), 81–113. Subsequent references to this work are cited in the text using the abbreviation *GR* and page number.

[51] This is still employed by the director Augusto Boal, who uses it as a means of changing an oppressive society for the better. In Boal's so-called *Theater of the Oppressed*, the non-actors in the "invisible theater" are not supposed to know that they are an active part of the performance around them. Yet they involuntarily participate and, through this, their opinions are put into question. See Augusto Boal, *Theater of the Oppressed* (1974) (New York: Urizen Books, 1979), translated from the Spanish by Charles A, and Marian-Odilia Leal McBride, p. 146.

8: Right-Wing Radicalism in Germany after Reunification

TWO YEARS INTO REUNIFICATION and its huge economic problems, the Germans, who were already disillusioned and disappointed, were confronted with another issue: the rapidly increasing number of violent attacks on asylum seekers and foreigners.[1] 1992 witnessed right-wing extremists riots on such an unprecedented scale that violence became a real problem, particularly in East Germany.[2] As analyses have shown, the attacks in East and West rose from roughly 300 per month in 1990 to 961 in October 1991, and in September 1992 more than 1100 were registered. In June 1993 the number peaked at more than 1,400 attacks.[3] These crimes included the desecration of Jewish graves, damage to property, bomb attacks, personal assaults, and manslaughter.[4] The four most important riots took place on 17 September 1991 in Hoyerswerda; 22 August 1992 in Rostock; 22 November 1992 in Mölln; and 25 May 1993 in Solingen. The last attack in Solingen forms the background to John von Düffels' play *Solingen* (1995) which indirectly blames an inadequate educational system for the rise of right-wing crimes. Von Düffel presents us with two teachers who prove unable to react to the springing-up of neo-Nazi ideology in their classes, until, as in Solingen, Hoyerswerda and Rostock, the homes of asylum seekers are attacked with the aim of scaring off further applicants for asylum.

It took several days to bring the riots under control, and the news reports were confusing, for they contradicted each another. On the one hand, a camera team was allegedly surrounded and challenged, yet on the other hand it is claimed that journalists offered money to those who were willing to act violently in front of the camera. In Mölln and Solingen, homes of foreigners who had lived in Germany for several years were set on fire during the night. This was the first time that people had been deliberately killed following a planned attack.

In his collage of scenes entitled *Ich bin das Volk* (I am the People, 1993), Franz Xaver Kroetz depicts all the facets of right-wing radicalism, ranging from the dull skinhead on the street to the judge who is prone to fascist thinking. According to Kroetz, fascism is, sadly, so common in Germany that the violent arson attacks do not come as a surprise. Gundi

Ellert's *Jagdzeit* (Hunt, 1994) tells the story of young neo-Nazis who terrorize the nearby village by arson, mugging, and looting. They capture a foreign girl, torture her, and bury her alive. Although their crimes come to light in the end, they are hushed up, for it turns out the fathers of the teenagers are influential local politicians.

The atrocities shocked Germany, and saw large-scale repercussions in the media.[5] Since then, it has been impossible to deny the existence of a minority of roughly 7,500 violent extremists.[6] However it has been pointed out that right-wing radicalism is by no means organized:[7] on the contrary, it is characterized by spontaneous gatherings and ad-hoc violence against foreigners. In contrast to right-wing political parties that are anxious to convey an outwardly peaceful image, independent right-wing youth defines itself through violence. In the search for identity, terms such as manhood, white nationalism, obedience and hard work (which is often a self-betrayal, because many are jobless) become important.[8] In the play *Heilige Kühe* (Sacred Cows, 1992), Oliver Czeslik focuses on the precarious relationship between right-wing radicalism and the media. A journalist who visits a couple of skinheads to produce a documentary film is taken hostage and tortured in front of his own camera, thus involuntarily taking the main part in the sensational film that he wanted to shoot.

In reaction to this trend, many measures against right-wing violence have been introduced, offering special help and advice to victims and potential target groups. Churches have held *Lichterketten* and other peaceful demonstrations in order to demonstrate solidarity with foreigners and to show public disgust at the murders in Mölln and Solingen. Strong opposition soon met right-wing violence, not least through the plays presented in this book. Sadly, however, it is only since the drastic changes of the *Asylrecht* in 1993[9] that such violence has ebbed away, as it has lost the reason for its existence.[10]

1995 saw the fiftieth anniversary of the capitulation of the Third Reich, which was remembered by vigils, inaugurations, speeches, and official celebrations focusing on the Holocaust. Following Kohl's attempt to "normalize" Germany by encouraging a new national identity, the Germans waged many a debate about whether young people were still to be held responsible for the Nazi past.[11] However, both intellectuals and writers agreed that the memory of Auschwitz and the concept of "normalcy" could not be reconciled.[12] Many writers engaged in the debate, arguing that this memory must be kept alive. In the same vein, Jorge Semprún pointed out that the "unnamable horrors" of the concentration camps were simply a pretext and that writing about the Holocaust was a must.[13]

Xenophobia:
Klaus Pohl's *Die schöne Fremde* (1991/93)

Pohl's play *Die schöne Fremde,* written in 1991 and revised in 1993, deals with the gruesome "normality" of xenophobia in everyday Germany shortly after the "Wende": A small provincial town turns out to be fertile ground for the upsurge of violence. In this conventional five-act play, Pohl confronts the audience with a set of negative stereotypes and clichés; his aim is to shake the Germans out of their complacence, forcing them to recognize what is really going on at the lower end of the social scale, because, according to Pohl, Germany is "ein leerer Kopf auf vollem Bauch."[14] The action is situated in Bebra, a small provincial town near the former German-German border. As the style of the play is conventional, the plot is of primary importance.

During a heavy snowstorm, Margrit, a young American woman, is forced to spend the night in Bebra, because her train has got stuck. In act 4, during a conversation with her husband, the audience learns that she is of German-Jewish origin, and that she has come to Germany in order to bring back the happy memories of her mother — an attempt that has failed miserably. Although she simply intends to spend the night there, she witnesses the brutal killing of a Pole, is sexually harrassed, and has to flee the next day. However, a month afterwards, she decides to return to Germany in order to take her revenge.

The play opens as she walks into the foyer of a shabby hotel, where the drunken Maul brothers are enjoying mistreating Christian Maul's wife. In a projection of their own desires, the brothers immediately classify her as a prostitute. While she tries to phone her fiancé abroad, a friend of the two brothers, the dog-owner Lutter, and the Maul brothers beat a young Polish man to death because he has blocked in their car. A foreigner who dares to violate the German parking rules is too much for their pettiness, and German thoroughness literally runs riot. They disappear quickly, leaving him to die in the arms of the perplexed and flabbergasted American. It is telling, however, that the only concern of the hotel owner is to keep the place tidy. Frau Mielke's worries echo the common complaints concerning the negative effects of the opening of the border on Germany. "If only the Wall had remained standing" was a frequently voiced comment at that time.

After the incident with the Polish man, the American woman retreats to her room, but, failing to lock her door, she is attacked by Lutter. Using his aggressive German shepherd to prevent her from escaping, he insults, humiliates and, finally, sexually abuses her. During this, it is clear that he is mentally disturbed. When the woman confronts him about the death of the Pole, Lutter reacts with a violent outburst of xenophobic stereotypes:

LUTTER	[. . .] Polen. Russen. Rumänen. Juden! Vietnamesen! Neger! Es werden täglich mehr. Die wollen unser Deutschland zerstören. Die wollen uns Deutschland wegnehmen. Wenn wir nicht aufpassen!
DIE FREMDE	Sie sind geistesgestört!
LUTTER	Aber so! Aber gründlich! Die Politiker lassen das ganze fremde Gesindel herein. Wenn das normal ist — dann bin ich jeden Tag ein Stück mehr geistesgestört. Bis ich irr bin und dann brennt es aber wirklich! Dann brennt es wirklich! Dann brennt das ganze undeutsche Gesindel![15]

In this passage, Lutter's twisted xenophobic thinking gets the better him. He is a common, frustrated, and impotent man, who seeks to compensate for his sexual needs in a strangely sadistic manner. The following day, he turns the tables on her, claiming that she is really a prostitute, and that he only came because of her "ad." When the woman seeks legal support the morning after, a web of lies waits for her: allegedly, the Pole was drunk, and died in a car crash.

In act 5, she returns to the shabby hotel, this time pretending to be friends with the drunken men who are still lusting after her. Cunningly, she persuades them to undress, and, wrapped in table-cloths and grunting like pigs, the four Germans happily lick the floor, on which she has just poured wine. While the men indulge in their masochistic crawl, Margrit remains in control of the situation. Promising them a night in which their desire will be fulfilled, she lures them into a trap: while Lutter is upstairs collecting her underwear, the Maul brothers kill Lutter's dog by gassing it in the stove. In a symbolic inversion of the Holocaust, the Germans are duped and humiliated. Docile and sheep-like, the men fall over each other to obey Margrit's orders. However, when Lutter learns about the killing of his dog, he stabs Christian to death and attacks Margrit, who just manages to escape.

In conclusion, it can be said that the play paints a clichéd image of the German frame of mind. In Pohl's eyes, half a century after Hitler, the Germans are still dull, macho, pernickety, violent, and filled with hatred of foreigners. In accordance with all negative stereotypes, the natives merely reiterate "Stammtischgeschwätz" (regular pub-goers chatter), thus displaying the same level of intelligence as their dogs; indeed, they are just as aggressive.

Media and Skinheads:
Oliver Czeslik's *Heilige Kühe* (1992)

Czeslik is one of few playwrights to tackle the problem of skinheads and neo-Nazis in Germany. The eighteen scenes of the realistic play, *Heilige Kühe,* tell of the misfortune of Karl Klementi, a Jew who is lured into a trap by the two neo-Nazis Gero von Wilfenstein and his girlfriend Ulrike.[16] While he is held hostage, Karl is tortured and brainwashed until, finally, he begins to love the perpetrator, Gero. Because it deliberately ignores political correctness, the cruel treatment of Klementi shakes the audience out of its complacency.[17]

The play was first published in April 1992, at a time when extreme right-wing violence had reached a worrying peak in anticipation of the anniversary of Hitler's birthday.[18] *Heilige Kühe* premiered at the *Schaubühne Berlin* in April 1992, and came out as a film (director, Uwe Janson) a year later. Under the pretext of providing him with insider information about the right-wing scene, Gero invites Karl, a well-known journalist and representative of the 1968 generation, to an abandoned slaughterhouse in a suburb of Berlin. Their meeting begins fairly harmlessly with a few takes of the video-camera, but Ulrike then secretly removes vital parts of Karl's car engine, thus forcing him to stay overnight. While he is asleep, Gero makes him a prisoner by securing a chain around his foot. Karl is to be put on trial and sentenced to death. In the days leading up to this, Karl is systematically tortured and humiliated, until his will becomes so broken that he even begins to love his torturer.

In *Heilige Kühe,* film as a medium plays an important role, as it not only reflects the artificial character of the meeting, but also implicitly criticizes the search for evidence, for filmed proof of what is believed to be true. Czeslik's play explores the relationship between the medium of film and the "actors" on the one hand, and the interdependence between film and everyday violence on the other. In the first scene, the verity of Karl's feature film is questioned, for it transpires that he offered five thousand marks for the interview.[19] The relationship between film and violence in the play underlines Czeslik's belief that journalism has a notable feedback effect and inspires further violence. Recently, researchers have openly blamed journalists for adding fuel to the fire, and according to recent studies, newspaper and television coverage of such crimes often encourages imitation.[20]

Like a child, Gero enjoys role-playing and games, and wears costumes and uniforms to make the games feel more real. In an unbalanced manner, he slips from one role to the next, imitating Nazis such as the notorious doctor Mengele, Hitler and other SS-officers. The problem, however, is that Gero does not simply imagine these roles, but acts them out. In scene 6, he asks Karl to direct the video camera at his right foot and takes sadistic pleasure in shooting the foot while Karl is forced to provide the evidence by filming the shooting. Next, he assumes the role of the doctor, while Ulrike comments on his actions. Again, she makes sure that the camera is switched on before Gero's "visit" begins. Dressed in a white coat, Gero struts around like a film-star in a hospital drama, pretending to examine rows of patients in beds. Although the only real "patient" is Karl, who is cringing on the floor, Gero rejoices in acting for the camera. Nonetheless, he does not simply pretend, but cruelly removes the bullet from Karl's foot. After the sadistic surgery, the skinheads leave Karl to suffer. Although they pretend to care for his wounds, they never really do so; on the contrary, they rejoice in his deterioration.

In the early hours of the morning, Ulrike appears to make a surprising confession, but, first of all, she insists that the camera be switched on again. This being done, she confesses that she is actually a student of the social sciences, working as an undercover agent in order to reveal the truth about the neo-Nazi Gero. Suffering from a high temperature, Karl can hardly grasp what she is saying, and before he knows it, she is gone, having taken the videotape with her. During the following scenes, she leads him to believe that he will be rescued in time by other journalists. During breakfast, she informs Karl that she has information about a right-wing conspiracy with a mafia-like structure that operates on a centralized basis.[21] In order to provide evidence of her findings, she needs video material about Karl's "trial." Although Karl begs to be released, her own ambition as a journalist comes first. Her missionary zeal is stronger than any empathy she may have for Karl. However, her real identity remains dubious, not only because the journalists never arrive, but also because she brutally pokes Karl's eyes out, thus reducing him to a helpless, humiliated creature. It is highly likely that her confession is a fake, made to win over Karl's confidence. As innumerable reports by Amnesty International and similar organizations have shown, it is a common fact that the perpetrator needs the emotional support, if not love, of the victim, if he wants to successfully break the victim's will.

Karl is also far from the embodiment of a positive figure, as he reveals himself in front of the camera to be a dogmatic and infatuated left-wing intellectual.[22] He questions his former life as a talk-show star who used to make large amounts of money by reiterating left-wing statements. Meanwhile, however, his belief in the left's ideology is shaken. Moreover, he admits that he has never really been in touch with reality, as he has always kept people and events at a distance through the camera lens. Through the satanic initiation rite that Gero and Ulrike inflict on him, he discovers his other self, or rather as the torture gradually changes his frame of mind, he abandons his former identity.

In a so-called rehearsal of the trial, in which Gero acts as the judge, he plays an associative language game with Karl. For each mistake that Karl makes, he receives a broken finger, and finally a broken left arm.

> ULLI *spricht ins Dunkel*   Der Ringfinger der rechten Hand.
> Knicka di knack. Und der Ehering hängt an einem
> schlaffen Halt.
>
> *Es wird wieder hell. GERO begibt sich an seinen Platz, die Kamera wird von ULLI eingeschaltet.*
>
> GERO   So schwer ist es doch nicht. Also: B!
>
> KARL   Brecht . . . Blockpolitik . . . Basisdemokratie . . .
>
> GERO   K!
>
> KARL   China . . . Christentum . . .
>
> ULLI *leise*   K, nicht C!
>
> KARL   Der Mittelfinger der rechten Hand?
>
> GERO   Nein, der kleine.[23]

As Karl can hardly think any more, he receives a few more broken bones, before, in total panic, he obediently starts to answer all the questions like an automaton. His body resembles a puppet, his broken limbs dangling uncontrollably over the brim of the box into which he had previously been forced. Mutilated and crippled, he is treated like an animal.

In scene 18, Gero enters with a chain around his foot and lies down in front of the monitor, while Karl is still sitting in the box, blinded. The role of the victim is the only one which Gero simply pretends to play, instead of taking it to the extreme. Here, he acts as a spectator who obtains a masochistic thrill by reliving Karl's suffering. As Karl is now blind, he is forced to see the world, or rather the documentary, through the eyes of the skinhead. However, Gero does not talk about Karl's situation, but instead describes a concentration camp, and his ranting betrays his greatest wish: to take part in the National Socialist genocide. While torturing Karl, he imagines himself to be carrying out ethnic crimes on a larger scale.

In the last scene, Gero destroys the box and begins to stroke Karl's naked and crippled body, evidently enjoying the perverted pleasure of his game. Meanwhile, the former journalist has lost any self-esteem, and, full of gratitude, tells Gero that he has become everything for him. In this highly dubious and frequently criticized scene, the two enemies seem to become friends. Yet it should be remembered that this perverted relationship has robbed Karl of his freedom as well as his mental and physical health. Gero's strange sexual tastes also become evident earlier in he play, when he comments on Ulrike's sexy legs while she is washing the floor around Karl's box. It is clear that one of the most typically German of "virtues," namely cleanliness, is the reason for Gero's arousal.

Against the backdrop of satanist crime and torture, *Heilige Kühe* depicts the theatricality of the taboo skinhead scene, in which the perpetrators' unbalanced mind is revealed while they play a perverted sadistic game with the Jew Karl Klementi. Czeslik displays the psychological mechanisms driving Gero's behavior, namely the urge of "the nobody" to heighten his self-esteem through a game of military grandeur, in which reality is blotted out. During the course of the play, Gero's strong esoteric line of thinking becomes increasingly evident, until, at the end, he describes his own face as the complexion of a "real Satan."[24] He obviously perceives himself to be an Antichristfigure who, like Hitler, intends to inflict pain on others, if only for the fulfillment of misguided sexual pleasure.

German Chauvinism:
Franz Xaver Kroetz's *Ich bin das Volk* (1993)

Kroetz wrote his play as an immediate reaction to the rise in right-wing radicalism in 1992/93. After a none-too-successful premiere on 25 September 1994 in Wuppertal,[25] it moved to the *Berliner Ensemble* on 10 December 1994, and was a success.[26] However, controversy surrounded the Berlin production over the way it was advertised, as the theater chose to use outrageous racist slogans to catch peoples' attention. Finally, the Berlin transport authorities banned the advertising campaign, for its offensive content could all too easily be misread. However, this provocative advertising generated a large amount of interest in the play. Moreover, even before the play premiered, Kroetz fell out with his publishing house, the *Suhrkamp Verlag*, which refused to print the play, maintaining that it lacked quality. The following day, Kroetz cancelled his contract and switched to *Rotbuch Verlag;* in the meantime, the *Berliner Ensemble* made *Ich bin das Volk* available as a special publication.[27] The director Peter Zadek supported Kroetz's view, for he also believed that a politically committed theater should not be dismissed because of a "low" style. According to Zadek, this would eventually stifle any creative initiative among contemporary playwrights to engage in political debate.[28]

As Kroetz points out in his introductory remarks to the play, the main topics of *Ich bin das Volk* are xenophobia, neo-Nazis, misery and cowardice. Playing on the famous slogan "Wir sind das Volk," which was coined at the Montagsdemonstration in Leipzig in October 1989, and was later to become "Wir sind *ein* Volk," thus calling for reunification, Kroetz links reunification to growth in German nationalism. The play shows the various ways in which united Germany serves as an "Ichmacher," a maker of an aggressive national identity. Kroetz explained this in more detail during an interview, but some of his remarks caused a negative reaction:

> Ich habe sehr viel Verständnis für soziale Verwerfungen und ich habe auch gerade deshalb sehr viel Verständnis dafür, daß Menschen in unserer Gesellschaft immer teilfaschistisch waren und bleiben werden.[29]

However, Kroetz qualified these controversial remarks, which could easily be misread, by repeatedly venting his anger about the conservative political climate:

> Aber das gesamte Klima, die Politiker, die Gerichte, die Berichterstattung in der Presse, dieser hilflos feige Staat — all das hat mich so wütend gemacht, daß ich diese Szenen hingefetzt habe.[30]

Although it is perhaps a little short-sighted simply to blame the state for the neo-Nazi violence on the streets, Kroetz's anger is genuine. Indeed, some of his statements, outrageous as they might seem, are rather sarcastic. Although Kroetz might be familiar with the fascism he sees around him all the time, he is nonetheless vehemently opposed to it.

The play consists of twenty-four scenes that can be rearranged for staging purposes.[31] It is thus clearly not a traditionally structured five-act play, but a review of everyday situations that could occur at any moment and in any place in Germany. The scenes are, however, all connected by the theme of right-wing radicalism. The play is not entirely realistic, for it contains supernatural elements, for example in the scene "Ich wünsche mir eine Arbeit/ eine Familie/ und ein Glück."[32] Here, a skinhead harasses and assaults a veiled woman while she remains silent. Finally, he violently pulls her veil off and is confronted with a grinning skull. Another scene that draws on surreal elements is "Dachau Fantasie," in which asylum seekers gather in a "Versöhnungskirche" in order to be granted refuge. However, they are expelled by the police, an action that was, of course, only possible with the assistance of the prelate, who proves to be more bureaucratic than truly religious. When the church is empty, they discover a man who has taken refuge on a cross, an image that is in itself highly symbolic. The prelate, however, ignores the first commandment, which tells us to love our fellow-men, thus ensuring the transportation of the last asylum seeker. When the prelate is left alone in the church, Christ appears on the cross and spits in his face. Embarrassed, he looks around to see whether anybody has witnessed the scene, then quickly kisses the spit on his hand, an act that evidently alludes to the German word "Speichellecker" (sucker). Hypocritical as he is, the man of God remains obedient and docile.

Some of the dialogue in the play resembles black-humored cabaret rather than theater; this results from both the theme of the play and the use of dialect. As far as dialect is concerned, Kroetz refuses to follow in the footsteps of Horvath, a figurehead of the new *Volkstheater,* a fact he made clear as early as 1971.[33] Horvath bans dialect from the stage in order to avoid irony and satire,[34] an effect that Kroetz is successful in achieving, albeit to make the audience feel uneasy about their laughter. For Kroetz, form comes second to content. In contrast to Horvath, Kroetz reintroduces dialect on the stage in order to reveal the psychological condition of his characters without having to expand on them theoretically. Every native speaker in the audience will subconsciously understand what Kroetz is aiming to achieve, namely the dismantling of a "we"-mentality that is based on dullness, injustice and racism. Dialect is thus used extensively throughout the play, serving to depict the characters' sociological background in a more realistic way. Some of the educated characters, such as barristers or politicians, speak a peculiar mix of Bavarian and High German. In the scene "Justiz," for example, we witness a meeting between several lawyers and a judge: the case in question is that of a right-wing youth who is accused of killing a foreigner. The judge pleads for a milder verdict according to the "Jugendstrafrecht," as he has been blackmailed by other extremists who have threatened him with further violence. The state officials, however, demand severe punishment in order to convey the image of a democratic Germany to the world:

> MINISTERIALDIREKTOR   Die Welt will von uns Taten und keine Psychologie. Mir ham auswärtige Investitionseinbrüche in Millardengröße, der Ami zieht sich vollkommen verschreckt aus Ostdeutschland zruck, und wenns aso weitergeht, is Made in Germany in da Welt drausn bald so verlockend — *(kollegial)* wia das Arschloch von am AIDS-kranken Stricher — wie der Herr Minister im kleinen Kreis zu scherzen pflegt.

KAMMERPRÄSIDENT   Deutschland braucht ein deutliches Zeichen.
Mir miassn klar macha, daß die von Ihnen geschilderten
Verhältnisse abnorm san, und ned mit wohlfeilem
Psychologismus so tun, als gäbs des an jedm deutschn
Straßeneck. (*V*, 489)

In this passage the alternation of dialect and High German marks the
change between official government policy and private opinion. Official
statements are inserted into the dialogue in correct German, but they swim
on the surface of muddy waters. It is a highly cynical passage, for the strict
penalty is only insisted upon for fear of losing foreign investors, such as the
United States of America, referred to here in a colloquial way as "der
Ami." The mere suggestion of any association between Germany and
right-wing radicalism must be prevented, whatever the means. It is paradoxical that the punishment is not meant as a warning to other criminals,
but rather as a safeguard for public relations. As one of the officials emphasizes, the harsh punishment will be a signal to other nations that the German state itself has nothing to do with the rise of right-wing extremism.
Through the juxtaposition of these two levels of language, Kroetz thus
reveals the biased nature of the legal system, and unmasks the hypocrisy of
official policy that obscures the origins of the problem in hand.

It is not only lawyers and judges, but also politicians, who are more
or less directly accused of promoting right-wing ideals. In a scene called
"Gedenktag," a politician works on a speech that he intends to give on
the occasion of a non-specified memorial day. Although he will address
problems such as unemployment, foreign workers and xenophobia, he
believes that they would not exist if the foreigners stayed at home. Towards the end of his speech, the outlook darkens further, for he mentions necessary changes to sections of the basic law (*Grundgesetz*), such
as the paragraph that secures the equality of men ("Alle Menschen sind
vor dem Gesetz gleich"). According to him, however, the lazy, the sick,
criminals, and anyone who is different should fall under a different cate-
gory. What is also highly dubious is that he calls into question the foun-
dation paragraph of the basic law that reads: "Die Würde des Menschen
ist unantastbar." In his opinion, it is high time to alter this and grant
dignity only to those who "deserve" it. Due to their obvious Nazi overtones, these opinions naturally make the audience shudder.

Another politician who is openly attacked in the play is the chancellor
and head of state at the time, Helmut Kohl. In "Thema verfehlt," a student reads out an essay on Kohl's visit to the controversial writer Ernst
Jünger that took place on 22 July 1993, the forty-ninth anniversary of the

failed attack on Hitler's life. Kohl's attitude towards the past is already notorious due to his controversial remark concerning the "Gnade der späten Geburt," which inferred that the young generation could no longer be held responsible for the Nazi past, and should start looking to the future. Here, Kohl becomes the "Geisterfahrer der deutschen Geschichte," because of his naive attitude towards the Nazi past.[35] As the student analyzes in some detail, Jünger's attitude towards the Nazi regime and its war crimes was rather favorable, a fact that reveals the more dubious nature of this state visit — even if did take place on the occasion of Jünger's 104th birthday.[36]

In Kroetz's kaleidoscope, even writers are not exempt from criticism. In the scene "Wenn der Hahn kräht," he depicts an intellectual who phones a friend in order to seek some legal advice on the content of a poem. Although the writer sees himself as a critical spirit, it soon becomes obvious that he is extremely anxious not to violate the law, even if this means not telling the truth. Thus he effectively practices censorship on himself, racking his brain as to whether he can call the Bavarian Minsterpräsident Stoiber a Nazi without being taken to court. Although the writer comes across as a fairly conformist and timid character, Kroetz indirectly achieves his aim of accusing the politician Stoiber of being a Nazi and a racist, simply by letting the poet discuss the various versions of the poem in every detail. As if talking to himself, the writer concludes that although he might not be allowed to write the poem — in fact he has only said the words onstage — he regards Stoiber as a "pure Bavarian Nazi of 1993."

The majority of the shorter scenes focus on troublesome youths and their right-wing tendencies. Focusing on the unemployed and ill-educated sector of the young generation, Kroetz is concerned with unmasking the mechanisms of prejudice and xenophobia,[37] and in various scenes, the absurdity of right-wing radicalism is depicted.[38] In the scene "Aufklärung," three young male prostitutes chat about Nazis and strangers and agree on the fact that having an enemy does not imply that one is a Nazi. All in all, the dialogue is characterized by dull prejudices towards foreigners that lack any logic whatsoever:

EINS *(laut, blöd)* Heil Hitler.

DREI Du lernst es nia, Heil Hitler is verbotn, Sieg Heil kennas uns ned nehma. (*V,* 494)

The three youngsters employ the racist language of National Socialism, including the so-called "Hitlergruß," as if it were absolutely normal. Number one, however, is told that this is not allowed. The fact that "Heil Hitler" is forbidden, whereas "Sieg Heil" is obviously not, makes an important difference to Number three and also demonstrates Kroetz's opinion that laws and rules alone cannot change people's minds. As Kroetz's play mirrors the language and problems of both the average German and the educated Bavarian, he depicts a convincing portrait of right-wing extremism in contemporary Germany.

Neglected Youth: Gundi Ellert's *Jagdzeit* (1994)

Gundi Ellert's play *Jagdzeit* is about young and old neo-Nazis in Germany.[39] It reveals the mechanisms behind hatred, violence, and brutality, and also shows how youngsters learn inhumane behavior in their childhood. The drama touches on a variety of key issues that play a crucial role in the rise of neo-Nazism today, such as unemployment, lack of parental care, and broken homes. It also points to the distressing fact that so-called minor offenses such as stealing and mugging are played down, and that the majority of offenders do not face any charges at all.

At the center of the play is a gang of teenage robbers, who are trying to save money in order to start a large-scale anti-democratic campaign. In the end, they remain victorious, as the leader of the gang, Robert, escapes prosecution and manages to found a right-wing party. What is more, none of the other members are charged for their criminal offenses, although they are found out by their fathers. Despite the fact that they have burgled several houses, including those belonging to their fathers, and seriously injured two people, fathers and sons agree not to make their crimes known to the public. As their fathers hold strong right-wing opinions themselves, and are afraid of endangering their careers as local politicians, the crimes are glossed over. Both generations are xenophobic to the core, and they quickly decide to blame foreigners for the burglaries and muggings. It is indeed "Jagdzeit," and it is definitely the weak, the mentally ill, the helpless, or, more generally, the "others," symbolized by the quiet, foreign girl, Sophie, who are pursued and tracked down.

The play was first staged on 16 September 1994 at the *Residenztheater* in Munich,[40] and as one of very few efforts to get to grips with the origins of right-wing radicalism in Germany, it aroused considerable interest.[41] It depicts a society that is permeated by violence, in which, perversely, the "ideal" virtue is, as Robert points out, showing contempt for empathy and affection. Above all, it is important to kill the "evil weak spot" inside oneself, the "evil animal" that insists on loving and caring.

Like his real-life model, Hitler, Robert talks and behaves as if he were a messiah, whose task it is to open other people's eyes to the greatness of the future.[42] His language is littered with religious images that he contorts to fit a Darwinian worldview.[43] He therefore tells the group that they are the chosen ones, like Jesus's followers, who should brace themselves against hardship and humiliation. Instead of preaching a social attitude, Robert tells them that they are knights in a holy war against the evil in the world:

> [. . .]
> Ich zeige euch den Weg
> Folgt mir getrost
> Ich führe euch
> Folgt mir
> Richtet eure gekrümmten Rücken auf
> Geht stolz und aufrecht
> Wir sind die Flamme die das Feuer entfacht
> (*J*, 36)

Like Hitler, he borrows phrases from the Bible and combines the apocalyptic threat with the promise of a better future. Finally, Robert secretly takes all the looted money and quietly disappears, abandoning the others. The small-town savior thus shows his true colors.

According to Ellert, this degenerate and inhumane group of youngsters is typical of the lower classes in German society; she offers a rather pessimistic view, as the few kindhearted characters do not survive. Vinzenz, the man who cannot silence his guilty conscience, and informs the fathers of their sons' crimes, slashes his wrists in fear of being "slaughtered" by Jens, who is the butcher of the town. In the end, the likable although slightly demented girl Kathi and the foreigner Sophie are buried alive in the bunker, as the others close the doors on them. Xenophobia, or simply violence, smolders in a dull little town, a town that could be anywhere, with a typical set of characters that could be anybody.

The Failure of Education:
John von Düffel's *Solingen* (1995)

Although the subject of Düffel's fourth play *Solingen* is the rise of right-wing radicalism in Germany, it does not feature any violence.[44] The main characters are a teacher and his girlfriend, a trainee teacher, who both work at the same school in Solingen. There are no other characters, only a "schweigende Mehrheit," represented by various silent people, including a student and a policeman. It is only through the couple's conversations about classes and teaching that the audience learns that right-wing radicalism is on the increase in certain classes. However, the teachers so are intellectual that they have lost touch with the real problems of their classes.

In Düffel's earlier play *OI* (1995), right-wing radicalism is portrayed differently, as neo-Nazis communicate through a sound language that resembles the squealing and grunting of pigs.[45] In *Solingen*, however, the playwright presents us with two people who are always anxious to appear politically correct. This is particularly true of the older man, who is burnt out by the demands of administration, a fact that becomes evident in a scene where he marks essays, wondering whether he should reprimand a student for sporting nationalist ideas by quoting the notorious "Horst-Wessel-Lied." Absurdly, the teacher is so caught up in his academic thinking that he wonders whether the pupil has quoted the National Socialist song correctly, instead of being outraged that it has been used at all. As he is no longer fit or intellectually sharp enough to survive the day-to-day harassment of his students, he decides not to make a fuss. His classes mainly serve the purpose of keeping the children off the streets, and his stranglehold stifles the possibility of frank discussion. His disgusted girlfriend, however, accuses him of tolerating neo-Nazi ideas in students' essays. Yet, it is telling that she does not promote a fruitful exchange of opinions either, for she believes that skinheads should be put behind bars. In her blind idealism, she rejects the opinions of everyone who refuses to adopt her way of thinking. Instead of placing the model of adult control and hierarchy under scrutiny, she supports the idea that successful education is based on an organized and traditional school life.

The teacher's reaction to his girlfriend's outrage remains rather evasive, and he resorts to pseudo-pedagogical principles. As he refuses to become involved in problems concerning his classes, he chooses to play them down and remain distanced from them. In the same vein, the couple exchange their ideas through literary quotations, thus maintaining a certain distance from one another. Similarly, the girl also underpins her enthusiastic attitude by frequently resorting to Friedrich Schiller's ideas regarding freedom of speech and democracy. In his turn, the teacher hides behind Heinrich von Kleist's *Kohlhaas* (1810), a character who sought revenge for any injustice inflicted on him. Nonetheless, the teacher's aggression is merely hot air, and he acts like the downtrodden horse in George Orwell's (1903–1950) *Animal Farm* (1945), who has given up on revolution long before it is even in sight. Indeed, his blinkers prevent him from realizing that he is promoting National Socialist propaganda:

LEHRER	Vorgestern habe ich sie gefragt, wer die deutschen Autobahnen gebaut hat
REFERENDARIN	Hitler
LEHRER	Genau das ist das herrschende Vorurteil.[46]

The teacher is so entangled in his pernickety correctness that he insists on the fact that it was not Hitler alone, but all his people, who built the motorways. He does not realize, however, that the watering-down of history can distort basic historical truth. What is more, he does not even care if enraged grandparents who witnessed the Third Reich come to tell him the truth.

As the example of the teacher shows, schools still tolerate latent fascism. It is therefore not surprising that neo-Nazi violence increases during the play, at the end of which the couple learns of a fatal arson attack that killed four members of a Turkish family in Solingen on 29 May 1993. However, the news practically becomes part of their bed-time routine, for, in the usual fashion, he comes to tell her about the latest news on television. Thus he mentions the arson attack only casually, and silences her questions with his stale, pseudo-erotic mixture of quotations taken from Goethe's poems "Wilkommen und Abscheid" (1771), "Der Fischer" (1778), and from Heine's *Buch der Lieder* (1827):

REFERENDARIN: Daß so etwas heute passieren muß

LEHRER   Pst; denk ich an Deutschland in der Nacht, bin ich
             um den Schlaf gebracht.

REFERENDARIN (*reagiert nicht*)
             [. . .]

LEHRER   Die Nacht schuf tausend Ungeheuer, doch frisch
             und fröhlich war mein Mut, in meinen Adern
             welches Feuer, in meinem Herzen welche Glut

REFERENDARIN Aua

LEHRER   Halb zog sie ihn, halb sank er hin
                    (*S*, 85–86)

In this passage, the original meaning of the citations are distorted, such as Heinrich Heine's famous lines in his last poem "Nachtgedanken" in *Buch der Lieder* (1827): "Denk ich an Deutschland in der Nacht,/ dann bin ich um den Schlaf gebracht./ Ich kann nicht mehr die Augen schließen,/ und meine heißen Tränen fließen."[47] Heine's intention was, of course, not to stop worrying about Germany in order to enjoy a peaceful sleep, but to remain aware of the nationalist developments of the nineteenth century. Moreover, the teacher in *Solingen* does not make a connection between the "Ungeheuer" of the night and the right-wing radicals. Von Düffel thus compares the couple to the sleepy and brain-dead "Michel," who was symbolic of the Germans' refusal to engage in political action in Heine's lifetime. Instead of being politically aware, they sleep with one another. The play thus shows that in the long run, political indifference will lay waste to the human landscape.[48]

In the face of the rapid increase in violent neo-Nazi crime in the early 1990s, playwrights vigorously opposed right-wing tendencies, and demonstrated how neofascist thinking works. In *Die schöne Fremde* (1991/93), Klaus Pohl depicts a young American Jew who visits Germany, the home country of her mother, and becomes the target of hatred and xenophobia. Although the local men are not even aware that she is Jewish, they resent her because she is foreign, beautiful, and out of their reach.

In his play *Heilige Kühe* (1992), Oliver Czeslik looks at the relationship between neo-Nazism and its media coverage, presenting us with an encounter between a journalist and two neo-Nazis. The journalist, who is trying to gather sensational film material for his documentaries, is taken captive and tortured in front of his own camera. *Heilige Kühe* thus asks whether or not intensive representation in the media fuels violent behavior. This has been the subject of much discussion, for journalists are believed to have bribe neo-Nazis to show the Hitler salute, just to obtain a story that sells.

Torture also features in Gundi Ellert's *Jagdzeit* (1994), where a couple of young neo-Nazis lure a foreign girl into a deer-trap, and take her to their hideaway. While she is raped, beaten, and starved, other members of the group commit crimes and arson attacks in the village nearby in order to raise money to found a new right-wing party. Although the youngsters are finally discovered, no legal measures are taken, for their fathers are local politicians who are eager not to spoil their careers.

In *Ich bin das Volk* (1993), a collage of short scenes, Franz Xaver Kroetz highlights the fact that fascism and xenophobia pervade society and politics, and can be detected everywhere. Judges and ministers, journalists and readers, estate-agents and artists, politicians and soldiers, teenagers and old widows are all prone to fascist thinking. Written in a mixture of Bavarian dialect and High German, the collage paints a gloomy picture of contemporary Germany. *Ich bin das Volk* shows that neo-Nazism does not originate on the street, but in the minds of an approving majority.

The fatal legacy of a society that looks away and retreats into the private sphere is also portrayed in John von Düffel's *Solingen* (1995). The play focuses on the relationship between a teacher and his girlfriend, still a trainee teacher. Neither teacher knows how to react to the increasing neo-Nazism among students in their classes The man is exhausted and the girl is more interested in the theoretical aspects of Friedrich Schiller's writing; and yet she proves unable to teach Schiller's ideal, freedom of thought, to her students. Von Düffel's play blames the rise in neo-Nazi crime on both the shortcomings of the education system and the indifference of teachers.

Notes

[1] This is also addressed in Werner Fritsch's play *Fleischwolf* (1992), set in a bar frequented by German soldiers, who are depicted as a bunch of half-demented, aggressive and xenophobic brutes; Werner Fritsch, *Fleischwolf* (Frankfurt am Main: Suhrkamp, 1992).

[2] This is mainly connected with the fact that denazification played a much less important role in the GDR and that guest workers in the East were kept segregated from the native population; see Marianne Krüger-Potratz, *Anderssein gab es nicht: Ausländer und Minderheiten in der DDR* (Münster, New York: Waxmann, 1991), 6–13; Marcus Neureither, *Rechtsextremismus im vereinten Deutschland. Eine Untersuchung sozialwissenschaftlicher Deutungsmuster und Erklärungsansätze* (Marburg: Tectum, 1996), 36–38.

[3] See the table: "Entwicklung der ausländerfeindlichen Straftaten Januar 1991–November 1993," quoted in Marcus Neureither, *Rechtsextremismus im vereinten Deutschland,* appendix, page XXI, table 29.

[4] Ruud Koopmans and Dieter Rucht, "Rechtsradikalismus als soziale Bewegung?" *PVjS,* Sonderheft 27 (1996), 265–87, here: 276–77.

[5] Thomas Ohlemacher, "'Wechselwirkungen nicht ausgeschlossen': Medien, Bevölkerungsmeinung und fremdenfeindliche Straftaten 1991–1997," in *Rechtsextremismus und Fremdenfeindlichkeit,* eds. Frieder Dünkel and Bernd Geng (Godesberg: Forum, 1999), 53–68, here: 56–59. Ohlemacher argues that the discussion in the media at some point caused a further increase of violence.

[6] Bundesministerium des Innern, ed., *Verfassungsschutzbericht 1999* (Berlin/Bonn: Bundesministerium des Innern, 2000), 18.

[7] Armin Pfahl-Traughber, *Rechtsextremismus in der Bundesrepublik* (Munich: C.H. Beck, 2000), 75–79.

[8] Wilhelm Heitmeyer, *Rechtsextremistische Orientierung bei Jugendlichen* (Weinheim and Munich: Juventa, 1995), here: 91–103.

[9] Every asylum seeker who has traveled through a secure country before arriving in Germany is automatically sent back (*Drittstaatenregelung*), so the only means of reaching Germany is to arrive by aircraft. Moreover, the entire procedure of decision-making has been considerably speeded up.

[10] Ohlemacher, "'Wechselwirkungen nicht ausgeschlossen,'" 62.

[11] See, for example, the interview with Hermann Langbein, president of the international Auschwitz committee: "Die späte Geburt ist eine Bürde . . . ," *Frankfurter Rundschau,* 25 January 1995.

[12] See, for example, Ulrich Beck, "Auschwitz als Identität. Gedanken zu einem deutschen Alptraum," *SZ,* 27 May 1995. Beck writes: "Auschwitz war nicht, Auschwitz ist. Auschwitz ist überall heute in Deutschland gegenwärtig. [. . .] Die Gnade der späten Geburt ist eine Legende. Die Wunde Auschwitz ist offen." See also Christian Meier, "Der letzte Tag. Auschwitz duldet keine Normalisierung," *FAZ,* 27 May 1995.

[13] Jorge Semprún, "Der Rauch aus den Öfen hat die Vögel vertrieben," *FAZ,* 26 January 1995.

[14] See Klaus Pohl, *Das Deutschlandgefühl* (Reinbek: Rowohlt, 1999). During two journeys through Germany, in 1994 and 1998, Pohl talked to people on the street, waiters, workers, and artists, and gives a lively impression of Germany and the Germans today. In his notes on his travels, he portrays the positive as well as the negative aspects of the new Germany.

[15] Klaus Pohl, "Die schöne Fremde," in Klaus Pohl, *Karate-Billi kehrt zurück. Die schöne Fremde. Zwei Stücke* (Frankfurt am Main: Verlag der Autoren, 1993), 89–158, here: 112. Subsequent references to this work are cited in the text using the abbreviation *SF* and page number.

[16] Axel Schalk, "Vom Voyeur zum Akteur," in *Stück-Werk 3*, eds. Christel Weiler and Harald Müller (Berlin: Zentrum Bundesrepublik Deutschland des Internationalen Theaterinstituts, 2001), 35–37, here: 35.

[17] Sabine Reinhard, "12 Anmerkungen," in *Stück-Werk 1* (Berlin: Internationales Theaterinstitut, 1997), 22–25, here: 23.

[18] It has frequently been pointed out that the year 1992 saw a rise in neo-Nazi crime. See, for example, Richard Stöss, *Rechtsextremismus im vereinten Deutschland* (Berlin: Friedrich-Ebert-Stiftung, 2000), 160; Ruud Koopmanns and Dieter Rucht, "Rechtsradikalismus als soziale Bewegung?" *PVjS* 27 (1996), 265–87, here: 279.

[19] The incident where journalists literally bribed neo-Nazis to show the Hitler salute in front of the camera is increasingly openly discussed. See, for example, Thomas Ohlemacher, "'Wechselwirkungen nicht ausgeschlossen': Medien, Bevölkerungsmeinung und fremdenfeindliche Straftaten 1991–1997," in *Rechtsextremismus und Fremdenfeindlichkeit. Bestandsaufnahme und Interventionsstrategien*, eds. Frieder Dünkel and Bernd Geng (Godesberg: Forum, 1999), 53–69, here: 54.

[20] See Ohlemacher, "'Wechselwirkungen nicht ausgeschlossen,'" 56; Hans-Peter Brosius and Frank Esser, "Massenmedien und fremdenfeindliche Gewalt," *Politische Vierteljahreschrift* 27 (1996), 204–20. Based on empirical data, the study by Brosius and Esser argues that the influence of the media on right-wing extremism can be explained by different theories, for example, 1. simulation, 2. social learning, 3. the suggestive and contagious effect of violence, 4. the model of priming which means that news stays in a person's mind for a certain period of time.

[21] Although this assumption is denied by the *Verfassungsschutz* and other researchers, rumors about an organized neo-Nazi scene persist. See Bundesministerium des Innern, ed., *Verfassungsschutzbericht 1999* (Berlin and Bonn: Bundesministerium des Innern, 2000), 25–27; Armin Pfahl-Traughber, *Rechtsextremismus in der Bundesrepublik* (Munich: C.H. Beck, 1999), 75–78.

[22] Michael Merschmeier, "Jenseits von gut und böse. Oliver Czeslik und sein Skinhead-Stück *Heilige Kühe*," *Th* 4 (1992): 42–43, here: 42.

[23] Oliver Czeslik, "Heilige Kühe," *Th* 4 (1992): 44–49, here: 48.

[24] Despite the fact that any official link between satanism and neo-Nazis is constantly played down, the odd exception paints a different picture. See, for example, the article by Kate Connolly, "German satanic couple held after ritual murder," *G*, 13 July 2001 and John Hooper, "Blood-drinking devil worshippers face life for ritual Satanic killing," *G*, 1 February 2002. On the Satanist and neo-Nazi Hendrik Möbius, see "Töten für Wotan," *Sp*, 18 September 2000.

[25] Franz Wille, "Rechts vor links?" *Th* 11 (1994): 11–13. Wille complained that the production was hardly more than boring anti-fascist propaganda that lacked any subtlety.

[26] Franz Wille, "Jeder ist sich selbst sein Volk," *Th* 2 (1995): 13–14.

[27] See the letters printed in Franz Xaver Kroetz, *Ich bin das Volk. Volkstümliche Szenen aus dem neuen Deutschland* (1993), ed. Berliner Ensemble, Drucksache 13/14 (Berlin: Alexander Verlag, 1995), 473–561, here: 563–64. Subsequent references to this work are cited in the text using the abbreviation *V* and page number.

[28] Peter Zadek, "In der Kunstfalle," *Th* 2 (1995): 12.

[29] Franz Wille, "Mit dem alltäglichen Faschismus selbstverständlich umgehen. Ein *Theater heute*-Gespräch mit Franz Xaver Kroetz," *Th* 10 (1994): 4–8, here: 7.

[30] Wille, "Mit dem alltäglichen Faschismus selbstverständlich umgehen," 6.

[31] Kroetz remarks that the sequence of the scenes simply mirrors the writing process, and leaves it up to the director to make any necessary changes. (*V*, 473)

[32] David Barnett, "Tactical Realisms: Rolf Hochhuth's *Wessis in Weimar* and Franz Xaver Kroetz's *Ich bin das Volk*," in *"Whose story" — Continuities in Contemporary German-language Literature*, eds. Arthur Williams, Stuart Parkes, Julian Preece (Berne: Lang, 1998), 181–95, here: 189.

[33] Franz Xaver Kroetz, "'Form ist der Teller von dem man ißt,' Programmheft *Stallerhof*, Deutsches Schauspielhaus Hamburg, Spielzeit 1971/72," reprinted in *Franz Xaver Kroetz*, ed. Otto Riewoldt (Frankfurt am Main: Suhrkamp, 1985), 88–92, here: 89. Kroetz is above all concerned with showing the cracks in the glossy surface of contemporary Germany; his aim is therefore to criticize the socioeconomic developments by portraying its pimps and would-be intellectuals.

[34] Ödön von Horvath, "Gebrauchsanweisung," in *Materialien zu Ödön von Horvaths Kasimir und Karoline*, ed. Traugott Krischke (Frankfurt am Main: Suhrkamp, 1973), 103–7.

[35] A "Geisterfahrer" is someone who deliberately drives the wrong way up the motorway, a phenomenon which renders driving on German motorways very dangerous.

[36] It may be worth mentioning that after the Social democrats took over in the *Bundestag* in 1998, Kohl became the center of a huge party finance scandal, in which former MPs and ministers swore false oaths, and files were deliberately deleted from state computers on an unprecedented scale. Even today, Kohl refuses to name the anonymous donor who gave more than 3 billion Deutschmarks to the Christian democrats — an act that is illegal if it is not openly declared. It is suspected, however, that the money stems from illegal arms deals.

[37] Yet it should be noted that Kroetz does not believe in the common prejudice that holds the younger generation responsible for the rise in right-wing extremism. Recent research has established that right-wing extremism is deeply rooted in society, and tolerated, if not supported, by the fifty-five to seventy-year-olds. Still, violent crimes are mainly committed by the eighteen to thirty-year-olds. See Bundeszentrale für politische Bildung (ed.), *Argumente gegen den Haß 1* (Bonn: Bundeszentrale für politische Bildung, 1993), particularly the table: "Rechtsextremismus — ein Jugendproblem?" 141; see also: Christoph Butterwegge, "Gewalt — Randgruppenphänomen, Jugendproblem oder Produkt der ganzen Gesellschaft?" in *Braune Saat in jungen Köpfen 1*, ed. Manfred Büttner (Hohengehren: Schneider, 1998), 163–78, here: 163.

[38] It is believed that the right-wing ideology of superiority is based on the following elements: racism and belief that one's own nation is morally superior, a totalitarian understanding of norms that automatically excludes strangers, belief in the principle of the survival of the fittest, a set of negative images of the enemy, a refusal to negotiate problems, and a strong inclination towards violence. See Wilhelm Heitmeyer, "Jugend und Rechtsextremismus," in *Argumente gegen den Haß 2,* ed. Bundeszentrale für politische Bildung (Bonn: Bundeszentrale für politische Bildung, 1993), 133–47, here: 134.

[39] Gundi Ellert, "Jagdzeit," *Th* 9 (1994): 30–42. Subsequent references to this work are cited in the text using the abbreviation *J* and page number.

[40] Franz Wille, "Zur Strecke gebracht," *Th* 10 (1994): 9–11. However, the production directed by Matthias Hartmann was heavily criticized for its bad acting.

[41] "Die grausamen Opfer," interview of Gundi Ellert by Anke Roeder, *Th* 9 (1994): 29–30.

[42] The parallels between Christian liturgy and National Socialism are examined by Otto Söhngen in *Säkularisierter Kultus* (Gütersloh: Bertelsmann, 1950). On the liturgical features of the Third Reich, see, for example, Klaus Vondung, "Die Apokalypse des Nationalsozialismus," in *Der Nationalsozialismus als politische Religion,* eds. M. Ley and J. Schoeps (Bodenheim: Philo Verlagsgesellschaft, 1997), 33–52.

[43] In the language of National socialism, you had "Maid" instead of "Mädchen," "Mark" instead of "Grenzland," "Gau" instead of "Provinz," "Jungmannen" instead of "Männer," "Sippe" for "Familie." Anti-Semitism was expressed by biologically masked phrases like "Volkskörper," and "Gift im Blutkreislauf des Volkes." Jews were referred to as "Blutegel" or "Parasiten." See Siegfried Bork, *Mißbrauch der Sprache. Tendenzen Nationalsozialistischer Sprachregelung* (Berne and Munich: Francke, 1970), 40–45.

[44] For a brief overview of von Düffel's plays, see Isabell Janack, "Der Autordramaturgdozent," in *Stück-Werk 3,* eds. Christel Weiler and Harald Müller (Berlin: Zentrum Bundesrepublik Deutschland des Internationalen Theaterinstituts, 2001), 46–50.

[45] John von Düffel, *OI* (Gifkendorf: Merlin, 1995).

[46] John von Düffel, *Solingen* (Gifkendorf: Merlin, 1995), 9. Subsequent references to this work are cited in the text using the abbreviation *S* and page number.

[47] Heinrich Heine, *Buch der Lieder* (Stuttgart: Reclam, 1998), 170–71.

[48] In the 1990s, people's indifference to political parties and politics became apparent and was hotly debated. See, for example, Hildegard Hamm-Brücher, "Wege in die und Wege aus der Politik(er)verdrossenheit," *Aus Politik und Zeitgeschichte. Beilage zur Wochenzeitung Das Parlament,* 30 July 1993.

9: Media and Politics

Ever since the Third Reich, the Germans' relationship to the media and any possible manipulation of information has been understandably tense.[1] To this day, the skepticism of the Frankfurt School is still very influential. The criticisms of the "culture industry" that Theodor W. Adorno and Max Horckheimer voiced in *Dialektik der Aufklärung* (Dialectics of the Enlightenment, 1944), developed into the dominant paradigms of German media theory. Only Hans-Magnus Enzensberger qualified the indictment of the German left in 1970. He pointed out that the resistive autonomous art of the Frankfurt School, which was supposed to penetrate the manipulative smoke screen of industrial culture, was probably just as obscure as the industry it was trying to fight.[2] Its highly elitist art thus simply duplicated the ideologically overdetermined mass culture, and did not offer the individual room for thought.

In the late 1980s, Siegfried Zielinski observed that the advent of video recorders, CD ROMs, laser discs, satellite and cable reception, and the Internet, rendered old projections of a uniform culture industry meaningless. However, he predicted that even more non-public retreats would be established in order to resist the control of the media.[3] Karl Ludwig Pfeiffer's theory of the media provides a different viewpoint, for he maintains that any catastrophic spectacle that the media report, regardless of whether it is real or simulated, is a basic element of any society. He argues that these catastrophes simply adopt the function of former public rituals, such as public hangings. These spectacles thus serve as a release for the subconscious hunger for excitement.[4] In the same vein, Florian Rötzer argues that catastrophic breakdowns in media-generated cyberspace have become necessary for mankind. For him, only the extreme experience of pain is a reliable link between the body and its surrounding world.[5]

Enzensberger also addresses the question of television, and states that all complaints about the shallowness of television culture eventually become pointless, a view that Daniel Call's (1967–) *Wetterleuchten* (Summer-Lightning, 1997) expresses. According to Enzensberger, viewers tune in because they want to be bored, and because they want to switch off their brains and be distracted.[6] This view is depicted in Albert Ostermeier's (1967–) play *The Making of B.-Movie* (1999), where the ill-mannered and fake poet Brom does not shy away from causing public outrage to sell literature. Ostermeier criticizes the mechanisms behind the media industry by having the media use Brom's rude behavior to boost their otherwise rather meager percentage of viewers.

In his theoretical approach, Norbert Bolz goes much further than Enzensberger, and maintains that the so-called Dionysian potential of media-generated reality springs from a human desire for entertainment. And if this need is not fulfilled, it will become uncontrollable and finally end in war.[7] In his subsequent books, Bolz is even more radical, and argues that the simultaneous, non-hierarchical processing of data that we find in hypermedia is, in fact, analogous to the ways in which the human brain works.[8] In the media age, the book has become the bottleneck of human communication. It is problematic, however, that Bolz gets rid of the traditional concept of humanism at the same time, and states that we should no longer look for a meaningful way of applying new techniques, but enjoy ourselves instead.[9] Falk Richter's (1969–) play *Peace* (2000) addresses this view, pinpointing the problematic fact that the over-intensive media coverage of war atrocities can also fulfill people's perverted need for sadism. Moreover, the play highlights the fact that the first victim of war is always the truth, since journalists do not hesitate to doctor the images of war.

In contrast, Hartmut Winkler wonders why the Internet leaves us with a feeling of desire, and concludes that it is a "wish machine."[10] He states that browsing the Internet is often a far from pleasurable experience and arrives at the conclusion that the web is nothing more than a large texture of texts. In *www.slums* (2000), a series of plays modeled on soap-operas, René Pollesch (1962–) looks at a group of people who grew up with the ideals of the 1968 movement, yet have relapsed into a state of utter dullness. The seven plays, which premiered in the foyer of the upper dress circle of the *Deutsche Schauspielhaus* in Hamburg, presented the audience with a group of young people who have lost their identity in the world of the Internet. As Pollesch successfully combined television and theater in an entertaining manner, the play received glowing reviews.[11]

As Chancellor Gerhard Schröder pointed out, Hitler's shadow becomes longer as time elapses, so that it is not surprising that writers mainly adopt Adorno's rather melancholy view of the media, instead of embracing the cyberspace age. The fact that the Germans have been manipulated once in their history to such disastrous effect has left a scar on their collective memory. The stain of the Third Reich will not wear off, and this is one reason why the concept of being "intellectual" is largely associated with being left-wing. It is a means of distancing oneself from crimes committed with the backing of the media. Even today, there is an unspoken consensus among the left that the Third Reich and its massive media presence and parallelization of all levels of communication (*Gleichschaltung*) must be remembered. This forms the background to Rainald Goetz's (1954–) play *Festung* (Fortress, 1993) which accuses today's media of actively taking part in the attempt to gloss over the Nazi past. If the Germans appear to be overreacting in their defense of the individual who sits passively in front of the screens, it is surely due to this experience.

Fascist Tendencies: Rainald Goetz's *Festung* (1993)

Rainald Goetz brings a particular sensitivity to the way in which the German theater uses and abuses language. His play focuses on the ways in which the shape of words can detach themselves from their real meaning, particularly as a result of the media culture.[12] The trilogy *Festung* is part of a larger project of the same title that also includes a collection of experimental prose called *Kronos* and a collection of material entitled *1989*.[13] The drama trilogy consists of the plays *Kritik in Festung* (Criticism in Fortress), *Festung* (Fortress), and *Katarakt* (Cataract), the first part of which premiered in 1993 at the *Deutsche Schauspielhaus* in Hamburg.[14]

In *Festung*, Goetz returns to the theme of war and destruction that he had previously tackled in the so-called "text massacre" *Krieg* (War, 1987). This was voted best play of the year by the journal *Theater heute*, because it demonstrated the fatal mechanisms of war.[15] Most of his works concentrate on the failure of the individual in modern society, and his fifth play, *Jeff Koons* (1998), is no exception.[16] However, this is not a reconstruction of the artist's biography, but a montage of loosely connected scenes that highlight single events in Koons's life. Goetz is above all concerned with language and its dissolution in the media age, yet he does not work according to a deductive principle himself, and his work is based on an associative style of writing.[17]

Festung focuses on the German trauma of the Holocaust, the problematic German repression of the Shoah, and the tendency to push the horrors of mass murder out of collective memory. In numerous short scenes, which do not hang together as a conventional plot, but are grouped together according to the principle of the postmodern pastiche, Goetz criticizes the relationship between memory and media culture.[18] In particular, he uncovers the mechanisms behind the desperate attempt to forget while pretending to discuss the past. The deliberately fragmented, disrupted, and defective language is further highlighted by the layout: the arrangement of words and the line breaks. As a result of the "Stimmenkonzentrat," philosophy and superficial phrases mix until language becomes meaningless and shallow.[19] True emotions and meaningful conversations drown in nonsensical media communications. As the metaphor *Festung* suggests, the Germans lock themselves up in the neurotic fortress of their own worldview and are unable to approach history in an open-minded manner. In the play, the trauma is evident in different ways: in part 1, the extreme horrors of extinction, the torturing and gassing of millions of victims, are expressed through defective language; in part 2, communication deteriorates into small-talk on television; in part 3, an old man soliloquizes about history and death without even having anyone to talk to.

Festung could be described as a radical postmodernist experiment in which people and names are largely missing; the setting is not specified and the theater itself is referred to. Instead of addressing the theater as a whole, the play focuses on the "Rampe," a highly ambiguous German word, as it both denotes the "fourth wall" of the stage and alludes to the selection ramp of the concentration camps.

As the deliberately defective language of part 1 underlines, the Holocaust is still beyond description, and it remains an unspeakable yet naked truth that everybody avoids talking about:

SCHWESTER	nicht auszu
BRUDER	Stille
SCHWESTER	zu verschw
BRUDER	und nichts zu
SCHWESTER	beschr (*F,* 50)

In this failed dialogue, the second parts of the verbs "aussprechen," "verschweigen" and "beschreiben" are cut off, indicating that the characters are avoiding talking about the Holocaust in even the most basic of ways. Communication about extinction, or "die klärende Ausspr," frank conversation (Aussprache) about the Nazi past, are literally impossible. Both the unfinished words and the missing nouns symbolize the inability to engage in true dialogue with the past, and thus the failure to create a collective memory.

The second part of the trilogy is modeled on various TV shows that are molded into inconsistent and petty gossip. The opening resembles a live show, with a number of celebrated German TV presenters and singers acting as hosts of a quiz show called "Criticism in Germany Times Table Talk Evidence." Everything must be fun, and because the Germans are anxious to present themselves in as positive a light as possible, they play down the mass murder.

By means of linguistic idiosyncrasies, Goetz highlights the fact that dialogue on television has become more or less restricted to a pattern of superficial phrases. In keeping with their social roles, the game show hosts literally show the "frontstage" part of their personality, to use Goffman's influential term.[20] In *Festung,* public discourse about the Holocaust deteriorates to a set of ritualized phrases, revealing both inertia and ignorance. In an absurd scene with the subtitle "ICH BLEIBE DABEI ICH KANN MICH AN NICHTS ERINNERN," memory work (*Erinnerungsarbeit*) is presented as an absurd game in which teams score points for pointless remarks. Throughout the game, numerous interruptions mock live commentaries and introduce a dimension of parody.

In an ironic comment on a talk show called "Das literarische Quartett," a well-known TV-program chaired by Marcel Reich-Ranicki, in which critics discuss recently published books, a chorus of girls addresses the evidently demented poets with empty phrases such as "wonderful," "interesting," and "very nice." The poets are not concerned with the content of their prattle, but are anxious to know if and when the interview will be broadcast. The scene employs ritualized social behavior and language alongside sharp critical remarks about media culture, thus creating a comedic effect because the characters do not seem to know what they are talking about.

In view of this negative scene, it is not surprising that *Festung* refers to reunification as "die Geburt des deutschen Gaskammergeistes aus dem klassischen deutschen Ideal." Here, Goetz intertwines the famous terms by Nietzsche, "Die Geburt der Tragödie," and Goethe, the "Klassische Ideal," and lends a sinister twist to them. Tragedy does not emerge from a musical spirit (Nietzsche) and neither does humanism result from German idealism (Goethe). According to Goetz, a notorious hunger for power and hegemony dominates contemporary German writing. He is painfully aware of the disastrous effect that idealism, namely nationalism and military expansion, had on politics. Reunification is therefore an excuse for forgetting the Holocaust in order to justify nationalistic feelings. In Goetz's view, the November revolution of 1918, Hitler's failed putsch in Munich on 9 November 1923, the pogrom on 9 November 1938 ("Reichskristallnacht"), and the fall of the Wall on 9 November 1989 all speak of a nationalistic continuity.[21]

Goetz sees the writing on the disappearing Berlin Wall, and criticizes the hypocrisy with which people exploit famous German poets as advocates of a humane Germany, while indulging in self-congratulation and lavish celebrations in order to conceal mass murder. Instead of coming to terms with the idea of being born guilty, the Germans carry on talking. However, their real aim is to forget the past, and to gloss over the horrible events with a pseudo-dismayed attitude. *Festung* is therefore not only a "Kommunikation über Vernichtung," as the subtitle of part 2 suggests, but also a destroyed communication.

To conclude, *Festung* is a passionate and critical picture of post-reunification Germany that shows how today's media culture transforms the memory of the Holocaust into superficial trivia. Through a multitude of voices, some anonymous, some borrowed from the world of the media, Goetz blames the banality of television programs for the destruction of memory. Instead of honest emotions and true intelligence, the speakers' trite remarks reveal ignorance and hypocrisy, particularly in relation to the Holocaust. Despite the fact that the Germans continue to rant about their Nazi past, their hidden aim is to repress the horrors of the Shoah. Infected by the idle babble of the media, disciplines such as philosophy, poetry, and science also become superficial, as the language of allegedly erudite speakers in *Festung* is equally dull, and their attitudes are conspicuously "adornohaft" and pseudo-left-wing. Goetz's play thus depicts a failed attempt to create a true collective memory that would ideally also take the dignity of the victims into account.

TV and Trivia: Daniel Call's *Wetterleuchten* (1997)

Since the beginning of the 2000/2001 season, Call has worked as a director for the *Volkstheater* in Rostock, yet he can look back on almost twenty years of theater experience that includes the *Triplex* in New York, the *Almeida* in London, the *Staatstheater* Aachen, and the *Renaissance-Theater* in Berlin. Call started writing in 1991, since which time he has completed seventeen plays, which largely focus on the downside of a society dominated by consumerism and the media. In *Gärten des Grauens* (Gardens of Horror, 1993), for example, the playwright presents us with a small town in which subconscious violence smolders, ready to break out into a neighborhood war.[22] *Tumult auf Villa Shatterhand* (Turmoil in Villa Shatterhand, 1997) depicts the romantic world of the American Indian created by the bourgeois writer Karl May (1842–1912), through the lens of a soap-opera.

In his thirteenth play, *Wetterleuchten,* Call presents us with Molli, Hanni, and Kitty, three elderly women who accidentally meet because Molli's car has broken down. Molli is a stereotypical saleswoman, who lives alone after her second divorce; Hanni looks after a run-down restaurant in the middle of nowhere, and is the guardian of her mentally disturbed sister Kitty. *Wetterleuchten* premiered at the *Theater Dortmund* in April 1997; reviewers criticized the production due to the overacted nature of the characters and the cluttered stage.[23]

Although critics often accused Call of staging nonsensical trivia,[24] he provocatively insists that emotions are the only key to people's hearts: "Ach ja, ich denke, das ist was fürs Herz, und ich denke nach wie vor, daß der Weg in die Köpfe übers Herz führt. Kitsch ist eine Urstruktur."[25] It is therefore only logical that Call chooses popular forms of theater, such as the *Traditionelle Volksstück* or the comedy, to express his opinions, because humor permits the disclosure of painful incidents while simultaneously deflecting that pain.

Indeed, the content of his plays is not to be confused with the inherent criticism of the phenomena that Call portrays. According to the playwright, society has deteriorated into a real-life soap-opera, and the ad-laden television has influenced cultural life. In his generally pessimistic view of history, Call follows the verdict of Enzensberger, who dismissed mass media due to their negative influence,[26] yet also relates to the theories of Norbert Bolz, who claimed that there is no longer anything behind the reality of the media.[27] In *Wetterleuchten,* the three women who live in, and through, the world of media find themselves completely at a loss when a power-cut forces them to make conversation:

MOLLI   [. . .] Ich schweige selbst sehr gerne. Ich genieße das.
Nichts ist schöner, als vertraut miteinander zu
schweigen. Es wird ohnehin zuviel geredet auf dieser
Welt. Nichtiges Geblubber. Wortkaskaden. Sondermüll
aus Versatzstücken. [. . .] Reden gegen den
Weltuntergang. Und nur aus Angst vor der Stille. Denn
Stille bedeutet Stillstand. Dauerberieselung. Man kommt
heim und schaltet Radio, Fernseher und alle
Haushaltsgeräte ein.[28]

In fact, Molli's endless litanies are hardly more than an ironic copy of the media-prattle, the purpose of which is simply to fill the emotional void inside her. Men, although physically absent from the play, infiltrate this world as memories that are brought up in conversation. The audience learns that Molli has of course accepted her limitations and restricted career possibilities, yet has decided to be a successful businesswoman. In an ironically pathetic outburst of tears and words, she informs the other two that it was she who wrote the lyrics for the songs of her first famous husband, and invented the advertising slogans for her second husband. These slogans were so popular that even Kitty remembers them:

> Wischi Waschi blitzeblanke
> Kleines Bitte, großes Danke
> Kleine Flecke, großer Dreck
> Wischi wischt auch Tränen weg.
> (*W*, 51)

By borrowing ideas from television and presenting them within the framework of an absurd plot, Call expresses his criticism of the mass-media in a non-dogmatic manner. The dialogue that results is a kind of layered conversation, where the superfluous remarks on the surface belie the pain beneath, thus creating a subtext that the audience senses on a subconscious level.

While Molli and Hanni indulge in the advantages of the electric age, Kitty refuses to use electrical appliances altogether, let alone understand how they function. She is unshakably convinced that Hanni's modernized household is an ill-disguised conspiracy of spirits that are after her life. Wrapped in her mad fantasies, Kitty lives in the nineteenth century, yet she enjoys watching television — if Hanni switches it on for her. Although Hanni claims to have sacrificed her life in order to take care of her sister, her self-stylization as the good Samaritan becomes a little dubious in view of the modern household that bursts with appliances that Kitty cannot touch. It does not come as a surprise, therefore, that Hanni admits to having acquired all the electrical equipment to drive her sister finally round the bend, and thus to control her.

The sisters are involved in a lifelong quarrel that has taken on the shape of a domestic war, a metaphor which, according to Call, aptly described the state of modern-day society. *Wetterleuchten* ends with a parody of the knight in shining armor, a scene that is inspired by advertising. Instead of a knight, however, Molli's high-tech car suddenly appears on its own, opens its doors, and takes Kitty away. The play thus presents us with stereotypes and well-known symbols, yet puts them in a comic environment that becomes increasingly absurd. Call thus employs the devices of popular entertainment, but only to criticize the effects of the mass media by presenting trivia on the large canvas of the stage.

A Star is Born:
Albert Ostermaier's *The Making of B.-Movie* (1999)

Like Goetz and Call, Albert Ostermaier holds the contemporary media culture responsible for the devaluation of conversation and understanding. Despite the fact that he is one of the technomusic generation, he compares the uniformity of techno to totalitarian structures. In an interview in 1998, he maintained that his dramas undermine the consumerism of the television addict, the so-called "Zapphaltung," first by restoring a high level of style, and second by abandoning the postmodern collage:

> Die Emanzipation der Konsumentenhaltung gegenüber dem genauen Hören oder der Präzision von Bildern löst die Texte oder den Wahrnehmungsapparat letztlich auf. Gegen diesen Trend muß einfach eine hohe Konzentration von Sprache behauptet werden, die auch überfordern kann. Theater existiert eben auch durch Sprache. Das Textgebäude, das man als Autor herstellt, muß in sich konsequent und stringent gearbeitet sein, um es dem Regisseur bzw. dem schnellebigen Kulturbetrieb zu verunmöglichen, die ästhetischen und politischen Spitzen zu kappen.[29]

His aim is therefore to create highly sophisticated plays that stretch the audience to the limit but are entertaining at the same time. *The Making of B.-Movie* mocks the relationship between art and commerce. It premiered at the *Bayrisches Staatsschauspiel* in Munich in May 1999, where reviewers received it with some misgivings.[30] The criticism, however, mainly concerned the staging, as the director Minke took the idea of the play within a play, which is simultaneously produced as a film, a little too seriously. This resulted in a confusing mixture of simultaneous projections, a "Mediensalat," that made it difficult to follow the plot.[31] By contrast, the press praised the production at the *Kölner Schauspiel* in November 1999 (director, Volker Hesse), because it honed in on the filmic aspect of the play and because of the brilliant acting.[32]

The Making of B.-Movie, Ostermaier's first dialogically structured play, presents writing as cleverly advertised plagiarism, thus criticizing postmodernist attitudes. The play follows the path that Ostermaier has paved in earlier works. In *Zwischen zwei Feuern: Tollertopographie* (Between Two Fires: A Topography of Toller, 1993),[33] for example, the expressionist writer Ernst Toller is confronted with his other self, Tollkirsch, who forces him to reflect upon the process of writing. Harking back to Shakespeare, his third play, *Tatar Titus* (1997), presents us with the problematic relationship of language and power,[34] and in *Death Valley Junction* (2000),[35] the main character, Desmond, becomes the victim of a self-constructed surrealist nightmare, from which he is unable to escape.[36]

The title of *The Making of B.-Movie* suggests that the play presents us with the production of a work of art, in the tradition of the play within a play. But Ostermaier adds another dimension, as a film team takes shots of the staging, thus breaking the fictional surface for a second time. The making of the film also includes the artist, here the young untalented writer Andree, who suffers from writer's block. He is picked up from an African village by his old friend Silber, who wants Andree to act as the author of his plays.

At the beginning Andree lacks convincing media presence, and so Silber sends him to a military training camp, where he is "made to be a real man" and taught the cynical laws of war. When Andree is finally presented to the flashy media circus for the first time, he has not only a new name, Brom, but also a completely new image. For the shy and desperate young man has become an ill-mannered bisexual sex-maniac, who constantly insults the rich representatives of the culture industry.

However, Brom and Silber depend on one another, like the ingredients of silver bromide, a chemical substance used in photography to produce flashes. Only as a team can they produce a flashy appearance, and make a big impression on the public. While Brom acts in accordance with his name — brome is a stinking, poisonous gas — Silber recites his cynical war poems. Ostermaier describes the setting of Silber's poem recital as follows:

> *Unter ihm, um ein ausladendes Buffet gruppiert, atmet die Gesellschaft seine Stimme, während ihre Blicke Brom gelten, der, die Beine auf dem Tisch, eine Sonnenbrille über den Augen, in einer Ecke sitzt und sich langweilt, raucht, die Frauen beobachtet, müde lächelt, sie mit einladenden Gesten zu sich zu locken sucht und dabei Hummerschwänze aufbricht, um dann provozierend obszön ihr Fleisch aus dem Panzer zu saugen. Silber merkt, wie die Aufmerksamkeit sich immer mehr zu Brom hin verlagert, und versucht sie durch dramatische Gesten und Stimmführung zurückzugewinnen, es ist ein Kampf zwischen ihnen.*[37]

Yet the presentation is a great success, mainly because Brom behaves badly, assaults a young man, and conspicuously invites women back to his apartment.[38] Brom is a hybrid of several misanthropist poets, for example, Antonin Artaud, whose *Theater of Cruelty* had aimed to physically torment the audience. Like Arthur Rimbaud, Brom seems to have lost his identity; this reminds us of Rimbaud's famous remark "Moi, c'est un autre" (My self is somebody else). Like him, Brom is fascinated by poetry inspired by the experience of war. Ostermaier shows, however, that in contrast to the 1970s generation of angry critical writers, Brom/Silber's war game is just an empty, meaningless bubble. This becomes evident in several allusions to Hans-Magnus Enzensberger, who announced that his poetry was the knife with which he would cut open the foul body of society.[39] In the same vein, a critic announces: "Ehemaliger Legionär stürmt die Bühne. 'Die Worte sind meine Waffen jetzt'" (*BM*, 48).

As Ostermaier was commissioned to write this play for Brecht's Centenary in 1998, it is appropriate that Brecht's *Baal* (1919) inspired both the plot and the main character, Andree, alias Brom. Brom is a misanthropistic sex-maniac, akin to the rude poet Baal, and like his fictional forerunner, he beds practically anybody, regardless of their sex. Indeed, the scenes in Brom's room are modeled on parallel scenes in Brecht's play, as both Baal and Brom treat themselves to a few girls, whom they kick out after having had sex with them. In *The Making of B.-Movie,* the poet even seduces the female lover of Mäzen, the lesbian supporter who funds his writing, and then persuades her to give her girlfriend to the young waiter who loves Brom. Although Ostermaier vaguely recreates the atmosphere of Brecht's play here, he makes it very clear that it is hardly more than a cheap remake, a B(recht)-Movie. This is particularly true of the scene called "Soirée. Mäzenatenparty," which shows the extent to which Ostermaier is inspired by *Baal.* The "Herrschaften" and the "Gastgeber" stem from the 1919 version of the *Baal* scene "Soiree," but are updated for the world of media, and thus transformed into stereotypes of critics (Müller-Schuppen) or TV presenters (Gil Mattis), or simply remain as the "Junge Mann."[40]

Despite the fact that Brom behaves as badly as he possibly can, the critics are intrigued, and praise the convincing union of author and work. This is even more ironic because Brom has nothing to do with Silber's poetry. Wherever he goes, Brom causes scandals and public outrage in order to sell the postmodern play of blood and gore about war that Silber has written in his name. Brom threatens to cancel their deal, thus forcing Silber to both revise and direct the play, albeit as Brom wants it, with an all-female cast that wades through horse blood.

In the scene "Talkshow," Ostermaier mocks the shallow culture industry that is always hungry for scandals and the media presence of writers, regardless of the quality of their work. It is modeled on a notorious television program called *Das literarische Quartett,* in which four critics, who seem to behave according to a pre-written script, yet pretend to quarrel spontaneously, review books by young writers. As it is late at night, the compère Mattis attempts to keep the audience awake by means of interactive games, such as phoning in for questions or a ticket for the premiere. During a short break off-air, Mattis admits that it is his job to sell culture by presenting it in the most exciting manner possible, and it is for this purpose that the agent provocateur Brom is useful.

It does not really matter what Brom says, as long as it is outrageous and provokes the anger of viewers at home. For it is not the written product that counts, but the marketing, and because Brom's strategy is successful, it is tolerated. No matter how inventive the so-called avant-garde proves to be, it will soon be digested and advertised for sale.[41] At the end of the scene, Ostermeier even mocks his colleague Rainald Goetz, when Brom imitates Goetz's first public appearance, during which Goetz cut his forehead.[42] In *The Making of B.-Movie,* however, Brom fakes this with theater blood, much to the disappointment of the TV presenter, and thus the pseudo-revolutionary attitude of Brom exposes the money-grubbing attitude of the media industry. This underlines the repetitive aspect of the postmodern culture industry that Ostermeier is criticizing here, since postmodernism lives merely by portraying itself.

Media and War: Falk Richter's *Peace* (2000)

In *Peace,* the director and playwright Falk Richter presents us with the problematic relationship of reality and illusion, a theme that he has already explored in previous plays. His first play, *Alles: In einer Nacht* (Everything: In One Night, 1996) depicts a woman who tries to work out a system, using the numbers in the local phone book, in order to find her ideal date. Her efforts fail, and in the end the numbers occupy her mind to such an extent that she becomes mentally ill. In *Kult! Geschichte für eine virtuelle Generation* (Cult! A Story for a Virtual Generation, 1996), a man and a woman desperately try to be authentic, despite the fact that the world around them has taken on the features of a talk show. *Gott ist ein DJ* (God is a DJ, 1999)[43] tells the story of a couple who live in a museum, and are therefore forced to perform their private thoughts and actions before the eyes of the public.[44] Pitting illusion against reality, Richter shows that true emotions no longer exist in our media-dominated age.[45]

Richter himself staged and directed his play in June 2000 at the *Schaubühne am Lehniner Platz* in Berlin. The reactions were mixed,[46] and ranged from dismissing the play as an "obscene mystification of war"[47] to enthusiastic approval because of its vehement criticism of the "Kriegsgewinnler," the journalists.[48] Soon after the premiere, however, the *Berliner Schaubühne* and the *S. Fischer Verlag* were taken to court, for Detlef Urban, a journalist whose name appears in the text of the play, claimed to have been insulted. The matter is still undecided, as Urban won the case, but the ruling was overturned on appeal, a decision based on the freedom of works of art.[49]

The setting of *Peace* is the reception area of an agency that produces news, documentaries, art films, and advertisements connected to war, highlighting the fact that the truth is always the first victim of war. The agency is run by seven young people aged between thirty and forty, except for Marc, who is only twenty-five. As the characters live and work there, they constantly meet, and their hectic conversations reveal that they have difficulty in keeping up with the pace of war. In an interview, Richter describes the characters as follows: "Dargestellt werden acht Figuren, die man als Gewinner des Systems bezeichnen könnte, vielleicht als Extremform der Karrierekrieger."[50] Most of the scenes of *Peace* take place in the night, when those who are working, having sex, or quarreling wake up others. As the hectic events in the war zones dictate their lives, all the characters are on the verge of a nervous breakdown. The flat is crammed full of enlarged photographs of dismembered corpses and ruined buildings, and the atmosphere in the flat resembles a war zone itself, especially since Marco's installations provide a background of warlike noises and images. This is further highlighted by the fact that the characters wear army-inspired clothing, and to all intents and purposes look like soldiers.

Although they can barely work fast enough to transform the events of war into a digestible product, and the atmosphere becomes increasingly chaotic, their team-work still functions: Laura and Stefan travel to the war zones in order to shoot new films and photos, and Marco uses the data to produce tasteless art films by mixing it with porn and images of fake torture. These fake tortures are inflicted on Marc, the youngest of them, who does not realize that he is being abused, since everyone sleeps with him. Tim, the agent for culture and public relations, dashes from one public event to the next, producing harmless but allegedly moving drivel that the culturally-interested want to hear.

Tim's task is to turn war into exhibitions that present random collages of texts and pictures. The "Kulturmensch" Tim is responsible for presenting modest criticism in a pseudo-sophisticated manner, in order to calm down peace campaigners. As a consequence, he is employed by the government to convey a positive image of the war, so that public opinion remains favorable. It is interesting that during the war in Kosovo, the speaker of NATO, Jamie Sheah, expressed the need to manipulate public opinion.[51] In this sense, Richter's play is symbolic of the increasingly skeptical attitude of many Germans towards the war in Kosovo.

Since the team manages the representation and misrepresentation of atrocities, the characters have become cynical and numb to the horrors of war. For example, Laura desperately searches for a photograph of dead babies for her new campaign, while Marco places Marc in the middle of a fake war scene:

LAURA *dazu* Scheiße wie schreibt man eigentlich
"Kollateralschäden"? wir sollen da jetzt fürs
Innenministerium irgend so ne flächendeckende
Kampagne starten die besonders Jugendliche
zwischen 14 und 18 ansprechen soll und diese
erfrorenen Säuglinge, wo sind die, ich find die nicht
mehr, die müssen doch morgen in den Druck

MARCO legt MARC so hin, daß es aussieht, als läge er in einer zer-
trümmerten Landschaft, filmt ihn, während MARC sich weiter
auszieht, auf der Leinwand sehen wir, wie MARC in Trümmern liegt:
verwundet, mit einem PEACE-Zeichen auf der Brust, CALVIN-
KLEIN-Unterhose, MARCO kippt ihm noch etwas Blut übers Gesicht,
macht dann Fotos.

"Bodentruppen," auch so n neues Wort, das
plötzlich jeder gebraucht, Wolfgang hat mir
irgendwas von "doppelter Auschwitzlüge" notiert,
keine Ahnung, was das nun wieder bedeuten soll,
seit wann benutzen wir überhaupt diese Wörter, so
reden wir doch gar nicht

Zu Tom.   Sag mal, kannst du nicht mal hier aufräumen?

TOM   Was?

LAURA   Kannst du nicht mal für Ordnung hier sorgen, ich
find hier echt nichts mehr wieder, ich verlier hier
alles, diese Mütter, die ihre erfrorenen Säuglinge
durch den Schnee tragen, und hinter denen fliegt
diese Brücke in die Luft, wo sind die, die sind
verschwunden[52]

The missing punctuation mirrors the breathless haste with which the words are spoken, and, occasionally, Richter even abandons the use of capitals. Due to her haste, Laura does not realize how cynical her technical language is when she refers to the victims of war. What counts for her is whether the dying are presented in an emotive manner, so that she can use them in her new campaign. Since she is desperate to finish the texts in time, she appears to have lost track of what she is writing at all. The fact that she is unable to make sense of Wolfgang's rather philosophical notes shows that she does not think in terms of content, but is mainly concerned with the sound of her texts.[53]

In the same vein, Marco employs Laura's images and film clips for his performance art that is nothing short of hard-core pornography. While the sexy young boy rolls about in theater blood, Marco's projections show a chaotic sequence of war documentaries, video ads for the army, military fetish parties, and the mass raping of women. In a perverse fashion, Marco's art turns war into something that he finds strangely pleasurable. As moral categories were long ago thrown overboard, it is not surprising that Julia will to transform the film material into an advertising campaign for a large clothing company in order to launch a new range of military fashion.

The characters are all united by the fact that they make large amounts of money because the war provides them with pictures of sensational horror that sell extremely well. If they are concerned with anything, it is the quality of the pictures, and after enlarging them, Laura is very annoyed when she finds out that the babies on the photograph were still alive. As she can only think in terms of how shocking the effects are, it does not even occur to her to have pity or feel relief for someone who survived.

It is the dead who count for her campaign, a fact that we are once again made aware of when Stefan complains that most of the mass graves he was shown in Kosovo were not genuine. War has taken on a new dimension, for corpses can even be sold to the media. As a consequence, the misrepresentation of facts begins in the war zones themselves. In 1999, this had its real counterpart in the deliberate manipulation of parliament by the Minister of Defense at the time, Rudolf Scharping. He presented the MPs with a photograph that allegedly showed the massacre of innocent people by the Serbs in order to influence the parliamentary decision regarding the bombing of Kosovo.[54] *Peace* shows how information is further processed in news agencies until it has no connection with real events. Not even eyewitnesses are reliable; Stefan can only think in terms of money, and is simply annoyed that his films are now so worthless that he has to shoot them again.

However, as Richter focuses on the deaths of human beings instead of the destruction of buildings, he contradicts the representation of war common since the Gulf War, which was generally referred to as a "clean war."[55] In *Peace*, we are thus confronted with personal loss and pain. Still, the conspicuous doctoring of the news expresses the playwright's distrust of the representation of war in the media. Indeed, none of the images or films in *Peace* are reliable accounts of the real events, highlighting the fact that the viewers at home are not eye-witnesses, but are being manipulated into believing that what they are shown is what really happened.

Rainald Goetz's *Festung* (1993) focuses on the impact of the mass media in Germany today. Like Kroetz, he links the popularity of anti-Semitism and neofascism to reunification that allegedly paved the way for an uninhibited pride in being German. Goetz's postmodern pastiche, which features many television presenters, singers, and other celebrities, is a hefty tirade against the media-dominated attempt to gloss over the Third Reich in order to present Germany as a "normal" state. In the critical tradition of the Frankfurt School, Goetz maintains that Germany cannot escape its fascist past and that the German nation as a whole must bear responsibility for the Holocaust. In contrast, Daniel Call's comedy *Wetterleuchten* (1997) presents the effects of the media on everyday life in a mock-ironic tone. During a power-cut in a thunderstorm, three elderly ladies meet in a run-down country pub, and it turns out that they are unable to communicate on any level other than in terms of television gossip. Albert Ostermeier's *The Making of B.-Movie* (1999) also focuses on the influence of the mass media, depicting the career of a nobody who becomes famous due to a cleverly conducted media campaign. While Ostermaier and Call look at the private and artistic aspects of media culture respectively, Falk Richter's *Peace* (2000) concentrates on the relationship between war and the media. In view of the misrepresentation of the war in Kosovo, Richter portrays the ways in which documentary material is manipulated until it no longer bears any connection to the reality it is supposed to represent.

Notes

[1] This becomes evident in an analysis of the mass media of the year 1969, in which the abuse of the media in totalitarian regimes was given special weight. See Hermann Meyn, *Massenmedien in der Bundesrepublik Deutschland* (Berlin: Colloquium, 1969), 9–10.

[2] Hans-Magnus Enzensberger, "Bausteine zu einer Theorie der Medien," *Kursbuch* 20 (March 1970), 159–86. Translated as "Constituents of a Theory of the Media," in *The Consciousness Industry. On Literature, Politics and the Media,* ed. Michael Roloff (New York: Continuum, 1974).

[3] Siegfried Zielinski, *Audiovisionen. Kino und Fernsehen als Zwischenspiele in der Geschichte* (Reinbek: Rowohlt, 1989), 240.

[4] Ralph Kray and Karl Ludwig Pfeiffer, "Paradoxien, Dissonanzen, Zusammenbrüche: Vom Ende und Fortgang der Provokationen," in *Paradoxien, Dissonanzen, Zusammenbrüche. Situationen offener Epistemologie,* eds. Hans-Ulrich Gumbrecht and Karl Ludwig Pfeiffer (Frankfurt am Main: Suhrkamp, 1991), 13–31, here: 27.

[5] Florian Rötzer, "Mediales und Digitales. Zerstreute Bemerkungen und Hinweise eines irritierten informationsverarbeitenden Systems," in *Digitaler Schein. Ästhetik der elektrischen Medien,* ed. Florian Rötzer (Frankfurt am Main: Suhrkamp, 1991).

[6] Hans-Magnus Enzensberger, "Das Nullmedium oder Warum alle Klagen über das Fernsehen gegenstandslos sind," in Hans-Magnus Enzensberger, *Mittelmaß und Wahn* (Frankfurt am Main: Suhrkamp 1989), 89–106.

[7] Norbert Bolz, *Theorie der neuen Medien* (Munich: Raben, 1990), 100.

[8] Norbert Bolz, *Das kontrollierte Chaos. Vom Humanismus zur Medienwirklichkeit* (Munich: Econ, 1994), 117.

[9] Bolz, *Das kontrollierte Chaos,* 194.

[10] Harmut Winkler, *Docuverse. Zur Medientheorie der Computer* (Regensburg: Boer, 1997), 11.

[11] See Roland Koberg, "Upgrade deine Realität!" *BZ,* 10 November 2000; Nele Zawada, "Seifenoper live," *BZ,* 25 November 2000; Frieda Karl, "Schöne neue Arbeitswelt," *Mopo,* 7 November 2000. The play is not yet available as a book, but it is scheduled for 2003: see Rene Pollesch, *www.slums* (Reinbek: Rowohlt, 2003); because of this, the play is not analyzed here.

[12] For a brief introduction to the first part of the trilogy, see Thomas Betz and Lutz Hagestedt, "Im Himmel der ruhelos ungeordneten Rede. Texte und Kontexte von *Kritik in Festung,*" *Spectaculum* 69 (1994), 265–74.

[13] Rainald Goetz, *Festung. Stücke* (Frankfurt am Main: Suhrkamp, 1993). Subsequent references to this work are cited in the text using the abbreviation *F* and page number.

[14] The staging in Frankfurt in January 1993, directed by Hans Hollmann, was received with some misgivings; see Franz Wille, "Zeitgeistshows: Sinn oder Stuß? Rainald Goetz *Festung* und *Katarakt* in Frankfurt, Volker Brauns *Iphigenie in Freiheit* in Frankfurt und Cottbus," *Th* 2 (1993): 12–17.

[15] Hubert Winkels, "The Texas Chainsaw Textmassacre. Zur Trilogie *Krieg* von Rainald Goetz," *ThJ* (1988), 61–66.

[16] "'Ein Hau ins Lächerliche.' Der Schriftsteller Rainald Goetz über sein Theaterstück *Jeff Koons,* den US-Skandalkünstler gleichen Namens und den Mut, über die kitschigen Aspekte des Lebens zu schreiben," *Sp,* 50 (7 December 1998), 250–53, here: 250.

[17] This becomes evident in Goetz's thoughts on the productive aspects of "Worthaufen"; see Rainald Goetz, "Abfall für alle," in *Theater*Kultur*Vision* (Berlin: Theater der Zeit, 1998), 43–45, here: 45.

[18] In his first novel *Irre,* the critique of media culture also plays an important role; Rainald Goetz, *Irre* (Frankfurt am Main: Suhrkamp, 1984). Moreover, Goetz's intention was to destroy shallow talk by cutting the surface of language; for a discussion of this, see Julia Bertschik, "Theatralität und Irrsinn," *Wirkendes Wort* 47 (Fall 1997), 398–423; Hubert Winkels, "Krieg den Zeichen. Rainald Goetz und die Wiederkehr des Körpers," in Hubert Winkels, *Einschnitte. Zur Literatur der 80er Jahre* (Frankfurt am Main: Suhrkamp, 1988), 221–59.

[19] Goetz also explored this topic in a text entitled "Hölle," published in *Manuskripte* 86/1984. In "Subito," Goetz attacks the meaningless gossip of the so-called "Kulturbetrieb"; Rainald Goetz, "Subito," in Rainald Goetz, *Krieg/Hirn,* 2 vols. (Frankfurt: Suhrkamp, 1986). This text received some media attention, as Goetz cut his forehead with a razor blade during the first public reading of "Subito," thus expressing his despair. For a discussion of Goetz's criticism of the media in his earlier works, see Jürgen Oberschelp, "Raserei. Über Rainald Goetz, Haß und Literatur," *Merkur* 41 (Summer), 1987, 170–74.

[20] In his famous book, Goffman examines the divide between the private ("backstage") and the public ("frontstage") of the individual. See Erving Goffman, *The Presentation of Self in Everyday Life* (Garden City New York: Doubleday Anchor, 1959).

[21] For a both critical and informative overview of the problematic continuity in German history in view of 9 November see Peter Steinbach, "Der 9. November in der deutschen Geschichte des 20. Jahrhunderts und in der Erinnerung," *Aus Politik und Zeitgeschichte*. Beilage zur Wochenzeitung *Das Parlament*, 22 October 1999, 3–11.

[22] For a brief introduction to Call, see Axel Preusz, "Fickparzelle mit Kampfgraben," in *Stück-Werk 3*, eds. Christel Weiler and Harald Müller (Berlin: Zentrum Bundesrepublik Deutschland des Internationalen Theaterinstituts, 2001), 26–30.

[23] Franz Wille, "Schöne neue Fernsehwelt. Ein Porträt des Jungdramatikers Daniel Call," *Th* 9 (1997): 41–44, here: 44.

[24] A review of the production of *Wetterleuchten* at the *Renaissance-Theater* in Berlin dismissed Call's play as popular comedy for elderly people, "Komödienstadel"; see Detlef Friedrich, "Neualtes Spaßtheater," *BZ*, 31 August 1998.

[25] Quoted in Wille, "Schöne neue Fernsehwelt," 43.

[26] However, in view of the fact that Call announced that the generation of 1968 playwrights should be overcome, it is somewhat paradoxical that Call should adopt the views of the Frankfurt School.

[27] For a short introduction to media theory in Germany, see the introduction to this chapter.

[28] Daniel Call, "Wetterleuchten," in *Th* 9 (1997): 45–52, here: 49. Subsequent references to this work are cited in the text using the abbreviation *W* and page number.

[29] Frank Raddatz, "Sprache muß sein. Interview with Albert Ostermaier," in *Stück-Werk 1* (Berlin: Internationales Theaterinstitut, 1997), 85–86, here: 86.

[30] Petra Hallmayer, "Das Stück vom Film vom Dichter," *BZ*, 3 June 1999. Hallmayer complained that the homoerotic relationship between Brom and Silber was not portrayed convincingly; see also "Herr Baal ballert Bilder," *Sp*, 31 May 1999.

[31] Jürgen Berger, "Wenn der Schwanz mit dem Hund wedelt. Albert Ostermaiers erstes Dialogstück *The Making of B.-Movie* im Münchner Residenztheater, *Th* 7 (1999): 32–33.

[32] Jürgen Becker, "Die Dürftigkeit des medialen Scheins. Albert Ostermaiers *The Making of B.-Movie*, nachgespielt in Köln," *Th* 1 (2000): 46–47; Roland Koberg, "Danke, gestorben," *BZ*, 29 November 1999.

[33] Albert Ostermaier, "Zwischen zwei Feuern. Tollertopographie" [1993], in Albert Ostermaier, *Tatar Titus. Stücke* (Frankfurt am Main: Suhrkamp, 1998), 15–82.

[34] Albert Ostermaier, "Tatar Titus," in Albert Ostermaier, *Tatar Titus. Stücke* (Frankfurt am Main: Suhrkamp, 1998), 123–86.

[35] Albert Ostermaier, *Death Valley Junction* (Frankfurt am Main: Suhrkamp, 2000).

[36] For a brief introduction to Ostermaier's works, see Christel Weiler, "Konstruktion — Komposition — Spiel," in *Stück-Werk 3*, eds. Christel Weiler and Harald Müller (Berlin: Zentrum Bundesrepublik Deutschland des Internationalen Theaterinstituts, 2001), 113–16.

[37] Albert Ostermaier, *The Making of B.-Movie/ Radio Noir. Stücke* (Frankfurt am Main: Suhrkamp, 1999), 46–47. Subsequent references to this work are cited in the text using the abbreviation *BM* and page number.

[38] In the second production of the play in Cologne, the director made the actor playing Brom leave the stage in order to assault two women, much to the shock of the audience.

[39] Hans-Magnus Enzensberger, "Scherenschleifer und Poeten," in *Mein Gedicht ist mein Messer. Lyriker zu ihren Gedichten,* ed. Hans Bender (Munich: Paul List, 1961), 144–48.

[40] Bertolt Brecht, "Baal" (1919), in Bertolt Brecht, *Werke. Stücke 1. Große kommentierte Berliner und Frankfurter Ausgabe,* eds. Werner Hecht, Jan Knopf, Werner Mittenzwei, and Klaus-Detlef Müller (Berlin, Weimar, Frankfurt am Main: Aufbau/ Suhrkamp, 1989), 17–82, here: 22–26.

[41] "Und wenn doch jemand aus der Deckung kommt und antritt, wirft sich die 'Bewußtseinsindustrie,' wie Diederichsen die Medien nennt, mit aller Macht der Beschleunigung auf die neuen Protagonisten, um ihre Geschichte zu erzählen, um die Dramen von Aufstieg und Fall, von Hoffnung und Katastrophe zu schaffen, von deren Verkauf sie lebt. Hier holt die Beschleunigung ihre Protagonisten ein und zerstört den Stoff, von dem sie lebt." See the programmatic essay by Thomas Ostermeier, the new manager of the crisis-ridden *Berliner Schaubühne,* "Das Theater im Zeitalter der Beschleunigung," *TdZ* 7/8 (1999), 10–15, here: 14. See also Diedrich Diederichsen, *Der lange Weg nach Mitte. Der Sound und die Stadt* (Cologne: KIWI, 1999); Diedrich Diederichsen, *Loving the Alien. Science Fiction, Diaspora, Multikultur* (Berlin: ID, 1998).

[42] See the chapter on Rainald Goetz in this book.

[43] Falk Richter, "Gott ist ein DJ," *Th* 5 (1999): 62–73.

[44] For a brief introduction to Richter's works, see Ulrich Seidler, "Du sollst dir keinen Begriff machen," in *Stück-Werk 3,* eds. Christel Weiler and Harald Müller (Berlin: Zentrum Bundesrepublik Deutschland des Internationalen Theaterinstituts, 2001), 121–23.

[45] The play was premiered in Mainz in April 1999, directed by Richter himself, yet the production was found to be inadequate; see Franz Wille, "Fun ist ein Stahlbad," *Th* 5 (1999): 59–61.

[46] Matthias Heine, "Verlorene zwischen 'Fuck!' und Fax," *W,* 15 June 2000; Irene Bazinger, "Club-Kids im Kosovo," *BZ,* 8 June 2000.

[47] Roland Koberg, "Abbitte bei Peter Handke," *BZ,* 15 June 2000.

[48] Hendryk M. Broder, "Weltschmerz der Warmduscher," *Sp,* 21 September 2000, 267.

[49] This is discussed in an article by Susanne Leinemann, "Der ungestillte Appetit auf Wirklichkeit," *W,* 9 November 2000.

[50] Frieda Karl, "Die totale Überforderung," *Mopo,* 10 November 2000.

[51] "Nach den ersten 'Unfällen' fiel die Zustimmung in vielen Ländern, auch in Deutschland, um 20 bis 25 Punkte. Wir mussten sechs Wochen lang hart arbeiten, um die öffentliche Meinung zurückzugewinnen." Quoted in a film by Jo Angerer and Mathias Werth, *Es begann mit einer Lüge,* Westdeutscher Rundfunk, 2001.

[52] Falk Richter, "Peace," in *TheaterTheater: Aktuelle Stücke 11,* eds. Uwe B. Carstensen and Stefanie von Lieven (Frankfurt am Main: Fischer, 2001), 207–88, here: 241. Subsequent references to this work are cited in the text using the abbreviation *P* and page number.

[53] See a speech by Philip Knightley, "A Triumph for the Military, a Disaster for Journalism," given in 2000; quoted in Dušan Reljic, "Der Kosovo-Krieg und die deutschen Medien," in *Medien zwischen Krieg und Frieden,* eds. Ulrich Albrecht and Jörg Becker (Baden-Baden: Nomos, 2002), 64–74, here: 66. Knightley concluded that journalists support lies by the government out of patriotism, personal beliefs, and economic interest.

[54] Lampe, "Medienfiktionen beim NATO-Einsatz im Kosovo-Krieg," 96–102, 96.

[55] Lampe, "Medienfiktionen beim NATO-Einsatz im Kosovo-Krieg," 97.

Conclusion

THE MAIN CHARACTERISTICS of political drama and the developments that have taken place in this field over the last two decades can be summarized as follows:

As the 1980s in West Germany saw a conservative turn in society and politics, and a feeling of inertia became stronger, playwrights reacted by advocating the cause of the lower classes, mostly through the new *Volkstheater* and postmodern pastiche. Moreover, the new social movements, such as the fight against the armament race and environmental pollution, debated issues that playwrights adapted for the stage and presented for discussion.

In the GDR, the increasingly rigid political structures in the 1980s provoked a series of theatrical responses, although it was difficult to avoid censorship, and plays were sometimes staged after a delay of several years. Using the veil of mythology, playwrights more or less directly attacked the clampdown on freedom of thought and speech.

In both decades, the Nazi past played an important role, yet with a difference. While West German playwrights focused directly on the Third Reich in the 1980s by putting historical characters on stage, the playwrights of the united Germany of the 1990s looked at the disastrous consequences of the upsurge of right-wing violence on the streets, which playwrights such as Franz Xaver Kroetz perceived to be grounded in a new nationalist pride.

Reunification affected writers in the GDR to a large extent, and many East Germans expressed their feelings of loss and disorientation in a representation of the lost "Heimat." The chorus of criticism, which many West German writers have also joined, generally saw capitalism to be the origin of all misery.

Following the culture clash of the two Germanys, plays have drawn upon a set of "Ossi-Wessi" stereotypes, such as the "Wendehals" (opportunist), the "Fernsehrevolution," the "looting" of the East, and the "rape" of the helpless GDR by the potent West. Many plays presented the East as the victim, while the West Germans mainly featured as greedy and overbearing colonizers.

Although the feminist movement slowed down in the 1980s, female playwrights remained on the scene and contributed to a new type of drama that discarded old male-female clichés in favor of an unbiased portrayal of society. By contrast, male playwrights continued to address discrimination against women in a fairly traditional fashion, for they were conscious of the need to remain politically correct and not be accused of chauvinism.

While responses to September 11 are still muted, writers tackled terrorism in several ways, pinpointing the origins of terror both inside and outside the family. More than twenty years after the fatal wave of terrorism in Germany in 1977, playwrights are finally trying to come to terms with the traumatic experience of terror on the streets.

Due to the enduring influence of the skeptical Frankfurt School, criticism of the mass media is still popular, and even more so since the Berlin Republic has redefined its role in military conflicts. Politicians, scientists and journalists hotly debated the relationship between the media, politics and war, a discussion that has found its way into today's plays. In the same vein, contemporary drama reflects the consequences of reunification and the discussion about "normalization and nationalism."

Towards the end of the 1980s, and boosted by the events of 1989, a generation change appeared on the horizon, and with the advent of new playwrights, a fresh view of history entered the arena. In contrast to older playwrights, who owed much to the spirit of 1968, the young generation has moved away from presenting world-encompassing issues in a postmodern manner, to focus on the individual instead.

Parallel to this, the taste for dramatic forms has changed. While pastiches, farces, and also the new Volkstheater thrived during the 1980s, the 1990s saw the reemergence of forms developed in the late nineteenth and early twentieth century, such as surrealism, realism, expressionism, and particularly Brecht's *Verfremdungseffekt*.

Despite allegations that German drama has become a dramatic self-centered prattle about art, it can be concluded that it always has been essentially political, and has never ceased to address crucial developments in the political arena by means of a political stage.

Epilogue

ON 21 JUNE 2001 the run of Botho Strauß's latest play, *Der Narr und seine Frau in Pancomedia* (The Fool and his Wife in Pancomedia, 2000) at the *Treptower Arena* in Berlin, closed early, as it had failed to attract sufficient audiences. As one critic pointed out, Peter Stein's production flopped despite, or rather because of, the immaculate portrayal of postmodern prattle in the foyer of a hotel symbolic of society.[1] Strauß's attempt to bring some sense into the world of unimportant know-it-alls and want-to-bes by introducing a mythological aspect has proved to be unsuccessful.[2] In a similar way, Rolf Hochhuth's latest production, *Hitlers Dr. Faust* (2000), which he produced at the *Schlospark Theater* (owned by Hochhuth himself),[3] received mixed reviews. It portrayed the life of the engineer Hermann Eberth (1894–1989), who worked on a strategic missiles program, first for Hitler, then, after his emigration in 1940, for the US. However, critics thought that both the plot and the dialogue suffered as a result of Hochhuth's pedagogical ambitions, which reduced the characters to mere purveyors of his views.[4]

At the turn of the millennium, German theater faced a period of change, and the fact that Frankfurt's commercial sector felt the impact of September 11 caused subsidies to be cut, leaving managers and directors to redefine the stage. However, German drama has a long tradition to draw upon, based on a highly esteemed theater that has produced vibrant regional and national plays. Both playwrights and directors thus seized the opportunity to change, and reintroduced their belief in the centrality of the dramatist — and the audience. Despite critical media attacks on the theater as outdated and irrelevant, recent developments suggest otherwise. With the advent of a new type of director such as Thomas Ostermeier, who advocates a return to realistic theater, fanciful experiments are increasingly frowned upon. In the production of Shakespeare's *Hamlet,* for instance, the director Christoph Schlingensief cut the text until only a few rudimentary pieces were left, and then inserted them between blatant displays of Nazism and right-wing extremism. This prompted Diederich Diederichsen to exclaim: "Muss ich mir den Scheiß anhören," for he found it difficult to make sense of Schlingensief's apparently random and obscure style.[5] A reviewer of Martin Kusej's belatedly postmodern, yet radical, production of Marlowe's *Edward II* also pointed out that it could just as well have been Shakespeare's *Richard II,* for the "zerhackte text" was drowned in a flood of meaningless effects, inappropriate costumes and technomusic.[6] In view of such developments, it is understandable that Thomas Ostermeier, who has turned his back on abstract concepts to do justice to both text and actor,[7] has become so popular.[8] Thanks to him, contemporary British playwrights such as Mark Ravenhill and Sarah Kane have had a considerable impact on the German theater.[9] Kane's "monologic dialogues" inspired Gesine Danckwart, for example, and Ostermeier's production of Mark Ravenhill's *Shopping and F***ing* was a huge success at the *Baracke* of the *Deutsche Theater* in Berlin in 1998, thus becoming the benchmark for a new style of theater.[10] Consequently, the search for promising young German authors appeared under the head-line "Deutsche Ravenhills erwünscht" in the *Berliner Zeitung.*[11] In May 2001, Falk Richter successfully staged Caryl Churchill's (1938–) *Far Away* (2001) at the *Berliner Schaubühne,* a production that received glowing reviews.[12] *The Lieutenant of Inishmore* (2000), a black comedy written by the Irish writer Martin McDonagh (1971–), which presents Irish terrorism as a war about two pet cats, caused positive repercussions in the media.[13] However, English theater is not the only source of inspiration,[14] and German theater, having a strong tradition of being open to international influence, also saw inspiring productions by the American playwright Neil LaBute (1963–).[15] In 2002, audiences in Berlin and Munich were enthralled by the Norwegian Lars Norén's (1944–) *Träume im Herbst* (Dreams in Autumn, 2001).[16] Not surprisingly, critics praised *norway.today* (2001), written by Igor Bauersima (1964–),[17] for its acute portrayal of a young couple who meet to commit suicide together,[18] and the plot of Bauersima's latest play, *Tattoo* (2002), owes much to Neil LaBute's *The Shape of Things* (2000).[19]

Meanwhile, Ostermeier has strengthened the cooperation between the *Berliner Schaubühne* and the *Royal Court Theatre* in London, and German plays are regularly presented once a year during a German week in London.[20] Marius von Mayenburg's *Feuergesicht* and Theresia Walser's *King Kongs Töchter,* for example, came to London, and Mark Ravenhill's *Some Explicit Polaroids* (1999) was translated immediately after completion[21] and produced in Zurich.[22]

Although the critic Hella Kemper has already voiced fears that the new generation of playwrights, who are mostly in their thirties, will soon die out,[23] Theresia Walser, Dea Loher, John von Düffel, and Albert Ostermaier, to name but a few, continue to be productive, as a glance at any theater program proves. Contemporary plays focus on the concrete situation of human beings in the twenty-first century, thus indicating that the postmodern trend, which presents a whole range of global problems in one evening, is gradually dying out.[24]

With respect to postmodernism, Dea Loher, one of the most successful German playwrights today, states: "Ich habe die Schnauze voll von dem postmodernen Orientierungslosigkeitsgefasel, das die gesellschaftliche Funktion des Theaters letztlich auf Null setzt, weil es wurscht ist, was gespielt wird."[25] As a consequence, Loher continues her sharp portrayal of those who were left behind by modern society in *Der dritte Sektor* (The Third Sector, 2001), a play that features two elderly house servants who rebel against their position by putting their employer into the freezer.[26] In *Täglich Brot* (2001), Gesine Danckwart presents us with today's cold working environment, depicting the egoistic and competitive climate of a firm through a couple of intertwined monologues.[27] In a similar manner, John von Düffel's *Elite I.1* (2002), depicts the effects of the new economy on a handful of top managers by means of "monologic dialogues."[28]

In *99 Grad* (99 Degrees, 2002), Albert Ostermaier explores the world of genetic engineering from the viewpoint of a researcher who invents a drug that makes anyone who takes it fall in love with the next person who happens to be around — as in Shakespeare's *Midsummer Night's Dream*.[29] Ostermaier thus follows the path that Igor Bauersima paved with *Future de luxe* (2001), which also focuses on the controversial issue of genetic engineering.[30] By contrast, Theresia Walser's *Die Heldin von Potsdam* (The Heroine of Potsdam, 2001) does not look into the future, but is based on a true story dating from 1995. The play offers insight into the mind of a woman who claims to have been injured by a group of neo-Nazis when she tried to protect an old woman.[31] However, after a few days journalists revealed that the woman had invented the whole story, simply because she enjoyed the attention of the media.

If German theater began to prosper again during the last decade, it was due to one circumstance: the tensions within society itself. Many a debate was waged over "normalization" and the Nazi past, and increasing right-wing extremism sent shock waves through the country. Since the "Wende," the *Berliner Republik* has not only been struggling with the deep frictions between East and West, but has also been attempting to redefine Germany's role within Europe. As this book has shown, however, fresh talent is emerging to tackle the problems of a highly industrialized, yet multicultural society in the rapidly changing media age.

Notes

[1] Franz Wille, "Begegnungen auf der Standspur. Das Generationen-Ding — Bemerkungen zur Dynamik der Verhältnisse," in *ThJ* (2001), 101–15, here: 106.

[2] The premiere in Bochum (director, Matthias Hartmann) was also received with misgivings; see Sibylle Wirsing, "Totentanz auf Nummer Sicher," *Th* 5 (2001): 46–49, and Andreas Schäfer, "Vom Schicksal ausgelöffelter Joghurtbecher," *BZ,* 9 April 2001. Later productions in Vienna and Munich were also considered to be fanciful; see Franz Wille, "Kein Schönes ohne sein Gutes," *Th* 6 (2002): 16–19.

[3] Hochhuth himself was also heavily criticized for his rather biased views of modern theater, and with respect to his policies, a journalist pointed out that an author-centered theater really meant a Hochhuth-centered seasonal program: see Roland Koberg, "Kasperl und Krokodil," *BZ,* 29 August 2000.

[4] Ernst Schumacher, "Zeitlebens in die falsche Richtung," *BZ,* 23 October 2001.

[5] Diederich Diederichsen, "Muss ich mir den Scheiss anhören?" *Th* 6 (2001): 20–23.

[6] Franz Wille, "Der Kopf fällt immer nach unten," *Th* 12 (2001): 16–18, here: 18.

[7] "Ich muss es einfach versuchen. Ein Theater Heute-Gespräch mit Thomas Ostermeier, dem designierten künstlerischen Leiter der Berliner Schaubühne," *Th* 5 (1998): 26–30, here: 30.

[8] (No author), "Neue Theatergeneration in der Berliner Schaubühne bejubelt," *Mopo,* 23 January 2000.

[9] Michael Merschmeier, "Endzeitlose. Über Sarah Kane's *Gesäubert* und die Aufführungen in Hamburg und Stuttgart," *ThJ* (1999), 107–11.

[10] Roland Koberg, "Und dann kommt diese Szene," *BZ,* 19 January 1998.

[11] Christian Hunziker, "Deutsche Ravenhills erwünscht. Wie das neue Uraufführungstheater junge Autoren fördert," *BZ,* 11 November 1998.

[12] Ulrike Kahle, "Krokodile sind immer im Unrecht," *Th* 6 (2001): 14–15. The German translation of *In weiter Ferne* was published in *Th* 4 (2001): 56–59.

[13] The first staging in German took place in Bochum and was celebrated for its wit; see Gerhard Preußer, "Sterben für die Katz," *Th* 11 (2001): 44. In September 2001, it was staged at the *Deutsche Theater* in Berlin, where it was also warmly received; see Christian Kühl, "Splitter und Splatter," *taz,* 1 October 2001.

[14] Patricia Benecke, "Nach dem Hype. Aktuelle Eindrücke und neue Stücke aus London," *Th* 12 (2001): 42–43.

[15] Peter Zadek's production of *Bash* at the *Hamburger Kammerspiele* was enthusiastically received; see Michael Merschmeier, "Im Herzen die Mördergrube," *Th* 6 (2001): 12–13.

[16] However, the reviewers did not always share the audiences' opinions; see Franz Wille, "Mord aus dem Augenwinkel," *Th* 1 (2002): 15–17.

[17] Igor Bauersima, "norway.today," *Th* 1 (2001): 48–58.

[18] It was premiered at the *Düsseldorfer Schauspielhaus* in December 2000 (directed by the author himself), where it was enthusiastically received; see Barbara Burckhardt, "Fake ist total real," *Th* 1 (2001): 44–47.

[19] The German translation *Das Maß aller Dinge* was published in *Th* 7 (2002): 50–63.

[20] Carola Dürr, "Vom Tragischen ins Komische. Neue deutsche Dramatik am Royal Court Theater London und Mark Ravenhills neuer Reißer," *W,* 19 November 1999.

[21] The translation *Gestochen scharfe Polaroids* was published in *Th* 2 (2001): 55–67.

[22] The German premiere was in Zurich in January 2002 (director, Falk Richter); see Franz Wille, "Call-a-drama, mit Idee oder Käse?" *Th* 2 (2001): 44–47. It was also staged in Lübeck in June 2002; see Till Briegleb, "Weltdrama in der Nussschale," *Th* 7 (2002): 38.

[23] Hella Kemper, "Stirbt mit den letzten Dramatikern das Theater aus?" *W,* 18 June 2002.

[24] Simone Schneider, "Worte, so passend wie Springerstiefel. Aufgetaucht aus dem Meer des Verschwindens: Die jungen deutschen Dramatiker," *W,* 27 July 2002.

[25] Quoted in Birgitta Willmann, "Kalter Blick auf menschliche Tragödien," *SoZ,* 18 January 1998.

[26] *Der dritte Sektor* was premiered at the *Thalia Theater* in Hamburg in May 2001 (director, Dimiter Gotscheff), yet the critics reacted with some misgivings; see Stefan Grund, "Die Herrin in der Tiefkühltruhe," *W,* 18 May 2001 and Henning Rischbieter, "Dinosaurier der Dienstleistung," *Th* 7 (2001): 49.

[27] *Täglich Brot* was premiered in Jena in May 2001, directed by Christiane Pohle. It was warmly received, due to its well-executed production; see Eva Behrendt, "Die höchste Schmerzstufe," *Th* 6 (2001): 52–55.

[28] Barbara Burckhardt, "Stellenmarkt der Eitelkeiten," *Th* 7 (2002): 42–46, here: 42–43.

[29] Burckhardt, "Stellenmarkt der Eitelkeiten," 44–45.

[30] The production in Hanover in April 2002 was received with misgivings, for the plot and the ideas were considered to be too complex for the stage; see Barbara Burckhardt, "Igor Bauersima Future de Luxe," *Th* 5 (2002): 46

[31] The production by Volker Hesse was premiered at the *Maxim Gorki Theater* in Berlin in September 2001, and was received with some misgivings; see Franz Wille, "Nischenbewohner auf Treibsand," *Th* 10 (2001): 54–55.

Index

Achternbusch, Herbert, influences on, 14, 15; political views of, 14, 15, 86, 88
Achternbusch, Herbert, works by: *Auf verlorenem Posten*, 83, 86–88, 128; *Frosch*, 14–17
Arendt, Hannah, banality of the evil, 45
Asylrecht, 187
Auschwitz, 42, 50, 119, 187
Ayckbourn, Alan, 1

Baader-Meinhof-Gruppe, 167, 170
battle of Stalingrad, 120
Bauersima, Igor, works by: *Future de luxe*, 231; *norway. today*, 230
Beckett, Samuel, works by: *Waiting for Godot*, 35
Bewegung 2. Juni, 167
Brasch, Thomas, influences on, 64; political views of, 62, 65
Brasch, Thomas, works by: *Lieber Georg*, 62–66; *Rotter*, 63
Braun, Volker, influences on, 108; political views of, 66, 84, 95
Braun, Volker, works by: *Böhmen am Meer*, 84, 108–10; *Iphigenie in Freiheit*, 84, 92–95; *Die Übergangsgesellschaft*, 66–69
Brecht, Bertolt, *Verfremdungseffekt*, 53, 116, 156, 160, 217, 228
Brecht, Bertolt, works by: *Der Aufhaltsame Aufstieg des Arturo Ui*, 5, 118; *Baal*, 217; *Coriolan*, 119; *Galilei*, 119
Brokdorf, 31, 36

Büchner, Georg, works by: *Leonce und Lena*, 72
Bukowski, Oliver, influences on, 122; political views of, 122, 125
Bukowski, Oliver, works by: *Gäste*, 85, 121–25; *Die Halbwertszeit der Kanarienvögel*, 122; *Hinter den Linien*, 122; *Intercity*, 122; *Lakoma*, 122; *Londn-L.Ä. Lübbenau*, 122

Call, Daniel, influences on, 213; political views of, 207, 214
Call, Daniel, works by: *Gärten des Grauens*, 212; *Tumult auf Villa Shatterhand*, 212; *Wetterleuchten*, 207, 212–14
Chekhov, Anton, 2
Chekhov, Anton, works by: *The Three Sisters*, 68
Chernobyl, 32, 33, 36–38
child abuse, 145–47
Churchill, Caryl, works by: *Far Away*, 230
collage, 8, 64, 83, 85, 89, 119, 128, 186, 202, 215
crisis of the theater, 5
culture industry, 61, 144, 207, 216–18
Czeslik, Oliver, influences on, 178; political views of, 187, 190
Czeslik, Oliver, works by: *Gaddafi rockt*, 169, 178–80; *Heilige Kühe*, 187, 190–93

Danckwart, Gesine, influences on, 155, 160, 230; political views of, 156
Danckwart, Gesine, works by: *Arschkarte*, 154; *Girlsnightout*, 143, 154–56, 160; *Täglich Brot*, 231
demonstrations, Leipzig, 82, 83, 85, 194
domestic violence, 145, 146, 148
Dorst, Tankred, works by: *Merlin oder das wüste Land*, 70
Dukovski, Dejan, 2
Dürrenmatt, Friedrich, works by: *Die Physiker*, 32

Eichmann, Adolf, 43–47; "Eichmann-attitude," 45
Ellert, Gundi, influences on, works by: *Jagdzeit*, 187, 198–99, 202
Endres, Ria, works by: *Der Kongreß*, 144
emotional crisis of the East Germans, 93
environmental crisis, 31, 74
Evreinov, Nicolai, 155

fascism, 129, 168, 188, 194, 201, 202, 221
farce, 43, 49, 50, 55, 83, 86, 88, 89, 95, 128, 153, 176
Fassbinder, Rainer Werner, 36; Minutendramaturgie, 174
Fels, Ludwig, influences on, 21, 26; political views of, 3, 14, 20
Fels, Ludwig, works by: *Lieblieb*, 20–23; *Soliman*, 20
female aesthetics, 145
female theater, 144–45
female writing, 145
Frauenbewegung, 143, 145, 153

GDR, 60–63, 64–75, 82–86, 87, 89, 91–95, 97–99, 102, 104–8,
111–113, 116, 119–21, 125, 127–30, 225, 227
gentle revolution. *See* Wende
glasnost, 62, 66, 70, 82
Goetz, Rainald, influences on, 209, 222; political views of, 209, 211, 221, 222
Goetz, Rainald, works by: *Festung*, 209–12, 221; *Jeff Koons*, 209; *Krieg*, 209
Gorbachev, Mikhail, 62, 66, 70, 71, 82
Grass, Günter, works by: *Die Blechtrommel*, 87
Greens, Green Issues, 13, 31–36, 39
Grips-Theater, 43, 52–53

Hatsor, Ilan, works by: *Vermummte*, 2
Hein, Christoph, influences on, 69; political views of, 4, 116
Hein, Christoph, works by: *In Acht und Bann*, 85, 125–27, 130; *Randow*, 85, 115–17; *Die Ritter der Tafelrunde*, 62, 66, 69–72, 74
Hitler, Adolf, 42, 43, 46, 47, 49–52, 55, 94, 114, 117, 118, 120, 129, 190, 191, 193, 197–202, 208, 211, 229
Hochhuth, Rolf, influences on, 111; political views of, 17, 85, 129, 130
Hochhuth, Rolf, works by: *Hitlers Dr. Faust*, 229; *Wessis in Weimar*, 7, 85, 111–15
Holocaust, 42–55, 187, 189, 210, 211, 212
holy war, 178; intifada, 179
Honecker, Erich, 61, 62, 70, 71, 82, 83, 114, 127

Jünger, Ernst, works by: *Auf den Marmorklippen*, 115

Kane, Sarah, works by:
Blasted, 7; Crave, 160
Karge, Manfred, influences on,
89; political views of, 90, 138
Karge, Manfred, works by:
Mauer-Stücke, 83, 89–92, 138
Kipphardt, Heinar, influences on,
43, 45; political views of, 43, 44
Kipphardt, Heinar, works by:
Bruder Eichmann, 43–47; Joel
Brand, 44; Die Sache Robert J.
Oppenheimer, 32
Kohl, Helmut, 3, 13, 14, 17, 26,
32, 42, 55, 84–86, 96, 99, 103,
106, 111, 187, 196, 197
Koltés, Bernard-Marie, works by:
Roberto Zucco, 1
Kosovo, war in, 2, 4, 219, 221,
222
Krechel, Ursula, 144
Kresnik, Johann, works by:
Ulrike Meinhof, 1
Kroetz, Franz Xaver, influences
on, 18; political views of, 17,
169, 194, 221, 222
Kroetz, Franz Xaver, works by:
Bauern sterben, 14, 17–20, 26,
38; Ich bin das Volk, 186, 193–
98, 202

LaBute, Neil, works by:
The Shape of Things, 230
Lasker-Schüler, Else, works by:
Die Wupper, 21
Loher, Dea, influences on, 170;
political views of, 145, 170, 231
Loher, Dea, works by: Der Dritte
Sektor, 231; Leviathan, 167,
170–73, 180; Tätowierung,
145, 146–48, 159
Ludwig, Volker, influences on,
52; political views of, 52
Ludwig, Volker, works by: Ab
heute heißt du Sara, 43, 52–54

McDonagh, Martin, works by:
The Lieutenant of Inishmore,
230
media, mediatized society, 18, 97,
190, 202, 207–9, 210, 217–19,
221, 222
media theory, 207
Meinhof, Ulrike, 1, 144, 167,
168, 170, 173, 176
Meinhof, Ulrike, works by:
Bambule, 144
MfS, Ministerium für
Staatssicherheit. See Stasi
montage, 86, 90, 112, 119, 209
Mueller, Harald, influences on,
34–35; political views of, 33
Mueller, Harald, works by:
Totenfloß, 32, 33–36, 38
Müller, Heiner, influences on,
117, 118; political views of, 118
Müller, Heiner, works by:
Germania 3 Gespenster am
Toten Mann, 85, 117–21, 128;
Germania Tod in Berlin, 120
Müller, Elfriede, influences on,
101; political views of, 103
Müller, Elfriede, works by:
Goldener Oktober, 84, 101–5,
128

National Socialism, Nazis, 46–51,
54, 64, 94, 97, 190, 200
NATO-Doppelbeschluss, 32, 65
neo-Nazis, 43, 85, 116, 187, 190,
194, 198, 200, 202, 231
neonconservative turn in politics,
42
neue Mensch, der, 65, 178
new social movements, 36, 227
Norén, Lars, works by:
Träume im Herbst, 230
normalcy (Normalitätsdebatte),
129, 187, 188
nuclear war, fear of a, 31–33, 65

opportunist (Wendehals), 83, 87, 90, 103, 110, 116, 127, 227
Ostermaier, Albert, influences on, 216, 217; political views of, 215
Ostermaier, Albert, works by: *Death Valley Junction*, 215; *99 Grad*, 231; *The Making of B.-Movie*, 214–18, 222; *Tatar Titus*, 215; *Zwischen zwei Feuern. Toller-Topograhie*, 215
outcasts, 13–27, 34

pastiche, 3, 64, 74, 102, 119, 129, 155, 209, 222, 227
peace campaigners, 32, 35, 36, 219
perestroika, 62, 70, 82
Pohl, Klaus, influences on, 105; political views of, 4, 107, 189
Pohl, Klaus, works by: *Karate-Billi kehrt zurück*, 62, 105–8, 128; *Die schöne Fremde*, 188–89, 202
Politbüro, 63, 69, 70, 71, 75, 83, 126, 127
postmodernism, postmodern, 1, 2, 3, 6, 7, 8, 64, 74, 92, 102, 119, 123, 128, 139, 154, 155, 209, 125, 217, 218, 221, 222, 227, 229, 231
poverty, 15, 17, 121

Rasterfahndung, 169
Ravenhill, Mark, works by: *Shopping and F***ing*, 7, 230; *Some Explicit Polaroids*, 230
Red Army Faction, Rote Armee Fraktion, RAF, 112, 167–71, 173, 176–78, 180
Reinshagen, Gerlind, works by: *Sonntagskinder*, 144
reunification, 92–130, 186, 211, 227; colonizing of the GDR, 92, 128; marriage, 84, 86, 88, 89, 91, 105, 130; Mauer im

Kopf (wall inside the head), 7, 84, 129; Treuhandanstalt, 111, 112, 168
Revolutionäre Zellen, 167
Richter, Falk, influences on, 218; political views of, 219
Richter, Falk, works by: *Gott ist ein DJ*, 218; *Kult! Geschichte für eine virtuelle Generation*, 218; *Peace*, 208, 218–21
right-wing radicalism/extremism, 42, 43, 115, 186–203, 229, 231

Schatrow, Michail, works by: *Die Diktatur des Gewissens*, 1
Schiller, Friedrich, 4, 112, 115, 200, 202
Schiller, Friedrich, works by: *Wilhelm Tell*, 90, 91
Schimmelpfennig, Roland, 7; influences on, 166; political views of, 158
Schimmelpfennig, Roland, works by: *Arabische Nacht*, 156; *Fisch um Fisch*, 156; *Push Up 1–3*, 143, 156–59, 160
Schreibtischmörder, 45
SED, Sozialistische Einheitspartei Deutschlands, 60–63, 67, 70, 116
Seidel, Georg, influences on, 72; political views of, 72
Seidel, Georg, works by: *Jochen Schanotta*, 61, 72–74; *Königskinder*, 72
Sicherheitspaket I und II (anti-terrorist laws), 169
skinheads, 187, 190, 191
society in transition, 60, 67
Specht, Kerstin, influences on, 23; political views of, 23, 153
Specht, Kerstin, works by: *Froschkönigin*, 145, 152–54; *Lila*, 23–26

Spiegel affair, 172
Srbljanowic, Biljana, 2
Stasi, Staatssicherheit, 62, 63, 68, 71, 89, 105–8
stations of the cross (Kreuzweg), 19
Strahlenangstpsychose, 31, 36, 38
Strauß, Botho, influences on, 98; political views of, 97
Strauß, Botho, works by: *Kaldewey. Farce,* 95; *Der Narr und seine Frau heute abend in Pancomedia,* 229; *Schlußchor,* 83, 88, 95–101, 129
Strittmatter, Thomas, influences on, 47; political views of, 47
Strittmatter, Thomas, works by: *Viehjud Levi,* 43, 47–49, 54
suicide bomber, 169

Tabori, George, influences on, 49; political views of, 52
Tabori, George, works by: *Mein Kampf,* 43, 49–52, 55
terrorism, 167–81, 228, 230
theater of the absurd, 15, 68, 108, 109, 159, 214
Todesstreifen, 113, 114

unemployment, 3, 14, 15, 18, 21, 23–26, 43, 47, 122, 195, 227, 228
Uraufführungstheater (UAT), 122

velvet revolution. *See* Wende
Volkstheater (critical), 14, 15, 18, 21, 23, 24–26, 43, 47, 122, 195, 227, 228
Von Düffel, John, influences on, 177; political views of, 178
Von Düffel, John, works by: *Born in the R.A.F.,* 168, 176–78, *180; Elite,* 231; *Solingen,* 186, 199–201, 202

Von Horvath, Ödön, 195
Von Mayenburg, Marius, influences on, 174; political views of, 176
Von Mayenburg, Marius, works by: *Feuergesicht,* 169, 173–76, 180, 230; *Haarmann,* 173
Von Wysocki, Gisela, 144, 159

Waldsterben, 61
Walser, Theresia, influences on, 148; political views of, 149
Walser, Theresia, works by: *Die Heldin von Potsdam,* 231; *King Kongs Töchter,* 145, 148–51, 159, 230; *Kleine Zweifel,* 148; *Das Restpaar,* 148
Weiss, Peter, works by: *Die Ermittlung,* 36
Wende (gentle revolution, velvet revolution), 63, 66, 72, 74, 82–86, 87–89, 91, 93–94, 98, 100, 105, 110, 115, 116, 121, 122, 128, 188, 231
Wende in der Wende, 83
Wendehals, 83, 87, 90, 103, 110, 116, 227
Wendestress, 116
Weyh, Florian Felix, influences on, 36; political views of, 37
Weyh, Florian Felix, works by: *Fondue,* 31, 36–39; *Ludwigslust,* 36; *Stirling,* 36

xenophobia, 23, 26, 47, 188, 194, 196, 197, 199–202

Zeitstück, 36, 38, 102